# PURSUITS AMATEUR AND ACADEMIC

THE COLLECTED WORKS OF E.J. PRATT

GENERAL EDITORS: SANDRA DJWA, R.G. MOYLES, ZAILIG POLLOCK, AND W.J. KEITH

---

The aim of this edition is to present a critical annotated text of the collected works of E.J. Pratt – complete poetry; selected prose and correspondence – fully collated and with a textual apparatus that traces the transmission of the text and lists variant readings.

E.J. PRATT

# Pursuits Amateur and Academic: The Selected Prose of E.J. Pratt

Edited by Susan Gingell

UNIVERSITY OF TORONTO PRESS
Toronto Buffalo London

Toronto Buffalo London
Printed in Canada
Reprinted in 2018

ISBN 0-8020-2907-8

ISBN 978-1-4875-8114-5 (paper)

Printed on acid-free paper

**Canadian Cataloguing in Publication Data**

Pratt, E.J. (Edwin John), 1882–1964.
Pursuits amateur and academic

(The collected works of E.J. Pratt)
Includes bibliographical references and index.
ISBN 0-8020-2907-8

I. Gingell, Susan, 1951– . II. Title. III. Series:
Pratt, E.J. (Edwin John), 1882–1964. The collected works of E.J. Pratt.

PS8531.R23A16 1995 C818'.5208 C94-932190-7
PR9199.2.P73A16 1995

University of Toronto Press acknowledges the financial assistance to its publishing program of the Canada Council and the Ontario Arts Council.

This book has been published with the help of a grant from the Canadian Federation for the Humanities, using funds provided by the Social Sciences and Humanities Research Council of Canada.

For my children,
Lee, Carrie, and Jesse

# Contents

# Preface

Gathered in this volume are selections from the published and unpublished prose of the Canadian writer E.J. Pratt. The first volume of the Collected Works, *E.J. Pratt on His Life and Poetry* (1983), offered a comprehensive compilation of Pratt's autobiographical writings and commentary on his own poetry, and the present book is a companion volume, providing representative samples of his stories, theological writings, literary and general interest essays, commentaries on both classics of literature and newer entries into the literary world, editorials, reviews, forewords and introductions, and lectures and addresses.

E.J. Pratt's commitment to poetic craft was certainly his most important as a writer, but poetry was far from the only dimension of his writing life. He had a varied career as a theological student, demonstrator in psychology, and professor of English, the latter post involving the collateral activities of editing; reviewing; and writing introductions to, and commentaries on, other people's work; and in each of these capacities he produced a partial record of his work. All these fields of activity are represented in the writing collected here: extracts from both the master's and doctoral theses in theology, an essay in defence of the new science of psychology, and a broad sampling of his varied literary writing.

I have had the help of many people and several institutions

in preparing the work. My colleagues on the E.J. Pratt Editorial Project deserve a good deal of the credit for whatever merits this volume may have, but its shortcomings are, of course, my own. I owe special thanks to Lila Laakso, who kept me informed of any Pratt prose she discovered as she compiled her authoritative descriptive bibliography of Pratt's work, often supplying me with photocopies or transcriptions of new pieces she and her research assistants uncovered; to Gordon Moyles for his scholarly advice, generosity, and unfailing encouragement; to David Pitt for alerting me to and supplying me with some reviews and other materials I had not uncovered, as well as for some discerning editorial advice; to Bob Gibbs for his careful reading of the typescript; and to Sandra Djwa for her queries and suggestions, which helped me strengthen the work. I also owe thanks to Zailig Pollock and W.J. Keith, who joined the editorial board when the book was being copy-edited, but set aside their other work to lend their expertise to help improve this volume. The staff of the E.J. Pratt Library at Victoria University in the University of Toronto were always most helpful in accommodating my requests, and thereby facilitated my research work considerably. I am also grateful to the Pratt Library for permission to publish the extracts from Pratt's MA thesis.

Many of my colleagues at the University of Saskatchewan, Professors William Bartley, Len Findlay, Ann and David Hiatt, John Lavery, Terry Matheson, Barry Popowich, Rob Scott, Peter Stoicheff, Claud Thompson, and Lisa Vargo, spent time and effort in trying to identify or track down some of the references and quotations in Pratt's text. Professor Terry Whalen of St Mary's University, Halifax, kindly provided me with information about Bliss Carman, and the scholars who read the typescript for the University of Toronto Press and the Canadian Federation for the Humanities offered most cogent advice. This book has also benefited substantially from the skilled eyes and attentions of my editors at the Press, Theresa Griffin, David Smith, and Margaret Allen. Further thanks go out to the University of Saskatchewan Department of English secretaries Peggy Smith and Sharon Ford for the repeated assistance they gave me with word processing.

The patient support of my family and many kinds of help from William Robertson have also been crucial to the completion of the project. This volume would also not have been possible without Ms Claire Pratt's kind permission to print or reprint the prose I had selected.

The Social Sciences and Humanities Research Council of Canada helped fund a sabbatical year in which much of the early work was done. The College of Arts and Science at the University of Saskatchewan provided me with both a time-release grant, which enabled me to work more rapidly on the book than would otherwise have been possible, and a small research grant that helped with photocopying and mailing costs. I am also grateful to the University of Saskatchewan for two sabbaticals, part of each of which was dedicated to the preparation of this present work.

S.G.
Saskatoon
June 1994

# Introduction

E.J. Pratt's eminence in Canadian literary history rests on the firm foundation of his poetry, but, as both David G. Pitt's two-volume biography *E.J. Pratt: The Truant Years, 1882–1927* and *E.J. Pratt: The Master Years, 1927–1964* and Lila Laakso's 'Descriptive Bibliography' have documented, Pratt also wrote extensively in prose.[1] Undeniably of interest for the light it casts on Pratt as poet, his prose also has merit in its own right. The title I have created for this selection of his prose, 'Pursuits Amateur and Academic,' is intended to reflect two dimensions of his character and writing: the more playful side represented in personal and informal stories and essays like '"Hooked": A Rocky Mountain Experience' and 'Golfomania,' and the scholarly side evident in his formal theological, psychological, and literary prose.

The 23 August 1907 edition of the St John's *Daily News* carried Pratt's earliest known publication, a prose work entitled 'A Northern Holiday.'[2] Though in most respects amateurish, it already displays what was to become a characteristic of Pratt's narrative technique, namely, the laying of a groundwork of realistically described circumstances or phenomena (in this case a description of Notre Dame Bay in Newfoundland, where he had gone to peddle his notorious Universal Lung Healer in order to finance his education) before a flight of comic fancy. The fanciful flight here is an account of Newfoundland's answer to the mainland rattlesnake: an oversized mosquito with an equally oversized appetite.

Pratt's planned career as a clergyman provided him with a pretext – and the financing – for a visit to the prairies, but his passion for the secular word prompted the literary reconstruction of the adventures and misadventures of that enterprise. The title of the piece, 'A Western Experience,' suggests that Pratt conceived it in the same mode as, and perhaps even as an extension of, the earlier newspaper article. The humorously presented dramatic struggle between the East, in the form of a tourist disguised as a student minister, and the West, embodied in a creature 'qualified, by both heredity and education, as a broncho' (6), is again characteristic Pratt. His exploiting the comic potential of juxtaposing Canadian character types anticipates the Leacock who makes humorous fare of such comparisons as that of city with town or Maritimers with Mariposans in the Pupkin episodes of *Sunshine Sketches of a Little Town* (1912). Moreover, Pratt's bringing together of Eastern and Western Canada predates by over a quarter century Leacock's *My Discovery of the West: A Discussion of East and West in Canada* (1937), of which the opening and closing chapters and intermittent paragraphs share the exuberant spirit of Pratt's comic exposé of East gone West.[3]

Like 'A Western Experience,' '"Hooked": A Rocky Mountain Experience' can be read as high-spirited autobiography – in this instance slightly transmuted – and readers can find an account of the factual basis of all three early works in *The Truant Years*. However, the precedence given to character-typing over facts invites a different kind of reading. Instead of full names and exact dates, the reader is first offered the information that 'three men were seated around a blazing log-fire one cool, still night in June ...' (11), and then invited to know the men as a Westerner by the name of Dan and two Easterners identified only as 'Scotty' and 'Irish' or 'the Hibernian.' As a portrait of male camaraderie of the type Pratt so clearly enjoyed, 'Hooked' has its interest, but the understated ironies and hyperbolic diction of the narrative also encourage the attention of those studying the development of Pratt's characteristic tone and style.

The ironic tone and blending of fact and comic exaggeration in these stories prompt further comparison with such Leacock prose as those sketches gathered under the subtitle 'Travel and Movement' in *Winnowed Wisdom* or the later work 'What Can Isaak Walton Teach Us?' from *Last Leaves*. The Smiths and Joneses of Leacock's 'The Gasoline Goodbye,'[4] for instance, are as generic and subservient to comic narrative purpose as Scotty and Irish of Pratt's 'Hooked.' The strong sense of a speaking voice, which is a hallmark of Leacock's narrative style, is also a feature of the Pratt prose gathered in Section A, though Pratt's narrators are less studiously funny than the characteristic Leacock persona. The cultivated but whimsical personality projected through the speaking voice of 'What Can Izaak Walton Teach Us?'[5] is, however, markedly like that projected in Pratt's 'A Northern Holiday' and 'A Western Experience.'

David Pitt has already pointed to the Leacockian touches in Pratt's early prose (TY 80 and 94), but the opportunity for a more detailed comparison exists and will, I hope, be facilitated by the present work. Less prolific a writer than Leacock, Pratt none the less can usefully be compared with him on several grounds in addition to those just sketched. Leacock published extensively both as a 'professor of political science and economics' and as a humorist, and Pratt, the erstwhile theologian-and-psychologist-turned-literary-scholar, left a written record of his work in all three academic disciplines, in addition to the poetry for which he is primarily remembered. As professors, both were generally indifferent scholars, though their academic writing on occasion records memorable insights and ideas. Their popularity as lecturers, however, probably rested a good deal more on their skills and reputations as witty speakers than on their originality of thought in their respective disciplines.

Academic writing is the foundation of Pratt's multidimensional career as a prose writer, and much of his later work is of this type. His earliest academic prose extant is the result of his study for the Methodist ministry. His master's thesis, 'The Demonology of the New Testament in Its Relation to Earlier Developments, and to the Mind of Christ,' was shaped by contemporary progressive Christian theology's concern with reconstructing the historical Jesus. The demystifying work of scholars like David Friedrich Strauss, author of *Das Leben Jesu* [*The Life of Jesus*] (1835–6, trans. 1848), must have appealed to that dimension of Pratt that sought to bring together scientific methods and humanistic concerns. Undoubtedly the value of Pratt's own theological writings today is largely if not exclusively limited to their ability to illuminate one part of the intellectual background of his poetry.

In *E.J. Pratt: The Evolutionary Years*, Sandra Djwa links Pratt's master's thesis with his need to come to terms with the demonic forces of nature that assault humankind from without, and, in the form of atavistic impulses, threaten civilization, or at least civilized behaviour, from within.[6] The portions of the thesis extracted here, however, show that the interest of this material for Pratt scholars extends beyond such links, because the thesis studies the relationship between myth, allegory, and history, as well as the psychology of interpretation. Pratt expressly dismisses wholly mythic, allegorical, or reputedly objective historical accounts of the demonological narratives, and offers instead his own 'natural' explanation of how these narratives function: 'The natural explanation is not the choice of one and only one alternative, not all myth or all history, all allegory or all fact, but rather an historical incident coloured by subjective prepossessions, and reported through the medium of a crude popular vocabulary, steeped in mythical notions inherited from the past' (18). Clearly the work Pratt did for his master's thesis offered him an early opportunity to understand some ways in which elements of myth, allegory, and history could be blended in a compelling narrative, a lesson that would stand him in good stead when he came to write his historical narrative poems.

The master's thesis is also of interest for the indications it gives of a mind already fascinated with language and poetry, and quite capable of recognizing sentimental excess in 'the poetry of the Christian pulpit' (20) when he encountered it. The thesis makes clear Pratt's well-developed awareness of the crucial link between form and meaning, when, in seeking to establish the grounds on which an argument about Christ's view of demons could be built, Pratt asserts, 'The form of the language in which Christ expressed his thought would make all the difference in the world to a question of interpretation' (24).

Pratt's doctoral dissertation, *Studies in Pauline Eschatology and Its Background*, yields even more evidence of the incipient poet, for his attraction to Paul seems in no small part to have been based on his admiration for the apostle's skills with language: 'The figures of speech, the striking similes, the illuminating illustrations that light up the epistles are a lasting monument to his skill in driving home a message as they reflect the range of his intellectual insight, and practical sagacity. His burning ethical exhortations place under tribute the whole field of Jewish, Roman, and Greek metaphor' (33). The work dwells at some length on the imagery that both Paul and his spiritual forebears used to convey certain theological concepts, and is in fact primarily an examination of Paul's language, most centrally the terms 'spirit' and 'soul.' In support of his particular line of inquiry Pratt cites Adolf Deissmann's assertion that '[o]ne might write the history of religion as the history of religious terms, or more correctly, one must apprehend the history of religious terms as being a chapter in the history of religion' (31). Moreover, in discussing the evolution of the meaning of the theological terms that Paul employs, Pratt shows himself sensitive both to the relation between language and socio-cultural situations and to the problems and results of translating the Bible.

The temptation to speculate about the significance of Pratt's being drawn to the study of 'Last Things' is strong; undeniably, death is a central preoccupation in Pratt's poetry, as it was a recurring feature of his Newfoundland experience.[7] However, we can be on firmer ground in discovering more narrow but precise parallels in such things as Pratt's treatment of theophany in both a theological context and the poetic context of the conclusion of *The Iron Door: An Ode*. The response of Paul and writers before him to the problem of representing the divine was a tradition on which Pratt could draw, but the more sentimental manifestations of the tradition he emphatically rejected. One of Pratt's letters to William Arthur Deacon, the literary editor of the Toronto *Globe and Mail* and a member of Pratt's circle of friends, discusses the problem of closure in his ode, a problem which was, no doubt, partly a matter of theological scepticism. The letter speaks of the dead gathered before the door to present their cases to 'the unseen Warders, or God or the Governor of the Universe whoever he may be,' before going on to explain:

> To my mind it would be a cardinal artistic and moral blunder to end it in complete gloom. The setting I think requires the conclusion, but I did not feel, on the other hand, that the requirements would be met by anything like a conventional heaven, harps or angels or such outworn paraphernalia. The only demand I make is that there shall be life and light with continued life effort on the other side. Hence I never see inside the door. I only judge by the reflection on the faces of human beings and by certain sounds which intermittently break through that there are vast stretches beyond. I do not aim at solutions. I only wanted to give an imaginative and emotional interpretation of what I feel myself ...[8]

By comparison, in the dissertation, Pratt provides from the Epistles numerous examples of Paul's representations of God, and then concludes, 'The terms which sum up the description are those of glory, radiance, power, and form et cetera. It is easy to see that to construct a more precise formula of definition is an impossible task' (28). Regarding Paul as an accomplished poet in his own right, Pratt can appropriate and modify according to his own lights the images of theophany Paul had formulated, though Pratt's images are broadly intertextual, not simply restricted to the Pauline field.

Pratt's non-theological writings offer readers the opportunity to trace different kinds of development and discover other kinds of connections. There are, for example, affinities between the stories collected in Section A and the essay 'Golfomania,' since the autobiographical persona given to comic exaggeration is present in both. However, the generic coding of the opening sentence of 'Golfomania,' 'Is golf a game or disease?' followed as it is by a reference to the medical column of a newspaper, suggests the mode of the informal essay.

Another kind of essay altogether resulted from Pratt's early interest in the study of the mind. 'The Scientific Character of Psychology' argues that the discipline deserves to be taken seriously as a science because of its empirical methodology, though the essay also acknowledges the discipline's foundations in theology. The very name 'psychology' indicates that the discipline was first conceived of as 'an inquiry into the operations of the soul in its manifold activities' (39), etymology therefore helping to explain what to late twentieth-century observers might appear a radical shift in career on Pratt's part, from theology to psychology.

Most of the essays selected for this book are of a literary nature, ranging from profiles of individual authors to extended treatments of an author's work, a literary movement, or a literary era. Pratt shows himself willing to devote serious attention both to writers working in well-established modes and to those whose work was more experimental, without being radically so. He finds Marjorie Pickthall's work strongly and largely negatively influenced by the pre-Raphaelites and the writers of the Celtic Renaissance, but he acknowledges that she has never been surpassed in her ability to express and control the 'tender moods' (67). Pratt reserves his greatest enthusiasms, however, for modernist poets like Leo Kennedy and Dorothy Livesay and the modernist work of W.B. Yeats. Though he rails against the obscurantist excesses of modernism, he shows considerable sympathy with the anti-romantic tendency of this movement, thus displaying the catholic tastes that governed his selection of material when he was editor of the *Canadian Poetry Magazine*. As he put it, 'Tradition and revolt are inevitable complements like rain and sun: the first by itself mildews; the second burns or explodes' (79).

I have sampled rather than comprehensively reproduced the monthly 'Literature' columns Pratt published in *Canadian Comment* from June 1933 to December 1934, and then followed up with contributions in March and October of 1935 and March of 1936.[9] Though a few of these columns are simply reviews, and could therefore have been included in Section F, most are broader in scope; together they represent a significant dimension of Pratt's prose-writing career. The columns most often were a response to his recent reading, which of course included poetry, but also collections of essays (a form he felt was particularly neglected in Canadian letters), literary theory, memoirs, and biographies and anniversary publications relating to British writers such as Lord Macaulay, Francis Bacon, and Samuel Pepys.

The poet's image-making power enlivens the prose of these commentaries, as his choice of a maritime metaphor (rather than the clichéd image of a movement or school) to describe the contemporary prevalence of realism illustrates: 'A tide of realism has simply swept over the world, invading fiction, drama, and poetry. The stretches which have remained immune have been in the high altitudes occupied by the older and established writers' (85). Readers of Pratt's prose will also on occasion encounter phrasing that so effectively distils Pratt's thought that the phrasing later will have found its way into a poem. For example, in speaking of representations of Satan in twentieth-century literature, Pratt cites him as 'the classical example of degradation of energy ... pictured more frequently in the role of a bacillus than that of a Titan' (87). The diction here is characteristic Pratt, but one part of the phrasing has a particular connection to 'The Truant,' in which the little genus *homo* defiantly speaks to the great Panjandrum of the future 'degradation of your energy' (*CP*, Part 2, 130).

Grace, vigour, the freshness of contemporary diction, and, above all, clarity characterize the best of Pratt's prose style. His representation of twentieth-century writers' handling of myth is exemplary in that it includes the observations 'We have the domesticities of the ancient heroes and heroines disclosed. Helen of Troy has had her private life written up' (88). Resolutely unpretentious like their author, Pratt's essays and commentaries are warmly appreciative of work quite unlike his own (witness his valuation of Marjorie Pickthall's work or of the early Dorothy Livesay), yet scepticism and frank impatience are his responses to anything he judges in the least grandiose or, worse still, obscurantist.

As editor of *Canadian Poetry Magazine* from the first number in 1936 until 1942, Pratt not only found himself obliged to prescribe 'birth control' to ten million versifiers who were sensitive with regard to their 'spiritual babies' (75), but also was responsible for fostering young writers like Earle Birney and Dorothy Livesay, whose promise he detected and acknowledged by publishing some of their early work. The editorials he wrote while at the helm of the magazine explain why the magazine came into being, the state of Canadian poetry at the time, and the difficulties encountered in editing such a publication. They are thus important documents of Canadian literary history.

One of the recurrent themes of Pratt's editorials, essays, and reviews was his defence of the right of poets to use whatever form of expression best suited their cast of mind and their poetic purpose, a defence which included a concomitant plea to readers to be catholic in their tastes. As he affirmed in one editorial, the *Canadian Poetry Magazine* had 'no other objective than the enlargement of the poetic vision of Canada,'[10] and for Pratt enlargement meant retaining an appreciation for traditional forms of poetry, while opening the door to more experimental forms.

Unlike his more prolific contemporary the poet-reviewer A.M. Klein, Pratt devoted nearly as much of his reviewing energy to works of Canadian literature, especially poetry, as he did to non-Canadian works.[11] His period of greatest activity as a reviewer coincided with his term as editor of the *Canadian Poetry Magazine*, so he encouraged young writers both by publishing their work and by offering critical comment on it.

Pratt was characteristically a generous reviewer, tending to the descriptive rather than the critical.[12] In the light of his views that the interaction of critical and creative intelligences was necessary for the health of literature (242) and that criticism should have at least as strong a fermenting as a preservative effect (70), his own practice as a literary commentator and reviewer is often decidedly conservative and at times even cloudy-eyed. Given his argument in the foreword to Samuel Morgan-Powell's *Down the Years* that the critic's job is to make 'discriminations between flaws and excellences in a work of art' (168), judgments like the one he makes on Bliss Carman's *Wild Garden* – 'There is little sign of decadence or failing vision in this volume' (134) – contradict his own critical principles. Not surprisingly, he was much more inclined to exercise the sharp edge of his critical intelligence on those writers he did not know than on his friends or acquaintances. As his review of Laura Riding's *Contemporaries and Snobs* (122-3) attests, Pratt could be scathing about critics who dismissed work he valued; habitually, however, he would look for features of the work to praise rather than for weaknesses to castigate.

If some of the poets Pratt so generously encouraged failed to live up to his best expectations of them, his reviews can nevertheless send us back to the work of those who may have disappeared from sight but deserved a different fate. In selecting the reviews to be reprinted here, I included all those that dealt with the writers who have become a part of the Canadian literary canon, but I also chose two that led me to discover the work of two women writers whose poetry seems to me deserving of renewed attention, namely, Verna Loveday Harden and Mona Gould. I have, moreover, tried to reflect the broad variety of non-Canadian books Pratt reviewed.

If Pratt was in demand as a reviewer, he was also called on to attest to the merit of others' books in a different way. His work as a writer of forewords is largely an index of his capacity for warm and broadly encompassing friendship, but it is also a measure of his stature in the cultural community of his day. He was of course asked to lend his name in approbation of many collections of verse, but also to endorse such books as Sir Ellsworth Flavelle's *Photography, A Craft and Creed* and William Sherwood Fox's *Saint Ignace, Canadian Altar of Martyrdom*. The principle of selection for the forewords reprinted here was that they throw some light on Pratt's own sense of how the imagination of the creative writer or critic works. For example, in his tribute to Jack McLaren's *Our Great Ones*, Pratt refers to the new forms of Canadian comedy as an indicator of the country's new intellectual maturity, arguing that the comic muse's being asked to 'throw a bag of salt into the cauldron of romance' (168) suggests that Canada is finally growing up. Likewise, his foreword to Samuel Morgan-Powell's collection of poetry *Down the Years*, as I have indicated, sets out Pratt's position that the work of creative writer and critic are interdependent, a theme he would return to in an address entitled 'The Outlook for Poetry.' He argued there that 'a renaissance of Canadian poetry can only be effected by a conjunction of public interest, the operation of critical taste, and of poetic productivity.' Regarding the creation of the second factor, Pratt said, 'we do not half appreciate what we owe to reviewers, columnists, and literary critics' (242).

The introductions to the novels of Herman Melville and Thomas Hardy, which represent another dimension of Pratt's prose, were no doubt commissioned work Pratt undertook to supplement his relatively meagre income, but they are valuable for the light they shed on his view of two writers whose work has obvious and well-documented affinities with his own.[13] *Moby Dick* Pratt calls 'one of the most original books of the world' (177), convincing readers as it does that 'Chaos itself is subject to architectural treatment' (180). Its place in the canon, Pratt maintains, 'springs from the underlying feeling of mystery, the sense of clash between vague titanic forces' (178).

That a writer's criticism is likely to illuminate that writer's own work as well as, or better than, the work putatively being addressed is a critical commonplace, so it is not surprising to find that much of what Pratt says of Hardy could be said of himself, but two comments seem particularly transferable. The first is the statement that in Hardy's work 'the life of an individual is merged in the life of his race, and that of the race is placed against geological history, and the geological against the solar and astronomical' (181); the second, that in his work 'the dark tones are relieved by the personality of Hardy himself, by his immense sympathies and by his perception of the fine grain in the human material' (184).

The introductions to the novels of Melville and Hardy are teaching documents, so there is a similarity in stance between these and the undergraduate lectures, despite the difference between written and oral styles. The undergraduate lectures are generally mundane and highly derivative, being little if anything more than the competent working notes of a professor of English who lacked extensive formal academic training in literature but who had obviously read widely in the discipline. Amid the largely unremarkable prose, however, readers will every now and then encounter an arresting phrase or a thought that seems notably felicitously expressed. Witness Pratt's grudging admiration for the work of D.H. Lawrence summed up in the brief but evocative asssertion 'He has a jungle imagination, rich and luxuriant' (194).

The subject range of the lectures is similarly largely unremarkable, though Murdo Mackinnon's account of Pratt 'The Man and the Teacher,' which refers to Pratt's teaching Shakespeare and modern poetry and drama, might lead readers to expect a narrower range than in fact exists.[14] The lecture notes in the Pratt collection show that his undergraduate teaching covered Renaissance drama other than Shakespeare, the early canonical novelists, and eighteenth- and nineteenth-century non-fiction prose writers, as well as those subjects Mackinnon recalls as Pratt's special territory.

From this body of material I have selected those lectures which deal with writers who in some significant way shaped Pratt's thinking or aesthetic (like T.H. Huxley); who addressed the same subjects, albeit sometimes in a different manner (like Robinson Jeffers); or to whom he expresses an antipathy that throws into relief his own position (like D.H. Lawrence).

The extant scripts of Pratt's public lectures are relatively few in number but show the poet's mind grappling with some of the greatest poetry written in English – work by Shakespeare, Milton, and Wordsworth – and with broader and more significant issues – the function of the university and the role of the humanities in the post-Second World War era, for example – than those addressed in the undergraduate talks. These public lectures offer evidence of Pratt's strengths as a critic, in showing him capable of originality of approach and perception.

Pratt discusses *King Lear* by examining the way Shakespeare adapts the speech of the play's characters to their mental states, and in doing so Pratt makes a number of acute observations. Of Goneril and Regan's conversation at the end of I.i, for example, he remarks, '[It] has all the slangy flavour of underworld thugs' (204), citing Goneril's 'Let's hit together' as evidence. And Regan's remark after the blinding of Gloucester, 'Let him smell / His way to Dover,' Pratt designates the most 'brutal sentence in all literature' (202). His tracing of the way the play unfolds and its cumulative construction of meaning seem, at least to this non-Shakespearean specialist, a subtle and revealing analysis of *Lear*, grounded in a detailed knowledge of the structure of Shakespearean tragedy.

Pratt's admiration for Milton and Wordsworth is equally clear. His approach to *Paradise Lost* is again through style, and among the qualities for which he lauds the epic poet is one which is important to Pratt's own aesthetic: 'the musical roll of personal and geographical names' (219). His approach to Wordsworth, by contrast, concentrates mainly on the substance of his writing. While freely acknowledging the 'absurd lengths' to which Wordsworth pushed his theory of subject-matter and diction, his lack of humour, the bathos of some of his poems, and the eminently dispensable pathetic fallacy, Pratt 'confess[es] to astonishment at the manner in which a great theme summoned the trumpet to his lips' (226). Wordsworth's political prose and sonnets are particularly recommended to Pratt's audience as meaningful to contemporary readers, given the parallel political turmoil of Wordsworth's and Pratt's own age.

A recurring concern of the lectures on modern poetry, as of the essays, is the excesses of modernity. Irritated by those poets who strain for clever effects, Pratt reaches a climax of annoyance in discussing the work of the Dadaists and Surrealists, those writers who applied the theory of psychoanalysis to their practice in such a way that the literature produced was 'not governed by any kind of rational design' (251). He blasts Edith Sitwell and Ezra Pound for their use of private imagery, and arraigns Gertrude Stein for the kind of repetition that he finds 'the last word in banality' (257). All these facets of modernism seem to Pratt the antithesis of art because they obscure communication, which he saw as the primary purpose of art. The Golden Mean in poetry was attained, according to Pratt, when the poetry was 'complex, containing a number of elements in varying proportions, tune, ideas, and images and emotional suggestion' (243).

But if he abhorred the stylistic excesses of some of the moderns, he saw as the 'most vicious enemy' (258) to the arts the ideological prescriptions of communism. At the same time Pratt insisted on the moral and social value of the humanities, seeing it as their job to foster 'the rehabilitating process of love' and to diminish 'the destroying power of hate' (283). He was equally impatient with naïve optimism and unrelieved pessimism, again seeking a mean when he argued that 'messages of hope and faith need to be run through the bulletins of realism' (281).

Pratt responded with lavish praise to the work of some contemporaries, A.J.M. Smith and Roy Campbell among them, and to the 'Immortal Memory' of Robert Burns. Where hyperbole would ingratiate, Pratt was clearly willing to engage in it, and public occasions seem to have called this quality out in his assessments, as the Campbell and Burns pieces most clearly show.

In all Pratt's prose, his critical stance is that of the liberal humanist. Whether he is dealing with the lesser-known writers of his own country (writers whose contributions either creative or critical he wants to encourage and acknowledge), the more widely known giants of British and American literature, or the theologians of the Christian world; and whether he is attending to the literature of the present or the past, of romance, idealism, or realism, he measures the work according to a common standard: the extent to which it fostered what he saw as the 'discovery and reassertion of values for the human family, aesthetic or social or religious, or all three combined' (241).

1 David G. Pitt, *The Truant Years* [hereafter TY] and *The Master Years* [hereafter MY] (Toronto: U of Toronto P, 1984 and 1987). Lila Laakso, 'Descriptive Bibliography,' in E.J. Pratt, *Complete Poems* [hereafter CP], ed. Sandra Djwa and Gordon Moyles, Part Two (Toronto: U of Toronto P, 1989) 373–497; see especially sections D, G, and H.

2 TY 79. Though Pitt does not so indicate, the byline on this article is Rev. E.J. Pratt, and it therefore represents the lone occasion on which Pratt was published under this title.

3 Stephen Leacock, *Sunshine Sketches of a Little Town* (Toronto: Bell and Cockburn, 1912); *My Discovery of the West: A Discussion of East and West in Canada* (Toronto: Thomas Allen, 1937)

4 *Winnowed Wisdom* (Toronto: McClelland and Stewart, 1971) 95–8
5 *Last Leaves* (Toronto: McClelland and Stewart, 1970) 13–20
6 Sandra Djwa, *E.J. Pratt: The Evolutionary Vision* (Toronto: Copp Clark; Montreal: McGill-Queen's UP, 1974) 25
7 Djwa 27
8 Quoted in Clara Thomas and John Lennox, *William Arthur Deacon: A Canadian Literary Life* (Toronto: U of Toronto P, 1982) 80–1
9 For a comprehensive list of titles, see Lila and Raymond Laakso et al., *E.J. Pratt: An Annotated Bibliography* (Downsview: ECW Press, 1980) 160–1.
10 'Brighter Days Ahead,' *Canadian Poetry Magazine*, March 1937: 6
11 For a complete listing of Pratt's reviews known at the time of compilation, see section D of Lila Laakso's descriptive bibliography in Part 2 of CP 467–73.
12 A comparison of Pratt's review of Bliss Carman's *Wild Garden* (133–5) with that written by F.R. Scott for *Canadian Mercury* June 1929: 140–1, shows the latter's greater willingness to engage in sharp-edged criticism of established figures. Scott begins his review by asserting, 'Here are seventy-five pages of verse by a man who has written as good poetry as anyone in this country, and there is not one poem to be found among them.' The subsequent practice of anthologists and critics has by and large concurred with Scott's rather than Pratt's judgment.
13 See, for example, R.J. Gibbs, 'The Living Contour: The Whale Symbol in Melville and Pratt,' *Canadian Literature* Spring 1969: 17–25; Djwa, *E.J. Pratt: The Evolutionary Vision*, 79–80; Susan Gingell, ed., *E.J. Pratt on His Life and Poetry* (Toronto: U of Toronto P, 1983) 43–4; and David G. Pitt, 'Shades of Egdon,' TY 260–70.
14 *Tamarack Review* Winter 1958: 71–4

# Editorial Principles and Procedures

My first concern as editor has been to provide an accurate and readable text of selected prose by Pratt. In choosing the texts for inclusion, I aimed for broad representation of the many types of prose he wrote, and selected those pieces that could significantly enhance readers' knowledge of Pratt – his philosophy, aesthetics, or poetics – or of his cultural milieu. More detailed comments about how works were chosen for individual sections can be found in the Introduction.

Because the texts reproduced here were created in and for a variety of contexts, there is a considerable degree of variation in the accuracy as well as the house styles of the copy texts. I have made the punctuation practice consistent, by adding serial commas where they did not already exist, removing commas or dashes before restrictive modifiers, and introducing with a colon those quotations which exemplify a point just made; and I have added punctuation where the absence of it potentially obscures the meaning of the text. Moreover, I have not followed Pratt's early habit of placing a dash after a comma. Capitalization practice has likewise been normalized, and obvious grammar, typographical, and spelling errors emended. British spelling is used throughout, and Pratt's variant spellings of the same word regularized. The following categories of accidentals have been regularized in accordance with the house style of the University of

Toronto Press: capitalization of titles, quotation marks (single, with double quotation marks for interior quotations), and ellipsis points (triple throughout).

Abbreviations are expanded without comment, except in the stories, informal essays, and lectures, where the informality of abbreviation is appropriate. In the lecture notes, after initially referring to authors by their full first names, Pratt would frequently thereafter abbreviate the names to first initials; these I have also silently expanded. When Pratt refers to a word or term, he usually puts it in quotation marks, a practice I have retained and made consistent.

I have checked Pratt's quotations against their sources wherever possible, but Pratt was not a careful scholarly writer, and he often failed to identify sources. The sources of some three- or four-word phrases he quotes have not seemed to me important enough to justify spending long hours tracking them down, though I have noted those I was able to find. I have been unable to identify a number of the sources of longer quotations, even after hours of searching and consultation with colleagues. Pratt also frequently quotes inaccurately, so I have recorded substantive variants in the notes, and have corrected seriously misleading quotations or those that do not make sense as misquoted, and then recorded those changes in the notes.

Where Pratt made holograph additions to the typescripts of his lectures and addresses, they are included in the text only if he clearly indicated their place. In other cases these additions are relegated to the notes, where their intended places in the text are considered. Significant deletions are also noted. Where holograph passages or brief additions are unclear, I have so indicated by placing a question mark after the unclear word or words: 'Dowden [?]' indicates the reading is highly uncertain.

The title that appears at the head of each selection is Pratt's, with the exceptions of the reviews and Pratt's untitled lectures. I have formulated titles for the latter, and have placed the interpolations in square brackets. Information about each work's first publication or public presentation (including approximate dating where determinable and exact dating is not known) follows all titles.

Within each grouping of prose works, I have generally followed a chronological principle in ordering the material. In the case of the lectures and addresses, whose dates of composition and delivery are often indeterminable, I have grouped the undergraduate lectures first and the addresses intended for a wider audience second. I have arranged the former according to the time when the authors about whom Pratt was speaking lived and wrote, and the latter according to an increasingly broad focus of interest in subject matter.

# Biographical Chronology

| | |
|---|---|
| 1882 | Born at Western Bay, Newfoundland, 4 February; third child of eight of the Rev. John Pratt, Yorkshire-born clergyman, and Fanny Pitts Knight, daughter of a Newfoundland sea captain |
| 1888–1902 | Educated in outport schools and at the Methodist College, St John's, with a three-year intermission, 1897–1900, as a clerk in a dry-goods store |
| 1902–4 | Teacher at Moreton's Harbour, a fishing village in Notre Dame Bay |
| 1904–7 | Probationary minister in the Methodist ministry at Clarke's Beach — Cupids and Bell Island — Portugal Cove |
| 1907–11 | Student in philosophy, Victoria College, University of Toronto, BA 1911 |
| 1912 | Received MA degree, University of Toronto |
| 1913 | Received BD degree; ordained into the Methodist ministry |
| 1913–20 | Demonstrator-lecturer in psychology, University of Toronto; assistant minister in a number of churches around Streetsville, Ontario |
| 1917 | Received PhD from University of Toronto — thesis, *Studies in Pauline Eschatology and Its Background*, published in Toronto; *Rachel: A Sea Story of Newfoundland in Verse* printed privately in New York |

| | |
|---|---|
| 1918 | Married Viola Whitney (BA Victoria College 1913), 20 August |
| 1920 | Joined Department of English, Victoria College |
| 1921 | Birth of only child, Mildred Claire |
| 1923 | *Newfoundland Verse*, first commercially published book of poems |
| 1925 | *The Witches' Brew* published in London |
| 1926 | *Titans* published in London; *The Witches' Brew* in Toronto |
| 1927 | *The Iron Door: An Ode* published in Toronto |
| 1930 | Appointed professor, Department of English, Victoria College; elected Fellow of the Royal Society of Canada; *The Roosevelt and the Antinoe* published in New York; *Verses of the Sea*, with introduction by Charles G.D. Roberts, published in Toronto |
| 1930–52 | Taught summer school at Dalhousie, Queen's, and the University of British Columbia |
| 1932 | *Many Moods* published in Toronto |
| 1935 | *The Titanic* published in Toronto |
| 1936 | One of the founders and first editor, from January 1936 to August 1943, of *Canadian Poetry Magazine* |
| 1937 | *The Fable of the Goats and Other Poems* published in Toronto, winner of the Governor-General's Award |
| 1938 | Appointed senior professor, Victoria College |
| 1940 | *Brébeuf and His Brethren* published in Toronto, winner of the Governor-General's Award; awarded the Royal Society's Lorne Pierce Gold Medal for distinguished service to Canadian literature |
| 1941 | *Dunkirk* published in Toronto |
| 1943 | *Still Life and Other Verse* published in Toronto |
| 1944 | *Collected Poems* published in Toronto |
| 1945 | *Collected Poems*, with introduction by William Rose Benét, published in New York; *They Are Returning* published in Toronto; received D. Litt. from University of Manitoba, first honorary degree (others: LL.D., Queen's 1948; D.C.L., Bishop's 1949; D. Litt., McGill 1949; D. Litt., Toronto 1953; D. Litt., As- |

sumption 1955; D. Litt., New Brunswick 1957; D. Litt., Western Ontario 1957; D. Litt., Memorial 1961)

1946 Created Companion of the Order of St Michael and St George in the King's Honours List

1947 *Behind the Log* and *Ten Selected Poems* published in Toronto

1952 *Towards the Last Spike* published in Toronto, winner of the Governor-General's Award; awarded the University of Alberta Gold Medal for distinguished service to Canadian literature; member of the editorial board, from 20 December 1952 to 13 September 1958, of *Saturday Night*

1953 Retired from Victoria College; appointed professor emeritus of English

1955 Elected honorary president of the Canadian Authors' Association

1957 Received Canada Council award on 75th birthday

1958 *The Collected Poems of E.J. Pratt*, edited by Northrop Frye, published in Toronto

1959 Received Civic Award of Merit from the City of Toronto

1961 Received the Canada Council medal for distinction in the field of literature

1963 Elected honorary member of the Empire Club of Canada; elected first honorary member of the Arts and Letters Club

1964 Died in Toronto, 26 April

# PURSUITS AMATEUR AND ACADEMIC

# A / Pratt as Story-Teller

## 'A Northern Holiday'

(*Daily News* [St John's, Newfoundland] 23 August 1907: 5)

Seekers after health, pleasure, and natural scenery could find few places so generous in their supply of these blessings as some of the delightful little islands and harbours which impart so much beauty to the coast and waters of Notre Dame Bay. That this bay has been adjudged pre-eminent in this respect may be proved by the numerical advantage in reference to passengers which the SS *Clyde* has over her sister boats in the other bays of the island. The tourist never fails to realize his expectations in visiting this bay. The rivers which flow into it contain salmon, well able to sustain a high state of nervous tension for an hour and to advertise the strength and suppleness of his rod. A few miles inland the wild duck is to be found in great abundance, and deer are so plentiful that sportsmen in quest of them seldom return disappointed.

It is the beauty of the scenery, though, which so charms the admirer of nature who is fortunate enough to spend a few weeks in the delightful bay. Hundreds of picturesque islands lie a short distance from the mainland – objects alike of beauty and of safety – receiving upon their own little shores the force of the northern and eastern blast and thus giving convenience and safety to the harbours behind them. So narrow are the channels between many of these little islands, that the conversation carried on by the inhabitants is frequently overheard on board the steamer as she glides through the placid waters. The air is so clear and balmy that one fancies he is living in another zone and luxuriating in a southern climate.

Instead of being poisoned by the bacteria-laden dust and damp so characteristic of the city, the air is charged with the spirit of health and vigour, the breeze from the sea imparting a delicious coolness to the atmosphere even in the hottest weather. This transparency and purity of the air must, to a large extent, contribute to the wondrous splendour of the sunsets, seen from various elevations on these islands. August 15th witnessed one of the most glorious settings that the eye could possibly gaze on. It was towards the close of a beautiful day which succeeded a very heavy thunderstorm, and the sun slowly sank, amidst great billows of cumulus clouds, which assumed every possible gradation of colour that could be revealed by the spectroscope. The more immediate and heavier masses of cloud were flanked by lighter stratus of the cirrus kind, tinged with every hue from green to violet. Admirers of the beautiful in nature must have had their aesthetic sense enthralled as they watched the transient shades change, until they faded away into the dull grey, and final darkness of night.

But one must not be led into the deception that the pleasure-affording capacity of the country is not diminished by counter-balancing detractions. Perfect, indeed, it would be in this respect if it were not for the ubiquitous mosquito. The sand-fly may be bad enough upon a dull day when you are fishing by the side of a willow-shaded stream, but we think that even that species of fly is not so intolerable as his larger and most powerful brother – the nipper – the rattlesnake of Newfoundland. This diabolical invention of the Prince of the powers of the air does not confine his haunts to the river or the bog, but pursues the returning sportsman with attentions that are almost human in their affection right to his very door, and as if to furnish indelible proof of its loyalty to the human species, invades the sanctity of the bedroom with just as little compunction as it would a log cabin. No improvised apparatus is ingenious enough to keep him out. You spend an hour before going to bed in visiting summary vengeance upon the upper occupants of the room, and then in language more lay than clerical and in maledictions not strictly confined to Webster, but still wishing and trying to be orthodox, you lay your weary frame upon the bed and sink into a deep slumber. At 12 o'clock, or so, a mysterious sensation gradually rouses you to a dim consciousness that your blood supply is running rather short, and the first thing which strikes your awakening senses is that ominous buzz, revealing the terrifying fact that the enemy is in possession of the fort. For an hour or so that noise will continue around your ear, approaching and receding, making your nocturnal condition considerably worse than that of Tantalus in your frenzy to 'get at 'em.' Then when one finally settles on the face, your hand comes round like a twelve-inch shell and thunders down on the bitter spot with a fiery force which a trained pugilist would envy, and then you strike up the first chord of the 'Dead March' in *Saul* in honour of the passing away of the blood relation.

But the fight is not yet over. An inquest is generally held over the mangled body of the slain, and the would-be sleeper finds, owing to his presence in the room at the time of the tragedy, he is kept in a state of angry and persistent surveillance until dawn. The nipper or the mosquito offers a wide field for the inventive faculty of the scientist. Perhaps a future decade will pay tribute to the memory of some great humanitarian, equal to Pasteur or Koch, who discovered an anti-toxin to the sting of the nipper.

**'A Western Experience'**
(*Acta Victoriana* October 1910: 3–8)

I had often wished very strongly to see a little of the vast prairie stretches that lie on the other side of the Great Lakes, and as it was not altogether practicable, financially and otherwise, to take the trip out there just for the gratification of that personal wish, I entered quite enthusiastically into the plan of employment by which the student services could be distributed throughout Saskatchewan and Alberta. Estevan, in the southern part of Saskatchewan, and not far from the international boundary, became my objective.

When I arrived there my Superintendent, the Chairman of the District, outlined to me my plan of campaign, and generously supplied me with an abundance of data, amongst which geographical facts, racial characteristics, broncho eccentricities, and the fundamentals of the Methodist Discipline were all combined together in one bewildering confusion. Somewhat weakened rather than stimulated by this copious hypodermic of advice, I was led out to get acquainted with an animal called 'Jack,' upon whose travelling ability and other incidental perfections the Superintendent spoke with glowing emphasis. I must confess that when I entered the stable and saw my summer companion for the first time, I was most peculiarly impressed. As my shadow fell across the doorway he suddenly turned his head, brought the halter-rope up with a quick jerk, ignored my 'Super' completely, and focused his concentration upon me. I stood off at a safe distance of twenty feet and returned the stare. He was indeed qualified, both by heredity and education, as a broncho. The brand had been burned there, large and distinct. He was no beauty. Nature had designed him in a freak of architectural genius for a wild, nomadic life upon the plains and not for the purposes of civilization. He was short, thick-set, and of very disproportionate build. His hind legs had so far outstripped their front competitors in length that the result of this congenital infirmity was to slope the back in the direction of the head at such an angle as to give a prospective rider considerable nervous uneasiness. But it was not this so much that set me thinking. It was that critical, ironical look, that attitude of disdain for a tenderfoot, which boded trouble. And yet at times during my inspection it seemed to me that his features were disposed to relax into a look of semi-innocence – a disposition to conciliation, provided the proper means were used; but I found myself powerless to analyse this apparent alternation of expression, as I did not know how much subtlety of purpose ran beneath it.

However, as I did not feel like wasting my afternoon in those fruitless speculations, I immediately made preparations for a ten-mile drive to Hitchcock, a town along the railway. I was greatly relieved when I saw the ease with which my new friend was tackled into the buggy, and having received some further directions and well-needed good wishes from my fatherly Chairman, I at once struck the trail for the above-mentioned town. Nothing eventful happened at first. The little fellow travelled along famously; and for the first few miles, with the exception of a few slight starts at the shriek of an engine in the distance, I had no reason but to congratulate myself upon having secured a tolerably good roadster for my summer work. It is true that it felt a little embarrassing upon the way to hear the passing comments of people whose aesthetic tastes were continually being exercised upon the wondrous symmetry of this novel type of horse. But what of that? Jack did not understand the nature of the compliments, and as for myself I was not responsible for them.

I journeyed on for a few miles further, passing several homesteads upon the way and exchanging salutations with farmers who were hard at work with the drill and plough. After a while I got out upon the untouched open prairie, and found the driving somewhat rough and monotonous. No variegated scenery delighted the eye; no lake, no river, no hill; not even a geographical irregularity; nothing but yellow sod, broken here and there by an occasional trail. This absence of interest had as its only redeeming feature a desire to get out of it, and seeing a homestead in the distance I turned in the direction of it in order to secure full and accurate information. As I drew up I could see nobody around, so I jumped out of the buggy, tied Jack to the wheel of a big cart, the only thing in sight available for that purpose, and walked over to the door of the house. A man came out, and in answer to my question began to give me all directions necessary. While he was speaking my ears were suddenly deafened by a huge crash, and looking around I saw to my bewilderment my faithful friend, the broncho, starting off at a home stretch across the prairie, with the rope which he had broken from the wheel swinging from his neck, and everything on board – grip, overcoat, rifle, etc. I stood for a moment and stared; then I followed, but soon slowed down. As well try to catch an express. If the circumstances were different I might have admired his speed. But now I could only think of his destination. Would it be the Coast or the Yukon? Perhaps it was the Rockies he decided on as his summer resort. I walked on silently, my eyes fixed upon that buggy rhythmically rising and falling with the prairie bumps. On in that direction somewhere lay the track. Four unusually high jumps of the buggy in rapid succession revealed its position. Still no sign of a slower rate. Jack was making for the horizon, there being no other stopping place worthy of his notice. I walked on and picked up a part of the reins, the whip, and a hame-strap. These would be valuable as souvenirs, at any rate. One thing I knew, I was going in the direction of the town. I saw the top part of the Hitchcock grain elevator, and that relieved me of the thought of having to spend the night out. It only meant trudging on for an hour or two, and ruminating over the loss of all this world's goods, which was not much after all. I felt it quite pleasant to moralize upon the emptiness of worldly possessions, for in such an emergency that particular kind of philosophy has its comforts. It was not long, however, before I saw a horse and buggy, with a couple of men, coming towards me, and when they approached they asked me if I had lost my horse. Upon replying that I had, they told me that they had caught a runaway and brought him into one of the town stables. My relief was great. So he had made for the town after all; he had probably regarded it as a convenient side-station to get a supply of oats for his trip. The first thing I did when I got into the town was to buy a halter-rope calculated to hold an elephant. This, I thought, would at least check his ardour for summer excursions, although it would not guarantee the physical integrity of the buggy whenever he felt like trying conclusions with the new rope.

My troubles, however, were not yet ended. There were many lessons I had yet to learn before I could lay claim to a Western knowledge of horsemanship. It occurred to me that when I eventually arrived at my headquarters for the summer it would be a good idea to purchase a saddle, which brilliant idea was reinforced in my mind by the sorry plight of my poor buggy. Jack could not run away, at any rate, without his rider, and I knew enough about his weakness for oats to conclude that it would be generally in the direction of his home he would run, rather than away from it. I felt quite satisfied with my new plan. What a lot of bother it would avoid – the putting on of the harness, the exhaustion resulting from an exciting chase, my own convalescence, the expense of the buggy's repair, and so on. What health-producing exercise it would be, as well! During the whole of the following week I travelled a good deal, and a more docile, quiet, faithful horse could not be imagined. I was anxious, though, to test him on the canter, and one beautiful morning I secured a saddle and went out into the stable with my friend, Mr M–, who had the reputation of being one of the best horsemen in the country. Just as I was tightening the straps, Mr M– drew my attention to a very peculiar action on the part of the horse. He was taking a deep breath, and continued to take it until he had increased in size to almost twice his usual girth. I asked the reason for this very occult phenomenon, wondering whether the broncho, with his unusual penetration, was getting his lungs in readiness for purposes peculiarly his own. I suggested this as an explanation. 'No,' said my friend, 'he is just doing that so as to make the straps look tight at the start; but later on, when he gets well out on the prairie, he will blow out again, the straps will become loose, the saddle will shift, and the rider, well –.' I made some remark about the super-equine intelligence of such an animal, and following my friend's advice, I patiently waited for exhalation, and then instantly tied the strap. I mounted and rode off, feeling safe now that Mr M– by his valuable advice had precluded any possibility of sudden mishap. I began to enjoy the ride immensely. The air was invigorating, the road dry and fairly even. Every added minute of safety was a new source of self-congratulation. I took as my cavalry training ground the road to one of my appointments, so that I might familiarize myself with necessary future directions, and when I had ridden five miles

I was confronted by a very sluggish slough, too long to ride around, but yet narrow enough to render the passage of it apparently easy. Practically none of the sloughs in the country were too deep to ford, though some of them covered very muddy beds. The broncho hesitated to go across. Sure-footed though he was, he declined the prospect of a burial in soft mud. Still I knew it was the only alternative to a considerable circuit, with the probability of getting on a wrong trail. I coaxed him a little, then gave him a touch of the spur. The latter method worked upon his nervous system quite a bit. The surface of the slough was about eight inches from the bank, and after a little more urging Jack condescended to place his forefeet in the water. They sank several inches in mud. I felt sorry now that I had urged him in; so did he, for the next moment, without any warning beyond an indignant snort, his head suddenly dropped, those long hind legs of his shot up in the air like a flash, and I suddenly learnt more about analytical geometry – the path of a parabola, and the properties of curves – than I had ever learnt at the university. The exact height of my flight, the precise depth of my fall, I have never been able accurately to determine. I didn't feel in such a mathematical mood to draw so fine distinctions. All I know is that I have certain important data in my possession which is at the disposal of the Royal Astronomical Society at any time they wish to acquire it. I managed somehow to extricate myself from the bed of the slough, and when I had regained some composure I saw my broncho quietly munching the grass by the bank. I went up to him. He made no resistance, showed no concern, but looked at me with every feature stamped with cool and placid innocence. The only severe derangement I sustained was a serious dislocation of vocabulary which, had Noah Webster or Samuel Johnson been present, would have occasioned a very animated discussion upon the orthodoxy of verbal hybrids. I got in the saddle again and rode home. I met Mr M– at the door. I did not need to explain; he saw and understood. I made up my mind that I would ride every day, trusting that constant companionship would result in friendship. It proved afterwards to have been the only mishap of that nature for the summer.

Some time has passed since then. I do not know what has become of that broncho; neither do I care. Perhaps if some lone wanderer should pay a visit to Saskatchewan, and stroll over that particular part of the prairie, he might discover a little mound with a rough stone at the head of it bearing the words *Hic jacet*, in token of the commitment to the dust of the last remains of an eccentric broncho, slain in a moment of passion at the hand of an infuriated successor.

**'"Hooked": A Rocky Mountain Experience'**
(*Acta Victoriana* March 1914: 286–91)

Three men were seated around a blazing log-fire one cool, still night in June, when the Alpine Club was holding its annual camp in the district of Lake O'Hara. It was no mere accident which had brought them together. The gently rising bank upon which they reclined, so soft with its covering of moss, and shaded by its network of overhanging cedar, would, indeed, have made it the favourite spot for tired climbers wandering about promiscuously for rest. Here, however, it was genuine affinity of interest which was responsible for the grouping, as it was a certain native streak of laziness common to all three that led them first to the coveted nook.

For nearly two days they had been at the camp, and had watched the stream of climbers, both graduate and prospective, pouring in. There was a lot of excitement. All were talking about the coming climbs. Cathedral Mountain had been chosen as the qualifying peak, and all eyes were being constantly directed towards that upward slope of timber, rock, and snow, where, at an altitude of over ten thousand feet, the ice-clad summit flashed back to the sun its borrowed brilliance. Questions were upon all lips. Expressions reflective of the most varied emotions were upon all faces. Was there going to be any danger? Would there be any likelihood of getting caught in an avalanche, or in a storm? Usually, however, the sentiment expressed was one of joy at the prospect of conquest, the honour of graduation. In a country where the greatest attraction was a mighty chain of mountains, it was natural and inevitable that both thought and expression should be soaring somewhere between glacial summits and brooding thunder-clouds. Imagine, then, if you can, the bathos of the situation when an Easterner, known in the camp as 'Scotty,' came up and, accosting another Easterner, said: 'Say, Irish, old chap, that looks pretty tough, that climbing. Let's qualify tomorrow, and get it over. I came out here to get some good fishing, and here everybody is gone mad over that peak.'

'Well, now,' replied the Hibernian addressed, 'the very thing I was just thinking about. There's no logic that compels a fellow to die before his time. Five thousand feet of a drop tomorrow evening might be a painless way of getting rid of life's sorrows, but I prefer the end to come later. I brought a most elaborate outfit of fishing-gear with me, hoping to get a few stray salmon or trout, and that's what I'm after.'

A friendship strong and cordial at once sprang up between these two fishing sports, and they decided that they would see if, out of the two hundred members attending camp, there were any others of like sympathy. Their search disclosed but one, a Westerner, a business man from Edmonton, Dan by name, who specialized in camp and game outfitting, and who accordingly had brought with him a vast collection of specially designed flies, rods, reels, catgut, lines, floats, etc., etc. This trio announced their intention of supplying the camp with fresh fish for the remainder of the season, an announcement which was greeted with a great deal of encouragement mixed with chaff. Some of the more aesthetic amongst the campers thought that the introduction of the question of fish was both an emotional and intellectual descent from the sublime plane of soliloquy and meditation, occasioned and fostered by the presence of the mountains. Undoubtedly they were right, but a considerable number welcomed the idea after they had found out that the great staple of diet for the ten days was to be ham and black currant jam, either in sandwiches or without.

It was, then, for the formulation of plans for the purpose of depleting the waters of the Rockies of their finny treasures that the three men in question sought the quietude of the cedar-sheltered nook. The outcome of that little council was to the effect that two expeditions be made within the next week, one by Scotty and Irish, to Emerald Lake, the other by Dan and Irish, down the Yoho Valley, to see if the Kicking-Horse River would supply the need. The former trip is alone described here.

Great reports had been heard of famous fishing excursions to that lake. Hundreds of large speckled trout had been taken out of it. One lady in the camp stated that she had been there herself, and that at the remote western corner, just at the junction of the main mountain stream with the lake, she had landed several fish averaging between three and four pounds. That settled it. Early on the following morning those two adventurers, well supplied with bait and tackle, thanks to the generosity of their kind friend from Edmonton, struck the trail for Hector station, boarded a freight train for Field, and drove a distance of eight miles to where lay one of nature's loveliest spots - a lake encircled by massive ramparts of mountains, some of them forest-clothed, others ice-clad, with streams of clear and sparkling water rushing precipitously down, as if glad to unite their life with that of the fair lake beneath. Emerald Lake was worth the visit ten times over for its beauty. Its colour was bluish-green, of the richest hue; its name was well chosen. Rapturously they feasted on the scene before them, but the feast came to an end very abruptly as they suddenly thought of the utilitarian purpose for which they had come. The pledge made to the camp had to be redeemed. To face that crowd without a plentiful supply of fish would be infamy. A man was standing just a little distance away, cleaning out a small boat. They went over, made a bargain for the boat, and paid extra for the advice to select as the fishing-ground a point at the other end of the lake - advice which coincided remarkably with that of the lady who first volunteered the information. The boatman claimed a canny relationship with the habits of the fish. They were most methodical in routine; they ate with the regularity of clockwork; they swam processionally; they might be caught by ardent fishermen between nine and ten in the evening and between three and four in the morning, but, generally speaking, they were ascetically inclined, refusing to yield to the lure of the red-blooded worm, or to the flirtation of a daintily dressed fly.

Aflame with excitement at this strange account they launched the boat, and rowed directly towards the point indicated. Heedless of the fact that it was only three o'clock in the afternoon, the sportsmen began operations at once. The truth of the old boatman's remark in its negative phase was discovered when, after five hours of punishment, the lake absolutely refused to yield up one of her family. During that long time the two companions hardly uttered a word. The silence at length was broken when Scotty, in rather disconsolate accents, remarked: 'Say, Irish, that old guy up there told us we wouldn't get any fish till nine o'clock. Let's row over to that bank and get something to eat, and then we'll come back.' The suggestion sounded reasonable, and the next hour was spent accordingly. Returning to the same place they teased and lashed the waters till midnight, and yet every fish cooly ignored the summons to dinner.

Tired and dejected, Irish began to invoke the heavens to bear witness that he would not hold himself responsible for what might happen that night. Turning around to his friend he burst out: 'Look here, Scotty, let's go and lynch that boatman, or else scuttle this rotten old tub, and hike back to camp. He gave us to understand this pond was a fish-hatchery. Never a bite will we get here. Besides, 'tis raining. Let's round up the chalet, and see if we can get a bed.' To those expressions of a disorganized spleen, Scotty calmly replied that the boatman had laid particular emphasis upon the early morning hour as the usually successful time, and that if they were on the spot then there would be no question about the landing of a few fine trout.

The chalet was reached, and the proprietress, being aroused out of a peaceful slumber about the hour of midnight, needed considerable persuasion to let them in. The sight of two grotesque and dishevelled forms drenched with rain, dressed in the accoutrements of mountaineers, and with number ten climbing boots, rough-nailed, to waltz across a rich Brussels carpet and a varnished floor before getting to a room, looked, to say the least, forbidding. She finally consented after they had agreed to pay in advance a rate which was more of the nature of a fine than a fee, and which made them face bankruptcy on the spot. Their boots, however, caused enough compensating damage to satisfy their desire for revenge, and after three hours of very broken sleep they rose, and left the house with a clatter that occasioned a torrent of rugged polysyllables and poetic coinages from a score of boarders, who thought that a squadron of cavalry were attempting to make an exit.

The point was again reached, and four long hours were spent in the exasperating suspense of expecting something to happen and nothing happening. Scotty, who was becoming quite emaciated, at last remarked to his companion – 'Cripes! is there anything in this infernal pond? Why not try that patented fly that Dan gave you before we left? It may not be much good, but it is a last resort.' Irish immediately grabbed his pocketbook and extracted from it the most wonderful piece of fishing mechanism ever conceived. It consisted of two hooks so arranged that one might be used for bait while the other was utilized at the same time as a fly. The latter was of the most unique description. The rainbow might well have been envious of its colours. Dan had made a hobby for years of collecting fancy specimens of birds' feathers. He claimed to have in stock representative residua of every known bird existent or extinct, from the dodo to the jay, and, as a result, he had worked out with the most perfect execution this brilliant polychromate at a value that threw the question of its purchase out of all consideration. It was attached to a revolving silver disc, and this again to a polished sinker, which evidently was intended, contrary to usage, to display the attraction of the fly beneath the surface of the water. This precious product Dan had, in true keeping with his lavish and open heart, forced upon them. The two hitherto baffled sportsmen gazed admiringly at this miracle of colour for a few moments; then Irish, having attached it to his rod, reverently, yet sceptically, cast it into the lake. It sank. For five minutes they fixed their attentive gaze upon the fishing-line, when a slight jerk indicated that something had happened. Irish began to reel in impetuously; he had not reeled far before the pull on the line showed that here was a fish worthy of a night's toil. A monster had bitten. Telling Scotty to get ready with the dip-net he continued to reel. The strain on the line was great, a dead, heavy strain, with a few occasional jerks that resembled more the action of an eel than that of a trout. Up came the line, and finally arose before their humiliated and disgusted vision the advance guard of disappointment – the uneven points of a rotted stump – and then the stump itself. But why those intermittent jerks? Just a few inches below, safely held by the barbed point of that famous fly-hook, was a fish. That is all that could be said about it. They were sure of its genus; not of its species. They laid it on a small plank within the boat to examine it. As for its size, its length – well, Scotty took out a pocket-rule and attempted to measure it; he found its length could be estimated better in millimetres than in inches. The record is not given. It was big enough to suggest fish when they were pulling in the line, and they were thankful for the suggestion. Irish took out his watch; it was precisely five minutes after eight. He noted that fact in a memorandum. They sat down, looked at each other, and then at the something that lay before them with a head and a tail. They proceeded to discuss plans as to the disposal of their capture. Would it supply the camp? Yes, with sport. Would it not serve as a relish for some lady climber with delicate appetite? It might. Would it not then give evidence of *trout* in the pond? No; it was a *fish*, that was all.

It was at length decided that it should be returned, with fitting requiem, to its native home from which it should never, never have been lured away. That decision was not carried out. The best-laid plans of human contrivance are often frustrated by agencies beyond our ken. In a slight stumble Scotty had knocked it off the plank. At least that is the only deduction that they could think of. It fell, presumably, into the bottom of the boat. There was no other place for it to fall. After an attempt of half-an-hour with the assistance of a magnifying glass, the search was abandoned, and the two crestfallen sportsmen wended their melancholy way back to Lake O'Hara, where they met a reception too tragic to be entrusted to history.

# B / Pratt as Theologian: Thesis Extracts

**From 'The Demonology of the New Testament in Its Relation to Earlier Developments, and to the Mind of Christ'**
(Unpublished ts, E.J. Pratt Collection, Victoria University in the University of Toronto, 8.61.14–17, 20, 22–32)

When the Gospel narratives are examined there are found variant descriptions of what is evidently the same event. In the most remarkable case of demon possession recorded in the Synoptics, and the best authenticated according to the critical estimate of the New Testament scholars, namely, that of Gadarene, we are confronted with rather perplexing divergences. Matthew refers to two demoniacs meeting Jesus in the country of the Gadarenes, Mark and Luke to only one. The latter two Evangelists give a much fuller description, dwelling upon his fierceness and his extraordinary strength, and pointing out the thoroughness of the cure by describing the demoniac as afterwards clothed and in his right mind, sitting at the feet of Jesus (Mark 5:15; Luke 8:35). Matthew makes no reference to the cure beyond stating the expulsion of the demons.

Just how far a confliction of report on the part of the Evangelists would justify an incredulous attitude towards the main body of the narrative, is difficult to say. Strauss thought he saw a gradual accretion of myth forming around the reported incident as the Evangelists one after the other undertook the task of committing the oral data of the Gospel to writing. It is true that Luke and especially Mark have, as above noted, added impressive ornamentation to the simpler statement of Matthew, and under the belief that Mark was the latest Gospel, as well as from other evidence, Strauss endeavoured to show that all phenomena savouring of the miraculous could dissolve into fanciful constructions of the mythical imagination. The Gadarene incident was the typical 'show-piece' of this process. But the finding of most recent criticism has placed Mark first, and has shown that while the mythical theory might be to some extent justified, yet it cannot adduce this particular argument of chronological sequence as one of its supports. Other writers like Baur and Volkmar, feeling with what seems exaggerated force the presence of discrepancy viewed from the standpoint of the historian, have tried to show that the incident had only an allegorical application, that the healing of the Gadarene just symbolized the conversion of the Gentile races; the legion of demons represented the multitude of heathen gods; the request to enter the swine, the moral impurity of the heathen; and so on.

These interpretations seem to be in either direction too extreme. The natural explanation is not the choice of one and only one alternative, not all myth or all history, all allegory or all fact, but rather an historical incident coloured by subjective prepossessions, and reported through the medium of a crude popular vocabulary, steeped in mythical notions inherited from the past. It is next to impossible not to see current demonology giving some drapery to the narrative. It could be accepted as historical without a great deal of objection, the simple statement of Matthew given in the 30th verse – 'Now there was afar off from them a herd of many swine feeding.' There is nothing very surprising in that statement, for the prospect of gain from commercial intercourse with the Romans might lead lax Jews in that part of the country to ignore some of the prohibitions of the Mosaic law, but the remainder of the narrative awakens a critical spirit. The demons ask Christ to send them into the swine. The answer of Christ in Matthew is 'ὑπάγετε' 'Depart.' Mark and

Luke do not mention the actual word or words which Christ is supposed to have uttered, but use the words 'Καὶ ἐπέτρεψεν αὐτοῖς' 'and he gave them leave.' Evidently the command 'ὑπάγετε' is interpreted as permission. But why? It is certainly an interpretation upon whatever view we may hold. That such an interpretation must be infallible seems scarcely likely in view of disagreement on other details within the same incident. There is no more reason to suppose that the command must be interpreted as permission, than that it is a stern and peremptory charge to leave instantly the body, in entire disregard of the request made. Indeed it seems rather unlikely that Christ should have been guilty of such a wanton economic outrage as the destruction of so vast an amount of property. It can be shown beyond all reasonable doubt that expressions of Jesus were misinterpreted again and again throughout his career, even upon the explicit recognition of the disciples, and allowing that, it appears highly probable here that the Evangelists put a mistaken interpretation upon the command.

This is further borne out by the rest of the incident, which shows a high colour of interpretation. Reference has already been made to the native instinct for incarnation in the nature of demons, and their predilection for the unclean and unsightly. It is also known that it was a common Rabbinical notion that demons immediately after expulsion caused physical disturbances in the immediate area, though themselves generally invisible. If we grant for the sake of argument that the narrative in so far as it relates the presence of a herd of swine is correct, and also that the demoniac was cured of his disease, and again, that the swine actually perished, we are not on the ground of that concession forced to accept the reason given by the Evangelists. They took an explanation that was furnished as the ready-made product of their age, and which was to them the most natural one. The expulsion of the demons was forcibly corroborated from the Evangelists' point of view when their activity could be so powerfully displayed in some outside quarter. There is no reason to doubt that some destruction was done to a herd of swine upon that occasion. It might well be that there were two historic incidents, one following the other without any real connection between them, and the Evangelists, in accordance with a very common custom of ascribing the cause of some unusual event to some antecedent and proximate event of like remarkable character, may have placed the expulsion of the demons as the explanation of disaster to the swine, or perhaps the 'demoniac,' becoming greatly agitated as he caught sight of the coming of Christ, had by his furious gestures created a panic amongst the swine that resulted in the death of at least some of them ...

The poetry of the Christian pulpit has loved to dwell upon the wondrous transformation from disease into health, and clothed in picturesque detail the reviving of wasted tissues, the infusion of rich healthful blood, the radical cleavage with the past, and the elimination of its effects in their physiological bearing upon the future. With what argument the imagination could justify the free deduction of details such as these against which the records have nothing directly to say, it is not the purpose of this thesis to examine ...

So far an attempt has been made to examine the internal evidence of the narratives to find out upon what basis the reported cures rested. All the statements given by the Evangelists upon this point could be accepted with unchallenged assent, and yet there would still remain the problem fundamental as far as its theological implications are involved, namely, the relation of Jesus to the current belief as above outlined. The difficulties already hinted at, regarding the original facts and the subsequent reports, are in this question brought out with increasing perplexity. The magnitude of the task which lies before that department of scholarship today which takes as its watchword – 'Back to the historical Jesus,' it is extremely hard to estimate. We have the Synoptic problem facing us in an intensified form. Although it is generally held that Mark is the earliest Gospel, yet it is also just as convincingly believed that there is a primitive Gospel, unfortunately lost, from which the Synoptics derived some of their information – the original *logia*. None of the Synoptics are claimed to come from the circle of the Twelve Apostles. The teaching of the Apostles probably lingered in the memory of the early Church, and around that, oral tradition in all likelihood gathered, so that the first Gospels we possess, while they may reflect Apostolic teaching in faithful outline, yet could hardly resist the inevitable encroachments of a generation of tradition. The worries of historians plagued with the scientific instinct of exactitude and destined to live two thousand years following the events, were not anticipated in the busy labours of these early writers. If in the course of thirty years or more, soft memories of a departed one weaved unhistoric yet appropriate images into the web of their imagination, that such a product would baffle the efforts of future analysis, no one even dreamed of. With each Evangelist writing from his own point of view, it would be the most surprising anomaly in the history of human literature, if some transfiguration of the acts and sayings of Christ had not in all sincerity crept in. Of course there is a danger of pressing the point of subjectivity too far. It is indeed a radical tendency that would within thirty years so drape the great figure of Galilee in such an impenetrable mist that no historic form could be seen within. That seems a credible hypothesis only on the disproved supposition of the Synoptics having their literary origin in the second century. But on the other hand, the task of wrestling with the psychology of interpretation is none the less significant. All these writers had their own theological equipment assuredly, and the question of the relation of Christ to demoniacal possession must be faced in full recognition of the fact that it is narrated by men who were confirmed believers in such possession.

Scholars who felt themselves convinced of the absolute omniscience of Jesus, and yet who did not want to accept what seemed the naïve view of demoniacal origin, were driven to the invention of the Accommodation theory to preserve intact the former position. Jesus, coming into the life of a people with radical customs and inherited traditions, had necessarily to accomplish his work by entering into sympathy with popular ideas. In his contact with diseased persons who were believed to be afflicted by demons, while he knew otherwise, yet by yielding to the idea and by impressing upon the patient his power to exterminate the demon, he could work more effectively. The fact is well known that there are insuperable difficulties involved in reaching an adequate and satisfactory treatment of facts when the initial act of interpretation springs out of dogmatic presuppositions. The same set of facts might be appealed to to arbitrate a quarrel between two opposing hypotheses, and the arbitration result, not in the usual procedure of concession and compromise, but in fully rejecting the total demands of both rivals. With such a comparatively limited domain which it is the special business here to investigate, it is quite possible so to deduce from the larger territory of facts, certain theoretical standpoints, which, in their more circumscribed application to this smaller area, might lead us to hopeless cul-de-sacs, from which there could be no escape. The theory of Accommodation is based upon the belief in the omniscience of Jesus. Such a belief in its turn is claimed to be founded upon evidence presented in the Gospels and in other Apostolic literature, and obviously its validity must be proved, if at all, by a close examination of all the data in the New Testament bearing upon the subject of the extent of Christ's knowledge. There is no need here to undertake such a large task as this. It is only necessary to refer to the many statements of Christ, which are amongst the best accredited historical facts of his lifetime, that seem contradictory of a theory of Omniscience. All that is sufficient to point out here is that no evidence whatsoever in its favour can be derived from the closest scrutiny of the narratives of possession. Christ makes claim here neither to supernatural knowledge, nor to any adaptation of it to popular needs. The Evangelists certainly make no reference to Accommodation, nor had they any interest in doing so, seeing they never doubted for a moment the reality of possession. The narratives in question, on the other hand, furnish no evidence against the theory. Hence the investigation is begun with a perfectly gratuitous presupposition, of which the facts furnish neither proof nor contradiction.

Again there is the view which regards Jesus not as out of the line of national development and independent of a vast and varied religious experience, but as an inheritor of beliefs, resulting from the slow crystallization of ages and subject to historical antecedents. It is held that if we confine attention to the narrow field of the present investigation, and take the narratives just as they stand, we should scarcely ever be led to any other theory than that Jesus participated in a belief current amongst the people with whom he lived. 'Hold thy peace and come out of him' is the command given at Capernaum, and from the incident considered in itself and independent of any theory of personality, no doubt would ever be raised but that the command represented in its meaning what it indicated in its verbal form. When in Mark 3:14 Jesus appoints twelve that he might send them forth and that they might cast out demons, and again when a distinction is drawn between healing some who are sick with divers diseases, and others who are tormented with demons, the obvious conclusion is that he believed there were demons to be expelled and possessed bodies to be healed. When the seventy return and declare their success saying, 'even the demons are subject unto us in thy name,' Christ seems to regard this as an indication of the loosening of the foundations of the Satanic dominion.

This is indeed the impression that results from a survey of the narratives before an attempt is made to dissociate the actual words of Jesus from the entanglements of provincial interpretation. As the very heart of this investigation is to determine what Jesus himself believed, the final word cannot be the narrator's statement of that belief, as perfectly honest as it might be, for nothing short of penetrating as far as possible to the nucleus of testimony given directly by Jesus himself can be sufficient. In the account of the healing at Capernaum both Mark and Luke lead up to the statement of Jesus with a preparatory description which is given in the language and thought of the times. The fact is stated that the man has an unclean spirit and that Jesus rebuked him with the words 'Hold thy peace and come out of him.' The result is described in similar language. The demon first throws him down and then leaves him. By how much the command of Christ had its phraseology shaped by reason of being embedded in that popular and traditional setting, it is not easy to say. The same difficulty is seen in the case of the epileptic boy. Mark represents the father as describing in detail the symptoms viewed as demoniacal effects. Before and after the reported saying of Christ, the language of possession is unambiguously used. The words of Christ are 'Thou dumb and deaf Spirit, I command thee come out of him.' The actual historicity of this saying is somewhat impaired by the fact that while both Matthew and Luke describe the event, in somewhat similar detail, yet they omit the direct words of Christ and close the incident with just the simple account that Jesus rebuked the demon and healed the boy.

It might be claimed that the command of Christ has good historical value because Mark quotes it and he is the earliest writer, but then the difficulty still remains how, if it be true that Matthew and Luke came later and had access to Mark, they both failed to record the command. The words of Jesus to the Syro-Phoenician woman are also reported with some variation. In Mark, Jesus says, 'For this saying go thy way, the demon is gone out of thy daughter.' In Matthew the statement is 'O woman, great is thy faith, be it done unto thee even as thou wilt.' Luke omits the incident altogether. The reply to the Gadarene – 'Depart' – is given, as already noted, only in Matthew, the earlier Gospel, Mark, narrating no direct statement of Christ.

These discrepancies may not be so very important in their bearing upon historical essentials, but they are next to fundamental if we wish to discover the relation of belief in possession, to the mind of Christ. It is only these conversational nuclei which form the foundation of a theory as to Christ's mental attitude to the phenomena, and the form of the language in which Christ expressed his thought would make all the difference in the world to a question of interpretation. That the exact words of Christ were not absolutely fixed in the memory from the time of their utterance down to the writing of the Gospels has already been seen. The variations seem to indicate that the words spoken to the demoniac immediately preceding his cure were somewhat coloured by the idea of expulsion and by the idea of the command believed to be necessary for it. At any rate the theory that Christ shared the belief in possession rests upon rather slender evidence if we try to cut beneath the reported narrative to the actual statements. It cannot find any support in the conversation between Christ and the Pharisees concerning Beelzebub. When the charge is made that 'this man doth not cast out demons but by Beelzebub, the Prince of the demons,' Jesus with wondrous skill refutes the accusation by showing how intrinsically absurd it is. If the charge were true, it would attribute to Satan the very character which it is evident cannot be assigned to him – that of the grossest stupidity. 'If Satan casteth out Satan, he is divided against himself, how then shall his kingdom stand?' Christ then proceeds to ask the question 'If I by Beelzebub cast out demons, by whom do your sons cast them out?' It seems quite clear from this statement that it furnishes no proof that Jesus shared the belief. It is only a device of argument. The point at issue is not whether demons are cast out or not, but that if Christ casts out demons through the power of Satan, and if the sons of the Pharisees cast them out through the power of God, then both Satan and God are aiming at the accomplishment of the same end so that the Satanic Kingdom becomes divided in its aim.

To show, however, that the theory of Participation with regard to this particular class of phenomena rests upon none too stable a basis, does not necessarily carry along with it an apologetic for the omniscience of Christ. If there are internal reasons for believing that Christ held views regarding the nation's past which are now considered to be erroneous, then the belief that Christ held them must stand or fall with the evidence upon which these reasons are based. If the reasons are sound and there is no other recourse than to conclude that Christ held a belief which a united scholarship rejects, then that only points to Participation in the field covered by such belief. His references to the past history of his people do not give to the historian his great landmarks by which the slow development of a nation's life can be accurately surveyed. The archaeologist's spade still continues to throw aside the clay from buried monuments, and ancient history and literature become woven together into consistent wholes, and in turn become the standard by which the historicity of some of the statements of Jesus himself might be determined. The authorship of the 110th Psalm, for example, has to submit to the canons of scientific research independently of any claim of the New Testament for it, and so with all other claims of similar character. But on the other hand an argument for Participation in certain current historical conceptions does not subject Jesus to the demonology of his age. To seek an explanation by first assuming Jesus to be a product of his age is to place a dogma at the very threshold of critical inquiry and to run counter to the law of all scientific progress. The spirit of the Old Testament prophecy was that of continuous reaction against the static formulae of its day. It was keen reflection upon the presuppositions of the times in which the prophets lived that caused them to fling aside as unworthy many beliefs whose antiquity was the sole ground of their respect. And if there was any cause which led to the final tragedy in the life of Christ, it was certainly his attitude sometimes of indifference, sometimes of antagonism to Rabbinical traditions. The tower of Siloam did not fall only upon the guilty. No Sabbatic observance was held so rigidly by him that it made him look with intolerant gaze upon the action of his disciples in the grain-fields. The question 'Rabbi, who sinned, this man or his parents, that he should be born blind?' shows how deep-grained was the notion of disease being the effect of sin, seeing the question is not whether sin as such caused it, but rather whose sin. The answer of Christ satisfies neither alternative but stands in bold defiance against the whole root idea of the day. Why then should the phenomena under investigation bind him to an unreflective theory of possession? The conversational data of the records are not decisive in affording proof that he held it. Indeed, on the contrary there is evidence that the prevalent notion, at least in some of its phases received scant sympathy from Christ. If he believed in the activity of Satan and his vast confederacy of demons, then its most complete expression was to be found where the age never dreamed it to exist – in the cultural circles of the Pharisees. Moral profligacy was never for a moment ascribed to the alleged demoniacs. The man healed at Capernaum, the youth at the foot of the mountain, the little daughter of the Syro-Phoenician woman, stand as irrefutable evidence against such an imputation. Jesus would have been the last one in Palestine to have laid the charge of guilt at the door of the sins of these sufferers. There was a mighty chasm of which he himself was so well aware, between this particular kind of affliction and that malignant type which stained the Pharisaic heart. The unclean demoniacs driven to the wilderness were currently regarded as the standard embodiments of Satanic impurity, and if Jesus spurned such a point of view, as assuredly he did, and showed that the central seat of corruption where evil was doing its most finished work was in the hearts of his official antagonists, that fact alone would be sufficient to place Jesus outside the line of traditional succession regarding the belief in demoniacal agency.

Indeed, apart from interpreted report, the paucity of direct evidence that he actually shared this belief in possession may best be explained by the fact that his life was concerned with affairs of far weightier significance. The great parables are noticeably free from direct allusion to it. Probably he went through life in serene indifference to many of the theories which the schools had pieced together to explain phenomena of various kinds. He was too intensely in earnest in dealing with individual concrete cases of sin and suffering, and in drawing great moral divisions between the tithing of mint and anise and cumin, and the weightier matters of the law, justice, mercy, and faith, to speculate upon the abstract nature of sin. If an outcast demoniac approached him, it is more likely that with sane conversation and gentle treatment, he effected the recovery, than by issuing a command of expulsion and thereby committing himself to the belief that a demon was inside and alone responsible for the havoc wrought. Questions raised regarding origin were scarcely ever answered by Christ with a view of theoretical settlement. He very frequently refused to respond categorically to points of mere scribal dispute, but would convey the implication that the solution lay outside the reach of their argument altogether, and if some Pharisaic dialectician had inquired of Jesus the reason why those unfortunate persons afflicted with fever, epilepsy, and mental derangement had been so completely within the grasp of Satan and his legions of demons, he would in all likelihood have replied that such affliction was no more due to demoniac power, than the blind man's infirmity was due to his parents' sin or his own.

**From *Studies in Pauline Eschatology and Its Background***
(Published diss., Toronto: William Briggs, 1917: 107–18, 198–203)

The stars or the heavenly bodies may have afforded him the best pictures available to express the hope of glory awaiting Christians in the Hereafter, but nevertheless his usual method in representing the pneumatic body is to refer it to the likeness of Christ, but when we seek for precise description of this likeness of Christ, the regressus goes still further back to what is called the form or image of God. As illustrations of this, the following instances may be cited: 'For if we have become united with him in the likeness of his death, we shall be also in the likeness of his resurrection' (Rom. 6:5); 'If so be that we suffer with him, that we may be also glorified with him' (Rom. 8:17); 'For whom he did foreknow, he also foreordained to be conformed to the image of his Son' (Rom. 8:29); 'Who [Christ] shall fashion anew the body of our humiliation, that it may be conformed to the body of his glory' (Phil. 3:21). But to determine the character of the body of his glory we learn that Christ is the image (εἰκῶν) of God (2 Cor. 4:4). The 'light of the knowledge of the glory of God' is in his face (2 Cor. 4:6). He is the image of the invisible God (Col. 1:15), and pre-existed in the form (μορφη) of God (Phil. 2:6). The terms which sum up the description are those of glory, radiance, power, and form et cetera. It is easy to see that to construct a more precise formula of definition is an impossible task. To take the instances where the phrases 'in the heavens,' 'in the heavenly places,' 'the image of the heavenly,' 'above principalities and powers,' and others occur, as indicating definite spatial properties, is confronted by the difficulty involved in the transference of simile from human beings to Christ and thence to God. It is true that when the Old Testament prophets tried to give a description of their vision of God, imagery implying symbolic localization is employed. Isaiah pictures God as 'sitting upon a throne high and lifted up,' while his glory fills the Temple (Isa. 6:1). Resplendent light, glowing metal and fire, thunderous noise, and other awe-inspiring phenomena are the features of Ezekiel's vision. 'This was the appearance of the likeness of the glory of Yahweh' (Ezek. 1:28). The very circumlocution suggests the inadequacy of the symbols of portraiture. The picture has to do rather with the attendant circumstances of the Theophany. God himself is not regarded as being visible. The light and fire are his 'manifestations,' the effects of his power. The more developed became the view which subsequently was designated as the Transcendence of God, the more insistent became the teaching that He could not be brought within the comprehension of human knowledge: 'For what flesh can see visibly the heavenly and true God, the Immortal, whose abode is the Heaven?' (Sibylline Oracles, Proverbs 1:10, 11). Especially is this so in the Alexandrian speculation. Philo's adjectives are 'The Wise, The Divine, The Indivisible, The Undistributable.' In the 'Book of Wisdom,' God works through Wisdom which is 'an effluence from everlasting light' (Wisd. 7:26). Hence such expressions as 'the invisible presence,' 'the light encircling the throne,' 'the Glory of the Great One,' 'an insufferable blaze of light,' are invariably the symbols to illustrate the unapproachable presence of God. Philo thus pictures heaven: 'An eternal day without night and without shadow, for it is lighted by inextinguishable and unalterably pure radiance.' In his description of Wisdom the very language he employs scarcely admits comparison with anything of the nature of physical light. It is true that he uses such phrases as a 'vapor of the power of God, a pure emanation of the glory of the Omnipotent, a reflection of eternal light, a spotless mirror of the energy of God, and an image of his goodness.' But he further adds, possibly to prevent a literal construction, that 'Wisdom is more comely than the sun, and above all the ordering of the stars; compared with light she is found preferable for this is succeeded by night, but against Wisdom evil has no power.' The Fourth Book of Ezra transcends even this: 'Not mid-day or night or dawn, not gleam or brightness or shining, but wholly and alone the radiance of the glory of the Most High' (Ezra 7:42). In the Ascension of Isaiah (10:16, 11:32), God and the Great Glory (ἡ μεγάλη δόξα) are synonyms. And also the *pneumata* of the righteous as of the angels are regarded as being clothed, though of course to a less degree, with the same effulgence. The monarchical conception of God had become so developed that even the highest angels are assigned positions prudently remote from the throne. Enoch pictures God as surrounded by an impassable wall of fire and glory, so terrible that the nearest angels are not permitted to stand in his immediate presence nor even to see him (1 Enoch 12–16), but nevertheless, glory is the characteristic not only of God but of the heavenly host, whether of angelic or human existences. Philo will only allow human shape to angelic and heavenly beings when these pneumatic existences appear upon the earth: 'But it happens every now and then that on emergencies occurring, they have imitated the appearance of men, and transformed themselves so as to assume human shape.' But in their native abode they are bodiless, 'incorporeal, as living spirits destitute of any body.'

Now in Paul's treatment, while he uses the hierarchical machinery with its allocations of positions and functions, his language is too figurative to demand a literal construction. It is true that the righteous *pneumata* have their homes in the heavenly places. That conception had become very prevalent in the century before Paul. It is present everywhere in the thought of Posidonius and his school. Cicero refers to it in his 'Dream of Scipio': 'The souls of those who have deserved immortality will not descend to the depths of the earth, they will rise again to the starry spheres.' Compare the Latin epitaph 'My divine soul shall not descend to the shades; heaven and the stars have borne me away; earth holds my body, and this stone an empty name.' Paul certainly seizes hold of this belief, and adds that the righteous will become conformed to the εἰκών of Christ, but this must be construed in the light of the terms applied to Christ: 'If then ye were raised together with Christ seek the things that are above, where Christ sitteth at the right hand of God' (Col. 3:1).

'Which he wrought in Christ when he raised him from the dead, and made him to sit at his right hand in the heavenly places far above all rule etc.' (Eph. 1:20, 21). To rob the language of its metaphorical meaning by fastening a prosaic literalism upon these clauses collides at once with the more comprehensive Pauline expressions where Christ is conceived as 'filling all in all,' and as the one in whom the universe is created and sustained. Nothing is more perplexing than to try to assign the terms which Paul employs to a place in a definite philosophical scheme. If the investigation in his use of language discloses any conclusion at all, it is the fact that the fluid and popular usage is everywhere dominant. A given concept may not only be taken to cover quite a variety of properties, but these properties themselves may be designated by just as great a variety of terms. Paul gives no hint whatever that he possesses a technical equipment of scientific terminology. To take any term and begin to explore its etymology in the philosophical schools of the fifth and fourth centuries BC, and then insist upon grounding its Pauline significance upon the original content, is as hazardous as to run back a nineteenth-century refinement into the thought of the Middle Ages. The argument of derivation must reckon with the fact that the apostle, intimate as he was with the prophetic development of his race, and versed in the procedure of Rabbinical argumentation, yet quotes from the Old Testament in the language of the Septuagint, and thus brings to the formulation of his religious thought a mode of expression unknown to the very men who shaped Hebrew theology. And it is quite probable that over a century had intervened between the period of this translation and the time when Paul was borrowing its phrases. All these terms 'spirit,' 'soul,' 'image,' 'form,' 'body,' 'flesh,' and others had been used in a technical vocabulary, but from there they had passed into popular employment to serve distinctions more concrete. Deissmann remarks: 'One might write the history of religion as the history of religious terms, or more correctly, one must apprehend the history of religious terms as being a chapter in the history of religion ... The Greek Old Testament was no longer understood in the Imperial period as it was in the Ptolemaic period, and again, a pagan Christian in Rome naturally read it otherwise than a man like Paul ... The men of the New Testament resembled the Alexandrian translators in bringing with them from their "profane surroundings, the most varied biblical elements of thought and speech."' This pointed statement of Deissmann applies just as well to the development of any literature. The numerous shadings and transitions through which language passes, not only in philosophical developments, but also through popular media, are too well recognized to be challenged. This becomes all the more apparent when in the examination of the apostle's thought, the purely speculative tendency is seen to be a matter of merely passing consideration. It is true that, amidst so much of earthly suffering following in the wake of the new religious movement that broke at once with Jewish prejudice and the demands of an imperial cult, Paul directed the hopes of Christians to a future painted in radiant colours, yet inasmuch as such a future was by its very nature transcendent and heavenly, the description had frankly to be clothed in the symbols of mysticism. No theological schematism in which doctrines of Sheol, Paradise, Heaven and Hell, and of the σῶμα and πνεῦμα are elaborately systematized can be discovered in the epistles. The apostle has none of the speculations of Stoic naturalism, where the body, for example, is defined as that which acts or is acted upon. Such categories as active, passive, efficient cause, or such definitions as 'Body is that which is capable of extension in three dimensions' are not included at all within his religious horizon. His method is not that of a theorist who wishes to construct a view of the universe that might satisfy a logical test, but that of a missionary who brought a practical ingenuity to bear upon the multifarious moral and social needs that grew in proportion to the expansion of his churches, and demanded sometimes immediate adjustments. Solutions could never be given *in abstracto*. They had to shape themselves in accordance with situations of a definitely local character, and it is quite conceivable that in matters of provincial or racial concern, a Jew might readily dismiss a solution that would satisfy a Greek, or a Phrygian accept what a Roman would summarily reject.

But when the apostle having, however successfully, done his best to meet such contingencies, applied himself to his great soteriological task of making known what he designated as the riches of God in Christ to the heterogeneous classes that made up the Graeco-Roman populations of his time, he stated his case with definiteness and lucidity. And to accomplish this, he adopted the customs, modes of thought, and phraseology native to the peoples amongst whom he laboured. His language therefore would have more in common with current vernacular than with the terms of academies and eclectic circles. The figures of speech, the striking similes, the illuminating illustrations that light up the epistles are a lasting monument to his skill in driving home a message as they reflect the range of his intellectual insight, and practical sagacity. His burning ethical exhortations place under tribute the whole field of Jewish, Roman, and Greek metaphor. The institution of slavery afforded him not only the basis of an appeal for a more humane and considerate relationship between a δοῦλος and his master, but also helped to throw into relief the more radical serfdom of sin as opposed to that liberty which is the birthright of the heir of God and joint heir with Christ. From the pursuit of agriculture he took the figure of sowing and reaping, of germination and increase, of carelessness and diligence in husbandry, of the plough and the ox-goad, to set forth the law of harvest in the moral life, and the struggles involved in the old and new methods of salvation in the process of his own conversion. From the splendour of the sun, the moon, and the stars, he tried to illustrate the radiance that would characterize the transcendent life of the *pneuma* and its organism. From the magnificent temple of Herod, from the Pantheon, and from the structures in the great Greek and Roman cities, which, however costly and resplendent, would perish with the changes of time, he could direct the vision of his converts to an eternal temple not made with hands. From the stadium, the race-meet, and the gymnasium he could illustrate how a Christian agon might be fought and won, how a race if well run would receive a laurel still more honourable than the fading wreath of wild olive placed on the brow of an athlete, and how in the match with the adversaries not of flesh and blood a moral mastery might be achieved. From the garrison in a Roman barracks, from the soldiers on parade and on the battlefield, he could turn to the breastplate of faith and love, to the armour of righteousness, to the helmet of salvation, to the sword of the spirit, and indicate how necessary to the Christian were the watchful vigil, the martial steadfastness, and the iron discipline, that he might endure hardness as a good soldier of Jesus Christ. And indeed the great spectacle which, perhaps above all others, impressed most the imagination of Rome together with that of her subject peoples, namely, the historic pageant which periodically moved along the Via Sacra in honour of a returning conqueror, became the grand allegory by which Paul described the immortal triumph of Christ over all his adversaries. No one could fail to catch the apostle's meaning when such well-known symbols were harnessed to the strong ethical messages of his life. The discussion of the terms shows that he was not employing a rigid technique of anthropology. A clearly schematized system of concepts was not essential to his propaganda any more than it was to the preaching of the Hebrew prophets. Provided that a term had sufficient distinctness in a given instance to serve in the enforcement of an appeal, a warning, or a rebuke, or a message of comfort, it satisfied the needs of the case. The fact that in another situation, or in another environment, such a term might have a content seemingly opposed to former usage, when considered as entering into a problem of abstract classification, was of little moment as long as the present ethical issue was met. Difficulties would probably arise when later exegesis began to operate upon the problems of analysis ...

This summary deals, then, with what may readily be seen as a comparatively highly developed content of religion, a content which was naturally the product of centuries of reflective activity. It is clear that the religious ideas of the first Christian century cannot receive adequate treatment without being brought into the closest relationship with the national beliefs and customs forged out of the vicissitudes and struggles of the late Greek and early Roman periods. Likewise the formative conceptions of these two centuries, crystallizing as they do into fairly definite shape out of national crises, are in part the refinements of many of the leading ideas that constituted the teaching and outlook of the prophets. In fact, the memorials of ancient Hebrew religion attest to a growing complexity of religious thought wherein the beliefs and practices of a given age are seen to emerge out of the age anterior to it, though indeed to a greater or less extent remoulded by the social, political, and international movements then in progress. In this historical evolution, one cannot take a belief at a specific time, and consider it as a ready-made product whose genesis needs no further explanation or derivation, for a full analysis of the case demands an inquiry into religious origins as they are found in the roots of Semitic antiquity. And even here, further investigation is barred only by the paucity of data concerning so distant a past.

Now it would seem that in its most primitive types, religious life was expressed in a complexity of ritual and practical observances prescribed by tribal and local customs where the objects of worship were concrete natural phenomena as plants, trees, wind, and fire, et cetera, together with certain animals especially noted for characteristics intimately related to the idea of the perpetuation of tribal existence. None of the concepts that we are dealing with here can be said to have been formed at this stage in the history of religion, though such original rites and sanctions formed the data out of which the later concepts arose. Certain properties of such objects are abstracted from others, and synthesized into concepts which are then regarded as having definite objective existence in the mythical god, no longer seen but imagined. The period under review in this thesis already possessed such products as an inheritance from its past, but the point must ever be borne in mind that these concepts of imagination and reflection underwent similar developments in succeeding centuries, keeping pace with the intellectual progress of the people, with their social advancement and their international relations. And in the course of Jewish history they were the decisive factors in the advance of the nation's civilization in the widest sense.

The Messianic concept, for example, not only emerged out of the national hopes of a given state of society, but became again the ground of reinvigorated faith amidst long stretches of misfortune and disaster, and the analysis of this interplay between great religious beliefs and customs, and their underlying conditions in the social and political experiences of the Jewish people, may properly be called the psychology of their religion.

Some of these factors in the development have already been pointed out. Many words and phrases in the vocabulary of the prophets were carried over into apocalyptic, and finally these Hebrew terms were exchanged for Greek expressions. Now it is obvious that in the employment of a Greek term for the expression of a Jewish idea, for example, '*pneuma*' for '*ruach*,' or '*psyche*' for '*nephesh*,' or 'Parousia' or 'Day of the Lord' for 'the Day of Yahweh,' certain shades of meaning may have been taken up by the old term, and conversely, the former content of the Greek term may have been modified by its substitution for the Hebrew term which thus designated a basal Hebrew idea, and this factor is of supreme importance in the growth of all concepts religious and otherwise.

But influences other than those of the linguistic type had been constantly at work for many centuries preceding Paul's time in the transformation of old concepts, and in the production of new ones. The general drift of development shows at least two lines along which the process of concept-formation took place. The first is what might be called a process of attenuation, by means of which a given concept would lose much of its original content by normal refinement in the history of the Jewish religion. The second tends towards the gradual enrichment of the concept by the introduction of new properties contingent upon the many pressing issues emerging out of the critical periods through which the nation was passing. The concept of individual resurrection, for instance, can scarcely be said to have been definitely formed before the third century BC. If the term is used at all in the literature before this period, it can only apply to the restoration of the nation from exile, or to its deliverance from foreign oppression, or possibly to its reinstatement in the favour of Yahweh following general repentance. It was in the Maccabean times that the term stood specifically for the raising from the grave of a deceased individual that he might share with the survivors the blessings of the Messianic kingdom. In the earlier apocalyptic teaching, the body which was to be raised would possess to a remarkable degree its former earthly characteristics, but in later thought these properties were abandoned, and were replaced by others of a supra-earthly character. It is not necessary here to review the historical causes of this operation. It is but sufficient to indicate that the processes of analysis, abstraction, and synthesis were continuously operative in the concept-construction. The former was in evidence in the gradual abandonment of earthly content, a result of the developing pessimism of the Jewish outlook for the national future; and the synthetic process was exhibited in the combination of qualities to form a concept, for example, like that of the resurrected *soma* with its properties of eternal life and felicity, its garment of radiance and glory, its abode in the heavens or among the stars, et cetera. This period of apocalyptic, which may be regarded as accretive, is especially noted for its rich and varied development along the foregoing line. In one respect it differs from the prophetic age. Prophecy in the main had laid great stress upon moral duties, and its chief concept was the character of Yahweh in his relation to human actions. It had also developed others like the Day of Yahweh, the Messianic kingdom, but it showed a striking reticence in its treatment of the concepts of Sheol, Resurrection, and of the Ruach and Nephesh in their eschatological significance. Indeed with regard to these, it had by reaction from many current beliefs pushed the process of abstraction so far that the above terms possessed the barest minimum of content.

It remained for Jewish speculation of the Greek period to work out these concepts by an elaborate procedure in which, while not ignoring the process of analysis, it yet placed the greater emphasis upon the synthetic phase of the operation. How this analytic-synthetic method was perpetuated, amidst the new scenes and interests that formed the background of the Christian propaganda of the middle of the first century AD, may be seen in the foregoing treatment of the concepts in the thought of Paul. But it must be remembered that technical formulation was not his purpose. Practically all of the terms were current in the vocabulary of his time, and so little were they fixed in their connotation that they were often used in fluid substitution for each other. Hence the concepts which they covered would lack the precision of scientific definition, although in the preaching and epistolary activities of the apostle they readily lent themselves to popular interpretation.

# C / Pratt as Essayist

**'The Scientific Character of Psychology'**
(*Acta Victoriana* March 1913: 300–4)

The above title, had it appeared at the head of an article some years ago, might have occasioned a feeling of sceptical surprise, or have been immediately dismissed as a fanciful chimera of the imagination. Such an incredulous attitude might well have been pardoned, because the study of psychology has, until quite recently, followed definite traditional lines and, as if bent upon proving its loyalty to the etymology of its name, has regarded its function as an inquiry into the operations of the soul in its manifold activities.

Every department of human knowledge has in the course of its history undergone more or less radical changes in respect of its method and its point of view. In the transition some of the sciences have abandoned their former titles, and have assumed new names, more in keeping with their change of methods and less suggestive of crude and primitive associations. The science of the heavenly bodies repudiates the ancient term astrology, as well as its assumption of the influence of the stars upon human affairs, and has taken its modern name to indicate its metric and mathematical aims. Alchemy in a similar way was superseded by chemistry, and other of the special sciences have revealed in a like manner their break with the past and their new relation with the present.

Psychology, unfortunately, was very late in making an historical readjustment, and the retention of its hoary name still keeps alive the confusion in the minds of many people regarding its purpose and its method. The name with its various cognates suggests to some the idea of the telepathic – the weird, mysterious communication of spirit media, the uncanny results of mental concentration, table-rapping, and all the other hair-raising and nerve-racking accompaniments of the séance. With such methods psychology has nothing whatever in common. In so far as phenomena of that nature can be made the subject of careful and exact investigation freed absolutely from duplicity and charlatanism, they may come within the purview of the science, but if so, they stand only upon common ground with all other phenomena that go to make up our world of direct experience.

The present age may be pre-eminently characterized by its increasing reverence for the sanctity of facts, and the criterion of progress is becoming more and more identified with that tendency to place the construction of a theory after an exhaustive survey of actual data. Hence the justification of the scientific claim which psychology makes is based upon the fact that it enters into the field of experience with the minimum of presupposition. It undertakes to study the facts of life at first hand. Any fact which is intrinsically a fact, that is to say, an object of direct knowledge, is claimed by it as a part of its special territory. It approaches the great complex unity of experience and commences a process of analysis and classification. Into what elements is that experience resolvable? What is the nature of thought? Is it ultimately composed of sensational processes and spatial relations, or is it in itself elemental and different *in toto genere* from such data? It inquires into the character of the emotional side of human life, of individual and social morality, of the nature of the moral judgment, the basis of distinction between right and wrong, and it asks what are the elementary products which an analysis of such complexities will yield.

In the realm of aesthetics it takes the pronouncements of individuals with regard to the pleasant or unpleasant tone of artistic combinations and arrangements, and seeks to discover the uniformities which may run throughout the collective judgments. It stands close to the medical field in that it is interested in the facts of abnormal mentality, and by tracing genetic influences within the life of a psychopath it offers its illumination to the task of therapeutics.

Into those difficult problems psychology has brought the use of apparatus and exact experiment. Laboratories have been in operation in Germany for half a century, and the Western universities now following Germany's example have been installing their departments with ingenious mechanical appliances, in the effort to place upon a secure and scientific basis empirical conclusions which hitherto had been the subject of guesswork and airy deductions. The experiments have been of the most varied kinds. Tests have been made for accuracy and strength of memory. Association processes have been observed, and results registered with clock-like precision. Sensations of sight have been patiently explored. Thousands of colours, shades, and tints in great varieties of combinations, puzzling anomalies of colour-blindness have been investigated, and laws of colour-mixture and contrast formulated. Work has also been done upon the other senses, and statisticians have been busy compiling and classifying their numerous data. In all this research the experimental procedure of science has been rigorously followed. As far as possible all uncertain factors have been ruled out. Care has been taken to keep all conditions constant except the one whose effect is desired to be observed in its changing phases.

But it might well be objected that a comparatively small area of the territory covered by psychology is open to experimental treatment, that there are many important conscious processes that will forever baffle and escape the exactitude of mechanics. What about those soul thrills which the artist experiences as he gazes upon a grand panorama of natural scenery? Are you going, for example, to bottle up the spirit of Beethoven or of Wagner, and draw metric curves around sonatas and symphonies, nocturnes and arias? Is the lyric to be placed upon the dissecting table, and the stately march of the epic robbed of its majesty by measuring out the length of its strides and counting the number of its steps? And – worst of all unhallowed attempts – what laboratory is going to fetter with its mechanism the *Grande Passion* and explain its moods and its fancies, its attractions and repulsions, in terms of equations and logarithms? No experimentee has yet been found so devoted to the interests of science that he is willing to give an exhibition before the eye of his experimenter.

Some of these objections do indeed constitute serious difficulties. Attempts have been made to measure the extent of emotional processes by correlating them with changes in respiration, blood pressure, pulse-beat, et cetera, and instruments like the pneumograph and sphygmograph have been used to register arterial and muscular reaction under changes of affective stimuli. Such investigations, however, have not as yet been very successful, but even if the emotional side of life eludes the tangible test of apparatus, that does not deprive it of the possibility of scientific treatment. The other great method of inquiry, that of observation and analysis, can still be continued, and much of the data of other sciences are subject to this test alone.

The other objection is really not so serious as it has sometimes been considered. It indeed requires long and laborious work to take a very complex emotional experience, and to discover the many factors which go to make it up, but it is a false claim to say that such a close and far-reaching analysis has done away with the value of the complexity from which it started. No psychologist denies the significance of the original experience. Its beauty is still there to be felt and admired, or its ugliness is there to be disliked, as the case may be. Analysis no more derogates from the importance of the initial experience than does the study of anatomy lessen the worth of the human body.

There has scarcely been any department of investigation whose recent progress has been watched with keener interest than psychology. The problems facing it are numerous and important. It has abandoned the old methods of inquiry that delighted the heart of the medievalist by puzzling his intellect and leading him by circuitous paths and endless labyrinths from which there was little escape except by an uncertain return to the original starting point. In the adoption of a new method which is scientific in its very foundation, it tries to understand human nature in its manifold phases. No pains are spared in making the examination of facts as comprehensive and as penetrating as possible. The last few years have thrown light upon the attempted solutions of questions that are as old as the history of thinking, by fixing attention upon the inherent nature of the problem to be solved. The science, indeed, is only in its pioneer stages, but it has the strength and vigour of youth, the faith and hope of a great future development.

The universities of Harvard, Clark, Cornell, Chicago, Columbia, have strong departments of psychology, the equipment increasing in efficiency every year. Of the thirty-two subjects credited with the doctorate in 1910 in the above universities, psychology stood seventh, and ranked fourth among the sciences which led university students. It may have been late before it won its title within the classification of the sciences, but having been kindled by the modern spirit of progress, it has justified its claim to the title by its recognition and acceptance of hard and honest toil as the only path to success.

## 'Thomas Hardy'

(*Canadian Journal of Religious Thought* 1 [May/June 1924]: 239–47)

'The Greatest of the Moderns.' This is the ungrudging testimony paid to Thomas Hardy by the English poets of the twentieth century and expressed in the dedication of a recent anthology. And in view of the high position which he undoubtedly holds in the more venerable Hall of English Letters, no honest lover of literature will challenge the modesty of the tribute.

One would have to travel far back into the past to discover a parallel for sustained intellectual vigour. His first work, *Desperate Remedies*, came out in the same year as *Middlemarch* (1871), and before George Eliot died, in 1880, Hardy had published seven of his novels, including two masterpieces, *Far from the Madding Crowd* and *The Return of the Native*. Then for seventeen years, in short story and novel, he kept adding to this roll of achievement until, with the publication of *Jude the Obscure* in 1896, he definitely closed his career as a writer of fiction, taking his place with the nineteenth-century giants, Scott, Dickens, Thackeray, Eliot, Meredith, and the rest of them. This might have satisfied the climbing energy of a Titan, but Hardy now struck out in another direction. In 1898 he published *Wessex Poems*, a collection mainly of lyrics, some of them written in his early life; another volume four years later, and then, in 1908, when he was approaching seventy years, he gave to the world an almost unexampled proof of his creative stamina in *The Dynasts*, a work so original and so spacious that it can scarcely be classified under any recognized literary or philosophical index. This was followed by other volumes of poetry – *Time's Laughingstocks, Satires of Circumstance, Moments of Vision, Late Lyrics and Earlier, Tristram and Isolde*, and others, until today the wonderful old man, eighty-two years young, is setting the problem for literary criticism as to whether posterity will adjudge his prose or his poetry to be the more splendid monument of his genius. His recognition has been complete; the Order of Merit has been bestowed upon him; he has received the Freedom of the City of Casterbridge, and Max Gate, his house in Dorchester, is already, within the lifetime of the owner, taking on the character of a national shrine like that of Abbotsford, Grasmere, or Cheyne Row.

Hardy's work may be studied from two related angles of approach. The emphasis may be placed upon the question of craftsmanship – points of structure, characterization, literary affiliations, and so forth; or upon the broad philosophical issues that insistently emerge. With regard to the former, a chronological survey of the novels would indicate that Hardy had, from the beginning, a fine sense of the structural quality of fiction. *Desperate Remedies*, melodramatic as it may be with its closet horrors, its sudden surprises, and its rather romantically correct denouement, possesses the interest of a fast-moving plot singularly free of padding. This adherence to design, strengthened possibly by Hardy's architectural training, became more absolute with the growth of his mind, and is presented in its most evident perfection in *The Return of the Native*. But the symmetry of this work, like that of *The Woodlanders* and *Tess of the D'Urbervilles*, rests upon a deeper base than that of mere plot coherence. Nowhere in English fiction can we find more determinate interaction between the characters of a story, and a more logical projection of human life upon its elemental backgrounds. In his portrayal of peasant types, in his description and use of natural scenery, there is much in common with the tradition of Scott. His preference for rustic characters was explicitly indicated in one of his essays, where he uses much the same argument as Wordsworth in the 'Preface to the *Lyrical Ballads*,' that people in close contact with the soil reveal their natures by their common speech and action with much greater fidelity than do the upper classes in urban life, where the social mask is usually on the face. The portraits are as sharp and lifelike as those of the Waverley novels. And landscape for Hardy, as for Scott, has none of that detached, exotic quality which earlier Romance was fond of employing as a piece of mere decorative art. Still, if a scenic passage were taken from one of the most brilliant illustrations of Scott's descriptive talent, say the setting for the interview between Burley and Morton at the cave in *Old Mortality*, and placed side by side with a corresponding section from *The Woodlanders* or *The Return of the Native*, the differences would be more striking than the resemblances. There may be the same picturesqueness, the same solicitude for exact detail, for topographical accuracy, but you find an added feature in the Wessex landscapes which make them just as potently expressive of the author's individuality as his own profound characterizations. This is really the starting point for the inquiry into that phase of Hardy's work which is sometimes claimed to lie outside of the domain of literature and simply to be a problem for metaphysics. But since practically each one of Hardy's stories propounds a riddle, some description of the answer, blurred though it be, must be considered. For thousands of readers, Hardy's name is a symbol for a certain philosophy of life, and many articles written upon him, beginning with some appreciation of his literary power, soon warm up to a polemical climax, only to subside with a devastating crash upon his alleged negations of human faith.

It is true that one may be pardoned if he cannot escape from a feeling of depression at the iron chain that Hardy forges around the lives of his characters. And it would be a treasonable weakening of Hardy's outlook upon life if one, by reference to a few remarks in the Prefaces, were to explain away as an artistic device the rigidity of the Fate that broods over the Wessex woodlands and heaths. By express statement and by implication in poetry and prose the evidence is piled up for an unequivocal personal conviction. Causation is forced back into the immemorial past. Egdon Heath, in that marvellous introduction to *The Return of the Native*, is represented as a complex system of forces whose resultant is the destiny of the peasants that live upon it. Sometimes it is regarded as an impassive spectator, sometimes as the genius presiding over the human lot and actively lending a hand in the shaping of the clay:

Not a plough had ever disturbed a grain of that stubborn soil. In the heath's barrenness to the farmer lay its fertility to the historian ... It was as if these men and boys had suddenly dived into past ages and fetched therefrom an hour and deed which had before been familiar with this spot. The ashes of the original British pyre which blazed from that summit lay fresh and undisturbed in the barrow beneath their tread ... Indeed, it is pretty well known that such blazes as this the heathmen were now enjoying are rather the lineal descendants from jumbled Druidical rites and Saxon ceremonies, than the invention of popular feeling about Gunpowder Plot.

In addition to this Natural Determinism, or perhaps as another phase of it, there are the biological processes evident in family and racial history. An act or an impulse here and there described in *Tess* is a throwback to an 'obscure strain in the D'Urberville blood,' or to some outlaw expression of ancestral days. This continuity of life with the living past and with Nature is taught with all the cogency and wealth of Hardy's fund of illustration. The peasant has a relationship of marrow and blood with the soil itself:

Only a man harrowing clods
  In a slow, silent walk
With an old horse that stumbles and nods,
  Half asleep as they stalk.

Only thin smoke without flame
  From the heaps of couch-grass,
Yet this will go onward the same,
  Though Dynasties pass.

And again - though this is only an arbitrary division of the unending line - the human fate is irrevocably sealed by impulses and trends within the character of the individual. There is no escape from the millstones. Henchard, the mayor of Casterbridge, is as decisively wrecked by his own overmastering moods as an unnamed soldier in Napoleon's army is broken in battle by 'the viewless, voiceless Turner of the wheel.'

In most of the novels Hardy directly assigns the responsibility for tragic outcomes to the operation of circumstance, with whatever content such a term may be conveniently charged. But in two of his outstanding stories, *Tess* and *Jude*, the antagonist to justice and happiness is social convention. Still, even here, these two novels fall into line with the general body of the work in that it is the ultimate order of the Universe that is impeached. They are only the more poignant and searching examples of the bitter grasp that an ironic Fate has upon life, and they constitute the ground upon which the severest assaults have been flung at Hardy's philosophy. Fate pushes Jude forward to his destiny 'as a violent schoolmaster a schoolboy he has seized by the collar, in a direction which tended towards the embrace of a woman for whom he had no respect and whose life had nothing in common with his own except locality.' Birth itself is potential tragedy. That it is not only the dramatis persona who is speaking, but the dramatist himself, is seen by the consistent unfolding of the idea in his poetry, especially in such a poem as that upon an unborn pauper child:

Breathe not, hid heart; cease silently,
And though thy birth-hour beckons thee,
Sleep the long sleep;
The Doomsters heap
Travails and teens around us here,
And Time-wraiths turn our song-singings to fear.

Fain would I, dear, find some shut plot
Of earth's wide wold for thee, where not
One tear, one qualm
Should break the calm.
But I am weak as thou and bare,
No man can change the common lot to rare.

The logic of irony is so wrought out that it sometimes leaves the impression that Hardy has strained the mechanism of his method to an unwarranted degree. Whenever Fate seems by some freakish turn to run the danger of being spoiled of a victim, an accident is conscripted to depress the rising scale. The explanatory letter to Angel Clare which Tess slips under the door of his bedroom is not discovered till the day of the wedding, when it is too late. The same delay cancels whatever hope she entertained in the despatch of another letter to him in Brazil. Clym Yeobright's message to Eustacia never reaches her, for the same fatal reason. Certain scenes of the acutest poignancy spring out of the irony of coincidence. Clym's visit to his mother takes place on the same day as the mother's visit to the son, and this failure to meet is responsible for the blasting remorse afterwards experienced. Fanny Robin goes to meet Troy at the wrong place for the wedding, and this mistake, which could be retrieved in a few minutes, is followed by a series of disasters ending in her burial in the reprobates' corner of the churchyard.

This is the way the current of life is supposed to move. There may be quieter backwaters indeed, or eddies possessing a capricious desire to twist themselves back against the flow, but they are eventually pulled into the general gravitation, 'happiness being only an occasional episode in the general drama of pain.' It might well be argued that, since misfortune so persistently dogs the steps of human beings, as indeed of all sentient creatures, the Power in control of the world is positively malignant. But Hardy's usual implication is that it is a gigantic abstraction, an IT utterly uncaring and unintelligent, much like the alogical Will of Schopenhauer or the Unconscious Principle of Von Hartmann, which may in its development throw off as conscious derivatives, human beings toying with the illusion that the calculus of life will reveal a plus of happiness in relation to pain. This fact constitutes the supreme irony in Hardy. The satisfaction of the most compelling instincts is as destructive as a torch applied to gunpowder. Man is as determined as the whirling of a leaf in a gale, but he has somehow acquired this groundless belief that he is free, and the mockery of it is that he must feel the same remorse as if he were – 'the intolerable antilogy / Of making figments feel.' Over all action then broods this universal Will. It would be more tolerable, suggests Hardy, if IT were knowingly cruel. Then, at least, you would not have to add to this fault of cruelty the blunder of stupidity:

*Hap*

If but some vengeful God would call to me
  From up the sky, and laugh; 'Thou suffering thing,
  Know that thy sorrow is my ecstasy,
  That thy love's loss is my hate's profiting!'

Then would I bear it, clench myself and die,
  Steeled by the sense of ire unmerited;
  Half-eased in that a Powerfuller than I
  Had willed and meted me the tears I shed.

But not so. How arrives it joy lies slain,
  And why unblooms the best hope ever sown?
  Crass Casualty obstructs the sun and rain,

And dicing Time for gladness casts a moan.
These purblind Doomsters had as readily strown
Blisses about my pilgrimage as pain.

This is the picture painted in the darkest tones and hung with crape. How much of Hardy's power as an artist comes from this philosophy is hard to determine. It might, at any rate, be conceded that his work is all the more impressive by reason of it. The question of its adequacy as a view of life is part of the old historical debate concerning Determinism and Moral Freedom. Both are postulates that depend upon the individual's emotional as well as intellectual readiness for their acceptance, and they have not even today ceased worrying theologians and trustees of Church property. The rigour with which Hardy pursues this scientific Naturalism makes him the towering representative in literature of this school of thought, as contrasted with the Romantic outlook which caused Wordsworth to write that

Nature never did betray
The heart that loved her; 'tis her privilege,
Through all the years of this our life, to lead
From joy to joy;

or Browning to convey through the songs of a factory girl the New Year's message to Asolo's happiest four. The hold that the Wessex novels has upon modern English readers is deepened by the last decade of calamity through which the world has passed, and since an ultimate view so varies with the temper of an individual or an age it may be that the complete statement of the case belongs neither to Browning nor to Hardy. It has always been for the human race one quavering interrogation, sometimes ending upon the agonized note, sometimes uplifted into triumph: 'He hath walled up my way that I cannot pass, / And hath set darkness in my paths,' for Job; the Golgotha utterance for Christ; an idiot's tale for Macbeth.

Hardy, in an explanatory sentence which might be construed as a self-imposed limitation upon his point of view, states that it is his purpose to be vocal to tragedy – that Romance may be left to other writers with other temperaments. And so his tragic imagination is given full play from the moment that Cytherea Graye sees her father fall from the church steeple, to that 'strange and consummate horror' when Sue Bridehead discovers the bodies of her three child suicides. Along this gamut then sweeps his epic lament for human misery and waste, at times querulous and wistful, at times searing with defiant reproach. Nevertheless, for those who are convinced that the final word of pessimism for this generation has been spoken, there are certain values that must be asserted.

The first consists in those utterances already referred to, where Hardy indulges his hopes in a few lyrical interludes. The song of a thrush in the sombre twilight of a winter's day is a brave utterance of hope:

At once a voice arose among
  The bleak twigs overhead
In a full-hearted evensong
  Of joy illimited;
An aged thrush, frail, gaunt, and small,
  In blast-beruffled plume,
Had chosen thus to fling his soul
  Upon the growing gloom.

So little cause for carollings
  Of such ecstatic sound
Was written on terrestrial things
  Afar or nigh around,
That I could think there trembled through
  His happy good-night air
Some blessed hope, whereof he knew
  And I was unaware.

And in the famous passage to *The Dynasts*, the Pities, who throughout the drama have been articulating the human plea, sing their final chorus:

But a stirring fills the air
Like to sound of joyance there
That the rages
Of the ages
Shall be cancelled, and deliverance offered from the darts that were,
Consciousness the Will informing till it fashion all things fair.

Such gleams are, however, too fitful to be interpreted as heralds. They express longing, but possess not the flame of promise.

It may be a forlorn hope, a mere dream, that of an alliance between religion, which must be retained unless the world is to perish, and complete rationality, which must come, unless also the world is to perish; ... But if it be true, as Comte argued, that advance is never in a straight line, but in a looped orbit, we may, in the aforesaid ominous moving backward, be doing it *pour mieux sauter*, drawing back for a spring.

The more substantial rift comes from a quarter where one perhaps might least expect it. It is true that, with the attention too minutely focused upon the theory of conduct set forth in *Tess*, one may succumb to unrelieved pessimism. But the deliverance comes from the personality of Hardy himself. We may concede the historical truthfulness of these sombre pictures drawn. We have analogies in abundance, not merely in such contemporary fiction as that of George Eliot and Dickens, but in the drab documents of early and middle Victorian law, to convince us that we are not doing ourselves any violence in making the concession. But the way our fists are raised to support the anger of Hardy at the social prejudices that debased and exterminated Tess is at least an affirmation of the redemptive processes stirring in human hearts. We may reject as perfectly gratuitous the hypothesis that would fling back the ultimate guilt upon an unalterable arrangement of things, whether conceived as an Impersonal Casualty, or as a hierarchy with a President sufficiently actualized to take a body blow. Some of us have less difficulty in transferring the responsibility, in this novel, at least, from the personified machine to such heartless moral prigs as Angel Clare, who, under the mask of a self-righteous respectability, serves to perpetuate, at the same time as reveal, the hollowness of so much of social pretence.

This arousal of the passion for justice is accomplished by Hardy and is possibly all the more effective as there is no manifest use of propaganda. He does not fill up his chapters, as George Eliot does in her later novels, with long dissertations upon the nature of Duty, nor does he, on the other hand, leave us with the clotted dregs of an experimental Naturalism such as might be found in the Rougon-Macquart series of Zola. There is waste indeed, even on a scale that staggers, and the lives of the Wessex peasantry are often blighted by accident and by human design. But there are pictures also of the holiest forms of renunciation, of devotion in the midst of suffering that rises into the sublime. Matching the stratagems of Wildeve for the possession of Eustacia, in *The Return of the Native,* Diggory Venn, the reddleman, devotes himself by day and night vigil to restoring Wildeve to Thomasin Yeobright when every self-regarding interest of Venn's nature would tend to widen the cleft between them. Standing over against the infatuation or mania of Boldwood for the physical ownership of Bathsheba, or against the sensuality of Troy, the dragoon, is the staunchness of Gabriel Oak, who might very well stand as a paragon in literature of whatever is sound in an English heart. That faithfulness of love which is unto death is also enduringly shown in the character of Marty South, and is expressed in her lament at the grave of her lover, Giles Winterbourne:

'Now, my own, own love,' she whispered, 'you are mine, and on'y mine; for she has forgot 'ee at last, although for her you died. But I – whenever I get up I'll think of 'ee, and whenever I lie down I'll think of 'ee. Whenever I plant the young larches I'll think that none can plant as you planted; and whenever I split a gad and whenever I turn the cider-wring, I'll say none could do it like you. If ever I forget your name let me forget home and heaven! ... But no, no, my love, I never can forget 'ee; for you was a good man, and did good things!'

The imaginative grandeur with which Hardy can invest a figure, alone and in darkness, upon a heath, cannot surpass as an evidence of genius the lyrical passion of a cry like that. It is a proof of his absolute vision. His power to chasten our feelings and stimulate our moral judgments is one of his silent achievements. And the width of his sympathies is so great that his tragic sense, ranging outside the accepted field of human action, exalts without unduly sentimentalizing the life of the lower animals. To him they are fellow victims entangled in the same great snarl. His poem upon a songbird made blind by its owner that it might sing more effectively is a supreme example of the way he can universalize an appeal out of a momentary observation:

I stand and wonder how
So zestfully thou canst sing!

Resenting not such wrong,
Thy grievous pain forgot,
Eternal dark thy lot,
Groping thy whole life long,
After that stab of fire;
Enjailed in pitiless wire;
Resenting not such wrong!

Who hath charity? This bird.
Who suffereth long and is kind,
Is not provoked, though blind
And alive ensepulchred?
Who hopeth, endureth all things?
Who thinketh no evil, but sings?
Who is divine? This bird.

**'Golfomania'**
(*Acta Victoriana* November 1924: 9–13)

'Is golf a game or a disease?' This question was recently submitted to the medical column of an English newspaper, and the physician in charge replied – 'It is neither; it is a symptom.' He declined, however, to enter into further explanation on the ground that he would be surrendering the confidences of some of his most intimate and revenue-returning patients. Had he been able to break through his professional crust he would, in all probability, have discussed the ailments of a class of *Les Misérables* who end their days in institutions described as Hospitals for the Care of the Mentally Afflicted. It is only within the last ten or fifteen years that the word 'golf' has become a pathological term. Before this time the game could boast of an honoured and venerable history. Standard encyclopedias have treated it with seriousness and decorum. Whole libraries of respectable dimensions might be constructed from its biographical and expository output. It was placed upon the pedestal of an art or a science. Its principles appealed to the reason and contained no discoverable antagonism to faith. Even John Knox, it is believed, assigned a just position for it in the economy of things, and many an Aberdonian professor since his day has lovingly dwelt upon the moral quality of the game, ranking it second only to oatmeal in the up-building of the national character. But in some peculiar way – which I am at a loss to explain – it has suffered a most lamentable declension. Not that it has forfeited any of its popularity. Quite the reverse. It is rather a question of the point of view from which it is regarded. From the moment a man takes up the game today he acts as if he were bitten by it, and immediately the whole circle of his non-playing friends becomes transformed into spectators anxiously watching the curious behaviour of the virus.

This past summer I made up my mind that I would study golf in an approved and scientific fashion. One of the reasons was that in May I sent in a challenge to a certain member of the staff of this college. The arrangement was that the one who lost had to expiate by presenting a Dorothy Perkins rose-bush to the wife of the winner. I lost. But I determined that the time would come when the garden at the back of my house would be planted with rose-bushes from beaten opponents. My first idea was to get hold of the most recent standard textbooks and make a thorough investigation of the principles involved. That, at least, would be an orthodox academic position. I would test it later experimentally. The primary essential, I found, was to acquire what Professor Thomson calls the 'eurhythmic swing.' Up to this time I had developed a swing which in my own unauthorized judgment seemed to lack nothing in curvilinear beauty. It was absolute perfection in the drawing-room or kitchen. It had the most pronounced natural affinities with whatever was artistic in the room – the cut glass on the buffet or the Sèvres on the mantel-piece – and would sometimes sweep it into its orbit. But it had a profound aversion to gutta-percha and I concluded that while the swing was rhythmic it lacked Thomson's prefix. So I began to hunt for a complete definition of the term. In Cyril Tolley's new treatise upon the game I discovered this: 'Your perfect swing both back and forward should be both smooth and true, round like the edge of a plate which is standing on edge at an angle of about seventy degrees.' This perplexed me somewhat, but I thought that since I was after definitions I would get my fill of them. The following page described the perfect stand (stance) at the tee: 'You must keep your head at the same distance from the ball all through the stroke. This will tend to lock the top of your backbone. The other point is that you must try – it is very difficult – to keep your bottom waistcoat button also at the same distance from the ball all through the movement, and this will tend to lock the lower end of your backbone.' My perplexity now became panic. I asked the advice of an osteopath (a non-golfer) and his reply was that though it might be perfect golf it was vile anatomy and not meant for vertebrates. However, I tried out the formula on the Braid Hills course at Edinburgh. The result was an execrable score and a bill for spinal readjustment. I then resolved to reverse my pedagogical theory and not to play any more until I had seen human beings in action. Accordingly, one day in June I bought a ticket from Edinburgh to

Liverpool, where the open championship was being played on the Hoylake links. The finest golfers of the world were to be present – Hagen, Sarazen, and Macdonald Smith were certain of wresting the honours for the United States; Taylor, Vardon, Havers, and a brilliant player named Duncan, who held several world records, were defending Great Britain. For three days the contest lasted. I picked out the likely champions and dogged them around the course. The nonchalant manner in which those old-timers stepped up to the tee and drove the balls with slowly rising curves two hundred and fifty yards down the middle of the fairways, with neither pull nor slice, would have brought joy to the heart of a geometrician. There was none of that agony which I had witnessed on the faces of some of my friends when addressing their Dunlops in front of the hazards on York Downs – none of that superannuated 'waggle' resembling rigor mortis which takes the energy out of them before they hit. Everything was effortless rhythm and precision. But as the competition wore on it became evident that, in spite of the poise and assurance of the players, there was a large measure of the incalculable. Indeed it might be questioned whether any other game possesses so many variables – the topography of the course; the moisture on the fairways or in the sand bunkers; the strength of the wind; the vagaries of the 'slice,' where a comparatively small error sends you deep into tiger grass with heavy penalty, or a wild hit that puts you out of danger on an adjoining fairway; the temperament or digestion of the players; and all the rest of it. When ten thousand people at Hoylake were expecting Vardon to add one more championship to his many laurels, they had the surprise of finding that he failed even to qualify in the opening rounds, being beaten by at least seventy competitors. And Hagen, who won the championship, just escaped exclusion by one fortunate stroke.

But the most paradoxical element in the game was to be seen on the putting green. One may readily concede the difficulty of securing a three hundred-yard drive as direct as a rifle bullet, but why a man should take three shots to pot a ball within eighteen inches of the hole is a riddle that might pertinently be submitted to the Sphinx. I imagined that I was the only person in the world who had that kind of an experience. In fact, I had become addicted to the third shot, a habit which disturbs my sleep even yet. I had come to the conclusion that when a golf novitiate purchases his first club, at that precise hour a demon enters his soul. And now I have the firmest conviction that another one enters the golf ball. The first credo might explain my own futile efforts to hole out in less than three at a distance of, say, two feet. It needs the second to explain why Havers, the 1923 champion, took that precise number at the same distance. I felt a savage delight in watching the crotchets of that ball in this particular instance. I am absolutely certain that neither psychology nor physics can account for its behaviour. When Havers struck it ever so gently with that pendulum swing of his, it went straight from the centre of the putter towards the edge of the hole, then, slowly turning, it meandered to the other side about two feet or less from the edge. The champion proceeded to hit it back. This time it acted in exactly the same way as before, returning to its original position. Once again he putted it towards the hole. The ball seemed to stop almost dead upon the edge as if it would not be satisfied with less than four, but it came back to life, and with some uncanny *élan vital* it pirouetted around the complete circumference before taking an apoplectic dive into the abyss.

Further evidence that the game is in some way related to the phenomenon of demoniacal possession is in the effect it has upon the modern professional mind. Teachers who in the classroom are the mildest-mannered men possible show incredible belligerency upon the course. I have known Old Testament exegetes and many philologists who, of all individuals, should never transgress the boundaries of exact diction, become notoriously adjectival when the ball dribbles off into a ditch after a yard of turf has been scooped up by the mid-iron. In the majority of cases, the professional inflammation subsides upon the return to domestic or academic routine. Occasionally, however, the fever persists in a less violent but none the less suspicious form when it invades the organism of a student of English literature. One critic of the drama has actually discovered in golf nomenclature what he believes to be the key to many obscure passages in Shakespeare. We are all familiar with the traditional difficulty of old quartos, and how a happy emendation of a corrupt line may, as in the case of Theobald, bestow a kind of immortality upon the interpreter. But that scholar's accepted version of Dame Quickly's description of the dying Falstaff – 'His nose was as sharp as any pen, and a' babbled o' green fields' (*Hen. V* II.iii.16–17) has been changed into – 'His nase was as sharp as any niblick and he babbled o' green fees.' Similarly, other expressions – 'I am down again' in *Cymbeline* (V.v.412); 'By thy approach thou makest me very unhappy' in the *Two Gentlemen of Verona* (V.iv.31); 'Cursed be the hand that made these fatal holes' in *Richard the Third* (I.ii.14); and more passages – including original oaths, were used by Shakespeare when he was probably smarting with the bitterness that Ben Jonson had stymied him at the eighteenth hole. Indeed this Shakespearean critic accounts for the feud between the houses of Capulet and Montague as arising out of the differences in their respective handicaps. Personally, I feel very much attracted to this manner of reading Shakespeare as a large number of other passages not specified by this scholar – passages remarkably uncouth but robustly masculine – surrender devotedly to the golf hypothesis.

## 'The Fly-Wheel Lost'

(*Open House*, ed. William A. Deacon and Wilfred Reeves. Ottawa: Graphic Press, 1931: 246–55)

It would be interesting to know just what kind of tag the literary historians will place upon these decades. Someone with a gift for alliterative nicknames will fasten a label which will survive like the 'saucy sixties' or the 'naughty nineties.' It will be a safe guess that the adjective will have a mental rather than a physical or moral flavour – something suggestive of excess or hysteria, at least, of pathological symptoms.

Manias are multiplying fast, particularly on this continent, ranging from the more or less innocuous forms of riding a hobby, up to panics which take on the character of a dangerous national psychosis. They are the perversions of natural instincts, of energies which have torn through bit and bridle. No record must be left unchallenged: it exists only to be broken by the next speed demon. The last altitude must be scaled and passed. The climax must be capped. Everything must be bigger and better every year like the national debt.

Apologists explain that these stresses are necessary to growth, that in any case they are inevitable, and no dykes may dam back the flow for any length of time. This may be true to the degree that forces are not always going to move along authorized channels; that they will, and occasionally should, expend themselves with heavy chances of risk. But this is a different matter from assuming that there is no need of a rational purpose behind exhibitions of daring and enthusiasm, fitting them in as constitutive processes of organized human effort.

There is no word which has become more abused today than the term 'marathon.' The competitive element has become secondary to the insane character of the objectives. We have dancing marathons, talking marathons, and eating and drinking marathons. An individual wins a prize for the number of pork pies he eats within an hour; another for the number of raw eggs in the shell he can swallow in half that time; another becomes the champion of his county for his endurance in standing motionless without blinking an eyelid or drawing a breath. Notoriety is so easily gained through the tabloids, and non-stop championships are so available, from polar flights to Charlestons, that stunts and freaks reap far greater material harvests than slow structural achievements. The favourite form of amusement is the circus; and the trapeze swing that forfeits the provision of the emergency net is the star performance. The craze for the sensation of novelty has become epidemic.

The bacilli have invaded literature, especially poetry, to such an extent that whole schools of criticism have devoted themselves to fostering the culture. If it were merely an idiosyncrasy on the part of an occasional writer it would not attract much attention. It is the concerted critical attempts to base the outcroppings on some presumably solid aesthetic that challenge the concern of those who have a genuine interest in literary development. The defence is put forward that since fashions and genres, now thoroughly established, were mercilessly assailed at their origins, there is a presumption of value for new forms in the very fact that they invite assault from the conservative batteries. This is an old argument fortified indeed by any amount of precedent. But it has been much overworked. It has forgotten that for every bark that found port, a hundred found the shoals – a most devastating ratio springing not at all from the spirit of adventure but from sheer lack of ballast or even from deliberate scuttling. The itch for the new has become so acute that it has tortured both form and subject-matter. Obviously, it is form which has suffered more, though the distortion must leave its twists upon the content.

This criticism is not a plea for directness and simplicity in speech, though it might well be argued and sustained that most of the great passages in world literature possess such qualities. Nor is it by any means a protest against subtlety where, as in the work of metaphysical and mystical writers from John Donne to George Russell, a reader comes under the spell of 'secondary suggestion,' not immediately conveyed by the face currency of the language. The objection is to making a cult of the unintelligible. This has grown into a monstrosity and is the absurd reduction of the otherwise legitimate vogue of imagism. The principle laid down is fair enough – that a writer must search his vocabulary for the precise word to express his own individual impression. But the trouble is that so long as he satisfies himself upon the precision of the description, it matters little or nothing if it is communicable. The audience is viewed with indifference or contempt.

It is difficult to see how any permanent values can be derived from the logical exploitation of such a standpoint inasmuch as, implying a taboo upon transmitted ideas and emotions, it is only by chance that aesthetic responses can be awakened. The direction of the drift may be followed without much strain. It is away from the trite, the commonplace, and by all manner of means from the sentimental. The initial impulse is healthy enough – to avoid the platitude. The chief target for its scorn is the syndicated magazine and newspaper banalities served up for mass consumption, frothy moralizings which decorate calendars and almanacs and the run of family albums. The reaction is salutary provided the pendulum moves back upon its arc, but it has violently swung out of its rhythm and is splurging about the four walls of its case.

An outstanding example of this attempt to confound the usages of words is seen in 'Work in Progress' by James Joyce. This work far outstrips anything Joyce has previously written in its novelty and experimentation. His most fervent admirers have gagged in their dutiful efforts to swallow the last dish he has placed before them. When these sections, now in serialization, are completed, the total volume will reach many hundreds of pages where there will be scarcely one paragraph that will not possess the most grotesque neologisms; and scores of little Joycians will strive to imitate the master in manner and bulk. Indeed they are already doing it, justifying themselves with the high-sounding claim that it is time to push back the language to its more primitive usages; to move away from the abstract to the solid, earthy connotations which words possessed in bygone centuries. Very good: but where is the evidence of such recession? And if it did succeed, would it not rob speech of all its contemporary flavour? One might just as well take a Hindustani script as a medium to reach the Anglo-Saxon consciousness. There is a good deal of talk about the tyranny of words, of punctuation, of sentence conventions, but, whatever the substitutions, the newcomers must in time establish their own habits of control. Syntax is as much an evolution as the human larynx, and, under violent wrenches, as much subject to haemorrhage. One man may create a word as he may build a hut, but one man cannot make a language any more than he can build a city. It may be a spectacular method, but a wholly artificial and destructive one, of laying hold upon the modern spirit – to force alien habits upon an organism whose very genius demands protracted processes for its growth.

The situation is more perplexing in verse, as the contagion is more easily spread. A writer may here display his wares or his symptoms in a more economic fashion. The public is made accessible through the magazines and there is a very insidious element in the belief, extensively propagated, that such a mode of writing is especially difficult and that its apparent facility leads a horde of tyros into flattering themselves that they have mastered a craft. The difficulty, however, is not in the writing: it is in the interpretation. Any one with a good supply of dashes and interrogation marks, a fountain pen and a pad, may establish himself as a prophet, and lament that his generation has not recognized him. His reputation must be left to posterity, who will see more clearly when the fogs have settled. A comforting thought!

An examination of the better anthologies, holding the concentrates of the 'new poetry' of twenty years ago, will reveal how much survival depends upon the assimilable quality of the content. The other types disappeared without as much as leaving a trace of their driftwood. I have before me a page devoted to an alleged poem entitled 'Afterwards.' It is one out of thousands of its ilk. It consists of seventeen words, twenty-four asterisks, and three blank lines not intended, I gather, to indicate stanza or paragraph divisions. I defy Minerva to extract any sense from it. A castor containing words instead of pepper could as easily have sprinkled the mess upon the page. Had the title been 'Hope Deferred' or 'Great Expectations' or 'Bleak House,' the author would, at least, have scored an ironic triumph.

We are all aware of the importance of literary eccentricities in furnishing amusement. There is an eloquence in silence, a teasing virtue in adroitly used mannerisms. Sterne juggled a masterpiece out of a bag of tricks, and no one questions the psychological adequacy of the perfectly blank chapter to describe the scene where Toby makes love to the Widow Wadman. But the pathetic side of the modern picture is the stone seriousness with which the literary occultists assert their pretensions. The appearance of a work in print must surely contain the postulate that there is something which may be apprehended in one form or another. If a writer says, 'I have my own restricted audience which will understand. I am not interested in universality of appeal. My work is esoteric,' he means that he has passed along the key of his combination to his favoured group. Either that, or he is just thumbing his nose. But how can a literature be based on such a procedure?

This is a different matter from the artistic exclusiveness which relies upon the 'cultivated minority' for appreciation and evaluation. Here the appeal is made to the sensitiveness of a reader, not to his possession of a key which has been constructed beforehand to fit a lock. The latter reduces the literary experiment to the level of a crossword puzzle; certainly much below that of a chemical or algebraic equation where the symbols are potential with light.

One source of irritation in this vogue is the effrontery accompanying the manner. Only two months ago there appeared in an important United States magazine a body of verse which displays the extreme feather tips of the left wing. The whole issue was placed in the hands of a group who styled themselves 'the objectivists of 1931.' The program set out to realize 'the desire for what is objectively perfect, inextricably the direction of historic and contemporary particulars.' The editor, in his explanatory comments, claims that he is initiating an age of real poetry after a period of darkness, quoting the words of the Chinese sage – 'Then for nine reigns there was no literary production.' The strictures are placed on most of the leading modernists of the past two decades – Sandburg, Masters, Lindsay, Robinson, Amy Lowell, and many others. These are now to be considered as arid conservatives, absolutely bleached.

I cut open the pages of the number with a definite sense of nervousness; read through the somewhat long poem of the editor; reread it, and then passed the issue around to some twenty lovers of poetry, art, and music. The comments ranged from boredom to scurrility and blasphemy. Even those hospitable to revolt grew profane and turned pale. cummings himself would have gone into mourning over the number. Here are two stanzas taken from the poem, 'A (Seventh Movement)':

Am on a stoop to sit here tho no one
Asked me, nor asked you because you're not here,

A sign creaks - Laundry-To-let (creaks - wind) - SUN -
(Nights?) the sun's bro', what month's rent in arrear?)
Aighuh - and no manes and horses' trot? butt, butt
Of earth, birds spreading harps, two manes a pair
Of birds, each bird a word, a streaming gut
Trot, trot - ? No horse is here, no horse is there?

Says you! Then I - fellow me, airs! we'll make
Wood horse, and recognize it with our words -
Not it - nine less two! as many as take
To make a dead man purple in the face,
Full dress to rise and circle through a pace
Trained horses - in latticed orchards, (switch!) birds.

The rest is of a piece with these extracts. The further one reads into the context the deeper becomes the swale. I know of only one thing comparable in infamy to this sort of utterance, and it is situated at the other end of the catalogue of crimes - a Rudy Vallee croon. I prefer the raw egg marathon to either. This was the proclamation of the New Renaissance after the nine reigns of darkness. If the mode were offered with any tincture of modesty befitting an experiment in new territory, it might be received with respect. But it is the blatant temper which is so revolting, a narcotic assurance that epochs are being ushered in when ink merely is being spilled. Another writer classifies himself (forbearingly enough) with Whitman and Lawrence and Proust.

Here is the fundamental illusion. A controversy might spring up around any one of these really massive figures because of divergent outlooks on society and life or because of opposite approaches to literary evaluations, but their works are, and always have been, assessable and within the critical horizon of the reader. What is deplorable today is the rampant spread of confusion as a creed, where the intellectual sterility has not even the compensation of beautiful rhythm or of imaginative phrase. And there is the economic protest that, in view of the plea for conservation of our vastly depleted forests, the pulp plants should be operating for the mutilation of the language.

## 'Canadian Writers of the Past: Pickthall'

(*Canadian Forum* June 1933: 334–35)

It is not difficult to understand the impression which the work of Marjorie Pickthall made upon the Canadian public when her first volume, *The Drift of Pinions*, appeared in 1913. The poetic taste, of the kind which would appreciate her quality, had been greatly stimulated by two factors – the Celtic Renaissance, and the Pre-Raphaelite influence energized for a short period by the immense vogue of Francis Thompson. The library counters were busy dispensing *The Countess Cathleen, Deirdre of the Sorrows,* 'The Blessed Damozel,' 'The Shepherdess of Sleep,' and 'The Hound of Heaven.' The New Poetry, whether of the Imagists like Amy Lowell, Ezra Pound, and H.D., or of the Realists as represented by the Georgian anthologies, had effected little, if any, infiltration, while the industrial blasts from Chicago, even granted they were heard, were repudiated as outside the province of art.

That Miss Pickthall had mastered the prevailing styles was clear from an examination of both the form and content of her work. The title of the first volume was taken from 'In No Strange Land' of Thompson, and the influence of this poet was seen not only in her fondness for religious themes, but in the 'mystical approach,' and in the sumptuous imagery with which she invested and sometimes over-apparelled the idea. The Celtic spell was upon her in the definite Yeatsian rhymes and in her mythopoeic tendencies, though she turned her face to Palestine rather than to Galway for her poetic lore.

There are two strands discernible in the texture of her verse on the metrical side – the Swinburnian prosody combined with the earlier and decorative Yeats, this second feature being a phase which the Irish poet later abandoned in theory and practice. The chorus in *Atalanta* – the 'hounds of Spring,' and 'the lisp of leaves and rattle of rain' – echoes in the excessive alliteration and assonance, in the deluge of liquids and sibilants, though of course the vast tonal effects of Swinburne were impossible because of the nature of Miss Pickthall's briefer compositions. The Yeats influence was a somewhat dangerous one, though quite intelligible in a young writer working under the glow of the contagion. (Masefield himself was under it in the nineties, producing emasculated hybrids until he discovered the native measure of his stride.) As Miss Pickthall's first published material consisted of poems whose writing covered a term of many years, without conscious reference to their integration in a printed volume, these discrepancies stand out the more prominently. Mannerisms strike the eye on every second page. Multitudes of moths flutter through the poems. The horns of elfland are blowing persistently, if faintly. Phrases of the lush variety are recurrent: 'Little lilting linnets'; 'elfin trills'; 'honeying pipes of pearl'; 'honeyed dark'; 'moth-winged winds of sleep.' The alliterative structures, though beautiful when taken separately, cloy when they are pyramided. Examples of such 'verbal felicity' are 'Bega' and 'Armorel.' This latter poem Yeats, twenty years ago, described as his favourite in the collection. Nevertheless, the value of these and kindred compositions resides more in the mechanics of the movement than in the emotional rendering of the ideas.

It is not in this type of verse where Miss Pickthall does her best work. It is rather when she forgets Swinburne and leaves to other writers the task of attending to the flight of wild swans over the Irish loughs that she takes on significance. And poems like 'The Mother in Egypt,' 'The Shepherd Boy,' 'The Lamp of Poor Souls' started her reputation for the expression and control of tender moods, which no poet in Canada has surpassed. Certainly, no one has succeeded so well in exploring the sources of pathos and at the same time avoiding the slough of sentimentality. Whether it is the death of a bird or the death of a child, it is the utter simplicity of the speech which conveys the poignancy – a simplicity which unerringly finds its appropriate melodic setting. Strung to her own measures, her child themes have the authenticity of folksongs, as rooted in natural feeling as the best poems of Moira O'Neil, Katherine Tynan, or Charlotte Mew.

In 1919 she achieved a notable success in *The Wood-Carver's Wife*, a one-act play based upon a French-Canadian scene. The National Community Players produced it in Montreal and later in the Hart House Theatre to highly appreciative audiences. This play, the finest single accomplishment of her life, and hailed by so many critics as the one outstanding drama of Canada, may be taken as the best approach to the evaluation of her gifts. It was her own favourite and she lavished her resources on it. It exhibits her excellences and her limitations. As poetic drama, with the tonal climaxes of its blank verse sections, with its lovely fashioned phrases and the general harmony of the mood, it secured unstinted praise. And it might be unjust to demand qualities precluded by the form. Still, the impression left is that it is ideas rather than persons that are on the stage. It is the Andrea del Sarto conception presented again as an artistic thesis, but the dialogue, beautiful as it is, sacrifices dramatic tang and intimate characterization – always the peril of the mode unless superbly executed. Local colour has vanished. The scene, despite the references to familiar fauna and flora, might as well have been placed in Fiesole as in Quebec:

> Your face again. Why, now you are fulfilled
> You will make my Mary perfect yet, your eyes
> Now, now the barren houses of despair,
> Of the passion that is none, of dread that feels
> No dread for ever, of love that has no love,
> Of death in all but death ...
>                                         But first
> Turn me her head a little to the shoulder
> So the light takes the cheek, raise the calm hand
> Clasping the sword, set the door wide, and go.
> Now, now my Virgin's perfect. Quick, my tools!
> O Mater Dolorosa! O Dorette!

It may help to explain Miss Pickthall's disappointment expressed in a number of her letters that the Community Players had 'prettified' Shagonas, the Indian lad: 'I can hardly bear to think that they made that suave little brute, Shagonas, into a sugary child.' But it wasn't the Players' mistake. The little scoundrel is visible only through the rose mist.

The same strains appear in her fiction, less perhaps in her admirable short stories than in her ambitious novels. The permanent value of her prose work consists in her sympathetic portrayal of child life and in the poetry of her nature descriptions. She can people the air with tanagers and blue-bills, etch shadows under poplars and birches, make kingfishers dive through a circle of lily-pads till the splash is audible, describe brown snakes crawling with the 'rustle of dry leaves,' and unfold over pages at a stretch a panorama surpassed in richness of colour only by a Hudson or a Conrad. What she lacked was the broad psychological interpretation. Desirous of describing human struggle on wide areas, she never quite realized the oscillating crises. Nature was too close at hand with her medicinal plants to allow wounds to bleed sufficiently. And her Celtic love of symbolism was continually blurring our vision of the protagonists by intercepting barriers not less tantalizing because composed of ivory or sandalwood. The unlovely phases of life were repellent to her. Her expressed dislike of Ibsen and his school, the absence of any analysis of life on the side of its civilized contradictions, her complete immunity to cynical and satirical moods reveal a temperament which, common enough only twenty-five years ago, seems as far removed from contemporary psychology as the mental horizon of Galen would be from the thought of experimentation on the ductless glands.

## 'Canadian Poetry – Past and Present'

(*University of Toronto Quarterly* 8 [1938]: 1–10)

This article is essentially a record of the difficulty and embarrassment in selecting a title which would not presuppose too much or too little for the subject. In order to avoid duplication, an index of the specific field was consulted, which was found to contain such ominous captions as 'Some *Animadversions* on Canadian Poetry'; 'The *Plight* of the Poetic Craft in This Country'; 'Pegasus in *Need* of the Spur'; 'The *Drift* of Canadian Verse'; and other titles which prejudged the issue by innuendo in word and phrase. They savoured somewhat of the attitude of a critic who, his mind a blank on the subject, but at least technically complying with the needs of a curriculum, commenced his series of ten lectures with the announcement – 'Canadian Literature: it doesn't exist.'

That such a prejudice is part of the mental lumber of many reviewers cannot be denied. The source of it is harder to determine. It may spring out of a proverbial suspicion of the home-bred product and a willingness to accept and garnish any mediocrity provided it is produced by a foreign loom, or out of the feeling of Olympian detachment in which the critic will not judge anything beneath the measurement of his celestial yardstick. It is a very self-flattering point of view. He has been nurtured on the best of all ages. He has fought with Achilles, travelled with Aeneas, wept with Niobe, and sulked with Hamlet. He has seen swans and heard nightingales. So he asks – Where are Mattagami, Tantramar, and the Basin of Minas? Who was Tecumseh? What are wolverines and veeries and chickadees? Why the laughter of loons? He has heard of little Nell, but who is little Bateese? Criticism of this character may act as a preservative but hardly as a ferment. It is generally hostile or indifferent to anything in the contemporary world, and it is a safe guess that the traditional masterpieces now held in refrigeration would never have been discovered by members of such a celibate order.

At the other pole are those who, with little root in the cultural past, glorify the native blooms out of patriotic fervour – who think that poetry attains its finest expression in rhapsodies at civic anniversaries or in national anthems. The bard and the booster belong to the same species. Artistic values are determined by personal, historical, and political fallacies. Poetry here is the art of creating slogans.

Canadian poetry has been caught between the frost of the first and the heat of the second. What it needs is the support of temperate judicial opinion to observe and estimate its growth. It is quite true that the country has not produced poets or poetic movements which may compare with the close of the sixteenth, or the beginning of the nineteenth, century in England, but what modern country has done so? Shakespeare and Shelley are not sprouting from the Canadian maples, but neither are they from the English hedges. Nevertheless, considering the age of the country, its population, the absorption of its energies in physical maintenance, the leavened mass of the production can stand up well with that of the United States, and with that of England since Tennyson. It is not an extravagance to claim that, although no existing anthology has done it, one could be produced to contest the position of the *Oxford Book of Modern Verse*, edited by William Butler Yeats. It is only the copyright hurdles which bar the way.

The refusal to consider any works but masterpieces has a deterrent action on the growth of any literature. It not only blocks the rise of minor poetry but tends to prevent the rise of the masterpiece. It is based on a false idea of the afflatus, that 'flame-images glare in' on the soul of the genius and somehow, sometime, somewhere, eternal ultimates shine forth to enlighten the mind of humanity. The lonely brooding spirit, generating his own steam in silence and abstraction, is a rare spirit, if indeed he ever existed, and as far as one may gather from scientific discussions on the point, there is no biological analogy for this kind of incubation. Rather, the mountains come to birth out of the foothills and the climbing lesser ranges. The occasional instance, cited in literary history, of personal isolation ignores the context of spiritual companionship with books and causes and movements. It would be a more profitable matter to investigate the healthy influence of clubs and taverns upon productivity, with their socialization of energies and purposes towards common ends, and the inevitable drive which the 'big fellows' received from their competitors of the second and third ranks.

It is, therefore, no depreciation of the Canadian output to say that it is minor when stacked up against the English pyramids. The just comparison is to take the poets of the last fifty years and let them rub shoulders with their American and English cousins. The comparison holds mainly with the poets, for, whatever encouragement to production there may be for the future in the national festivals and trophies, the native dramatists (with one exception and he is out of the country) are just trying out their toddling paces between father and mother. Fiction has a better record, but even here the honours are divided among a very small number of living novelists, only one of whom may be said to possess a big international reputation. The analysis, accordingly, must be limited to verse.

In any classification of schools and movements in Canadian poetry, attention should primarily be focused upon 'the group of the sixties' – a group of eight to ten poets, all born within two or three years of one another, of whom the most notable were C.G.D. Roberts (1860), Carman and Lampman (1861), and Duncan Campbell Scott (1862). Whatever may be the biases and revolts of the present generation, whatever the tastes and interests derived, as likely as not, from non-literary springs, the period has yet to come which can equal in form and substance the aggregate production of these four. Much has been said, accompanied by derogatory shrugs, about the derivative character of some of their work: that the idyllic sensuousness of the Acadian landscapes reproduced the old Arcadian properties; that spiritual *émigrés* from the Trossachs and the Lake District took excursions through Nova Scotia and New Brunswick to breathe transcendental sighs over the vales and marshes. There is more superciliousness than truth in this attitude. That Wordsworth, Keats, Tennyson, and Rossetti are traceable atmospherically in the work of this school means little more than that Aeschylus, Shakespeare, Milton, and Rousseau fertilized the thought of the first half of the nineteenth century. The relevant point is that in two decades following 1881, the English-speaking world was compelled to acknowledge for the first time the existence of a national consciousness making itself heard and felt through a Canadian literature. And for the first time adequately a nature poetry came into being. The claim is made for nature poetry only. The larger human currents, the democratic visions, the creative impulses at work on myths and national origins are not so pronounced. We have not produced a Whitman or a Yeats, but in the field, immense in its own right, of natural description and interpretation, the poets of this school have nothing to concede to the work of the English poets during the same period, and certainly nothing to the writers of New England over a period twice as long.

The representative offerings before this time were thin and papery in comparison. Take two selections from poems often quoted and often praised in the name of the Muses - Sangster's 'Lyric to the Isles' and Mair's 'Fire-Flies.' There must have been weeping on Helicon when this stanza to Beauty was penned:

Here the spirit of beauty dwelleth
In each palpitating tree,
In each amber wave that welleth
From its home beneath the sea;
In the moss upon the granite,
In each calm, secluded bay,
With the zephyr trains that fan it
With their sweet breath all the day.
On the waters, on the shore,
Beauty dwelleth evermore.

And Mair's 'Fire-Flies,' rich enough in detail, is full of 'emerald sheen,' 'sylphids,' 'dreamy glass,' 'bounteous rain,' 'tremulous lights,' which 'gleam like trailing stars then sink adown.' Here is the painful interrogation at the end:

Where is thy home? On what strange food dost feed,
Thou fairy hunter of the moonless night?
From what far nectar'd fount, or flowery mead,
Glean'st thou, by witching spells, thy sluicy light?

Contrast this with selections taken almost at random from the collected volumes of the leaders in the Canadian Renaissance, where bird and animal life, flowers, trees, marshes, and lakes are made visible and audible by artists who are at once painters and musicians:

Broad shadows fall. On all the mountain side
The scythe-swept fields are silent. Slowly home
By the long beach the high-piled hay carts come,
Splashing the pale salt shallows. Over wide
Fawn-coloured wastes of mud the slipping tide,

Round the dun rocks and wattled fisheries,
Creeps murmuring in. And now by twos and threes,
O'er the slow spreading pools with clamorous chide,
Belated crows from strip to strip take flight.
Soon will the first star shine; yet ere the night
Reach onward to the pale-green distances,
The sun's last shaft beyond the gray sea-floor
Still dreams upon the Kamouraska shore,
And the long line of golden villages.

*

A vireo turns his slow
Cadence, as if he gloated
Over the last phrase he floated;
Each one he moulds and mellows
Matching it with his fellows:
So have you noted
How the oboe croons,
The canary-throated,
In the gloom of the violoncellos
And bassoons.

*

The scarlet of the maples can shake me like a cry
Of bugles going by,
And my lonely spirit thrills
To see the frosty asters on the hills.

The new poets went after Nature in dead earnest until by the time they had finished with her there wasn't a recess or a ligament in her anatomy left unexposed. They were naturalists in the best sense of the term – exploratory, microscopic, their observation informed with interpretative vision. Canada in its central and eastern provinces is known though their work just as accurately as it is revealed through the records of the geographers, zoologists, and botanists, and this assertion is a tribute because any poetic fire is but a flickering thing at the best when there is not an abundance of good solid material to burn.

What, then, is the present outlook? What are the influences shaping the thought of the younger generation? How far does contemporary poetry reflect contemporary life with its daily-changing horizons, its cockpits, its chess-boards, and its mortality statistics? Does it show a tendency to plunge into the arenas, to enlist its pen for causes or to seek calm in nature communion, in ivory towers of introspection and Anglo-Catholic retreats? I can answer such questions imperfectly and only through the examination of several thousand poems and letters which have come into the editorial office of the *Canadian Poetry Magazine* in the last three years.

The first impression is that there are ten million versifiers in this Dominion, all clamouring for self-expression and, what is far worse, for publication, and most of them extremely sensitive with regard to the critical reception of their spiritual babies. They demand for them immunity from the world's blasts and predict for them immortality. As such parents violently repudiate the suggestion of birth-control and abhor the advice given, I think by Quiller-Couch – 'Fathers, learn to strangle your darlings' – we can realize what an appalling arithmetic must be faced by Canadian editors. Of this number, needless to say, the overwhelming proportion pass out through rickets and anaemia. Many enjoy a fugitive appearance in newspapers; some live a little longer in chapbooks; a few hundred get inside cloth covers, and a few score inside the anthologies. Nine and a large fraction out of every ten in the astronomical total belong to the sentimental type, uttering little stomach cries, toying with fragile illusions, or whispering the consolation wafted into their souls by the zephyrs. Poetic diction dies the hardest death of all the flora and fauna, and most of the poetettes are in its grip. It is the surest sign of amateurishness, of literary inertia or incapacity – to have recourse to the stale perfumes and faded decorations of the old boudoirs and arbours. Thomson's *Seasons* and Gray's odes 'To Spring' and 'Eton College' have done incalculable harm to writers who have assumed that the imprimatur of important historic names can sanctify banalities of diction. Expressions may be used thousands of times without ever coming under the reproach of clichés. The very naturalness of phrases like 'blue sky,' 'green sea,' 'gray clouds,' 'fresh fields,' 'red blood' prevents them from becoming stereotyped. They never go out of fashion any more – to use Synge's illustration – than the blackberries on the hedges. What bores the human spirit are the 'azure domes,' 'the emerald mains,' 'the fleecy cloudlets,' 'the verdant growths,' and the rest of the paraphernalia. Moreover, the eyesight is physically impaired by the mutilations and evasions of speech springing out of the tyro's use of poetic licence where words are put in subjection to the mechanics of metre rather than metre put in service to the organic structure and order of language. Insistence on this point would be belaboured were it not that the nine odd millions of writers in this country are committing literary hara-kiri. It betokens a most pitiful condition.

A reaction has swung in with two tides. One, an extreme type, as might be expected, is endeavouring to expunge all traces of sentimentality in content and all conventions in form. The influence is obvious. Under a sound general instinct, but uncontrolled, some writers, hating the obvious and seeking freshness of vocabulary, are subjecting verse to shattering strains. The desire for originality has become a passion for the freakish and the grotesque, resulting in miniature 'Works in Progress.' Dots, asterisks, exclamation points, blank spaces, hyphenated barbarisms jostle legitimate words and phrases, striking the eye assuredly as something unique, but yielding no idea that can be properly assessed by finite intelligence. There may be little doubt that somewhere in the recesses of the writer's soul the barm is at work on the flour, but what loaves finally come from the oven! And what a challenge to the assimilative processes! The initial instinct, let us say, is commendable – to work out the suggestive function of poetry, the associational values, a function honourably exercised by the mystics and metaphysicals of every age. It goes without saying that such poetry is difficult to write – the result of spirit-searching and meditation – but what we are witnessing is not the perpetuation of the tradition but the cracking of it by writers who use not fountain pens but pepper castors to sprinkle the words on the pages. An opaqueness as impenetrable to sight as pitch is as much a symptom of deterioration in the craft as is the facility of the sentimentalists. It is not fine frenzy but stark, certifiable lunacy calling for direct action.

The other type manages to steer between the two shoals in navigable though occasionally stormy water. And here again there are two broad classifications which differ rather in choice of subject than in technique. This is the usual distinction between tradition and modernity and, incidentally, creates a very practical problem for the internal politics of a national magazine. A subscriber interested in silver thaws, iridescent pools, and scarlet maples cannot endure the smoke from a foundry or the taste of pork and beans. He can find that any day in the wards, he complains, and poetry ought to give him release from it. Another has a loathing for the moon and things like hepaticas and sequestered brooks, and thinks in terms of sweat and the infamy of the wage system. When, as sometimes happens, both cancel their subscriptions on those opposing grounds, it makes the sledding pretty rough for the business management. If only the objections did not take such a practical turn, the job would be fairly easy for the editor. He could say: 'Nourish your prejudices to your heart's desire, exercise your liberty of conscience but, for heaven's sake, pay up. We are not making the magazine the vehicle of a clique or a claque. We are interested mainly in expression. To huddle the same minds together in the same fold would soon inbreed them to death. Your points of view may not be aspects of immutable and eternal truths, but the significant thing is your power or subtlety in setting them forth.'

Assuming, then, this catholicity in approach to theme and treatment, is there any basis to determine which side is winning out in the clash? May one predict the direction in which the main current of Canadian poetry will move in the near future? As already indicated, the mere poll test is in favour of the sentimental tradition, an easy, languorous, pulpy pastoralism, but fortunately the numerical determinant is not vital. The concern is with two sound minorities which will always be needed as mutual correctives. Excellent work is done by writers following the liberal tradition, still wringing some juice from the mythical fruit, refurbishing legends, discreetly lending a little more apparel to Diana and Venus, putting Nature in technicolor, and massing the stars for chorales. There is no reason that productivity of this character should ever cease. The material is inexhaustible, for the interaction between human moods and natural phenomena may vary like the permutation of numbers, and the romanticist sensitive enough to record the complexities is in a position to add fresh triumphs under the traditional banners.

But this is not the prevailing wind today. A group of young writers relatively small in numbers, but compensating by their intensity of conviction and by their study of experimental forms, are infusing new energy into our literature. It cannot be said that their poetry is distinctively Canadian in the sense in which the Carman-Lampman movement is so described. But there is no derogation in that. The simple fact is that the issues inflaming their minds are worldwide. An incident in Barcelona, Canton, or Quebec vibrates with poetic appeal. The geographical element is casual, so to speak, but the detonation of a bomb or the clang of a padlock belongs to a perpetual scheme of discord which poets and musicians have ever tried to resolve. I have before me a letter from one of the most promising poets of the new generation. Completely out of tune with the Canadian warblers of the past, he writes: 'Let us get away from this "bird on the bough" stuff. Continents are blowing up. I am never going to use the word "dream" again, and all the cuckoos can burn up in their ruddy nests as far as I am concerned.' I have the greatest respect for this writer's talent. He is going to be heard from in the future. My answer was that there was no need for him to relinquish his convictions at all. He might cherish them but, above all, channel them through the poetic mould. He had the requisite passion and art to do it.

It is interesting to watch the action of this temperament upon the subject-matter. As already indicated, a few years ago under the influence of the much-lauded Oxford satirists, our young writers were outdoing their masters in dislocating verse-forms and word-orders. Confusion was rampant in creed and practice.

It is probable that there was never a decade like the last, which indulged in such obscurantism through verse composition. And the paradox was that the new writers assumed a prophetic role, having at heart social re-establishment. This role broke through their prose but, no matter how keen and honest the hidden intention, daylight never broke through the verse. Now, however, as discriminating critics foresaw, the technique is changing, for what is the purpose of satire, be it frontal or flank, if the enemy never sees or feels the point. The current mode was absolutely destructive of the social or prophetic end, and, ironically enough, the exponents were slapped sharply by the traditionalists for turning poetry into precious and dilettante exercises. It is a good sign to see verse once again becoming charged with meaning and emotion, and the work of this group should receive encouragement. Canadian literature has never been very strong in poetic satire. As another correspondent, with a flair for stinging couplets, remarked, 'What our poets need in their diet is liver, more liver.' We may be getting this balance redressed by half-a-dozen writers now in their twenties and thirties. To all appearances this is the way we are heading. The liver extract is colouring up the corpuscles.

But another consideration needs to be emphasized. There is no reason why the advocates of tradition and the apostles of revolt should not occasionally drink their respective wines and ales at the same table. Inspiration has been known to be associated with both. It may be added that the water-lilies are still going to bloom on the pools, and the anti-aircraft guns are not going to destroy all the cuckoos – at least, we hope not. Tradition and revolt are inevitable complements like rain and sun: the first by itself mildews; the second burns or explodes.

The task of criticism in this country, as in any other, is to cultivate both discrimination and tolerance. Neglect or curt dismissal is as bad as a readiness to accept a jacket blurb at its face value. Criticism at its best in Canada is seen in the review-sections of the Toronto *Saturday Night*, in the three university quarterlies, in the *Canadian Forum*, and in the literary columns of the *Globe and Mail*, where the tempered enthusiasms of the editor have done so much to promote the plants and delay the weeds in the Canadian garden. A sheer conservatism never makes any progress when it becomes blind to its own origins, when it fails to recognize that what is now a settled, respectable routine was once a cause fought on the barricades by ragged battalions. This is the lesson of toleration for the new. Give any cause its right of expression, its demand for a hearing, but after that, what? Examination and criticism, by all means. It is a mistake to claim that the heaviest fires today proceed from the conservative batteries. This attack is mild compared with the heat and scorn poured upon the older orders by the new schools. And it is an easy but fallacious reasoning to claim that the more violent and extreme forms of the present will be the accepted and orthodox modes of the future. What is more likely to happen, if one might make an inference from the analogy of literary history, is that the spasmodic and freakish varieties will subside and disappear like the effervescence on a tankard of Stein.

## 'Dorothy Livesay'

(*Gants du ciel* 11 [1946]: 61–5, trans. Susan Gingell)

In studying contemporary Canadian poetry, it is very fruitful to examine how the young poets group themselves into coteries, make themselves disciples, and assume the manner of their masters. Some of them rest loyally in the bosom of a school, others leave and annex themselves to hybrid groups, others work finally to free their own personality. Influences are inevitable. They are felt either deliberately or unconsciously, and when they are assimilated with a vigilant eye that avoids all danger of plagiarism, the results are salutary. But when a volume of verse bears too obviously the imprint of a model, so that on each page the reader finds before him an idea or expression that cries out to him, 'This is Eliot or Hopkins, Auden or Spender,' that becomes boring or revolting.

Dorothy Livesay is a poet who knew how to discover her own style and who knew how to think with a lively intelligence about the problems of her time. Her progress has been considerable. I remember her first publication, a little collection entitled *Green Pitcher* (1928). It was a modest début, which very naturally betrayed the influence of two important poetesses, Elinor Wylie and, an older and greater poetess, Emily Dickinson. The Imagists, whose influence was declining in the United States, had also found a favourable soil in Canada. Our poets exhausted themselves with sobs in treating of annihilation, separation, decadence, and death. But, above all, it is Emily who, thanks to her disciples, made fashionable metaphysical ideas and the image of the poet withdrawn into his ivory tower.

Miss Livesay connected herself to this tradition. Several quatrains from her next volume, *Signpost* (1932), seemed to be paraphrases of Emily Dickinson, even though one felt that the disciple meant to follow her own path. Compare the little poem 'Time':

The thought of you is like a glove
That I had hidden in a drawer:
But when I take it out again
It fits; as close as years before.

with this verse of Emily Dickinson:

We outgrow love like other things
And put it in a drawer:
Till it an antique fashion shows
Like costumes grandsires wore.

Miss Livesay takes from Imagism the precise clarity of her verbal images, the rigour of expression that leaves no room for any sentimental effusion. She has gone to the heart of Amy Lowell's manifesto on this subject. And it was a good school for a novice. It ensured a unity of vision. It permitted at the outset an apprenticeship in forms before plunging the paintbrush into an array of colours. The canvases would come later.

But since *Signpost*, the artist has revealed more ample gifts. 'City Wife' impresses us not only by its style, but also by its content.

The poem is written in flexible and colloquial blank verse that reminds one of Robert Frost's. Its atmosphere is rural, and one finds a remarkable objectivity in the pastoral passages full of 'sober evergreens, lombardies, and pale wild cherry trees.' Nevertheless, this poem was followed by a return to the old impressionistic experiences that give the volume its general character.

That which has prevented Miss Livesay from limiting her preoccupations to the simple recording of her personal sentiments is her intense social conscience. For many other writers, this passion has engendered dilemmas. Two important influences made themselves felt concurrently. The one led poets to put their pens to the service of a direct and immediate propaganda - with a view to the immediate establishment of an order, and to this end, no ambiguity was permitted in the expounding of the thesis. Poems written under this impetus had a tone of sincerity and fervour but frequently revealed a proclaimed purpose. The other influence operated on the style that betrayed too clearly the disciples' submission to the teachings of Eliot and Hopkins. We are certainly at an impasse when a poet conscious of his social responsibilities abandons himself to nihilism or to a mode of expression in which surrealism sacrifices all ideology to questions of form. A pure didacticism spoils the first, and unintelligibility destroys the second.

Miss Livesay overcomes this second danger. Some critics have maintained that the social-technical dilemma has sometimes impaled her, and some poems certainly justify this assertion. But, on the whole, it seems to me that her better poems have escaped this double danger. They have been faithful to a dialectic without giving way too much to the abstract: they have succeeded in combining warmth of feeling and tasteful style and images, and in satisfying, therefore, the exigencies of art.

Her last volume, *Day and Night*, is a remarkable illustration of this particular synthesis. The revolutionary ardour, which made her choose as a subject for a poem the execution of García Lorca by Franco, does not conflict with the search for the purity of style and exactitude of image which inspires her aesthetic conscience. Spurred by her outrage, she rises in the last verses to a remarkable lyric rage:

You dance. Explode
Unchallenged through the door
As bullets burst
Long deaths ago, your breast.

And song outsoars
The bomber's range
Serene with wind-
Manoeuvred cloud.

Light flight and word
The unassailed, the token!

There are in this collection two poems that appear to me to count among the best that have appeared in Canada for ten years, the 'Serenade for Spring' and the title-poem 'Day and Night.' These two poems could be seen as complements in the art of Miss Livesay. 'Serenade for Spring,' describing a childbirth, unifies to a rare degree force and emotion. The verse-form is one the author seems to prefer, brief and choppy, and the imagery recalls that of H.D. but expresses intense personal sentiments:

O God the knocking
The knocking attacking
No breath to fight it
No thought to bridge it
Bare body wracked and writhing
Hammered and hollowed
To airless heaving
...
Now it is done.
Relax. Release.
And here, behold your handiwork:
Behold – a man!

It is this same technique that gives to the poem 'Day and Night' its explosive force. In its setting of blast furnaces and machine shops move belts of men, men who 'do a dance to the machines.'

The metallic rhythms are admirably adapted to the whistles, the rotating machines, the flashes of the welding torch, the incessant hammering:

One step forward
Hear it crack
Smashing rhythm –
Two steps back

Your heart-beat pounds
Against your throat
The roaring voices
Drown your shout.

This poem is based on sonorous themes. It also demonstrates the gifts of interior observation, but the artist is joined to the reporter to give the definitive product. The ideas were carried from the senses to the conscience, and the reader finds that which his eyes reveal to him must be corroborated by a moral judgment. It is very difficult to attain this intimate fusion of the sociological and the poetic. The energy carried away in a torrent of passion must be controlled by the hand of the artist, and Miss Livesay has accomplished this literary task better than any other Canadian writer of our time.

# D / Pratt as Commentator: *The Canadian Comment* Columns

**'The Decay of Romance'**
(*Canadian Comment* July 1933: 24–5)

Were one to attempt an analysis of the literary output of England and North America during the last twenty years, it would be found that, as far as movements and schools are concerned, the approach has been definitely anti-romantic. A tide of realism has simply swept over the world, invading fiction, drama, and poetry. The stretches which have remained immune have been in the high altitudes occupied by the older and established writers, who have gone back to the past with its legends and myths and folklore, or who have treated contemporary subjects with the faith and outlook of the preceding generation. Examples of these solitary tendencies are furnished by the older Irish writers like Yeats and Russell and by the late Sir Robert Bridges in his *Testament of Beauty*.

This change is quite intelligible when one considers the stern background of life for the past eighteen years: the four years of the War; the decade following, with the crash of hopes for world reconstruction; and the present economic blight. One would not expect Romance to take root in such a soil. So we have adopted a phrase which describes two-thirds of our literature today – 'postwar disillusionment.' Realism is having its innings with a vengeance. It is seen in every department of literature. In biography, under the leadership of Lytton Strachey and pursued by Ludwig, Maurois, Hackett, and others, we have what is known as the debunking process, where the heroes of history are slashed from their pedestals, sometimes brought closer to our common humanity and sometimes distorted by false exaggeration. Napoleon, Burns, Carlyle, Nelson, Scott, in their present position are giving their admirers plenty of work in putting back the plaster. In drama, Shaw has been doing this for thirty years, driving his harpoons into the leviathans in his attack upon sentiment, romance, and the accepted British virtues.

Practically all of the War literature was of this kind – not perhaps that of the first year of the War where, under the inspiration of the bugles and of the call to the colours, martial enthusiasm was combined with the old appeal to the altar and the throne, to the patriotic sentiment of sacrifice for 'The Cause.' There was a brief flurry where the ancient tradition which ran its way from Drayton to Tennyson was maintained – the glorification of the unbroken British square: 'The Guard dies but never surrenders'; 'Was there a man dismayed?' which contained its own rhetorical negatives. That passed long before the curtain of censorship was lifted from the crosses on the battlefields. The literature which followed 1918 belonged to the order of C.E. Montague's *Fiery Particles* and *Rough Justice*, of Remarque's *All Quiet on the Western Front*, and of plays like *Journey's End*, *The Silver Tassie*, and the *White Chateau*.

Fidelity to fact has become the passionate note in this stern reversal of tradition. Take any contemporary anthology of verse in England or on this side of the Atlantic, and you do not have to turn over many pages before you come on a club-footed boy with a broken lamp, fumbling his way along the galleries of a mine and clutching hopelessly at a seam; or upon a woman looking hungrily through the Christmas windows of a store; or upon a scaffold where a rope swings with a rising wind at dawn, and then you discover how tight is the grip that Realism has upon the mind and sympathy of the modern writer.

The movement is in open revolt against the conventional middle and late Victorianism. It is against the optimism of the age, which was partly generated by the vast spread of wealth and power under the flag. It is true that we did not have to wait till the twentieth century for this change. It was initiated largely by Hardy and Housman, where the accepted social and religious beliefs were shattered. From 1910 to 1920 those two great writers towered above their contemporaries in forming the tastes and outlooks of the younger generation.

This modern viewpoint may be studied from many angles. One obvious approach is indicated in the handling of old themes like God, Freedom, Eternity, Sin, the human Soul. Contrast the Miltonic tradition perpetuated by Tennyson with the prevailing modes. The last time Satan was seen in the form of a planet was when Meredith trained his telescope upon him on a starry night. Since then, Satan has forfeited not only those qualities of ambition and brilliancy in design which once made him such a picturesque study in moral dynamics, but also his mass. He has become the classical example of degradation of energy, and is pictured more frequently in the role of a bacillus than that of a Titan. Take the treatment of Aurora. Milton's way, with its spacious beauty and rotundity of phrase and sound, is seen in the description of Abdiel's flight back from Pandemonium:

> All night the dreadless angel unpursued
> Through Heaven's high champaign held his way, till Morn,
> Waked by the circling hours, with rosy hand
> Unbarred the gates of light.

Put that over against the description of a writer who, a few years ago, was regarded as America's most typical modernist, Carl Sandburg, who composed nocturnes and rhapsodies, not upon nightingales and dying swans, but upon brickyards and abattoirs. This is his picture of Dawn: 'In the false dawn when the chickens blink, / And the east shakes a lazy baby toe at to-morrow, / And the east fixes a pink half-eye this way,' reminding one of the old simile: 'And like a lobster boiled, the morn / From gray to red began to turn.'

Twenty years ago! In some respects that period was antediluvian – long enough, in any case, for a protracted literary war to be waged, with the issue gradually favouring the heavier battalions of revolt.

## 'Changing Standpoints'

(*Canadian Comment* August 1933: 25)

One pronounced difference between the imaginative literature of this generation and that of the preceding one is in the treatment of myth. The old legends in the latter half of the nineteenth century lost nothing of their dignity with the craftsmanship bestowed upon them. The Knights of the Round Table were taken out of their pagan environment and transported to the Isle of Wight, where they fought and loved and died under more stringent moral codes. The classical figures were revived and their deeds set forth with all the splendour of preludes and epilogues with blank verse and the lyrical chorus. Whatever idols were broken in religious or aesthetic outlook, at least it might be said that there was veneration for the antique. But the twentieth century is remarkably versatile in putting old themes to new tunes. We have the domesticities of the ancient heroes and heroines disclosed. Helen of Troy has had her private life written up. She has been shown as old and toothless and haggard with virtue. Tristram and Iseult have been taken over and placed on Fifth Avenue. There are, indeed, a few writers of the order of Francis Thompson, who, before he attempted to catch a glimpse of the other world, invariably took off his shoes and tapped apologetically at the door that he might not 'perturbate the Paradisal State.' But, in general, the etiquette of admission has changed. Both realms formerly called Heaven and Hell have taken on the character of big public museums with the doors thrown wide open, but extending a special invitation to the antiquarian.

The conception of power, too, has changed from the time when Kipling wrote. The emphasis is no longer upon the speed and the grace of a battle-cruiser in the Pacific. Steam and electricity were once forces to be wondered at and admired – to be treated Homerically:

I'm sick of all their quirks and turns,
The loves and doves they dream,
Lord, send us a man like Bobbie Burns
To sing the song of steam.

But, today, the imagination is not so easily kindled by some high-sounding ode to the god of Progress: one is, rather, taken to the blast-furnace with its molten slag searing the eyes of a fire-man, or perhaps into the monotony of a printing-press turning white sheets into red and green and blue until the brain becomes subdued to the machine it works upon.

Social conditions have never been so relentlessly exposed in poetic literature, and the cry of the submerged tenth never been made so articulate. Theodore Dreiser, Sinclair Lewis, and a host of lesser writers have taken hold of this phase of life, subjecting it to exhaustive documentary analysis and blasting it with their own individual irony. The most powerful poet in this respect in America is Giovannitti. After leading a textile strike in Massachusetts, he was arraigned on a charge of sedition. Though he denied having urged violence, he was placed in prison through the course of a trial which lasted nearly a year. He was acquitted later, but the poetry which he wrote in prison was published under the title of *Arrows in the Gale,* which runs all the way from the most strident protest against American law and religion to the tenderest humanitarianism. He said that the verses were the 'blows of his own sledge against the walls of his jail':

All that you worship, fear and trust
I kick into the sewer's maw,
And fling my shaft and my disgust
Against your gospel and your law.

The achievement of the volume is 'The Walker,' where he describes the months in jail, hearing, day by day and night by night, the footsteps of the guard on the floor above his cell. The only description comparable to this is the third scene of Galsworthy's *Justice,* which takes nearly a quarter of an hour with not a word spoken – where the whole interval is taken up with the pantomime of a convict restlessly pacing his cell after years of solitary confinement, and listening to the blows of his fellow prisoners against the walls of their cells. The comparison is a valid one because, in both cases, the prisoners are far removed from the criminal type, sensitive, refined, highly wrought, essentially good in instinct.

## 'English Meat *and* Irish Gravy'

(*Canadian Comment* December 1933: 3)

The charm of the Irish poets consists largely in the simplicity and the naturalness of their poetic expression. Our contemporary English literature owes a great debt to the Anglo-Irish revival headed by William Butler Yeats, Lady Gregory, and John Synge, because these writers stood out against the mode which, very prevalent thirty years ago, assumed that the language of poetry should be different from the speech of life – that it should be very specialized, highly coloured, and full of the odour of sanctity. As a result there had grown up a distinct vocabulary – words and phrases descriptive of nature which were supposed to be more fragrant than those usually applied. It was thought to be more poetic to say, 'emerald main,' 'azure vault,' 'feathered songsters,' 'finny tribe,' for the sea, the sky, the birds, the fish, and so forth.

In addition to this, it was a common belief that verse should be allowed liberties denied to prose, an old-time theory that words ought to be slaves to the metre, and that the natural order of language, found in conversation, might be perverted in the interest of the verse scheme. That is, poetic licence was indeed licence, not freedom. Hence words underwent torture to fit into the stocks. When a poet could not jam into his lines words like 'against,' 'beneath,' 'among,' he simply beheaded them to make them read ''gainst,' ''neath,' ''mong'; or he made them commit hara-kiri like 'e'er' for 'ever,' or 'e'en' for 'even.' And sometimes the mutilation was caused by the tyranny of rhyme. A writer wanted to end a stanza with the line 'The birds among the trees.' Now, he had already used the word 'song' to end another line and required a rhyme. 'Among' rhymed all right but it was in the incorrect place, so he simply transposed it, creating the monstrosity 'the birds the trees among.' Such violation today would be at once condemned by the healthier taste demanding the integrity of speech. The English language, as it is largely uninflected, depends particularly upon the order of the words for its meaning and emotional tone, an order as insistent as that of soldiers in a platoon, and if the words get out of step the result is confusion or panic.

It is to the Irish poets and dramatists (not so much to the novelists) that we owe the revived respect for the organic quality of language as far as verse is concerned. Written speech should be, as Yeats pointed out, as simple and direct as a cry from the heart or, as Synge remarked, as flavorous as a nut.

The literature known as Anglo-Irish used English as a framework but with the everlasting Irish idiom running through it. What, then, is the nature of this idiom that makes it recognizable as Irish even in the printed word read silently, when the brogue hasn't a chance of declaring the racial identity of the writer? First of all, there are individual words that smack of the soil and have their native culture in peat and bog. There are certain mannerisms of speech which, so far as the grammar and syntax of the sentences are concerned, may be regarded as superfluous but which add piquancy to the expressions – thrown in like sauce on the pork. Note the use of the reflexives: 'Is it yourself indeed that is here? Herself is out in the garden'; the use of endings to sentences like 'maybe,' or 'at all'; or little religious invocations like 'God help us,' 'It's a fine day today, praise be to God.' 'Is it departed he is – God rest his soul?' 'I'll be after givin' you this little token, the way you won't be forgettin' me.' Then, too, there is the use of the superlatives. When a man is tired out he is said to be 'destroyed entirely.' You ask a sick Irishman how he feels and he is as likely as not to reply, 'I'm powerfully weak today, thank you.' It is the nature of an Irish bull to employ contradictory metaphors which, instead of neutralizing, enhance each other. How much of the charm and piquancy of contemporary Irish plays issues from just these little terms and oddities of expression – the English meat saturated with the idiomatic gravy.

One of the most delightful books put out recently is an autobiography written by a young Irishman, Maurice O'Sullivan, who has captured the old Celtic spirit of utterance in a most astonishing manner. It is written in fluid rhythmic prose with unstudied art. O'Sullivan would be the last person to expect that his work would be the discovery of 1933. *Twenty Years A-Growin'* will be reviewed in the next issue.

## 'New Notes in Canadian Poetry'

(*Canadian Comment* February 1934: 26–7)

To those who are studying the character of Canadian literature it must be a matter of deep interest to follow the developments which have taken place in poetry during the last four or five years. It is not too much to claim that we are witnessing a renaissance in the genuine sense of the term – a birth whose paternity cannot be laid at the door of any literary progenitor in this country but will show blood strains with the lusty foundlings exercising their Anglo-Saxon (and other) lungs in England and the United States.

This movement exhibits a general divergence from the main Canadian stream with its nature photography and diluted transcendentalism. It is, however, traditional and contemporary in the sense in which the modernism of writers like Eliot, Pound, MacLeish, and Jeffers can blend with the work of Donne, Sir Thomas Browne, and the metaphysical poets down to Emily Dickinson.

The vital centre of this energy is in Montreal. Most of the work has appeared only in magazines, but it is attracting wide attention for its originality, its strength, and its constant reflection of the ferments and moods which are stirring the emotional life of the world today. It has all the spirit of adventure, the zest of being in the intellectual and artistic advances of the age. We shall do well to watch the later and systematic production of the group composed in part of F.R. Scott, A.J.M. Smith, Abraham Klein, and Leo Kennedy.

The first contribution in volume form is by Kennedy – *The Shrouding* (Macmillan), a slim, modest collection indeed but of sterling poetic content, utterly unlike anything in our Canadian output up-to-date, and, considering that the author is only in his middle twenties, one might reasonably expect that the years ahead of him possess major fulfilments. It is not often that a first presentation displays such finished craftsmanship and a technical manner which forces interlinear meanings of a deep emotional cast upon condensed expression. 'The Gravedigger's Rhapsody' reveals a command of strong undulating rhythm with an ability to sustain the purity of the organizing idea in the midst of material which, at first sight, may not appear to contain much malleability. Indeed, the impression which remains after the reading of the poems is that of triumph over refractory content. The sense of the unusual sometimes springs out of the novelty of the subject or out of the freshness of the attack on familiar themes. Individual lines and phrases flash out on every page, indicating that Kennedy rarely suffers from the malaise of the majority of our younger poets – the acceptance of clichés, worn-out counters of expression which furnish the line of least resistance when inspiration is at a low ebb.

I think I may be anticipating one criticism of this volume when I point out – what the author himself would probably acknowledge – that the general emotional attitude towards life does not find sufficient relief or variety. The autumnal tones are consistently present though they are always impressive. This quality, however, distinguishes most of the characteristic poetry of the age, and one would expect to find a measure of it in any writer who is attempting to subject the world as it now exists to an honest analysis. What is more important is that whatever viewpoint is taken should be stated with conviction and sincerity, and I am sure that these poems attest the reality of the signature.

I do not find it easy to offer clipped examples of his power of poetic phrasing for, apart from the present limitation of space, the quotations would not contribute the full value shared by the context, and, moreover, an outstanding characteristic of his poetry is the cumulative appeal built up by masses of realistic detail. The imagery is so largely processional.

The final critical result is not simply an estimate of a poetic accomplishment. This in itself is considerable, I am convinced. It is rather the feeling of promise of what is to appear in future work. But enough of the ore has been sampled in this verse to indicate richness and depth. I should like to quote in their entirety such profoundly moving poems as 'Rite of Spring,' 'Prophecy for Icarus,' 'Reproach to Myself,' and 'Quatrains against Grief.' But there is space for only one:

*Words for a Resurrection*

Each pale Christ stirring underground
Splits the brown casket of its root,
Wherefrom the rousing soil upthrusts
A narrow, pointed shoot ...

And bones long quiet under frost
Rejoice as bells precipitate
The loud, ecstatic sundering,
The hour inviolate.

This Man of April walks again ...
Such marvel does the time allow ...
With laughter in His blessed bones,
And lilies on His brow.

## 'With Hook and Worm'

(*Canadian Comment* April 1934: 13)

One of the most difficult tasks confronting a writer who aims at achieving in his compositions more durable qualities than those attending overnight journalese is to transform technical information into literature. To add interest to instruction and to secure it by charm of presentation is a triumph of the literary art, for the very nature of a treatise tends to subordinate the graces to logical proofs and practical ends. The *Compleat Angler* is not only a treatise on sport but a beloved classic of the English language.

The book is almost unique in respect to the circumstances under which it was written. It cannot in any way be described as a 'period work' for, apart from its frequent references to songs and books with which Walton was familiar, it might have been composed in any age, and in any country possessing trout streams and genial human beings given to contemplation. The author was in his teens when Shakespeare was writing his later plays. When he died in his ninety-first year, the Stuart dynasty was nearing its close, and when he wrote *The Compleat Angler*, England was in the throes of the Civil War, but that long stretch of national change and upheaval finds practically no reflection in the quiet pools of his mind.

The style befits the pastime like peaceful, effortless, interesting conversation. It meanders along, discursive and pleasant, as if the thought were following the natural contours of a brook, something in the fashion of Thoreau's *Walden*. Description, meditation, casual observation upon virtue and contentment of soul, upon friendship and temperance, alternate with Arcadian references to flowers and landscapes and the songs of milkmaids and nightingales. Walton has caught from Sir Francis Bacon – whom he terms 'The Great Secretary of Nature' – the manner of expressing himself in pithy and memorable phrases that read like proverbs:

> As for money, neglect it not: but note, that there is no necessity of being rich: for I told you there be as many miseries beyond riches as on this side them.

> We may say of angling as Dr. Boteler said of strawberries: 'Doubtless God could have made a better berry, but doubtless God never did:' and so, if I might be judge, God never did make a more calm, quiet, innocent recreation than angling.

Come let's to supper. Come, my friend Corydon, this trout looks lovely; it was twenty-two inches when it was taken, and the belly of it looked some part of it as yellow as a marigold, and part of it as white as a lily, and yet, methinks, it looks better in this good sauce.

*The Compleat Angler* has always been a favourite with great writers even of opposed outlooks and temperaments. By its very buoyancy it rides above stresses and movements which accompany changes in artistic tastes and political prejudices. It belonged to the choice shelf of readers in the nineteenth as in the eighteenth century. Samuel Johnson put it in his list of thirty essential books, and Lamb, in a letter to Coleridge, remarked: 'Among all your readings did you ever light upon Walton's COMPLEAT ANGLER? It breathes the very spirit of innocence, purity and simplicity of heart ... It would Christianize every discordant, angry passion ... Pray, make yourself acquainted with it.'

Wordsworth wrote two sonnets upon him. Landor and Hallam claimed that, in Izaak Walton, the pastoral manner of writing had preserved all that was warm and rich in the tradition and, at the same time, excluded all that was affected and artificial.

Izaak Walton is known mainly through this classic, but he has another claim to literary recognition in his *Lives*, which contain the biographies of some of his great friends, most of whom were themselves 'anglers and very honest men.' The same style pervades both books, the same gentle, urbane point of view that a man's recreation is the key to his character. His dislike of bustle and agitation, of life's 'sick hurry and divided aims,' and his love of calm and contemplation are expressed in this characteristic passage:

I knew a man that had wealth and riches, and several houses, all beautiful, and ready-furnished, and would often trouble himself and family to be removing from one house to another; and being asked by a friend, why he removed from one house to another, replied, 'It was to find content in some one of them.' But his friend, knowing his temper, told him, if he would find content in any of his houses, he must leave himself behind him; for content will never dwell but in a meek and quiet soul.

## 'Simplicity in Poetry'

(*Canadian Comment* June 1934: 22–3)

Why does the poet persist in writing difficult verse filled with archaic words and classical allusions? Is it that he is forced to write for the well-educated classes who buy his books or is it that simple verse is extraordinarily difficult to write? The latter is the opinion expressed in the *Christian Science Monitor* by the American writer Harold Hobson, who writes:

> An English writer has had the pleasing fancy that the newest of entertainments may revive one of the oldest of the arts. He thinks that the radio's daily five-minute poetry readings may bring back popular poetry – poetry that is popular, not so much in the sense of being widely read as in being written for the people. The literature of every race begins with verse that is understandable by the entire nation; Homer was not the poet of a coterie, nor Langland the prophet of a clique. It is poetry of this type, though naturally of a modern cast, that is needed for reading on the radio – poetry that is universal in its appeal, and easily comprehensible. This writer is of the opinion that, with the exception of Burns and the Elizabethans, nothing of the requisite simplicity has been written in the English language for upwards of five hundred years. But now that the audience for popular poetry has been restored, he hopes that popular poetry will begin to appear.

When one comes to think of it, it is odd to reflect how difficult much of the best English poetry is, how confined to a certain class of readers its appeal must be. Wordsworth, almost alone among English poets, deliberately set out to make his verse from the words and phrases of uneducated people, and he wrote what Mr Gladstone is said to have regarded as the most beautiful line in the English language. Considering Wordsworth's theories, one would expect that line to be instant in its meaning to every reader; but what is the actual case? The line in question completes the famous sonnet on 'The World,' in which Wordsworth expresses his dissatisfaction with modern unrest and materialistic preoccupation:

I'd rather be [he says]
A Pagan suckled in a creed outworn;
So might I, standing on this pleasant lea,
Have glimpses that would make me less forlorn;
Have sight of Proteus rising from the sea;
Or hear old Triton blow his wreathéd horn.

'Or hear old Triton blow his wreathéd horn' – it is indeed a beautiful line; but more than a full half of its beauty is lost on the reader to whom it recalls no classical memories. This is not poetry for the people.

*Memorable* English poetry – that is the crux of the question. Our optimist of the BBC is somewhat mistaken in supposing that simplicity has quite gone out of poetry in the last five hundred years. It would be truer to say that the simplicity remains, in large measure, while it is the poetry that has gone. An abundance of simple verse has been written almost continuously since the days of Chaucer. But it has unfortunately risen only on the lower slopes of Parnassus:

Breathes there a man with soul so dead,
Who never to himself hath said,
This is my own, my native land?
Whose heart hath ne'er within him burned,
As home his footsteps he hath turned,
From wandering on a foreign strand?

Here at all events Scott conveys his meaning even to the least learned reader.

Is there, for honest Poverty,
  That hangs his head, and a' that?
The coward-slave, we pass him by,
  We dare be poor, for a' that!
  For a' that, and a' that,
Our toil's obscure, and a' that,
  The rank is but the guinea stamp;
The man's the gowd for a' that.

One scarcely needs to be a profound scholar to take the point of this, one of the most celebrated of Burns's poems. But alas! the clearness and admirableness of the sentiment are exceeded only by the pedestrianism of the verse. What modern English literature lacks, therefore, is plainly not simple verse, but simple verse that also happens to be poetry. The situation will not be improved by any modern development that encourages people to turn out quantities of easily comprehensible verse, for that is precisely what men of the most distinguished ability have been doing for several centuries. Only very little of what they have turned out has happened to be memorable.

The occasional victories are, of course, among the supreme treasures of the language. Othello's 'It is the cause, it is the cause, my soul,' Macbeth's 'Tomorrow, and tomorrow, and tomorrow,' Lear's cry, when the news of his Fool's passing is brought to him, 'Thou'lt come no more, / Never, never, never, never, never!' and even Burns's

> We twa hae paidl't i' the burn,
>   From mornin' sun till dine;
> But seas between us braid hae roar'd
>   Sin' auld lang syne,

have a keener poignancy than is within the scope of the most elaborate and scholarly of verbal harmonies. But passages like these are very rare; and this rareness, one suspects, is due, not so much to want of an audience for them, as to the extraordinary difficulty of writing them. One cannot really expect them to be any more numerous in the future than they have been in the past. All the more reason, therefore, for enjoying to the utmost such examples of them as exist.

After all, it is hardly surprising that most of the riches of English poetry yield themselves only to fairly experienced readers. Words and phrases that have received distinguished usage in the past, old and golden legends, memories of ancient literature – all these things are part of the equipment with which the poet makes his effects; the poet who does not employ them is deliberately sacrificing the most evocative section of his materials.

He is fighting with one arm tied behind him. Few, therefore, are his victories – but all the more resounding when they come.

## 'A Study in Poetic Development'

(I in *Canadian Comment* August 1934: 20; II in *Canadian Comment* September 1934: 21)

### I. THE EARLIER YEATS

There are not many writers in the English world today who have the capacity to blend creative production with sustained self-criticism in the manner of William Butler Yeats. In sheer content, only Hardy and Shaw may be placed in the same class. As a formative influence, moulding style and fostering discipleship, he moves with Hardy, Housman, Joyce, and Eliot. His fifty volumes, taken chronologically, furnish a comprehensive range of development, aesthetic and philosophical, a development which, as in the more concentrated and feverish case of John Keats, becomes a matter of searching analysis for the artist himself.

There are two broad divisions in Yeats's poetic career. The boundary is somewhere between 1904 and 1910, a period which marks a crisis in his intellectual life. Before this time he was under the spell of the Pre-Raphaelites and of the French Symbolists, an enthusiastic advocate of Art for Art's Sake, a student of theosophy and occultism, delighting in dreamy abstractions and, as far as the Irish Renaissance was concerned, surrendering himself completely to the passion for Celtic mythology. He had no sympathy with the practical and utilitarian currents of his generation. He would not become involved in the political strifes and clamours of his race. He hated anything which savoured of propaganda – an aversion which possessed him right through the Great War, for he would not write a line on the world upheaval. His artistic conscience made him dislike the sociological novel. The ultimate aim of the true artist should be the pursuit of Beauty, and the purest of all efforts was in the direction of myth, of primitive faiths, of the simplicity of folk-beliefs, long before science had clouded towns and cities with the smoke of industry. It was the 'Ireland of the heart' in which he was interested.

It is thought that the most enduring monument of Yeats's genius is to be found in this earlier period. This, at any rate, is the Yeats with which the literary world is most familiar. He began writing fifty years ago, became identified with the 'Young Ireland' Society, and soon, in drama and poetry, was at work upon the great Gaelic legends and the 'old wives' tales' which had been orally transmitted through generations of Irish peasants in the remote counties. That he was a lyricist of the first rank was recognized quite early, not only by virtue of his songs and lyrics but by reason of his plays, like *The Hour Glass, The Land of Heart's Desire, Deirdre,* and others, which illustrate his poetic virtuosity at the same time as they prove his lack of dramatic competence in the strict sense of the term. He brought his readers back to the lost ages in the spirit of the 'true romantic,' as he styled himself, nourished their hearts on symbols instead of facts, and haunted their imaginations with stories of elves and fairies and with cadences that were reminiscent of Blake and Keats and Rossetti.

How far removed was his verse from the noise and dust of the sweltering towns may be seen by the hundreds of lyrics and odes and narratives strewn through *The Wind among the Reeds, The Wild Swans at Coole,* and his successive volumes of *Poems* and *Later Poems.* All modern anthologies possess 'The Lake Isle of Innisfree,' 'The Song of the Wandering Aengus,' 'The Cap and Bells,' and 'The Rose of the World,' and the dreamy, languorous, melodic character of his compositions is perfectly expressed by such a lyric as this, which is pure Yeats:

Had I the heavens' embroidered cloths,
Enwrought with golden and silver light,
The blue and the dim and the dark cloths
Of night and light and the half light,
I would spread the cloths under your feet;
But I, being poor, have only my dreams;
I have spread my dreams under your feet;
Tread softly because you tread on my dreams.

What then constitutes the character of the later Yeats, which makes some of his admirers regret the change, and others to welcome it as an inevitable step in the development which tries to keep abreast of the age?

## II. THE LATER YEATS

There is an interesting parallel between the aesthetic development of Keats and that of the greatest of the Irish poets. If we discard the mere consideration of time – that Keats accomplished all of his marvellous work within four crowded years, while Yeats has taken fifty to accomplish his – we still have a crisis common to both in mid-career wherein there was a profound dissatisfaction with the earlier approach to poetry, a turning away from a mere sensuous impressionism where passing fancies were indulged, and an attempt to reach a more organic and philosophical understanding of life and art. With Keats it is well known that the last two years of his life yielded infinitely grander poetry than his earliest achievements. With Yeats it is a matter of dispute, for many people feel that the closer texture of the thought is not an adequate compensation for the alleged fading of colour and charm and music.

We might compare two representative selections, one written in the nineties – the incomparable 'Lake Isle of Innisfree' – and one from his latest volume, *The Winding Stair,* to illustrate the difference of manner:

I

I will arise and go now, and go to Innisfree,
And a small cabin build there, of clay and wattles made;
Nine bean-rows will I have there, a hive for the honey-bee,
And live alone in the bee-loud glade.

...

I will arise and go now, for always night and day
I hear lake water lapping with low sounds by the shore;
While I stand on the roadway, or on the pavements grey,
I hear it in the deep heart's core.

II
I am content to live it all again
And yet again, if it be life to pitch
Into the frog-spawn of a blind man's ditch,
A blind man battering blind men ...

I am content to follow to its source
Every event in action or in thought;
Measure the lot; forgive myself the lot!
When such as I cast out remorse
So great a sweetness flows into the breast
We must laugh and we must sing;
We are blest by everything,
Everything we look upon is blest.

The first belongs to a period which, for all its decadence and nostalgia and twilight inertia, lulled and caressed the senses like so much of the poetry of Yeats's early contemporaries, Wilde, and Dowson, and Lionel Johnson. It is poetry such as this that the anthologies will invariably select because of the lyrical value, the immediate appeal, and the completeness of the sentiment. The second, though a brief extract is obviously unsatisfying, is typical of Yeats's maturity, of his desire to shape his intellectual system rather than simply to round out his aesthetic impressions. And for the attainment of this, Yeats was conscious that the discipline involved a sacrifice – the very sap of his veins, as he describes it, where his youth blossomed with romantic 'joy and natural content,' and where his ambitions as a poet were all summed up in his intention to set myth to song, to wear poetic apparel – 'Covered with embroideries / Out of old mythologies.'

This new programme of life – 'to follow to its source / Every event in action or in thought' – has given more intellectual substance to his poetry. Like George Russell, he has developed a social conscience, realizing that the world of pure introspection and symbolism, however beautifully it may be expressed, was after all a narrow one where phantoms were substituted for realities. It is a sign of strength and growing capacity that both these writers have swung into the larger orbit of the national life in which not only the mystic notes are sounded but martial calls, if not from the battlefield, yet from arenas where the economic and sociological issues are being fought out. The only true unity for both of them is 'the unity of Culture in class or people' where all interests of value may find position. *The Tower, The Winding Stair,* and *Words for Music Perhaps* – the latest volumes of Yeats – represent this wider intellectual vision.

## 'The Comic Spirit'

(*Canadian Comment* November 1934: 17)

There is a certain type of philosophy which endeavours to explain the comic element in human nature on the biological ground of social defence – that laughter is a mechanism produced by evolution to safeguard society against excess in the individual. It is essentially critical, having as its aim the return of the prodigal to the fold. The most popular exponent of this view is the French philosopher and critic Bergson, who in his brilliant essay 'Le Rire' would make laughter a form of social snubbing in which there is an intention, explicit or unavowed, to humiliate and consequently to correct our neighbours: 'Any individual is comic who automatically goes his own way without troubling himself about getting into touch with the rest of his fellow-beings.' Laughter is the 'birch of the school-master' to bring the erring one into line, a method of discipline in which there is a sense of conscious superiority on the part of the one who administers it.

This is not an original standpoint, of course. It was stated by Thomas Hobbes in the seventeenth century: 'The passion of laughter is nothing else but sudden glory arising from a sudden conception of eminency in ourselves, by comparison with the inferiority of others, or with our own formerly.' But Bergson, with Darwin and Spencer preceding him, was able to adduce a mass of scientific evidence in support of his position. And there is no doubt that there is a large element of truth in ascribing the corrective function to comedy, but just as certainly it does not cover the whole process.

It applies emphatically to the comedy of manners where types which are more or less obnoxious to us, like the miser or the hypocrite or the fop, are held up to ridicule. In such cases, laughter may be more devastating than the lash or imprisonment as a mode of punishment. Most of the outstanding French comic plays fit into this conception, and the satirical English comedy, like that of Congreve, Wilde, and particularly Shaw, follows the accepted classical tradition. It does not apply, however, to what is described as the comedy of humour, exhibited in its highest form in Shakespeare. The contention that laughter is incompatible with sympathy has very little relevance to the Shakespearean creations, just as it has very little bearing upon the characterizations, say, of Dickens or Scott. The disciplinary quality may at times be present but it is not obtrusive.

If we analyse our own experiences in the theatre, or in real life, how often do we find satire running through our laughter? On occasions, admittedly, but in the majority of cases there may not be a trace of it. Indeed the comedies we most enjoy are those which expand our sympathies at the same time as they evoke our humour. And the gamut is long from the most temperate mood up to the wildest hilarity. One of the very obvious sources, one which probably accounts for three-fourths of comic expression, is the simple fact of the incongruities of life, summed up in the idea of contrast. Possibly this fact is an elemental one and all that a critic may do is not to attempt to analyse it but to point it out. We laugh when the orderly or normal sequence of things is disturbed, provided the consequences are not serious. Inverted positions and relationships, such as a man trying to stand on his head in a church or a battle-scarred pugilist appearing in court to sue his wife for non-support, or the appearance together of an exceedingly tall, thin individual and an exceedingly short, fat one - all these clownish, midway illustrations up to the most subtle social embarrassments stimulate mirth in every variety and are based upon eccentric position.

It is a matter of everyday observation how an irrelevant or incongruous remark may puncture the most heavily weighted argument. This underlies the psychology of heckling. It is reported that when Sir Oswald Mosley was addressing a vast throng at a recent meeting in England, he tried to furnish a dramatic conclusion to his speech by clicking his heels and lifting his arm in the fascist salute. Just when the act was finished, a little voice from the gallery piped up: 'Yes, you may go out.' The cause of fascism was lost from that moment, and the principle of incongruity uproariously vindicated.

## 'Slang – Why and Why Not'

(*Canadian Comment* March 1936: 28–9)

Just a little while ago a group of teachers met together in Toronto to form a society for the promotion and preservation of pure English. They had been very much disturbed over the invasion of our speech by hordes of unsightly and unsavoury colloquialisms, most of them imported from the United States. A few years before, the parent society had been organized in England under the leadership of Sir Robert Bridges, Henry Bradley, and Sir Walter Raleigh, Oxford Professor of English Literature, for the purpose 'of informing popular taste on sound principles, for guiding educated authorities, and for introducing into practice certain slight modifications and advantageous changes.'

The interesting words in this programme are 'slight' and 'advantageous' for they indicate two things: first, that some restriction should be placed upon the wild, unlicensed trifling with an organic language, and secondly, that some liberty should be allowed to what is inevitable in an organism – change and development. With regard to the first, it was felt that heavy and serious inroads upon the language were being made by the uneducated masses, that certain expressions which, after a few repetitions, created violent reactions in the gorge, seemed likely to become a permanent bill of fare at the common table. With regard to the second, it was recognized as an indubitable fact that expressions, bitterly opposed when they were introduced, fought their way into the acknowledged diction and structure of the tongue. On the one hand, it was seen that phrases like 'Oh Yeah,' 'I'll tell the cockeyed world,' 'You said a mouthful,' 'Oh boy, she's some baby,' 'Sign on the dotted line,' 'He's the prize cuckoo,' and countless others sent the purists into convulsions. On the other hand, it was just as indubitable that expressions like 'What on earth,' 'row' (a disturbance), 'grit,' 'plucky,' 'pussy-foot,' 'hard-boiled,' 'hot-air,' 'chiseler,' 'snooty,' 'sham,' 'stingy,' 'tiff,' 'budge,' 'wobbly,' all of them contested when first used, had become admitted into the drawing-rooms.

It was one of the purposes of this local society to study the legitimacy of language. Why are some words received almost immediately into the speech, some rejected at once like tramps with dirty faces, some held a long time on probation, and others invited in only to be kicked out later? What is slang anyway? What is a vulgarism? What is the procedure by which a wild or alien word is domesticated?

Slang has been defined by an American philologist as 'a peculiar kind of vagabond language, always hanging on the outskirts of legitimate speech, but continually straying or forcing its way into the most respectable company.' But this description does not show how the family proprieties are preserved or disturbed after the arrival of the vagabond; neither does it give any credit to the intruder for the vitality which in the course of time he occasionally imparts to the native stock. The first question then to be discussed was - Why does slang occur at all? What purpose does it serve?

There was general agreement that it springs out of the desire for novelty, for getting picturesque effects not attainable to an equal degree by the higher social levels of speech. It puts freshness into the formal and genteel modes. It is a form of colloquialism with the restraints taken off and made to hit the eye and ear with the slap of surprise. And obviously, the great proportion of slang emerges from the sporting columns where the attention of the readers must be seized and stimulated day by day and year by year through unfamiliar treatment of familiar subjects. The popularity of Ring Lardner grew out of his ingenuity in the manufacture of new, witty, and sometimes outlandish comparisons. I remember his forecast of the Dempsey-Carpentier fight, his whimsicality in writing up the anticipated rounds, finishing with the remark that Carpentier had as much chance of coming out alive after the bout 'as a celluloid cat in hell pursued by an asbestos dog.' Although that simile was only a variation upon the 'snowball in hell' figure, it was so strikingly funny that it couldn't be repeated without plagiarism. Nevertheless, the image has been adopted and altered indefinitely according to the resources of industrial chemistry to create inflammable and non-inflammable substances, or the resources of human wit to imagine anything faster in pursuit than a dog or in flight than a cat.

Well, to come back to the Society for the Promotion of Pure English, one of the group attending this meeting was a Frenchman who was spending a year in Canada to perfect his knowledge and use of the English idiom. His conversation was excellent and he had so divested himself of his native accent that he might have been any one of the Canadians taking part in the discussion. He was being complimented upon the precision of his speech and upon the social ease with which, presumably, he could travel through the country and engage in conversation on any level he chose. I offered, very respectfully, to introduce him to a level of English speech which might cause him to question his mastery. Had he ever been to a wrestling bout? No. Would he like to go? Very much indeed. Not that he cared for the show as a matter of personal taste, but if any new light could be shed upon the language he would consider the time profitably spent.

So to the Gardens we went to see a 'Greek god' from Ireland (not all the gods come from Greece) do battle with a hairy Russian known as 'the sabre-toothed Siberian.' Pierre took along with him his notebook to copy down expressions: I was to act as interpreter. This was to be an abysmal fight, for the Irishman, beautiful as he was, and heralded by the newspapers as 'the darling of the dolls,' was credited with terrific strength and endurance, well able to cope with the deadly double armlocks and paralysing crotch-holds of the Russian. The gladiators came into the square to the refrains of an Irish jig, which was drowned by the boos and cheers of fifteen thousand throats. The first expression my friend wrote down was – 'What a peach of a cauliflower,' which being lifted up one level might be construed as – 'What an extraordinary looking ear that Russian has.'

From the moment the wrestlers met, there was not one phrase which Pierre understood. Either the words were new coinages, or established familiar words used in a new sense. The arena became an excellent laboratory to demonstrate the nature of slang. Variety, surprise, highly specialized cant, grotesque transferences of words from one application to another, distorted, exaggerated meanings were all put on exhibit to the accompaniment of mass laryngitis. Never once was a normal term used in a normal setting. Words like leg, arm, stomach, head, chest, did not belong to this kind of anatomical classification. When a 'het-up' dame (a doll or whizz-whang) flung a pop-bottle and hit the villain on the head, she raised a 'walnut' on his 'bean' or a 'wow' on his 'coco.' When the Russian landed his knee in the Irishman's 'breadbox' (oven) the crowd gave him the 'raspberry' or the 'razzle-dazzle.' When the Irishman got a toe-hold, they roared, 'Turn on the juice, make him like it. It's a beaut,' and to the protests and canvas-thumps of the Russian, they yelled, 'Horse-feathers,' 'Boloney,' 'He's getting woozy; another turn and he'll "cry Uncle."' Finally, when the dramatic moment came for the champ 'to do his stuff,' 'show his class,' and hurl 'the mug' over the ropes to land on his 'pan' fifteen feet to the concrete, 'did the fans like it?' 'And how!' 'You're telling me?' 'No, I'm telling you.'

It was a bewildered Frenchman I took back to his lodgings that night. 'So that is English as she is spoke.' He realized how ambiguous were the congratulations which a few hours before had been offered to him by the Society for Pure English. He had listened, he said, to the native tongue of fifteen thousand lunatics, which was just as foreign to him as Hindustani – in fact, more foreign, because in the latter case there was a logic and a structure which he could understand. And he became aware that even if he did learn his lesson from his notebook, he would have to unlearn it in a few months when 'raspberry' and 'boloney' and 'Limburger' were abandoned in favour of other varieties of jam, meat, and cheese wherewith to plaster the gods and the demons of the sporting world. I tried to argue with him that the whole question had to be considered as much from the standpoint of psychology as of language. No one could deny that the fun and excitement of the evening were heightened by the use of these coinages. They were used as missiles and were substituted (sometimes) for pop-bottles. They helped the box-office. They served as a purgation to the pent-up emotions. And Toronto needed it. But my argument fell on deaf ears. When I called to see Pierre the next week, his landlady informed me that quite unexpectedly for herself and for him, he had purchased his ticket for Europe.

# E / Pratt as Editor: The *Canadian Poetry Magazine* Editorials

**'Foreword' to vol. 1, no. 1**
(*Canadian Poetry Magazine* January 1936: 5–7)

For some time past the desire has been growing among people interested in the poetry of this country for a national magazine devoted exclusively to verse. It was felt that though popular journals and academic reviews offered abundant scope for Canadian literary expression through the channels of prose, the general position for verse contributions was in the backyard spaces of the periodicals. The explanation given is the far greater marketability of short stories, sketches, and articles dealing with the political and economic issues of the day. After all, the concern is with public consumption, and fiction answers the appetite like a dinner gong.

It is hardly to be expected that anything like a corresponding demand may be created for poetry, but at least it is possible to stimulate interest in the art by drumming up a larger audience and by giving recognition to works of distinction through publication and awards. There still remains in the minds of some people the self-imposed doctrinaire notion that anything so precious and sacrosanct as a poem should never appear on the bargain counters or be tarnished with the trade and truck of the world. It is likely that such a notion had its origin in the psychological compensation which occasionally comes to a creator who, finding his work neglected on this earth, feels that the only Board of Assessors competent to pass judgment is a council of eternity. Of all the arts, poetry is the one which gets the least tangible results, but, while there may not be for many years to come a flattering balance struck between reward and the time and craftsmanship involved in creative writing, yet the disparity may be somewhat redressed by a wisely fostered interest in the art and by whatever returns in the coin of the realm may be secured through the help of finance committees.

Canada lags far behind other countries in this respect. Not indeed is the backwardness shown in regard to quality or quantity of production. We believe that the highest grade sifted from the mass can be placed without prejudice with what is in the best bins of other countries – but the intelligent sympathies of the public are indispensable to the future success of the craft. The United States, besides offering many substantial prizes, keeps alive, if not flourishing, more than forty magazines which publish nothing but verse and critical comments, and a few of these are responsible for the discovery of several major American poets of the twentieth century. The time is well advanced for Canada to initiate its own movements in the same direction.

To this end the *Canadian Poetry Magazine* is launched under the auspices of the Canadian Authors' Association. It is not intended to displace but rather to supplement the yearbooks which have already done excellent pioneer work in presenting regional output. Its policy is ambitious enough to formulate the following program. It will pay for all verse printed, although contributors are admonished against purchasing vacation tickets to Miami on the strength of the proceeds. The amounts will be determined by the volume of subscription and the generosity of guarantors. The magazine will be published quarterly and will consist of forty-eight pages containing the selected best from the submitted manuscripts together with notices, reviews, and critical discussions of whatever looks significant on the poetic horizon. It will be open to Canadian verse not before published in book form, but anything which has appeared in the magazines for one year preceding the time of presentation to the quarterly will be regarded as eligible. It will offer three or four prizes every issue for poems of leading merit. While not anticipating the Nobel Award before the end of 1937, yet we may safely assure the prize-winners that they will not be dismissed with copies of *Locksley Hall* or *Evangeline* bound in pigskin. In order to avoid too subjective a verdict, the democratic element is introduced of having the awards based upon the main judgment of an advisory board comprised of twenty representative persons. Writers of more established repute may exercise their option of remaining outside the prize contest, in which cases an asterisk will indicate the non-competitive character of the contributions.

## 'Comment' from vol. 1, no. 2

(*Canadian Poetry Magazine* April 1936: 5–6)

We enter upon the second issue of the *Canadian Poetry Magazine* with confidence. Many of the fears and hesitations which accompanied the January launching have been largely dispelled. Subscriptions have been encouraging and the critical comments of the press throughout the country have been stimulating and appreciative.

The task of sifting out forty pages of verse from approximately one thousand was a formidable one, especially when so much good stuff had to be omitted through the finest shades of discrimination. Should the magazine receive adequate support in the months ahead, it might be expanded into sixty-four pages, which would allow more liberal inclusion of verse and at the same time furnish room for critical articles and book reviews. For the present, however, such volumes of poetry and of criticism as currently appear cannot receive more attention than a notice of publication.

We have been particularly gratified by the extent and keenness of the interest displayed on the part of those who do not write poetry but read it. The most illuminating suggestions have come from this source and are welcomed. Anything but lethargy and complacency! Several correspondents have deplored the absence of humorous verse in the issue. To this we plead guilty but the remedy is a simple one. Send it along but make sure first that it is humour. Others have claimed that Imagism possessed too prominent a place and that the assumption of modernity was a trifle too obvious. Against this there was a large body of opinion that as tradition had already taken too firm a grip upon the minds of Canadian writers, now was the opportunity to break new ground and to create an experimental medium out of the national magazine. The demand was for contemporary poetry giving full expression to the time-spirit in theme, mood, and technique.

The accepted policy of the magazine is towards the tolerant consideration of genuine poetic effort and against identity with any form of aesthetic whether old or new. We believe that the long-established modes are far from their point of exhaustion and are everywhere giving evidence of fresh vision and vitality. We believe also that they have no monopoly on the creative spirit, for there is just as abundant proof that the various empirical approaches today are leading to results of indubitable poetic merit. Generous latitude should be given to subject-matter and points of view. No segment of life which has any significance ought to be discarded on the ground that it belongs to the *profane* areas of prose. And with regard to form the same hospitality must be extended, for there is no reason to affirm that there should be less diversity in the treatment than in the material – always subject, however, to the right of the blue pencil to go through the meaningless lay-out of a fatuous sentiment.

## 'Comment' from vol. 1, no. 3

(*Canadian Poetry Magazine* July 1936: 5–6)

The number of contributions submitted to the *Canadian Poetry Magazine* has now reached an approximate average of two hundred a week. With a very small staff, it has become absolutely impossible to answer requests for criticism, or to give instructions on how to write poetry, or to return manuscripts that have not been accompanied with self-addressed stamped envelopes. To all those, however, who have asked us if they are wasting their time writing poetry, a blanket answer is possible. No one ever wastes time writing poetry, for his own amusement, but writing and publishing poetry are very different matters. Thus there is a good side and a bad side to this flood of unpublished and for the most part unpublishable poetry. That so many people should want to write poetry is good; that they should all seek publication indicates that they have very little idea of the amount of craftsmanship necessary to produce a poem which can be read with profit and pleasure by a large number of people. Our job is to print the best of the material submitted to us, and thereby publish some of the best poetry being written in Canada. It is not our business to absorb the vast quantity of competent but undistinguished verse that every locality produces.

A poem can be written only by someone who knows how to write: there is no exception to that rule. Poetry is an exacting, difficult craft, and it takes years of hard work, and education, and a sense of the language. Rhyme and metre do not make a poem; they produce by themselves nothing but doggerel. The real flesh and blood of poetry lies in turns of phrases, vivid images, new and unusual thoughts and manners of expressing them. A good poem is good because it is an unusual, imaginative, arresting way of writing English. We do not speak in poetry, except at rare moments; and if a poet writes so simply as to give the effect of spoken language, that effect is all the more startling and novel.

To be able to use this language, one must learn it, and that takes, among other things, reading. Practically all the great poets of our language were very highly educated, and the majority were scholars of enormous learning, commanding a large number of languages living and dead. Shakespeare, Burns, and Keats are usually regarded as proving the contrary, but their capacity to respond to the books they did read was tremendous, and of no great poet is it untrue to say that his genius would have starved to death without books, for all his observation and experience of life. The reason is very simple: the poet is a literary man, and he has to know something about his trade. Too many of our contributions betray no familiarity with the great body of English poetry other than what has been printed in the school reader, and school readers are frequently more interested in moral sentiments than in poetry. Of course, reading the classics is not everything: this is the twentieth century, and just as anyone who has never heard of an automobile is likely to get knocked down crossing a street, so anyone who has never heard of a prominent living poet is likely to get a rejection slip. People will always try to resist reading modern poets, but very few ever succeeded in becoming good poets who took that attitude to the poetry of their own time. Contemporary poetry should be studied by everyone who wishes to add something further to it. It is to help such students that the *Canadian Poetry Magazine* has been started.

**'Entering the Second Year'**
(*Canadian Poetry Magazine* June 1937: 5–6)

This is the first number of our second volume, the start of a new year in the records of the magazine. The enterprise was begun in the spirit of faith on the part of a few people who gave voluntarily of their time, labour, and money, requiring no other return than the success of the publication in furthering the growth of an art. That faith, which struggled through months of doubt, is now being justified by freshening responses from all over Canada. The representative character of the interest is most encouraging, which is as it should be for a magazine that is ideally national.

This widespread appeal has been stimulated by a number of factors, two of which call for special comment. As announced in the March issue, His Excellency the Governor-General has taken an active interest in the welfare of the magazine by offering an award for the poem judged to be the finest over the four issues of the year. The award will take the form of a medal. He has also expressed his willingness to address a meeting some time next autumn on behalf of the *Canadian Poetry Magazine*, inasmuch as the magazine represents the first organized effort to furnish a national poetic medium.

Following this announcement came the offer of the Canadian Broadcasting Corporation to extend the facilities of the system to the magazine. At the request of the executive committee, the Corporation agreed to put on the air a number of programmes in which speakers might expound the nature and aims of Canadian poetry and read selections from the magazine. This is most helpful and encouraging because verse, by reason of the qualities which it shares with music, needs the ear as well as the eye to secure its most complete interpretation. Moreover, the width of the radio constituency is an immense advantage. For this, our thanks.

From the very first, requests have come in from subscribers that the magazine be expanded sufficiently to admit brief articles and letters upon subjects like the nature of poetry, the Canadian expression of the art, the relation of Canadian verse to contemporary movements in other countries, the native production individual and collective, the indications of change in outlook and technique, the points of difference between Romanticism and Humanism, and kindred topics. We are in the midst of literary controversies today which ought to be presented and clarified to our readers and especially to our younger craftsmen who are puzzled by the discipleship attracted to new and bewildering paths on Helicon, and are wondering whither the paths lead. It is true that the presentation of a problem may occasionally issue in greater confusion, but this is a minor matter compared to the intellectual excitement which attends an acute awareness of the strifes and ferments going on in the world around us.

We are heartily in accord with this demand and have waited only for favourable developments on the business side of the magazine to make the required expansions. This *first* issue of Volume *Two* is larger by fourteen pages than the foregoing numbers, and we are pleased to print an article from Dr Lorne Pierce, Literary Editor of the Ryerson Press, and one of the ablest critics in the Canadian field.

# F / Pratt as Reviewer

## **A.D. Watson's *Robert Norwood***

('A New Book,' *Christian Guardian*, 4 July 1923: 21)

The editors of this projected series have reason to congratulate themselves upon their first presentation of Canadian poets. This volume, even in its mere physical properties, is as lovely as a gem, and persuades the eye before the covers are opened. It is fitting that such an ambitious editorial plan should have had its first try-out by offering poetry-lovers a taste of a writer like Robert Norwood, who, without imitation, can truly manage to perpetuate old and vital standards. This task of interpretation has been accomplished with insight and refinement by Dr A.D. Watson. The volume consists of a biographical sketch, a brief but representative anthology of Norwood's best work, and an appreciative review.

The classical direction of Norwood's sympathies is seen both in content and in technique. Ancient themes with strong Biblical infusions possess a dominant attraction. 'The Witch of Endor,' 'Dives and Lazarus,' 'Judas,' 'The Man of Kerioth,' 'Melchizedek,' 'Giordano Bruno,' are illustrative titles. And these subjects do not break their moulds. There is a patterning, which, in its display of firmness and elegance, indicates the adequate craftsmanship of the author. The stanzaic structure is carefully wrought out.

Dramatic blank verse, the quatrain, and many delicate lyrical forms are employed in full recognition of their carrying capacity. But it is in the sonnet and its sequences where Mr Norwood has most clearly achieved his artistic distinction and revealed his filial contacts with the accepted workmen of a former age. In the words of the appreciation by Dr Watson, 'Great art is a suggestion of a new and fuller life based on a glorious reminiscence. Such is the benign function of a classic. It is a perennially-inspiring challenge to the ages to take it and make its beauty more beautiful.'

## Flos Jewell Williams's *New Furrows*

('An Alberta Novel,' *Saturday Night*, 4 December 1926: 8)

This is a story of the soil. A Belgian family migrate to Canada just before the war, settle on a farm in sight of the Alberta foothills, and receive their first taste of hail and drought with all the unadvertised variations of life in the New World. Marie Fourchette, the refined and beautiful daughter in a sordid home – a biological anomaly explained later – is the central figure, with Tom Canning, a debauchee, and Grange Houtain, a fine specimen of the Mounted Police, the rivals for her affections.

The scaffolding of the plot at first sight gives the appearance of a construction designed for a Romance, but before long we are faced with a picture where the conflicts are grippingly wrought out under the strict formula of a realist. The story is alive with incident, and the plot, notwithstanding that it has to carry the happenings of several years, is compact with an interest that leaves one guessing at consequences. Nothing is dragged into the narrative that does not spring out of the natural treatment of the theme. Immigration problems that crop up here and there are presented by dramatis personae in action on the prairies.

The dialogue is skilfully handled except in two or three places where Marie tests credibility by imagery and speech that would daze a Mercutio. Her comparison of her own mood with a garden of vegetables is a delightful fantasy which might easily spring from the author's brilliance, but scarcely from Marie, despite her accredited vocabulary. But the conversation in the critical, staccato moments becomes vivid, tense, and authentic.

The sense of background is one of the vital qualities of the book. There are some descriptions superb in style and movement. Nature is not merely identified with soil and climate inviting and resisting the human hand. It is that, of course, in part, for much of crisis in the Fourchette family is so conditioned, but artistically considered, it is rather a page on which the author finely records sharp vignettes of human mood, little stabs of passion in speech, as well as the larger and more arresting decisions that do not need language for articulation.

**James O'Donnell Bennett's** ***Much Loved Books: Best Sellers of the Ages***

('The Immortality of Literature,' *Saturday Night*, 17 March 1928: Lit. Sec. 2)

This work is a collection of sixty articles which appeared as weekly contributions to the Chicago *Tribune*, and were finally published in response to the wide demand of enthusiastic readers for a more durable presentation. Its distinctive quality lies in the task of the author to cover as a news assignment the best sellers of the world and of all time, under the space limitations in each case of two thousand words.

There is a half-concealed assumption that the great classics are still unfamiliar to millions of people who nevertheless may be conversant with a great deal of the modern output, and to such the *Agamemnon*, *The Canterbury Tales*, *Tom Jones*, *The Decline and Fall*, and their immortal kindred could be written up with the freshness of report attending at least the discovery of an important Egyptian tomb.

The books jostle each other most intimately in the topical order. *The Bible* is followed by *Treasure Island*; *The Three Musketeers* by *Hamlet*; *Faust* by *The Compleat Angler*; Boswell's *Life* by *Mother Goose*; *Robinson Crusoe* by *The French Revolution*. In vivid reportorial vein Mr

Bennett tells the reason for the composition of the book, relating it to biographical and historical events, and then asserts the flavour of the style by pungent extracts followed by his own comments, which really amount to vigorous hand-waving – Come and See; Come and Taste. To a person who has not read a given work of age-old reputation but who has still nourished his taste upon many good things in literature, this summons strikes the eye like a headline. Here is something which has resisted decay, and here is the secret of its life and perpetual flowering.

Each masterpiece is illustrated by its idiom: the eternal quality, suiting the twentieth century AD, as the fifth BC, of the soldier's speech in the *Agamemnon*; the abounding spread of Cellini, the gnomic moralizings of Bacon and Chesterfield; the 'Polonius-Montaigne' character of Pepys; the delightful inconsequence of Lamb; the wise ribaldry of Sterne; the exotic perfumes and brilliancies of *The Arabian Nights*, which made the youthful Carlyle pay surreptitious visits to the garden against the protest of his 'verra pious' old father.

The best chapters of the book, as might be inferred from the author's profession, are those which reflect the narrative energy of the originals or their piquancy of biographical revelations. The news element is the dominant one, and the systematic constructions of men like Goethe and Gibbon are here made less inviting than the more casual, picturesque, and saucy conversations recorded for the world's entertainment. The main virtue is the impression it gives of a much loved and leisured fingering of books. The treatment is unforced and as natural as a caress. 'The minute selection of characteristical circumstances' which furnishes the guiding principle of Boswell's method is also Bennett's key to your interest. If I had never read the *Life of Johnson*, but had simply brushed up against it in this short news article, I would have pawned my winter overcoat to buy the volumes. Boswell had just taken the count from Johnson but with enormous powers of resuscitation he came back with one more question:

'What did you do, sir? What did you say, sir?' to which the enraged Bear replied: – 'I will not be put to the question. Don't you consider, sir, that these are not the manners of a gentleman. I will not be baited with *what* and *why*; what is this? what is that? why is the cow's tail long? why is a fox's tail bushy?' Boswell, who was a good deal out of countenance, said, 'Why, sir, you are so good, that I venture to trouble you.' Johnson – 'Sir, my being so good is no reason why you should be so ill.'

## Laura Riding's *Contemporaries and Snobs*

('A Poor Case for Modernity,' *Saturday Night*, 26 May 1928: 9, 12)

The central idea of this volume is to show the danger to which the poetic faculty may be exposed, by being harnessed to contemporary criticism. Literature, it is generally recognized, has come to be defined as work which reflects the spirit of the age (the *Zeitgeist*), and all effort not in conformity with professional critical dicta must run the risk of social and intellectual ostracism. It is this authority which the writer attempts to expound and arraign, though with a great deal of obscurity.

The eighteenth century is taken as the famous historical example of literary tyranny, with Dryden as the prince of snobs. It is precisely the same condition which prevails in the modernist attitude towards literature and art – which is nothing but 'the will to extract the literary sense of the age from the Zeitgeist at whatever cost to creative independence.' There are, however, several means of escape from this domination. There is the satire mode, which at its inception bursts in on the age as a vigorous corrective to heroics and sentimentality, but this in its turn may ascend into the aristocracy of taste, and prescribe its own fettering canons. There is the nature mode, with the emphasis upon decentralization and romantic eccentricity. And again, there is the attempt to effect a radical dissociation from all trends and influences, a form of individualism which is called the *poetic absolute*.

These methods of expression, as far as they belong to poetry, are regarded as protective barriers constructed by the poet against the autocracy of the *Zeitgeist*. But the experiments and reactions themselves are pursued by a relentless nemesis. The very preoccupation with tradition, even when the writer is in revolt, destroys spontaneity, for 'creative self-consciousness is a contradiction in terms.'

Such appears to be the argument of the book. But the author, at the outset, has burdened herself with unnecessary trappings. Why should a writer's awareness of what is going on about him prejudice the aesthetic values of his work? This contact with his period is what Miss Riding calls the 'professional conscience,' a civilizing agency which makes for technical expertness, but loses in fire and vitality. It is difficult to extract much meaning from some of her illustrations. It may be true that Byron and Goethe were, in a sense, typical *Zeitgeist* writers, largely recording spirits of a period of revolution and reaction, but that 'their poetry died as it was written' is an absurdity. This sort of irresponsible writing is continued in her discussion of the poetry of Keats, his 'little hill of nonsense' as she jejunely describes it. Keats is supposed to have sacrificed himself to ambition, 'writing according to a layman's idea of how a poet should write, catering to society's snobbism toward poetry and to poetry's protective snobbism toward society.'

The whole treatise is marred by the prevalence of terms and expressions which are not merely ugly, but are only provided with meaning, if at all, when they are shoved back into a context of several pages. The opening paragraph of the book is one of many examples in which a cloud of words may darken understanding:

> There is a sense of life so real that it becomes the sense of something more real than life. Spatial and temporal sequences can only partially express it. It introduces a principle of selection into the undifferentiating quantitative appetite and thus changes accidental emotional forms into deliberate intellectual forms; animal experiences related by time and space into human experiences related in infinite degrees of kind. It is the meaning at work in what has no meaning: it is, at its clearest, poetry.

This might do as an intellectual teaser, but one finds with the further reading that the function of paradox – making truth stand up on its head – is not at all times sustained. The contortionist cannot right himself from his own knots.

**Robert M. Gay's *Ralph Waldo Emerson***
('The Oracle at Concord,' *Saturday Night*, 14 July 1928: 10–11)

This work is an attempt by an admirer and disciple to present afresh the life and message of a man who, very much in eclipse today, was regarded in the middle of the nineteenth century as the foremost philosopher that America had produced. It opens with the lament that an age concerned with the 'externalities of invention, expansion, efficiency,' and so forth, should have little in common with the transcendentalism of Emerson, his love of solitude and speculation, and the fine shadings of his philosophy which, stated with the finality of oracles, added confusion and often vexation to the minds of many readers.

The author contents himself with biographical statement and straight exposition. He intentionally ignores the critical side, thereby imposing a serious restriction upon himself, in that he forfeits a means of explaining in some measure the American neglect of Emerson, in terms of the advance of thought, religious belief, and national psychology. It would be interesting to examine a temperament which could look upon the world in 1859 (the time of the *Origin of Species*); accept the evolutionary hypothesis; and yet, while Huxley was proclaiming the tooth-and-claw opposition between the ethical and the cosmic orders, placidly extol the harmonies and correspondences between man and nature.

The main conceptions which governed Emerson's thinking are set forth in some fullness, usually by direct quotation from the *Essays*. Evil or error – it can scarcely be called sin – and pain find their adjustment under the law of compensation. 'The compensation of calamity is that it affords the measure of a richer, higher and more helpful life.' Whenever the natural world becomes a little too uncomfortable there is the second great refuge in the doctrine of self-reliance, where man is after all the captain of his soul. Emerson is a blend of Wordsworth and Carlyle, of 'Tintern Abbey' and *Sartor Resartus*, and his kinship with Joseph Butler is shown in the fertility with which he discovers analogies for design in the universe.

The most entertaining part of the book is the account of Emerson's travels to Europe, his evenings with Carlyle, Tennyson, Landor, and hosts of other celebrities. Carlyle he finds 'one of the most amiable persons he ever knew.' The seer must have had an excellent brand of tobacco in his pipe that night. Tennyson is a man of 'quiet, sluggish thought and sense, refined and good-humoured.' Macaulay is the 'King of diners-out.' Emerson relates an excellent anecdote about Landor, who in a fit of temper threw his cook out of the window into the garden, and then exclaimed – 'Good God, I never thought of those violets.'

**Emil Ludwig's *Goethe***

('The Greatest of the Germans,' *Saturday Night*, 13 October 1928: 8)

The secret of the charm exercised by Emil Ludwig, the master of biography in this age, is contained in the introductory dedication to George Bernard Shaw. The artistic standpoint which enlivens all his work, and which after all is the modernist approach at its best, is that there are to be no hidden sanctuaries of thought and feeling which may not be exposed in the interest of a dramatic realism. That this is the only faithful mode of treating any character of history, and pre-eminently a character like Goethe, is stated in so many words in the Preface: 'This book will display in a slowly-moving panorama the landscapes of his soul ... Thus he will be lifted above the sphere of national and moral prejudices – just as you [Shaw] have shown the world some historical figures who have not thereby been diminished, but only made more humanly comprehensible. Goethe himself wished to be not otherwise seen; for he inveighed against all delineations "which weigh merits and demerits with feigned impartiality, and thus are far worse than death in their obscuring of a personality which can only be made to live through the unification of such contradictory traits."'

This panorama begins to unfold itself by the same strong pictorial process which animates his Bismarck, William Hohenzollern, and Napoleon. Goethe, adolescent, erotic, vivacious, a dilettante concerned with the 'art of dress,' smiles forbearingly upon his lecturers in the physics classroom talking about monads – 'quaint little beggars.' His maiden speech, as an advocate at Frankfurt, in which he defended a son against a father in a property case, is a gem of literary affectation and extravagance, resembling Disraeli's first effort in Parliament, making wiseacres shake their heads in amazement or melancholy over the way the gods make people mad before destroying them. His debut, which was in this fashion, resulted in a severe snub from the Court:

> If blustering self-sufficiency can affect the decision of a learned judge, and the most malignant of invectives prevail against a well-established verity ... in such circumstances as these, how could I, how should I, be expected to add fuel to the fire which is to consume me? When jurisprudence, that mysterious veiled goddess, after long grievous travail has brought forth – what do we see? A couple of ridiculous mice that creep from the pages of some compendium of definitions and proclaim themselves her children. Run away, little mice.'

And so on for ten pages of a brief.

Three years were all he could stand of the Frankfurt practice, and encouraged by his father, he decided to enter definitely upon 'an imaginative career.' He had already published *Götz* at twenty, a work which won for him a European reputation, and now under the influence of Herder, he flung himself into the *Sturm und Drang* conflicts which exalted intuition and sentiment over reason, and searched for the sources of poetry in folklore rather than in the sophistications of court manners. At twenty-five he wrote his *Werther*, an even greater sensation than *Götz*. It ran through scores of editions in Germany, France, and England, and caused – it was claimed – such an epidemic of disillusion and suicide that the book was put under the ban by the Leipsic authorities.

Upon the crest of this popularity he was invited to the Court of Weimar – a parvenu who quickly gained the ascendancy over the nobility in the affection and confidence of the Duke. The complexity of his nature, his amazing versatility, the variety of his tastes, his prodigious intellectual gifts were displayed along with an independence of spirit which quite frequently threatened the harmony of his relationship. He entered the Council of State, at first backing up the Duke's progressive measures against the reactionary policies of the older officials. He became successively Minister of Public Works, of War, of Finance; and proposed plans for the reconstruction of mines and the establishment of factories, for the partitioning of Crown lands and for the general reformation of the financial system.

There was nothing human that was foreign to him. He could turn, after a fatiguing day in which he superintended the putting out of a village fire, and seek recreation in working out a theory of colour to combat the Newtonian principle of the composition of light. Or conversely, he would retire for a week to paint and sketch after days spent in original and brilliant anatomical research in which his whole being 'seemed to be concentrated between his eye-sockets.' Or again, he would take the advances and disappointments of his latest amour and sublimate them in the form of an ode or a drama. All this and infinitely more with *Wilhelm Meister, Egmont, Iphigenie, Faust,* and countless elegies, lyrics, and odes streaming from his pen. One has to go back to Leonardo da Vinci for a parallel in respect to multiplicity of interests.

The volume is alive to the fingertips with great reflections, passions, arguments, and encounters. Ludwig shows his mastery by the way he sets the stage for meetings between Goethe and other flaming personalities of the age. Witness the picture where he is sitting in a room near to a wretchedly built piano with Beethoven, 'devastated, pallid, ill and deaf, running his fingers over the keys.' And also that electric hour where Napoleon and Goethe 'mutually gaze into one another's starry countenance.' *Voilà un homme* is Napoleon's comment when the German is introduced into his presence.

The Life is dramatized in terms of a conflict in which the *genius* of Goethe is perpetually striving to obtain the victory over the restless, spirit-shattering energy of his *daemon*, and the serene reconciliations of his closing years reveal how intimately he took to heart his favourite maxim of Pindar: 'When you stand boldly erect in the chariot, and four fresh horses are tugging frantically at the reins, and you control their energies, whipping the fiery ones in, the unruly ones down, urging and guiding, with a turn of the wrist, a flick of the lash, pulling them up and then giving them their heads, till all sixteen hoofs are taking you at a measured pace to where you want to go – that's mastery!'

**J. Middleton Murry, ed., *The Letters of Katherine Mansfield***
('Intimate Autobiography,' *Saturday Night*, 1 December 1928: Lit. Sec. 22)

The purpose of the publication of these *Letters* is best stated in the opening paragraph of the Introductory Note by J. Middleton Murry: 'In arranging the letters of Katherine Mansfield for publication, I have had two distinct aims in view: to present as fully as possible all those of her letters which seemed to me to possess an intrinsic interest, and secondly, to retain such portions of other letters as would explain the various situations of her life. My hope is that, taken together with her *Journal*, the letters as now arranged will form an intimate and complete autobiography for the last ten years of her life.'

It must be a rare literary quality which is able to sustain the unflagging interest of a reader throughout six hundred closely printed pages of personal letters (practically a letter a day for ten years), but this is the achievement of Katherine Mansfield. When her stories were appearing some ten or fifteen years ago, English reviewers felt themselves somewhat at a loss to explain the attraction in a genre of fiction in which narrative and plot were almost negligible as factors of intrinsic interest. The mere tissue of the stories seemed at times almost invertebrate, and yet results of gripping intensity were attained. Analysis of her technique revealed that in place of action, adventure, climax, and the general apparatus of incident, she had substituted psychological moments and brilliant flashes of characterization. Not that incident was abandoned. Such a course in the strict sense would be physically impossible, but details served no other economy than that of spiritual portraiture.

The *Letters* are a luminous commentary upon her more deliberate production. The great majority of them are written to her husband, Mr Middleton Murry, and all, except the obviously casual ones, have this peculiar fixation point: 'God forbid that another should ever live the life I have known here, and yet there are *moments*, you know, old Boy, when after a dark day there comes a sunset - such a glowing marvellous sky that one forgets all in the beauty of it - these are the moments when I am *really writing*.'

As stated, the *Letters* comprise ten years of her life, from the summer of 1913 to her death in 1923 at thirty-four years of age. Apart from the compensations of these creative moments, the story is one of a battle with disease and depression. Arthritis, insomnia, tuberculosis and severe heart involvement, temporary hopes of recovery with a more favourable reading of the morning chart, followed by settling gloom with the next diagnosis, are the general outlines of the landscape. Only a few of her letters are repressed, such as were written from March 22 to April 11, 1918, when she was lying helpless in Paris during the German bombardment. Those Mr Murry has reserved as too painful and intimate.

Her sensibility is almost as exquisite as that of Keats. Indeed, one cannot resist the comparison between the two temperaments and, in some respects, the two environments. England, France, Switzerland, Italy, and England again were successively tried in the quest for health, and in every place her claim upon life and love and material and domestic happiness is accompanied by responses to Nature in all the variations of mood:

You know it's madness to love and live apart. That's what we do. Last time I came back to France, do you remember how we *swore* never again? Then I went to Looe - and after that we swore: never again. Then I came here. Shall we go on doing this? ... What have I done that I should have *all* the handicaps plus a disease, and why should we believe this won't happen again? This is to be the *last* time. We'll *never* let each other go again. We *could* not.

The nights here [Paris] are full of stars and little moons, and big Zeppelins – very exciting. But England feels far, far away – just a little Island with a cloud resting on it. Is it still there?

As soon as I have recovered from this cursed chill I'll write again. But at present my jaundiced eye would as lief gaze on the Fulham Road as on this lilac sea and budding mimosa. As the night wears on I grow more and more despondent and my thoughts walk by with long, black plumes on their heads, while I sit in bed with your pink quilt round my shoulders and think it must be at least 4 o'clock and find it just a quarter to 2!

Distributed through the personal records are numerous comments upon her daily reading: 'For some unaccountable reason I've got our Marseilles fever again, with all its symptoms, loss of appetite, shivering fits, dysentery ... I am a ragged creature today. If I hadn't got William Shakespeare, I should be in the ultimate cart, but he reads well to a touch of fever.' Keats, Shelley, De Quincey are people with whom 'she wants to live.' Her taste for Emily Brontë would be a natural inference even if it were not explicitly stated. It is because she writes without a disguise. 'Nowadays one of the chief reasons for one's dissatisfaction with modern poetry is one can't be sure that it really does belong to the man who writes it. It is so tiring, isn't it, never to leave the masked Ball.' Tchekof, Dostoievski, Tolstoi are the greatest of the moderns. Shaw is so uninspired, with no capacity to feed and refresh, one who can laugh *at* but never *with*. Her correspondence with Hugh Walpole is given in full. Walpole had been hurt by what he termed her unfair criticism of *The Captives*, and in her 'dead frank' reply she tells him that 'the movement is of one trying his wings, finding out how they would bear him, how far he could afford to trust them ... just an experiment.' Mrs Asquith is not worth Murry's reviewing pen. She is wearisome and insensitive, 'one of those people who have no past and no future.'

There is scarcely a letter which does not, in some delicate or vigorously sparkling way, reveal her characterizing stamp. Nothing is left unnoticed by day or by sleepless night, from the coming of the maid to unfold the shutters in the morning to the thunder of guns in the Northeast.

## Edwin Arlington Robinson's *Sonnets,* Elinor Wylie's *Angels and Earthly Creatures,* and Bliss Carman's *Wild Garden*

('Contemporary Verse,' *Saturday Night,* 25 May 1929: 9–10)

The reputation of Edwin Arlington Robinson has been a slow but solid growth, the result of an artistic conscience which would never allow the intrusion of sensationalism into his themes or his technique. His work has had a most austere and disciplinary influence upon a generation which exhibits at every turn its passion for modernity.

He received his first definite though limited recognition thirty years ago, by the publication of *The Children of the Night,* in which he manifested his power to describe states of soul with an intensity ever afterwards sustained in such volumes as *The Man against the Sky, Roman Bartholow,* and *The Man Who Died Twice.*

There are a few qualities which may be unfailingly discovered in the mass of his production. Irony is prevalent even in his most objective work, an irony which does not so much present for critical examination localized situations and actions as universal currents of feeling and prejudice. He has a flair for dramatic exposition in narrative form, resembling Frost and Masters in this one particular, and the Robinson quality in the sonnets of this volume is the manner in which character revelation is etched with subtle comment. The very personalities which furnish so many of his themes illustrate the cast of his mind – the brooding analysis, the element of soliloquy which merges the individual lyrical note into wide moral and religious issues. Zola, Crabbe, Hood, Verlaine are immediately recognized as offering appropriate texts, while 'The Pity of the Leaves,' 'The Dead Village,' 'L'Envoi,' 'Job the Dejected,' 'Karma,' and 'Glass Houses' anticipate the sombreness of their treatment. Many of the sonnets are variations in minor key of *The Children of the Night,* describing frustration and disillusionment: 'crowns lost before they are won.'

Sometimes he forgets his habitual role and writes a poem in which it is not philosophy so much as rhythm and beauty of imagery he endeavours to achieve:

*The Sheaves*

Where long the shadows of the wind had rolled,
Green wheat was yielding to the change assigned;
And as by some vast magic undivined
The world was turning slowly into gold.
Like nothing that was ever bought or sold
It waited there, the body and the mind;
And with a mighty meaning of a kind
That tells the more the more it is not told.

So in a land where all days are not fair,
Fair days went on till on another day
A thousand golden sheaves were lying there,
Shining and still, but not for long to stay –
As if a thousand girls with golden hair
Might rise from where they slept and go away.

Ever since the publication in 1907 of *Nets to Catch the Wind,* Elinor Wylie may be said to have found her place amongst the intelligentsia of American poets. Very few of her contemporaries surpass her for concise structure and brilliant finish. She took the sonnet form and made it the severest medium for the expression of thought, often submerging the emotional values.

Running through this volume, which she compiled for publication just the day before she died, one is struck with the relationship in theme and treatment, with the general standpoint of the metaphysical poets of the seventeenth century. Some of the sonnets might easily have been written by John Donne. There is the same reliance upon vague suggestion, upon a penumbra which grows darker as the poem nears the conclusion: the same tendency to pack the content into the smallest compass, preserving at the same time the hint that the reader, having captured the mood, would be led into the author's own interpretation. Her opening sonnet might indeed have been dedicated to the memory of Donne:

Although these words are false, none shall prevail
To prove them in translation less than true
Or overthrow their dignity, or undo
The faith implicit in a fabulous tale;
The ashes of this error shall exhale
Essential verity, and two by two
Lovers devout and loyal shall renew
The legend, and refuse to let it fail.

Even the betrayer and the fond deceived,
Having put off the body of this death,
Shall testify with one remaining breath,
From sepulchres demand to be believed:
These words are true, although at intervals
The unfaithful clay contrive to make them false.

There is meditative mysticism in such poems as 'Absent Thee from Felicity Awhile,' the 'Hymn to Earth,' 'Farewell Sweet Dust'; and in 'This Corruptible' she starts out in the company of Francis Thompson, without however reaching the same haven with his spread of wing and rapturous intensity. In 'The Lie,' she threads her way through the tortuous paths of a lover's mind, putting up psychological defences for an action which at first blush would call for condemnation.

Technical excellence is stamped on all her work. The lines are chiselled, the phrases resonant, the imagery striking, but one feels at the end of the volume that the hands have been left chilled before the excessive banking of the fires.

The laureate once more makes his bow, which, we trust, will not be the last. There must have been extraordinary sustenance in the oatmeal of the early sixties which could account for the literary longevity of those three best-known and best-loved of our Canadian writers: Charles G.D. Roberts, Duncan Campbell Scott, and Bliss Carman. There is little sign of decadence or failing vision in this volume. There is the same buoyant naturalism, the simplicity, and the fresh charm that won him his fame in his first *Book of Lyrics*, the Vagabondia collections, and the *Songs of the Sea Children*. He has his lapses occasionally. It would be too much to expect him to be always rising to the magic of his famous 'Spring Song,' and the 'Low Tide on Grand Pré.' Such poems are not written every day of the year, but after a pedestrian tramp he can come back by his capacity for rejuvenation when the 'old sorceries' are made anew.

The chief virtue of this collection is the directness of its unforced lyricism. Carman gets his effects out of the simplest material, without involution and without too much of introspective lumber. It is true that he does not shake us with passion very often, but he can induce the feeling of meditation and a quiet acceptance of things as few authors are able to do who are in our midst today. Nature for him is not a battlefield but a sanctuary with 'morning revelations and twilight oracles,' and it is the spirit of Wordsworth rather than that of Shelley which is invoked in the song of wood-thrush and field-lark, in the rhythm of falling water, and in the picture of landscapes covered with blue haze: 'Far fleeing the tumult of cities, the fever of fame.'

It is the pagan understanding of Nature which furnishes his Credo in 'The Largess of Life':

Because I have given my heart
To the joyance of living,
Its lords have given me life
Past their measure of giving.

Because I have given my soul
To the rapture of gladness,
They have taught me the simples of earth
For the healing of sadness.

Because I have given my years
To the service of beauty,

They have given me wonder and light
Without limit or duty.

Because I have followed their trail
Often faint yet unswerving,
They have given me guides in the way
Beyond all deserving.

**K.A.R. Sugden's *A Short History of the Brontës***
('Whom the Gods Love,' *Saturday Night*, 12 October 1929: Lit. Sec. 19)

The main reason for the writing of this volume is to present a precise biographical record to offset the legends which in the short space of seventy years have grown up about the life of the Brontë sisters. There is no intention of assessing the literary importance of their work, or of analysing the stories. The account is factual throughout: 'It seemed that there was possibly room for a slim, handy, frigid work, in which the details and events of the career of the Brontë family should be set out in order, without much embroidery or many theories, but containing most of the information now available, given in due proportion.'

Although the chief interest obviously centres in the careers of Charlotte and Emily, the story, beginning with the father's incumbency of Hartshead and soon after of Haworth, follows the birth, growth, discipline, and death of every child of the family, with the most sombre projections. The death of the mother occurred shortly after her marriage; the two eldest daughters died the one at ten, the other at twelve years of age; Branwell, the only son, virtually a suicide through drugs; then Anne, Emily, and Charlotte following each other with tuberculosis before they reached middle life. For environment physical and psychological, it would be difficult to discover anything more conducive to gloom than the Brontë situation. The parsonage faced a landscape covered with a 'multitude of gravestones, a few upright and ornate, but most of them flat and black ... The sweep of lonely moorland, grim slopes covered with coarse reeds, dark pools, and clumps of heather and bilberry, stretching out illimitably to the west.' The vicarage garden led into the churchyard, and scarcely a day passed without a reminder in and out of the house of the presence of death.

The three sisters sought some escape from the intolerable monotony by accepting positions away from home as governesses of girls' schools. It was 'hard labour from six in the morning till near eleven at night, with only one half-hour of exercise between,' and Charlotte describes her pupils as - 'riotous, perverse, unmanageable cubs.' They gave up their positions in order to start schools of their own, and to this end Charlotte and Emily went to Brussels to the Héger Pensionnat, controlled by M. Héger and his wife. Héger impressed Charlotte as a 'little black being with a face that varies in expression. Sometimes he borrows the lineaments of an insane tomcat, sometimes those of a delirious hyena; occasionally, but very seldom, he discards these perilous attractions, and assumes an air not above one hundred degrees removed from mild and gentleman-like.' Explain this impression as one may, Charlotte must have been fond of feline appearances for very soon she fell violently in love with him, and on her return to Haworth she began a most hectic correspondence: 'I have never heard French spoken but once since I left Brussels - and then it sounded like music in my ears - every word was most precious to me because it reminded me of you - I love French for your sake with all my heart and soul.'

The author relates the adventures of the sisters into the literary world. They published under the pseudonyms of Currer (Charlotte), Ellis (Emily), and Acton (Anne) Bell. The secret was kept very close for years, and though at first, bitter disappointment attended all their efforts, *Jane Eyre, Shirley,* and *Villette* aroused critical attention and achieved a considerable market, in spite of generally unfavourable reviews, of which the following twaddle, taken from the *Quarterly,* is a typical illustration. 'We have said that this book portrays a heart entirely lacking in grace. That is, in our opinion, the great, the horrible defect of Jane Eyre. It is true that she behaves well and displays great moral strength, but it is the strength of a soul which is utterly pagan and a law unto itself. We do not find in it a single trace of Christian grace. It has inherited the direst sin of our fallen nature, the sin of pride. It has pleased God to make Jane Eyre an orphan, without friends, without money, nevertheless, she thanks nobody – least of all her friends. It is an anti-Christian work.' Charlotte lived long enough to realize the public appreciation of her work, but Emily died without any recognition of her genius, and it took men of the critical stamp of Sydney Dobell, Matthew Arnold, and Swinburne to prepare the present generation for an adequate estimate of a book like *Wuthering Heights*, which, for imaginative intensity and its white core of lyrical expression, surpasses anything achieved by her more acclaimed sister.

## Mazo de la Roche's *Whiteoaks of Jalna*

(*Acta Victoriana* November 1929: 21)

*Whiteoaks of Jalna* is decidedly Miss de la Roche's most successful novel. A lively sense of humour; a keen regard for individuality of character; a sympathetic interpretation, as well as an exact portraiture of nature, combine to produce a novel of real interest and some power. The tragic atmosphere of *Jalna* has cleared: the characters breathe a more normal and consequently a more healthy air. The conflicting reactions of personality to personality are not as sharp, but the results, on the whole, are more satisfactory.

Finch, the lovable young dreamer, is the real hero of the book. His life is drawn closely into the web which the ancient, yet vigorous, Adeline has woven about her amazing brood at Jalna. Young as he is, Finch has early become conscious of the powerful forces which have moulded, and are continuing to mould, the lives of his uncles, his aunt, his brothers, and their wives. The complexity of life is felt rather than understood; it troubles his sensitive soul, yet stimulates in his whole being a longing to probe its mystery. The entire story hinges on his psychological reaction to these powerful, although apparently inexplicable, forces which dominate the household of Jalna.

A simple plot with action purposely subordinated to character development, a development which is not restricted to a few years, but to generations, combine to place *Whiteoaks of Jalna* in the Galsworthian, rather than the contemporary American, tradition. The Whiteoak family, like the Forsyte family, will provide fertile sources for further literary invention. *Whiteoaks of Jalna* is no more felt to be an entity than *The White Monkey*, nor, as a matter of fact, than *Jalna*, at its publication, was. One imagines the character of Wakefield, to mention the most obvious, capable of interesting development; his impish pedantry, his uncanny judgment of character, his highly sensitized enjoyment of the incongruous or unusual, provoke all manner of speculation.

It is to be hoped that Miss de la Roche will not refuse to appease the curiosity of her reading public, in regard to the future destinies of the great Whiteoak clan.

## André Maurois's *Byron*

('Poet and Cynic,' *Saturday Night*, 5 April 1930: Lit. Sec. 2)

No finer tribute could be paid to this new life of Byron than to assert that Maurois has fulfilled the expectations raised by *Ariel* and *Disraeli*. It is genuine biography reduced to readable dimensions by its refusal to be drawn into tempting excursions upon the evaluation of Byron's poetry. Only such analysis is offered as might serve to add form and colour to the portrait.

The first two or three chapters give the clue to the author's technique in the handling of biography. It is perfectly in accord with the modernist approach of drenching drama with psychology. The atmosphere is prepared at the outset with the same skill and with the same feeling for startling announcement as the chart of a storm by a meteorologist. We follow the genealogical tree with much the same interest as we would the history of the Jukes or the Kallikaks, with this difference, that the story of degeneracy and passion is lit by many passages of brilliant achievement. The birth of George Gordon, sixth Lord Byron, is registered upon an amazing family album.

The family, though run back into the Crusades, had its first prominent name in Sir John Biron, known as 'Little Sir John with the Great Beard,' who, as a faithful subject of Henry VIII, came into possession of Newstead Abbey in 1540, the time of Henry's spoliation of the English monasteries. The motto of Sir John, thereafter to be perpetuated, is especially significant of the careers of the descendants – *Crede Biron* (Trust in Byron). The Abbey was transformed at once into a castle and for two hundred years it became, under the watch of a revengeful black-hooded ghost, the seat of pillage, rapine, assault, and murder. One of the ancestors was made a Baron for charging too soon at Edgehill, and at Marston Moor, causing much harm to Royalist strategy, according to the journal of Prince Rupert. Another allowed the estate to go almost to ruin by improvidence. Another was tried for murder, and still another, a sailor known as Fairweather Jack, though beaten by the French in a battle on the sea, was promoted to the rank of vice-Admiral because his defeat was caused by the noble family trait of precipitancy. His son John, the father of the poet, nicknamed Mad Jack, triumphantly upheld the escutcheon by as dissolute a career as one might expect to find in the raciest of picaresque fiction. But the end is not yet. This last named roué, by his marriage with Catherine Gordon of Gight, a woman 'proud as Lucifer,' with royal blood in her veins such as it was, bequeathed to his son another genealogical document which reads like a Newgate Calendar: 'It seemed as if a Gordon of Gight had been strung up on every branch of their family tree.' In this way Maurois sets the stage for the actor.

Byron's early education was calculated to deepen those biological trends. His Scotch nurse, Mary Gray, was a Calvinist, and his schoolteacher, a stern melancholiac. All the consolation he may have derived from his repeating before going to bed – 'The Lord is my Shepherd, I'll not want,' was soon dispelled by Mary's account of Satan and God. Cain, too, had an overpowering influence upon his mind. How many Cains were there in the Gordon history? 'And the Lord said unto Cain – Why art thou wroth and why is thy countenance fallen?' sang in his head every night. 'All Scotland seemed full of ghosts, the house was close to a graveyard, and there was that awful Satan, and the Lord. In the darkness the child could feel evil things prowling about him.' Byron came to the conviction quite early and inevitably that he was among the reprobates predestined by the will of God. So he grew up, his idea of God and retribution in no way softened by what he saw in his own home. By the accounts, it would seem that his mother spent most of her time chasing him with other than maternal feelings, and the balance of the time smashing all the breakable household goods upon the heads of her servants. His growing detestation of his mother became the prologue to an attitude towards the world, more particularly towards women – an attitude which very readily grew into a cult to which Byron gave his name.

The biography from the time Byron came into the national focus by his vigorous attack upon the *Edinburgh Review* in *English Bards and Scotch Reviewers* is almost as amazing as that of Napoleon himself – at least regarded as a personal phenomenon. He dominated not only England but Europe for fifteen years. It was a Byronic fever. 'The subject of conversation, of curiosity, of enthusiasm of the moment,' wrote the Duchess of Devonshire, 'is not Spain or Portugal, warriors or patriots, but Lord Byron. The poem [*Childe Harold*] is on every table and himself courted, flattered, and praised whenever he appears ... he is really the only topic of conversation – the men jealous of him, the women of each other.'

Byron held the spotlight by virtue of his supreme theatrical gifts. His poses varied from the childishly ridiculous to the near-sublime. When he gave a farewell dinner to his friends at Newstead, the ceremony became a Saturnalia. The guests entered the hall just barely escaping the claws of a wolf-hound and a bear chained to the pillars. The vault echoed to the sound of pistol shots in salute. After dinner all had to drink burgundy out of a monk's skull dug up by the gardener, polished by a jeweller, and engraved with verses from Byron. When he left England on his first pilgrimage he departed like Timon of Athens brooding over wrongs real and imaginary. On reaching Albania, he wheedled the 'terrible Ali Pascha' into lending him a travelling retinue of Albanian warriors - bandits, corsairs, and robber-chiefs. From there to Greece, thence to Smyrna, and on to Constantinople, when English newspapers awoke with the news that Byron, emulating Leander, had swum the Hellespont - from Europe to Asia in one hour and a half, and against tide!

He came back to England in 1811, basked in popularity, and captivated women from duchesses to servant-maids with the famous 'Byron underlook' penetrating through a scornful aloofness. Most of the women were mad from the start; all were mad at the end - Lady Caroline Lamb, Lady Frances Webster, Claire Clairmont, The Countess Guiccioli, and the rest of the lugubrious procession - Byron himself celebrating their social obsequies in verses sometimes as scented as roses, but more often as rank as bilge-water. He published his sensational poems, *The Giaour, The Corsair, Lara,* during these years. In 1816 he left England, never to return, wrote the rest of the *Childe Harold, Manfred,* his masterpiece *Don Juan,* and many others, all of his characters being but portraits of the author in different poses. His influence was tremendous on the continent, especially in heightening the Romantic temper which everywhere was in the ascendant, the finest writers of the day putting him second only to Shakespeare in the English succession. In England, Byronism infected the younger generation like a bacillus.

And so to the fifth act. Time, 1824; scene, Missolonghi. Byron was in Greece in charge of a band of adventurers fighting for the independence of that country. If the conclusion had not been history but the fiction of a playwright, it would not have been staged with more effect. The curtain fell upon a real Byronic tableau, perfectly in keeping with the melodramatic elements that crowded the story of his race and his own career. His thirty-seventh year had just come, which in his own belief, based on an old prediction, was to be fatal to him. He signalized his birthday with his last important poem:

My days are in the yellow leaf;
The flowers and fruits of love are gone:

The worm, the canker, and the grief
Are mine alone.

Seek out – less often sought than found –
A soldier's grave, for thee the best:
Then look around, and choose thy ground,
And take thy rest.

His death was of the nature of a portent, ending a delirium broken by cries, 'now in Italian, now in English, as if he were advancing to the attack: "Forward! Courage! Follow my example! Don't be afraid!"' The finishing touch is a triumphant vindication of the pathetic fallacy. The spirit of Byron would have entered into felicity if it had been conscious of its own natural exit. Listen to this requiem from Maurois:

A few moments before, a terrible storm had broken over Missolonghi. Night was falling; lightning and thunderclaps came one on top of another in the gloom. Far off, across the lagoon, the fleeting gleam of flashes lit up the dark outlines of the islands. A scudding rain lashed the windows of the houses. The fatal tidings had not yet reached the Greek soldiers and shepherds who had taken refuge indoors; but like their ancestors they believed that the death of a hero came heralded by portents, and as they listened to the prodigious fury of the thunder, they murmured to each other: 'Byron is dead.'

## Frank H. Shaw's *Famous Shipwrecks*

('The Toll of the Sea,' *Saturday Night*, 5 July 1930: 3)

The author of this work is a man who, in the tradition of Dana, Melville, and Conrad, is well able to submit credentials for the job he has undertaken. He put in his apprenticeship on a 'windjammer,' sailed round the world four times, took part in the rescue of crews from foundering vessels, qualified for a master's certificate, served as a commander of a Q-boat in the Great War, and, possessed of a passion for literature, established himself as a writer of distinction upon adventure relating to the sea.

Captain Shaw makes no attempt to give the history of shipwrecks in chronological order but rather an account of a score of disasters which have attracted world attention since the closing years of the eighteenth century – disasters which not only exemplify the tradition of the sea in respect to courage and resourcefulness, but such as have been productive sacrificially in speeding the evolution of measures for the safety of life. The stories are told in splendid fashion and in perfect accord with the historical occasions. The whole work, moreover, has an imaginative undertone, for the sea is made to assume the character of a protagonist, baffled at times, but never beaten in the continuous struggle. Ships are treated from the sailor angle as animate beings possessing instinct and beauty, compelling the admiration and love of masters and crews.

Nearly all of the major tragedies have one feature in common. The ships that went down were launched with the boast that being at the time the last word in scientific construction, they were absolutely unsinkable – a belief that increased the stunning nature of the shock when the news reached the world. Some of them, like the *Royal George*, the *Victoria* (rammed by the *Camperdown* in the Mediterranean), the *Empress of Ireland*, sank in calm water, the task being left to the Courts of Inquiry to explain to an incredulous nation how it was possible for the inconceivable thing to take place.

The most terrible illustration of 'incredibility' in the history of ships is that of the *Titanic*. The White Star Line had, under declared intention, set out to build the most perfect ship for 'size, luxury, and maritime security.'

Here at last was the unsinkable ship: with every contingency provided against. Did fire break out in any part of her magnificent interior, what happened? A small electric tube in a teakwood box on the navigating-bridge changed colour; a buzzer sounded – at once the menaced compartment was indicated. There was not even need to turn the ship's fire-brigade and pumps loose to deal with the outbreak: by the mere act of adjusting a coupling, a small hose-pipe was attached to a copper pipe leading in to the seat of conflagration; and a fire-quenching gas was poured directly into the danger-zone ... Her very size rendered her inviolate from anything wind or sea could do to her; she was as ponderous as a solid chunk of the land that had created her. No Atlantic storm ever conceived could lave her high promenade decks.

How the *Titanic* foundered, with the *Californian* only twenty miles away, but ignorant of the catastrophe, is one of the ironies of scientific faith.

The finest chapter of the book is the description of the loss of the *Birkenhead*. The incident belongs to the annals of British courage and steadfastness even as Waterloo. The phrase '*Birkenhead* drill' or the '*Birkenhead* manner' has entered the language. It is 'the two o'clock in the morning courage.' Seven hundred on board; one boat only pushed off carrying all the women and children; the horses of the troopers thrust out of the gangway to be given a chance to swim to shore; their screams of terror as they were pulled down by the sharks; the deliberate discarding of the accepted right of '*sauve qui peut*,' which might result in the upsetting of the boat by the gunwale clutch of the swimmers; and then the magnificent tableau of the soldiers at attention and under the eye of their officers, awaiting their death.

Considerable space is devoted to showing the vicarious nature of the tragedies. It was the loss of the *Adventure* (1789) on the Northumbrian coast, in full view of thousands on the shore utterly powerless to help, which gave rise to the claim for a lifeboat – 'some form of vessel that will float in the roughest water and stand up against the fiercest gale.' And on the heels of this demand emerged the Royal National Lifeboat Institution. It needed the *Titanic* calamity to revolutionize the Merchant Shipping Laws regarding adequate lifeboats and efficient wireless telegraphy.

## Wilson Follett, ed., *The Collected Poems of Stephen Crane*

('An Early Imagist,' *Saturday Night*, 11 October 1930: Lit. Sec. 13)

The publication of this volume, thirty years after the author's death, is just another evidence of the revival of interest in the

American nineties. Crane was the leading exponent in his age of the naturalistic school of fiction, his novel *The Red Badge* curiously anticipating the grim photography presented to us nowadays in books on the Great War. His two books of poems, *The Black Riders* and *War Is Kind*, now published together in this edition, though lacking the popular interest of his novels, reflect none the less his characteristic attitude of mind, his open revolt against the current idyllic pastoralism, his irony, his naked impressionism. As slender as his poetic output may have been, and unspectacular as compared with his prose, it is the best illustration – apart from the work of his contemporary Emily Dickinson, whom Crane resembled in many respects – of the reaction against the movement represented by writers like Irving and Longfellow. The volume comes out today when his school has thoroughly entrenched itself behind the names of Amy Lowell, Masters, H.D., and the rest of the Imagists. The following poem in *The Black Riders*, besides being a specimen of his *vers libre*, is an epitome of his philosophy:

Once there came a man
Who said,
'Range me all men of the world in rows.'
And instantly
There was a terrific clamour among the people
Against being ranged in rows.
There was a loud quarrel, worldwide.
It endured for ages;
And blood was shed
By those who would not stand in rows.
And by those who pined to stand in rows.
Eventually, the man went to death, weeping.
And those who stayed in bloody scuffle
Knew not the great simplicity.

The world is altogether out of joint. Whatever activity there is in the world is directed towards futile ends. The book of knowledge is open but the characters are illegible. The idealist eats out his own heart. Courage is best illustrated in forlorn leadership, and always pursuit ends where it begins:

I saw a man pursuing the horizon,
Round and round they sped.
I was disturbed at this;
I accosted the man.
'It is futile,' I said,
'You can never –'

'You lie,' he cried,
And ran on.

There is the closest relationship between the man's life and his work. Twelve published volumes, besides numerous short stories in magazines – all before he had reached his thirtieth year – attest the high pressure under which he lived, the flaming intensity which wore out his body and sent him to the Black Forest in a hopeless quest for health. Both in form and material the poems indicate protest and struggle and unfulfilment. Underneath the defiance is his humanity, his hatred of militarism, the idea of the regiment whether for war or industrialism. His method is to present pictures not abstractions, just as in his *Red Badge* the 'heroic ideal' is sternly dismissed, and the psychology of fear exhibited in its demoralizing effect upon the mind of an individual soldier.

The verse suffers from the limitations of the imagistic modes, flow and rhythm being sacrificed for the sharpness of rifle shots. And when the style is caught, say, in the first ten or fifteen pages, the conclusions are too easily anticipated through the rest of the volume. Still, there is the compensating clarity and focus. The title-poem, 'War Is Kind,' is a long distance from the tradition of 'The Charge of the Light Brigade':

Do not weep, maiden, for war is kind.
Because your lover threw wild hands toward the sky

And the affrighted steed ran on alone,
Do not weep.
War is kind.

Do not weep, babe, for war is kind.
Because your father tumbled in the yellow trenches,
Raged at his breast, gulped and died,
Do not weep.
War is kind.

Mother whose heart hung humble as a button
On the bright splendid shroud of your son,
Do not weep.
War is kind.

## Dormer Creston's *Andromeda in Wimpole Street* and Émilie and Georges Romieu's *Three Virgins of Haworth*

('The Brownings and the Brontës,' *Saturday Night*, 8 November 1930: 8–9)

Current interest in the Brownings is attested by the publication in two successive years of a couple of substantial volumes. Last year a mass of correspondence between Elizabeth and her sister, Henrietta, was released and printed. And now, the story of Elizabeth and Robert is retold with a very vivid handling of the mutual love-letters. The first part of the book is devoted to a sketch of Elizabeth's life up to the time she met Browning – a very dismal family picture. Elizabeth and her ten brothers and sisters grew up under the hand of a father-manager whose discipline savoured almost of insanity. Barrett was the son and grandson of Jamaica slave-owners, and on the death of his father he became the absentee proprietor of the plantation. He must have transferred the exercise of his slave rights to his own home, for he made it a rule that not one of his daughters should marry: 'If a prince of Eldorado should come, with a pedigree of lineal descent from some seigniory in the moon in one hand, and a ticket of good-behaviour from the nearest Independent Chapel in the other –' said Elizabeth – 'Even then, it would not do,' finished her sister Arabel.

What love-making went on at all was surreptitious – only in the daytime, for at seven o'clock punctually the father came home. Nothing made him more furious than the suspicion that a man had been in the house, and when Henrietta showed a faint annoyance at his curt refusal to admit 'a friend,' her knees 'were made to ring upon the floor' to the accompaniment of screams and a fainting spell on the part of Elizabeth, who witnessed the punishment. Life dragged wearily along, Elizabeth – who was an invalid – attempting to keep up her vitality with daily doses of laudanum.

Such was the situation in 1845, when in walked Perseus, the Deliverer, in the shape of Robert Browning – 'a swift-walking young man, with a pale handsome face, entirely surrounded, according to one of the fashions of the day, with an orang-outang-like fringe of black hair.' Not much of a Perseus, one might say today, striking a triumphant blow at the fetters of Andromeda. Considering the circumstances, one might be tempted to stand behind the timorous Robert with a barrel-stave to try to get a little ginger into the love-making. One hovers between boredom at Elizabeth's conscience, and impatience at Browning's hesitancy in carrying the lady off – a course which she obviously expected. What we have is rather a slough of correspondence broken by occasional day visits, the polka-loving Henrietta entertaining three lovers downstairs, and Elizabeth interviewing Robert upstairs.

At last the vital moment arrived. Barrett had issued an edict that the family should vacate the house for a month during spring cleaning, and, taking advantage of the confusion, Elizabeth, attended by her maid, Wilson, staggered half-fainting to a church, stopping at a chemist's on the way to buy some smelling salts to support her. Then 'more dead than alive' she went through the ceremony. A few days later, she, Wilson, and Flush, her dog, walked silently down the long flights of stairs out of the Wimpole House – 'and as the front door shut behind them Elizabeth cut herself off at that moment from her past life as completely as if she had stepped into another world.'

The story is replete with romantic interest. Miss Creston has properly restricted herself to the biographical side without making those critical assessments which anyone may find in surveys of Victorian literature.

In the *Three Virgins of Haworth* the authors have well achieved their aim – of awakening the sleeping Brontë household that those 'odd, silent, solemn, unchildlike children' might be loved a little longer.

Dickens himself could not have created a more tragic story of stunted childhood than that of the Brontë sisters. Certainly, Salem House under the notorious Creakle, or Dotheboys Hall under Squeers, was not worse than Cowan's Bridge under the Reverend Carus Wilson, the thinly disguised Brocklehurst, the 'clergyman of black marble,' as he is called later in *Jane Eyre*. Tyrannized, starved, frozen, the two oldest girls, Maria and Elizabeth, died from its 'slow-fever,' and Emily and Charlotte were rendered semi-invalid for life. The home-life at Haworth Parsonage was practically the spiritual counterpart of the existence at the school, not from any positive brutality on the part of the father but from his stupidity and indifference. Not a child's instinct was ever satisfied or even considered. The very environment carried the suggestion of disease and death. Haworth Parsonage overlooked a cemetery and the six children made a game of counting the stones, and their only exercise was roaming over the moors later to be immortalized as 'Wuthering (Windbeaten) Heights.' Before the eldest child was ten, the father used to lead the discussion at the table about the King's laxity in dealing with the Irish question, about the too liberal tendencies of the new Prime Minister and the pros and cons of Catholic Emancipation.

After the death of the two sisters, the story is concerned with the efforts of the other four (the Quadriga as they are called by the author) to earn a livelihood. Charlotte and Anne became governesses – positions which they loathed; the dipsomaniac Branwell became a tutor; while on Emily fell the heavy household duties. Charlotte's visit to Belgium to study French; her infatuation for the married Héger, the principal of the seminary; her disillusionment; and her return to the Parsonage, 'islanded by the dead,' are a stark recital of fact and mood.

Rarely has fiction been more frankly autobiographical than in the Brontë novels. Anne told her story in *Agnes Grey.* Charlotte depicted her tragedy in *The Professor* and later in *Jane Eyre;* and Emily in what serious literary criticism today is regarding as the most powerful bit of realism of the Victorian period – *Wuthering Heights.* Emily died before anyone was aware of her genius. Charlotte lived long enough to taste the thrill of national recognition, claiming among her admirers such names as Thackeray, Arnold, Swinburne, and Maeterlinck.

### John Masefield's *The Wanderer of Liverpool*

('Queen of the Sea,' *Saturday Night,* 6 December 1930: 5)

It is fitting that John Masefield should have signalized his own appointment as Poet Laureate of England by a full-dress performance in the old manner. No one of the contemporaries could have made a more graceful acknowledgment of the keys of office and, at the same time, a more complete vindication of the national selection. The laurel was the gift alike of government and people.

It would be too much to claim that *The Wanderer* is the crowning achievement of Masefield's career. As fine as it is, few people will be found to put up an argument for its primacy amongst his masterpieces. The honours will go, according to taste, to *Dauber,* or to *The Everlasting Mercy,* or to *Reynard the Fox.* It would scarcely be expected that the qualities which make up this remarkable triad could be repeated with the same triumphant result. The new poem has not the speed of the first, the elaborate structure of the second, or the psychological appeal of the third. Yet in some respects, *The Wanderer* is unique. It registers, to a fuller extent than any other of his works, Masefield's search for the ultimate principle of Beauty in a world rocking with frustration and disaster. This has always been his quest, from his first amateur and Kiplingesque *Salt Water Ballads* right through his dramas, poems, and novels to this last production. It pervades all his prose. It came out royally in *Gallipoli*, where the departure of the troops from the peninsula was described in as exalted a style as anything offered in the literary output of the War. Masefield has lived up to the letter and spirit of his creed expressed in 'Consecration.' So the ship, the *Wanderer*, is a symbol in his mind of the finest thing that the idea of Beauty could evolve out of marine technology. It is even more - it becomes a pageant of life on the heroic scale.

He describes his first sight of her moving out of Liverpool:

> The sight of a new ship, setting forth upon her first voyage, was one often seen. I will not pretend that the heart of Liverpool was stirred by the first setting out of the *Wanderer*. Yet some hundreds of souls in Liverpool had taken part in her building, rigging and loading; and all those who were interested in ships knew her as the finest ship of her year. She was thought of and talked of a good deal. Even in Liverpool a sailing ship of nearly three thousand tons setting two skysails, of a great sheer, and of a noble beauty, was a rare sight. She was the last achievement in sailing-ship building and rigging; nothing finer had been done, or ever was done.

The poem exhibits Masefield, like his predecessor, Bridges, as an experimentalist. It is the first time that he has tried out this plan of structure. Only the prelude and the conclusion are in verse; the general body is in prose. The work is at once a poem and a document. It is a history - the biography of a ship from the time she was laid down at the yards of Liverpool in 1890, throughout all the adventures of her ten voyages, to the hour when she sank in collision with a German steamer in the Elbe in 1907. It is as if the author had been attempting, under a marine Bureau, to exhaust all the data of research. The pages are sprinkled with drawings and photographs describing in the minutest detail the plan of accommodation, the midship section, the main deck, the ship under full canvas, under bare poles in a cyclone, and then as a derelict upon the quicksands. The tonnage is given to the decimal point, the exact lengths of bowsprit, masts, and yards, the calibre of her wire ropes; the dates, the latitudes and longitudes when Capes or icebergs were sighted; the inventories of her cargoes; the daily weather reports; the findings of the Court of Inquiry; the assessment of damages, and so on – all stated with the precision of charts and graphs.

The documentary phase of the work is to some extent relieved by the luminous presentation of fact and by the human interest of many of the situations. For instance, it is stated that after the first disaster, in which the captain had been killed, the tradition began to be formed that the *Wanderer* was an unlucky ship, that the ghost of the captain periodically visited the bridge – a superstition which some of the apprentices used as a means of paying off a grudge upon an unpopular sailor:

> When this man was alone, on lookout, on the forecastle-head, they used to creep underneath him and smite three knocks with a handspike below his feet. Once, by wasting a great many phosphorous matches, one of the boys made his face and hands luminous, and crept into the forecastle in the dark as a spirit. Most of the crew left the ship in San Francisco.

In this change of narrative technique there are distinct losses and gains. In Masefield's earlier work, it was always a pleasure to watch him triumph so splendidly over his material, over the raw realism of the content: the more intractable the stuff, as in *The Everlasting Mercy*, the more complete the sense of mastery when the job was done. People have quarrelled with his 'unpoetic diction' in *Dauber* where, as in 'The Bosun turned. "I'll give you a thick ear. / Do it? I didn't. Get to hell from here,"' Masefield seemed to be testing to its logical limit his theory of realistic verse. But such lily-fingered criticism failed to appreciate Masefield's power of fusion, his capacity to make malleable, in the interest of a general atmospheric effect, items of content which as fragments were as tough as steel. It ignored the fact that when the work was accomplished, the final products simply enthralled the imagination.

In *The Wanderer* Masefield has felt that the statistical side of the performance should be allotted to prose. Perhaps here he is right, for it would be an appalling task to follow out his earlier technique. Had he done so, the story would have changed considerably. We would undoubtedly have been charmed with many fine transmutations, but we might also have been let down with many anti-climaxes. He does not give us his usual glossary to help the landlubber's reading. It is not so essential here, as the prose narrative lending itself, more than verse, to explanatory additions, carries with it quite frequently its own light. Nevertheless, to the uninitiated even the prose sections hold their perplexities. A recent writer in the *New Statesman* very wittily expresses his bewilderment over some of the details:

> Of course, sailor language may seem obscure to us poor landsmen, and when the Poet Laureate tells us that his lovely heroine was wall-sided, rather hard in the bilge, though sweeter aft, had a noble sheer and an exquisite elliptical stern, with heavy teak skirtings and a fully-laid wooden tweendecks; also that she had one peculiarity: the eyes of her lower stays fitted over the cleats in the doubles above her tops, some feet clear of the eyes of the shrouds – then we feel as puzzled as by the advertisement of a lady's fashion-plate. But that is only because our education as Englishmen has been so shamefully neglected.

This difficulty would have been insurmountable had Masefield tried to perform his whole task in verse – and perhaps it is an unfair measure of criticism to demand that he should have cleared up a vocabulary which applies to a specialized subject-matter and to a circumscribed audience. As it is, the prelude and the conclusion are built up out of fairly homogeneous material and comparatively untechnical; and as to the prose, such readers who find the stretches of fact hard sledding may be compensated by many illustrations of Masefield's peculiar quality of summarizing a prolonged factual description in a paragraph which falls nothing short of sheer crystallization. After the first disaster to the ship, he writes:

> In the morning of Sunday, the 25th October, in fine bright weather, she left the anchorage, an image of such glory and beauty in desolation as I shall never forget. Her broken spars had been secured in the swifters

of the lower rigging. The rags of her sails fluttering from her yards gleamed in the sun. I have seen much beauty, but she was the most beautiful thing. She was so splendid, and so distresst: she was also moving as though she were alive. She docked in the Queen's Dock, a heart-rending sight to all, from the broken glory aloft, and the blood of her dead and wounded below.

The versification of the poetic passages is, I think, new to Masefield – a five-foot dactylic measure unrhymed, a bounding beautiful form which combines the virtues of the stanza and the continuous narrative. And he handles it magically. In one section Masefield describes the welcome extended to the *Wanderer* by the *Watchers* – the many splendid ships of the past that had foundered in the Channel and on the Atlantic:

> And another voice rose from the water, the voice of the
> Queen, *Queen Margaret*, saying, '*O Wanderer* star of the sea
> I once was the glory of all the seas of the world,
> In sailing I set forty sails, I exulted, I strode,
> I rushed like the sea-streaming dolphin, the frigate-bird white
> Skimming over the measureless miles leaping wave on blue wave
> And crushing their blueness to greenness, the greenness to white
> In a track a mild broad rolling outward all glittering gay.
> And seamen remember my running the seas of the Horn
> Pursued by the toppling grey combers uplifted astern
> Forth thundering eastward all dim with the smoke of my spray.

## Joseph Auslander, trans., *The Sonnets of Petrarch*

('The First Modern Man,' *Saturday Night*, 12 December 1931: Christmas Lit. Supp. 8)

The unique quality of this volume consists in the fact that it is the first appearance in English literature of a translation by one author of the Petrarchan sonnets in their complete series. Justification is claimed for this piece of work on the ground of the far-reaching influence which Petrarch has exercised over English poetic thought, not only during the Renaissance of which he was one of the earliest prophets, but throughout the five centuries since his death. All of the greater English poets have acknowledged his influence – Wyatt and Surrey (who introduced the vogue into England in the early sixteenth century); Shakespeare, in thought and mood if not in form; Milton; Wordsworth; Keats; Tennyson; right down to the hundreds of present-day writers who are, or profess to be, smitten with the malady of love. For love is the master theme governing this kind of expression. Though it is true that under the influence of Milton preeminently, and scarcely to a less degree, of Wordsworth, the limits of the form were extended to embrace much wider content, such as moral duties, religious aspirations, and patriotic passions; still, the sonnet, as a sustained sequence, usually follows the traditional path.

The three hundred and seventeen poems contained in this volume are the longest series ever penned upon a given theme, more than twice the Shakespearean collection. It is still a matter of conjecture as to who is the Laura of Petrarch. Some have claimed that she is an ideal figure in an allegory, an embodiment of the poet's fancy; others, that there is an historical person basically, but developed into a symbol like the Fairy Queen of Spenser; while many students of the life of Petrarch point out that there was a thoroughly real individual, in the person of the wife of a notary of Avignon, who ensnared the poet's devotion for more than half a century of his tormented life. More than two hundred were written during her lifetime; the balance described the poet's grief after her death.

Her authenticity assumed, she takes, in respect to definiteness of features, an easy leadership over all the feminine immortals who have inspired the flow of ink. Lesbia, Corinna, Cynara, Beatrice, Julia are vague forms on the horizon compared to Laura. One may irreverently construct an anatomical chart from these poems which would give the most specific details with wearisome repetition: the colour of her hair and eyes; the ineffable pallor of her cheeks; the marvellous slimness of her hands, feet, and waist; the bust measurements; the temperature of her blood; the systole and diastole of her heart. The first sight of Laura compels Petrarch to scour earth and heaven for adequate imagery to describe her effulgence. The universe went black the first moment he saw her:

> Never so splendidly did the sun arise
> When the sky stood most purged of taint and mist,
> Nor, after rain, has the rainbow's amethyst
> In the washed air displayed so many dyes
> As are the colours that against my eyes
> Dazzled that day I strapped upon my wrist
> Love's load, that face (the florid I resist
> In speech) beyond all mortal rivalries.

Her beauty and virtue are heavenly derivatives, and all Nature is 'the theatre to her sorrow.' Had Homer and Vergil seen her, Achilles and Aeneas would never have been sung. Violets would have rejoiced to be crushed by her passing feet upon a hillside.

The acreage of love-poetry sown by Petrarch in Italy, France, Spain, and England is enormous, and the most exquisite flowers have grown in the same garden with the rankest and most noisome weeds. Where the greatest poets have placed their imaginations under tribute to evolve their finest specimens in this form of culture, the minor writers have succeeded merely in turning superlatives into the grossest conceits. And indeed, in England, we owe the Dryden period largely to the existence of a healthy national stomach which refused to drink any further from the viscous streams laid open by men of the Crashaw order. The Petrarchan sonnets should be read at widely spaced intervals, and in full reflection upon the age which engendered them. Only a student alike of Italian and English may pronounce upon the adequacy of the translation to mirror the original. Taking the three hundred as they stand in this volume, one may not withhold commendation for the structural excellence of the work. The metrical scheme, the most intricate and difficult of all sonnet variations, is pursued with astonishing skill, and only devotion to his subject, as persistent as Petrarch's to his lady, would have sufficed to keep the translator alive and breathing after such an analysis of the most exhausting of all mortal passions.

One illustration may be cited to show the permanence of the Petrarchan cult. He has been described as 'the first modern man.' Possibly the concluding couplet here may help to clarify the description:

Felicitous in dreams, to brood content,
To grasp at shadows, chase the summer gust,
Through shoreless fathomless leagues of water thrust,
To build on sand, write on the windy tent
Of air, gaze at the sun till these eyes, spent
And broken by his splendour, drop to dust,
To drive down some soft slope with empty lust
The storm-hooved stag with cattle slow and bent;
Sightless and faint, begging an end to all,
Which I seek day and night with heart on fire,
I call on Love and Laura, Death I call.
So through two decades bitter with desire
I have endured the worst, because I took
Under a sinister star both bait and hook!

## Kenneth Leslie's *By Stubborn Stars and Other Poems*

(*Canadian Poetry Magazine* April 1939: 44–5)

Kenneth Leslie has done his best work to date in this volume. *Windward Rock* was a fine collection of poems full of maritime flavour and native energy. But it was rather a promise of which this new work is the achievement.

*By Stubborn Stars* has richness, variety, and power. The first twenty-odd pages contain sonnets as good as any produced in this country during the last decade. They are marked by flashing, original turns of expression, by freedom under the control of the pattern, and by a happy mixture of introspection and objectivity. One quality which stands out notably is the solidity and massiveness of the figures of speech. They have weight and movement:

> The day reeled downward from a heavy blow
> ...
> The black spruce dragged her beneath the skirt
> of the low hill.

> these three,
> the solid sky, the water ramming the shore,
> thrusting its hills of green against the hills
> of grim set pride, and their engendering war
> from which life and my thought of life distils.

And there is that superb image taken from 'The Misty Mother,' which was published in this magazine a few issues back, describing the sea as the home of all life, to which all things must return:

> There is no mountain-top but must come home
> to taste the salt against her heaving side,
> no crag but is an exiled reef whose foam
> flashes a far white longing for her tide.
> And with our happy tears and tears of woe
> we too shall swell her song with what we know.

The miscellaneous poems possess much that is vigorous and also much that is tender and poignant: 'Sleep-Song for Robert Norwood,' 'The Old Man,' 'Halibut Cove Harvest,' and many others.

### Verna Loveday Harden's *Postlude to an Era*
(*Canadian Poetry Magazine* September 1940: 45–6)

The verses of Verna Loveday Harden are well known to readers of the various magazines of Canada. Some of her most distinctive work has appeared in the *Canadian Poetry Magazine*. Her characteristic note is that of the baffling conflict between good and evil, joy and sorrow, war and peace – the everlasting contrast between the roses and the thorny hedges, the agony and ecstasy of living.

These are old themes, obviously, but Verna Harden has the gift of ringing upon them new variations. She may retell the old story indeed, but suddenly one realizes that the story needs to be retold in terms of our present life clamouring for insistent articulation. There are moments when we feel that the human story is a tale told by an idiot who, by his intellectual incapacity, by his obliviousness to the real horror of the world in which we live, is a fortunate type amongst mankind. Ernest Dowson has treated this idea in reference to the insane – 'To One in Bedlam.' Verna Harden has such a conception, which contains more realistic philosophy than might appear on the surface:

Happy fool!
You can sit on your door-step and grin
As the harassed world goes by.
The threats of dictators
And the lives of little children
Alike leave you indifferent.
You can look to the sky at night
And laugh at the twinkling stars,
And have no fear that death
Will be showered upon you.
You have a peace that passes
The wise man's understanding.
O happy fool!

Her 'Martyrs,' 'Zero Hour,' 'Lost Autumn,' 'Gallantry,' 'Inland Waters,' disclose the ore-laden vein of the writer.

This little volume of verse has an excellent introduction by Nathaniel A. Benson, part of which we quote: 'In poem after poem, all of them metrically correct, even in quite intricate stanzaic patterns, she reveals not only the authentic gift of song, but the penetrating power of thought. Strong, sharp, incisive and highly articulate, she has not chosen, as so many women poets have, to "turn hell itself to mere prettiness." This is indeed a hard world now in which to simulate the nightingale – it has become one in which the raven himself is hoarse.'

## Watson Kirkconnell's *The Flying Bull and Other Tales*
(*Canadian Poetry Magazine* April 1941: 53–4)

These are verse-stories built upon the pattern of *The Canterbury Tales*. A miscellaneous group of travellers, snow-bound, meet in a Manitoba hotel and pass away the time recounting 'tall' yarns. A drover, a clerk, a butcher, a bus-driver, and many others, representing as many occupations, compete in the manufacture of thrills and incredibilities. 'The Flying Bull,' 'The Frog-King,' 'The Captain's Cat,' 'The Drifting Corpse' are a mixture of Chaucer and Paul Bunyan – racy, vivid narratives set to the swing of pulsing iambic tetrameters. There is not a dull page in the book. Humour and tragicomedy play over the scenes and incidents, and the local colour is given by the use of euphonic Manitoba names like Deloraine, Assiniboine, Plum Coulee, and Neepawa.

Kirkconnell makes us feel the heterogeneous character of the West in his description of those New Canadians of whom he is indubitably the best interpreter in this country. A very accomplished linguist, he has become familiar with the life and speech of Slovaks, Bulgars, Poles, Ukrainians, and the racial minorities whom he introduces to the Anglo-Saxons with the rare sympathy and understanding of a scholar and artist. Although this is not the primary purpose of the book, it is nevertheless there in interlinear fashion. What the writer has done so often in prose is here achieved in verse with the same simplicity and effectiveness.

It may be true that stories like 'The Flying Bull' and 'The Captain's Cat' are meant to appeal to our love of the farcical, yet there are many passages of human pathos and poignancy. The finest writing seems to me to be in the tale told of the Magyar violinist by the bus-driver:

In time, he told me all his hope
And all the story of his past;
And though the young lad did not mope
About those days that could not last,
Yet memories were his existence
And his poor soul found its subsistence
In recollections sweet and far
Of summer nights in Kolozsvar
When the acacias were in bloom
And through the tender twilight gloom
The babbling Szamos whispered low
To the two lovers wandering slow,
Till starlight touched their happy cheeks
Beneath the Transylvanian peaks.

**Alan Crawley, ed., *Contemporary Verse: A Canadian Quarterly***
(*Canadian Poetry Magazine* December 1941: 46)

We welcome the appearance of this little sheaf of verse which constitutes Volume 1, no. 1 of another Canadian quarterly. It is not brought out in competition or conflict with the *Canadian Poetry Magazine*, as its main concern is with contemporary techniques, while our own magazine, representing a national organization, has tried to preserve a balance between tradition and modernity. Moreover, we hail any progressive effort which would freshen the quality of our national verse.

All of the contributors have appeared from time to time in our pages and, we hope, will reappear. Any modern poetry magazine would be enriched by the best work of poets like Leo Kennedy and A.J.M. Smith, to mention only two of the nine writers. Smith, who has recently won the Harriet Monroe Memorial Prize of one hundred dollars for 'Three Poems' printed in the April 1941 issue of *Poetry*, is as notable for his criticism as for his verse. And if there is in any present-day magazine a more exquisite bit of verse-turning than the 'Carol for Two Swans' by Kennedy, I should like to come across it. All we say to those nine writers is that their affiliation with *Contemporary Verse* does not by any means preclude their connection with the *Canadian Poetry Magazine*. May good luck attend their exchequer.

## Earle Birney's *David and Other Poems*

(*Canadian Poetry Magazine* March 1943: 34–5)

The hearty acceptance of this volume by literary critics and general readers is not only a deserved tribute to the author but a reflection of the growing good taste on the part of the public. The enjoyment of the poems is primarily based, as it should be, on the artistry by which humour, satire, wit, and tragedy are made the vehicles for the emotional responses.

'David,' the title poem, is a masterly piece of work fashioned out of simple material. It has the directness and spontaneity of musical speech – the traditional hallmark of lyricism – combined with the strength and stride of good narrative. It has the authority of a personal experience. It is always gratifying to a reader to feel convinced that a writer has firsthand contact with the raw stuff on which he imposes the technical resources of his craft. The science of mountain climbing is here in detail and principle made subject to the art of poetry. The vast stretches, the towering peaks, the frozen 'ocean of rock,' the glaciers and skylines, the bighorns across the moraines, the prints of the grizzlies, are all woven into a beautiful tapestry against which a human story is poignantly related. The rhythms, pauses, bursts of speed, retardations, and the cunning use of the 'rove-over' lines are admirable, but the most impressive feature of the poem is the ironic foreshadowing of the catastrophe by the references to the Finger 'crooked like a talon,' to the 'splayed, white ribs' of a mountain goat, to the 'silken feathers of kites,' to the robin wing-broken, and then by the abrupt switch to the wider canvas – 'the glistening wedge of giant Assiniboine, heedless of handhold.' This is in the finest manner of tragic poetry leading up to the conclusion –

a story of youth (to use Professor Sedgewick's phrase) 'stabbed into age by a sudden and unintelligible agony.'

The shorter poems give variety to the collection. Some of them suffer by too much condensation – a cryptic virtue which may so easily pass into a mannerism – but on the whole the level of expression is extraordinarily high, as in 'Reverse on the Coast Range,' 'Hands,' and 'Vancouver Lights.' Canadian poetry has been truly enriched by the appearance in 1942 of *David and Other Poems*.

## Mona Gould's *Tasting the Earth*

(*Canadian Poetry Magazine* August 1943: 35–6)

This volume, with its appropriate foreword by B.K. Sandwell, is like an elaborate variation upon the title phrase, 'Tasting the Earth.' The songs seem to come not so much out of the air as out of the ground, with a low, rich timbre which recalls us to our physical origins, and at the same time suggests germination and struggle and life. The poems look exceedingly simple and may appear easy to write, but only a deeply stored nature, furnished with a gift for communication, could reveal those intimacies and make impressive what we so often take for granted. And then the easy, conversational free-verse constructions might delude us into regarding as artless what is really organic. The poems do not end anywhere except in the logical position. The conclusion *is* the final line, which rounds out the impression and makes any fragmentary quotation quite inadequate. The virtues, therefore, are not in the scintillating individual expressions, which sometimes occur, but in that unity of effect by which a succession of lines, each in itself plain, leads up to a fine emotional impact. This especially applies to the poem on her brother who was killed at Dieppe. The last line – 'And even Death must have been a little shamed / At his eagerness!' – needed for its poignancy the preceding biography in miniature.

'NostAlgia' is another illustration of the art in the final stroke.

It is the picture method of making an abstract term concrete and absolutely realizable to a child. No dictionary definition could accomplish anything like it. 'Immortality, 1943' is of the same quality, and also 'Blood Donor Clinic at 10 a.m.' All of the poems are woven from threads of common everyday colours, giving the pattern and manufacture of life.

## A.M. Klein's *The Hitleriad*

(*Canadian Forum* October 1944: 164)

Canadian poetry of recent years has been enriched by the work of A.M. Klein. He has not received the recognition in this country which he deserves, although, we may be sure, his appearances in the United States through the New York publishing houses will help greatly to build up his audience here. For ten years or so discerning readers have felt the imaginative glow and peculiar power of his poems as they came out in the *Canadian Forum*, in *New Provinces*, and in *Hath Not a Jew*. He stood alone in his own classification, no other poet writing like him in Canada and, according to Ludwig Lewisohn, no one in the United States. His uniqueness consisted in his being the representative of Jewish nationalism, practically every important poem dealing with some phase of the tradition, religion, culture, and outlook of the Hebrew race.

Such was the content and such the atmosphere enveloping it. But Klein also identified himself with a certain style which, though at first strikingly derivative of Eliot, brewed a tang of its own. It is true that a decade ago everybody was copying Eliot, just as today so many of our new writers are being Spenderized into a family album. And when the 'Soirée of Velvel Kleinburger' appeared, it was a little disconcerting to find that the voice of Velvel was that of Prufrock: 'My life lies on a tray of cigarette butts.' Still, Klein had a way of making us ignore the echoes by a manner of utterance which was imposed upon the material by the nature of the theme and by his own vivid personality. Despite the difficulties springing out of his scholasticism, his legalistic lore, and his Talmudic terms and references, which needed footnotes, Klein could appeal to us on the basis of a moral culture common to Jew and Gentile – that of the Hebrew prophet and psalmist. All of his best work possessed this appeal, whether it was the ringing affirmations of Isaiah or the subdued litanies of Jeremiah, Ecclesiastes, and David. Moreover, he added something which can scarcely be attributed to the Old Testament – a rocket wit exploding in ironic contrasts and brilliant caricature.

*The Hitleriad* (published originally by *First Statement*) extends Klein's range both in material and treatment. It is written basically in the heroic couplet. In it he has discarded the musical instrument which played the lovely Biblical interludes of his Spinoza poem and such lyrics as section vii:

I am weak before the wind; before the sun
I faint; I lose my strength;
I am utterly vanquished by a star;
I go to my knees, at length

Before the song of a bird ...

He has reverted to the more sinewy rhythms of his powerful 'In Re Solomon Warshawer,' although going beyond that war poem in fierceness of frontal assault. The pity and poignancy of 'Warshawer' are displaced by militant blasts of prophetic denunciation and Drydenian satire. Indeed it is Dryden of Zimri and of Achitophel, the politician, who is speaking in the lines. The satire is direct and unequivocal, leaving no room for any other interpretation than that of a face-to-face indictment, a bill of hate for the Nazi treatment of the Jew. Here is his picture of Hitler, the 'artist':

He drew a line, it was not crooked, so
He thought that he was Michelangelo!
Yet is it true that in due time, he would
Incarnadine him murals with much blood;
To Europe's marbled treasures adding his

Ruins out-ruining Acropolis;
Yes, with a continent for easel, he
Would yet show vicious virtuosity,
Would yet achieve the opus of his dream,
The classic painting, masterpiece supreme:
The Reich's *Last Supper* (out of stolen pots)
With quislings six, and six iscariots!

There are no qualifications, no flanking innuendos, nothing but the damnatory clauses pressed home to the hilt. Klein may be criticized here on academic grounds, that high satire involving some reformative element should not admit personal vituperation, but it is difficult to see how delicate, urbane shafts could be directed by a spokesman for the Ghetto against such targets as Hitler, Goering, Goebbels, Rosenberg, Ribbentrop, and Ley. As well sharpen a rapier for a lunge at a Tiger tank. Klein must have anticipated this criticism in his invocation:

Heil heavenly muse, since also thou must be
Like my song's theme, a sieg-heil'd deity,
Be with me now, but not as once, for song:
Not odes do I indict, indicting Wrong!
Be with me, for I fall from grace to sin,
Spurning this day thy proffered hippocrene,
To taste the poison'd lager of Berlin!

Klein has laid his plan of attack and has pursued it remorselessly. One may object to the stridency of some of the passages, to the punning, and to figures of speech which belong more to the vocabulary of oaths than of aesthetics, but few will deny the drive of the masculine thrust against the common foes of humanity. No other poet today in this country has used the heroic couplet with greater pungency. The subject has pulled the threnodist away from the wall of passive lamentation and placed the satirist in a colosseum with a grenade in his hand and a good round curse on his lips.

# G / Pratt as Prefacer: Forewords and Introductions

**'Foreword' to Jack McLaren's *Our Great Ones: Twelve Caricatures Cut in Linoleum***
(Toronto: Ryerson, 1932)

One of the most promising signs of the cultural progress of this country is that national biography should be recorded not merely through textbooks and romantic fiction, but through the medium of caricature. This album of prints by Jack McLaren, accompanied by the incisive and entertaining sketches of Merrill Denison, is a brilliant pioneer adventure in an art which in older countries has had a long and honourable tradition. It is the mark of intellectual maturity, when the comic muse is invoked to throw a bag of salt into the cauldron of romance, and it is a matter of common historical observation that any period which, out of an inflated seriousness, has too stridently advertised its vogue, has been most effectually corrected by a chorus of laughter.

The function of caricature is to place on exhibit, by controlled exaggeration, the quirks and salients of human character – mannerisms, it may be, which live longer in the public mind than the more sedate and self-conscious qualities. It does happen indeed that about the only thing which posterity remembers in the life of an individual is the size and colour of his nose, when all the other features of the proprietor have disappeared in the mist. Immortality in such cases is pre-eminently the gift of the caricaturist. It must not be assumed, however, that it is just the incidental lines that comprise the specialty of his art, and much less that it is the savagely satiric role which usually finds expression. Anyone turning over the pages of this portfolio will see that kindly though trenchant fingers have been probing into the recesses of our heroes with the purpose of restoring them to our streets and our homes. For, with our tendency to idolatry, we are inclined to forget that those dynamic personalities not only thundered in Parliament and from the rostrum, but that they were known to sleep, to eat, perchance to swear, to doff togas and don bathrobes, and it is therefore fitting that, in addition to striking their official gestures in oil and marble and bronze, they should be lured into giving their unguarded intimacies in linoleum. Moreover, it was an inspired judgment in selection when the Ryerson Press committed to the care of two such artistic surgeons as McLaren and Denison the task of operating on our national glands.

## 'Foreword' to Samuel Morgan-Powell's *Down the Years*

(Toronto: Macmillan, 1938)

The best friend of the literary artist is the literary critic. It is regrettable that through degeneration in popular usage the term 'critic' has come to be identified with the one-eyed fault-finder, prying into seams and crevices, and maintaining an attitude usually inimical to the practitioners in the crafts. Too frequently we have lost sight of its intrinsic meaning – that of a judge making discriminations between flaws and excellences in a work of art, and entering into genuine alliance with the artist seriously engaged in the pursuit of his ideals. Canada, however, is fortunate in possessing a group of writers who are upholding the finer traditions of the guild and whose cooperation with the 'producing' talent has made for the stimulation and enrichment of our native literature.

This brief foreword is offered as a personal tribute to a man who by virtue of his length of service and quality of work is recognized as the Dean of newspaper critics in this country. For thirty years the name of S. Morgan-Powell has been before the book-reading public through the circulation of the *Montreal Daily Star*. No argument is necessary to prove the range of his study and observation beyond the simple statement that during this long stretch he has covered the fields of drama, music, literature, and the screen, and that his present position as Assistant Editor-in-Chief of his paper reveals how closely he has kept in touch with world affairs. Any introduction of a man who in the early years of this century wrote up the Wagner Festival at Bayreuth, the Passion Play at Oberammergau, travelled up the Nile to describe irrigation schemes for a group of English papers, edited a paper in Demerara, served as a war correspondent, and free-lanced over half the globe, would be an impertinence were it not for two considerations. It gives one an opportunity of gratefully acknowledging the services of a distinguished critic – for many a youthful ambition on the part of Canadian poets, taking their first risk with the public, has been underwritten and ultimately vindicated by his signature. And he has challenged attention by bringing out a volume of poems as the most recent evidence of his versatility.

It has always been a matter of psychological curiosity to watch a critic step out of his professional tracts and enter a territory known to him only as an observer and analyst. It is quite easy to see how he might succeed as an essayist, biographer, or commentator, but not quite so evident how he would manage to construct a play, write a score, paint a picture, or compose a poem. It is therefore a pleasure to find a volume of verse which, already put through the critical mill of the author himself, carries for the reader the marks of finished craftsmanship. The themes, for the most part, are romantic – the time-honoured material of love, passion, nature rhapsodies, patriotic loyalties – but with sufficient realism to appeal to an age not prone to displays of sentiment. One gets the feeling through these pages that life has not been shredded into thin flakes of experience, but that it has been lived abundantly, and it is refreshing in a day of repressions and caveats to find poetry used as the vehicle of high-spirited animations. It is the poetry of reminiscence projected on the rich background with which readers of Morgan-Powell are familiar through his *Memories That Live.*

But romantic as the moods may be in colour and exuberance, the moulds are classical in their discipline of form. No tricks are played on the metre, and the feet run merrily unimpeded by artificial hurdles. The critic who has been making appraisals of poetry week by week for so many years is scarcely going to be caught out in his own practical techniques. Still, what is more significant is the fact that a critic in turning poet has not lost himself in the technician, but has put enough imagination and fire into his work to transmute the raw material of his themes into the substance of poetry.

## 'Canadian Poets in the USA – A.J.M. Smith'

(*Canadian Review of Music and Other Arts* April–May 1944: 5)

The recent recognition in this country of the work of A.J.M. Smith is an excellent sign of a developing Canadian taste. He is one of the few poets whose reputation entered Canada by way of the United States and England. His verse has been published in the *Adelphi*, the *Dial*, *Hound and Horn*, *New Verse*, *Poetry*, and many other periodicals, and has been acclaimed by critical reviews and by the award of substantial prizes. His publication last year of the *News of the Phoenix* (Ryerson) put into the hands of readers an original collection of verse of rare distinction. This volume is only forty pages, but its very slimness is an index of the mind and art of the author. His friends have tried for years to persuade him to make his bow to the public by an edition which would contain such superb pieces of composition as 'Prothalamium,' 'The Archer,' 'Good Friday,' and finely inspired as anything done by Yeats himself. The tardiness of Smith's appearance may be explained by a touch of personal timidity, but more, I think, by a scrupulous artistic conscience which submits the written word to revision, refinement, and too often to rejection.

A.J.M. Smith belongs to the Montreal group of poets and is unquestionably the ablest of them all. Although at present he lives in the United States, being on the English staff of Michigan State College, his interests are Canadian, and his influence is seen in much of the work of the younger writers. We hope that his manifold activities as Guggenheim research scholar, critic, anthologist, essayist, will not slow down his output in poetry, for it is in this creative field that his sensitive craftsmanship will yield the best grain.

**'Introduction to the Life and Work of Melville'**
(Herman Melville, *Moby Dick or The Whale* [Toronto: Macmillan, 1929])

One of the interesting results of literary criticism today is the rescue of submerged reputations. Writers, particularly of the nineteenth century, who for some inadequate reason escaped popular attention are now reaping deserved harvests in magazines, newspaper supplements, reading societies, and public libraries. Witness among others the names of Blake, Emily Brontë, Charles Doughty; the growing fame of Whitman and Emily Dickinson; the sound of the auctioneer's gavel over a first edition of Edgar Allan Poe; and the burst into international light of the name of Herman Melville.

The difficult thing to understand is not the stature which Melville has assumed in the last five or six years. That is easy for any person with normal sight. The problem is the almost utter neglect of his work, which makes his recovery today as dramatic as a great archaeological find.

Practically all of Melville's major work was based upon four years of crowded experience on the seas. In 1837, when he was eighteen years of age, he left his home near the Hudson River, and, full of the romance of the Old World, entered the service of the merchant marine as a ship-boy on board the *Highlander*, bound for Liverpool. Out of this voyage comes the fine story *Redburn*. Upon his return he spent three years school-teaching and writing occasional articles for the Democratic Press – occupations which bored him immeasurably – and for the sake of a holiday he started off again, this time from New Bedford, in 1841, on board the whaling-ship the *Acushnet*. Fifteen months was all he could stand of the bad fare, so he and his friend Richard Tobias Greene – Toby of the narrative – deserted the ship when she arrived at the bay of Nukuheva in the Marquesas. Here he spent four months among the cannibals of the island, and this account makes up the book *Typee*. He escaped from this place by reaching, with the smallest margin of safety, the *Julia*, an Australian whaler, but the general conditions on board this ship were as atrocious as those on the *Acushnet*, and the story of a mutiny followed by imprisonment at Tahiti, his escape and further adventures with his friend Doctor Long Ghost, furnish the theme of his third work, *Omoo*. He now joined the crew of another whaler, the *Leviathan*, bound for Japan. Nothing is known of this trip, but shortly after we find him shipping as an ordinary hand on a man-of-war, the *United States*, where he served for one year, getting his discharge at Boston, October 1844, closing a swift, adventurous record at the age of twenty-five. Out of this last voyage issues *White Jacket*. The rest of his life, apart from his writings, is taken up with his marriage, the care of children, the purchase of a farm in Berkshire, Massachusetts, two trips to Europe, and his residence in New York, with the anti-climax of a post as Inspector of Customs.

For a short while after the publication of his early volumes it seemed as if Melville were going to find his position as a ranking star in the American firmament. Few books published in the United States possessed so much of the vivid quality of romance. *Robinson Crusoe* itself was hardly more successful in putting the stamp of credibility upon the fictitious than *Typee* in making belief take hold of the incredible. The picturesque appeal of Polynesian savages – their modes of life, their methods of warfare, their opinions of Europeans, their table manners, was presented by a man who had actually lived in their midst. And then in the other books, mutiny on the High Seas, the brutality of captains, and flogging in the navy found a public even as the less tempestuous *Evangeline* and *Hiawatha*.

But the popularity was short-lived. The critical reception from the very beginning was decidedly adverse. He had done violence, it was claimed, to civilized feelings. He had taken the part of barbarians against Europeans and Americans; had like Rousseau endowed the savage with many of the virtues, and had put the white man in the pillory, charging him with the grossest forms of cruelty, sensuality, and greed.

The decline of his reputation began with these attacks in the early fifties. Other reasons contributed to his disappearance: his own aloofness and sense of loneliness, which withdrew him from association with writers and with literary movements in New York; his growing introspection, which tended to subordinate incident to philosophy. As long as he wrote and lectured upon cannibals he could be assured of a fair audience, but having abandoned that method of earning a living, the pinch of poverty took hold of him, and with the Harper fire of 1853, which destroyed both books and plates, Melville was considered too unpopular to merit republication. Then for more than half a century he had almost negligible standing among the men of letters. He barely received mention in the *Cyclopedia of American Biographies*. The *British Survey of American Letters* of 1892 granted him a few casual lines. In a later two-volume History he got one half page to Longfellow's forty-seven pages, and at his death in 1891, the New York papers accorded him only the perfunctory notice of the daily obituaries of the city.

Another long period of indifference, and then within the last decade Melville became crowned by the most discerning authorities in England and America with such laurels as 'the greatest Romantic writer of American literature'; 'as powerful and understanding an interpreter of the sea as either England or America has produced'; 'a master of allegory'; and readers began to wonder at the delay in recognition. One of the causes which stimulated his return was the rapidly multiplying interest in South Sea fiction written by men, some of whom had come under the spell of Melville, as Stevenson, Stoddard, O'Brien, and Jack London.

Melville's work may be examined as a process with three general stages of development which exhibit a general though not an absolute agreement with the dates of production. The first is illustrated in *Typee, Omoo,* and *Redburn,* where the interest is sustained at the highest pitch by a masterly objectivity. These are narratives full of incident showing superb dramatic selection, with a minimum of digression, and with characters sketched upon perfectly congruous backgrounds. The second is shown in *Mardi* and *Pierre;* the third in *Moby Dick.*

In one respect Melville stands alone among predecessors and contemporaries as a writer on the life of the sea. His common association is of course with Marryat, Cooper, and Dana, but Marryat and Cooper are acquainted only with the life of the naval service, and that from the quarter-deck. Dana's *Two Years before the Mast* came out in 1840, and he shares with Melville the reputation of being 'the first to lift the hatch from the forecastle.' But Dana had the empirical disadvantage of having a recognized social superiority to the common seaman; his birth and status were known to the captain; he had taken the trip for his health, though assuming the full duties of a hand; and accurate as is the account and worthy of 'a classic of the sea,' yet an immediate comparison of his work with Melville's will show the striking differences in the two modes of writing. Melville had aristocratic lineage on both sides of the house but was granted no concession on that score; in fact it worked definitely against him. It does not require much proof to see that it is this very contrast of pride and gentility with the brutal usages on board ship which gives the edge to his stories. Two or three pages of *Redburn* at the beginning and end would illustrate this, and in *White Jacket* it is precisely this acute sensibility which incites him to put forth his characteristic strength. Possessed by anger over a wanton act of cruelty he summons the archangels to witness his indictment. Narrative becomes drama when after watching a diabolical and undeserved flogging of a seaman, he himself is summoned by Captain Claret of the *United States* to take the same penalty for an offence of which he was completely innocent. So tremendous were the pictures he drew that it is claimed *White Jacket* became a potent influence in abolishing corporal punishment in the American Navy – a copy of the book being placed on the desk of every member of Congress.

A change now comes over Melville's style of writing, having its conspicuous beginnings in *Mardi* and its final baffling expression in *Pierre*. In a brief preface to the former work he says: 'Not long ago, having published two narratives of voyages in the Pacific which in many quarters were received with incredulity, the thought occurred to me of indeed writing a romance of Polynesian adventure, and publishing it as such; to see whether the fiction might not possibly be received for a verity; in some degree the reverse of my previous experience.' The first half of this book is in the style of *Typee*. It describes a whaling expedition, the author's escape from the whaler in the longboat, and the rescue from savages of a beautiful maiden. The second part is quite fantastic: *Mardi* becomes a name for an island representing the world; the maiden Yillah takes on the form of a demi-goddess who vanishes like an impossible ideal; and by the time the book comes to an end Melville's pursuit might be interpreted as a futile search for a religion. The next step, then, is *Pierre* – a definitely autobiographical piece of work propounding unanswerable riddles and ending in despair.

He did indeed, in one respect, return to the earlier vein when, in 1854, he wrote *Israel Potter*, with its vivid portrayals of Benjamin Franklin, Ethan Allen, and Paul Jones, and its description of the famous fight between the *Richard* and the *Serapis*, but the face of Israel Potter in his fifty years of exile is the face of Melville, and the conclusion is in the gloom of *Pierre*.

There were many factors which accounted for this radical change in point of view. The attacks often virulent upon his work, and inferences wholly unjustified against his personal character; the scantiness of his royalties; his growing debts, which made him picture the attempt to get hold of his manuscripts at death as a scramble between his executors and his creditors; his disappointment at the failure of even his admirers to see anything more in his work than a racy journalism (Stevenson, for instance, referring to him as a 'howling cheese') – these facts and attitudes partly determined his decision that he would not go down to posterity 'as a man who had once lived among cannibals.'

But there was a more fundamental reason, which had its roots in tradition and personality. It must be remembered that Melville sprang from Puritan stock; that he spent much of his life among a people to whose ancestors Jonathan Edwards had descanted often and long upon two characters of God – his righteousness and his anger. Whenever a doubt arose in Melville's mind, through his residence in New York, about the Divine Government, he found a solace in constructing a world of romance with its headquarters in London. Books were placed in his hands by his devoted parents, which fostered his idealism and caused him to look upon the countries of the East as the home of vision and fulfilment, but his ideals entered upon their first period of readjustment when he boarded the *Highlander.* He left home as a member in good standing and wearing the ribbon of an anti-smoking society organized by his Sunday School Principal, and one of his first acts in the carrying out of his pledges was to question a veteran shipmate as to the nature of his habits. The torrent of language he received in return was like the shipping of a sea. It staggered him and before he was three days out he quit his missionary activities in desperation and disgust. His experiences at Liverpool and London turned his soul into revolt. He saw starvation there in appalling form – women and children picking rags and refuse out of the garbage boxes; he witnessed criminality on the docks; and on the return voyage he was in daily contact with five hundred emigrants in the steerage, unclean and unfed, with disease and death growing at a fearful rate.

His acquaintance with life in the next three years of travel shattered many a romantic notion. He had indeed his heroes – a few starry figures like Jack Chase (the 'Captain of the maintop' in *White Jacket*), Toby, and Doctor Long Ghost, men whom he loved and rhapsodized over in exalted prose, but these are highly exceptional. The crew on the *Acushnet* he described as 'a parcel of dastardly and mean-spirited wretches, divided among themselves, and only united in enduring without resistance the unmitigated tyranny of the captain.' Melville was aghast at the refinements of discipline amounting to torture: the terrible 'flogging through the fleet'; the treatment of the sick; the harshness of the criminal code where even the milder refractions of the law were visited by death. The periodic reading of the statutes by the captain to the crew, where each clause ended with the phrase 'shall suffer death,' sounded for years like an infernal tune in his head. In addition to this were the crimes of the white race against the savages of the South Seas, which plunged him into despair. All these things, with his natural aptitude for philosophy, accounted for the gloom of much of his later writings, for the interruption of his narrative by fiery propaganda and by comment upon the cosmic order.

But strange as it may seem, these very elements, producing such strife in his mind, for once gathered together to result in a magnum opus, which for dimensions and drive and climax can be compared only to a storm. *Moby Dick* is one of the most original books of the world. If the term 'unique' has any application, here is its significance. As Raymond Weaver, Melville's biographer, has expressed it, the book is of the 'order of Melchizedek, without issue and without descent.' The most heterogeneous descriptions may be applied to it. It is a vast miscellany in which masses of fact stated with the utmost scientific precision are mixed with the liveliest allegories. Narrative, fable, philosophy, anatomy, the technique of the whale chase, comedy and tragedy, digressions which scramble through whole chapters, soliloquies which Hamlet would have coveted for their concentrated dejection, conversations which Bedlam alone would pronounce authentic, are all heaped together without stint, but such is the elemental vitality, such the imaginative burning underneath, that a masterpiece issues from the fire. In *Mardi* each separate part is striking enough to command respect, but the elements will not unite; in *Pierre* the heat is intense, but there is little ore; in *Moby Dick* the fusion is complete.

'Call me Ishmael' is the opening sentence of the book, and this mood of spiritual orphanhood is never completely absent even in the incidents of greatest objectivity. The work was, to use his own expression, 'broiled in Hell Fire.' But the allegorical purpose Melville had in mind has left commentators guessing. That matters were not running smoothly in the world may be inferred from a statement of Melville that 'though in many of its visible aspects the world seemed formed in love, the invisible spheres were formed in fright'; but beyond working out the broad implications of this belief, it becomes unnecessary to demand that a specific and sustained parable was in Melville's mind. It is perhaps sufficient to regard the work as an allegory of conflict between factors in the ethical constitution of the universe, or between ideal and actuality. Melville had indeed stated to Nathaniel Hawthorne that the story was susceptible of allegorical interpretation, without indicating, however, that it might be systematically pursued; and the best that might be said for Ahab, who would 'strike the sun if it insulted' him, is that he represents the human soul driven to distraction by injustice and seeking satisfaction by the pursuit of revenge upon the source of the injuries, typified by that snow-white hump whose home was in the sea. This much should be allowed even if the problem admits no further clarification, because the appraisal of *Moby Dick* as an immensity in our English literature springs from the underlying feeling of mystery, the sense of clash between vague titanic forces – the feud which, as Melville says, 'Time has with the sons of men.'

It has been asserted that in mere content *Moby Dick* has sufficient merit to establish the reputation of half-a-dozen writers of narrative fiction. If that is so, then it is because there is little in the story that is not touched by a Dantesque imagination. The daily routine aboard the *Pequod* is like the procession of the seasons. There have been many descriptions of the rendering of blubber into oil where the chief concern was with the mechanical procedure, but there is no parallel anywhere to Melville's account of the tryworks. It is typical of his general treatment; the incident becomes a scene in Tartarus, and drawn to scale. And Ahab scanning the horizon, his ivory leg braced in an auger hole on the deck, brooding over his hate, becomes a figure one-third Rabelaisian, two-thirds Miltonic. The closest analogy at hand is Lucifer taking the measure of Chaos, pondering his voyage.

The appeal of the comic element in the work, strange as it may seem, is irresistible. It follows hard upon the trail of the gloom, and sometimes mingles with it in the weirdest fashion. There is very little need for comment upon such characters as Stubb and Flask: the humour in their exhortations to the crews is comparatively simple. It is in situations which, in their movement towards the sublime, receive a strong dash of the grotesque where the Melville vein is disclosed. A good deal of it is apparent in the relations between Ahab and the Fedallah. What a scene where Ahab, standing in the cabin scuttle, his hat drawn heavily over his forehead, gazes the whole night upon the fixed stare of the Parsee, who keeps the same unslumbering watch by the mainmast! In the same way, though to a less degree, this curious blend is achieved in the descriptions of the swart, 'tiger-yellow' savages who make up Ahab's boat-crew. They are as much symbols as individuals. In other places the riddle of it all may be less obtruded on our minds, but the sardonic is nearly always present, as in the more obviously comic pictures of the black cook preaching the sermon to the sharks, and of the immortal Queequeg, the tattooed cannibal, who is fond of steaks, 'likes 'em done rare,' who shaves himself with a harpoon, and who when ill sleeps in a coffin. The more boisterous the laugh, the more bronchial the accompaniment.

Another important element in Melville's style springs from his gift for apostrophe and for elaborate generalization. Elsewhere than in *Moby Dick* this becomes a disturbing usage, like an eruption from the narrative, connected as it is at times with propaganda. But in the great whale story it has its harmonic justification. The passages move with the rhythms of noble chants. Many of them are preludes with a considered dramatic quality – the most notable, as far as concerns his power to awaken the sense of terror, being the prose-poem upon the nature of whiteness.

Into this grand allegory, then, he pours all the resources of language. We can discover from the frequency of quotations in his books, letters, and journals his formative literary influences. Sir Thomas Browne possibly is his favourite, for the cadences of *Urn Burial* are abundantly manifest. Burton is seen in his cetology; in his regard for masses of particulars. John Donne throws sepulchral shadows. Hamlet and Lear meditate and invoke. Milton directs the fighting; Rabelais, the humour. Paley is hard-pressed to account for design. Rousseau accompanies him to the South

Seas. De Quincey fashions his nightmares; and the fire of many a passage is derived from the imprecatory Psalms. The style nevertheless is by no means to be regarded as an imitation; the synthesis is Melville's – or rather Melville should be considered in the light of a conductor of an orchestra in which the masters here mentioned play willing parts. The great achievement is the final impression left on the reader's mind that Chaos itself is subject to architectural treatment. Direction is given to the drift, and the mass, despite its complexity, is endowed with feature and articulation. The structural difficulty was to give adequate finish to a work begun with huge design and soon covered with an amazing show of scaffolding. We are kept in a state of speculation as to what kind of a conclusion could justify the elaborate and imposing setting. The crew of the *Pequod* are not ordinary men. They do not talk like sailors. They are mariners bound for eternity. Ahab and Moby Dick are two Homeric characters with supernatural endowments of courage, endurance, will, and fighting urge. And when they finally meet on the blue arena the catastrophe measures up to a collision of planets. If it is the impossible which occurs – then it occurs. There is no resisting the invitation to enter Melville's world, and having entered, the hands go up in token of surrender to the conditions. There is something overpowering in the final tragic picture, transcending all current tests of realism; in the face of the Parsee tangled up in the snarl of the harpoon lines; in Ahab's last curse cut short by the foul of the rope; and in the fluttering of the sea-hawk about the uplifted hammer of the Indian as he nails the flag to the last surviving inches of the spar.

## From 'Introduction' to Thomas Hardy's *Under the Greenwood Tree, or The Mellstock Quire*

(Toronto: Macmillan, 1943)

### THE WESSEX NOVELS

Of all the masters of English fiction Thomas Hardy may be claimed to be the most local and at the same time the most universal. He chose a very small part of the world as his parish, a peasant district in southwestern England between Oxford and the Channel and between Windsor and Cornwall, and designated it Wessex – the ancient Saxon name. There was something deliberate about the selection of place and name. Hardy had the most emphatic sense of the continuity of life. His characters are rooted in their environment. Their habits and instincts and superstitions come out of the blood of their ancestors. The life of an individual is merged in the life of his race, and that of the race is placed against geological history, and the geological against the solar and astronomical. Hence the inhabitants of Wessex, though living in the nineteenth century, might well belong to the ninth century. They have a pagan, earthy background, a Druid perception of life and nature. In *The Return of the Native* Hardy compares the lighting of a bonfire to a ritual: 'Festival fires to Thor and Woden had followed on the same ground and duly had their day. Indeed, it is pretty well known that such blazes as this the heathmen were now enjoying are rather the lineal descendants from jumbled Druidical rites and Saxon ceremonies than the invention of popular feeling about Gunpowder Plot.'

So in *The Woodlanders* he indicates the feeling for Nature possessed by Giles Winterborne in the planting of the pines: 'He had a marvellous power of making trees grow. Although he would seem to shovel in the earth quite carelessly, there was a sort of sympathy between himself and the fir, oak or birch which he was operating on; so that the roots took hold of the soil in a few days.' This conception of human kinship with Nature, of the permanence of passion and instinct, is expressed in its most succinct form in the poem 'In Time of the Breaking of Nations':

Only a man harrowing clods
In a slow silent walk
With an old horse that stumbles and nods
Half asleep as they stalk.

Only thin smoke without flame
From the heaps of couch-grass:

Yet this will go onward the same
Though Dynasties pass.

Yonder a maid and her wight
Come whispering by;
War's annals will cloud into night
Ere their story die.

The name Wessex is thereby made to transcend locality and chronological restrictions and to represent peasantry in its eternal breath and pulse.

But this close-knit connection of man with the soil, important as it is in the thought of Hardy, is secondary to another conception which pervades his mind and art from the beginning to the end of his career, and gives to his work its characteristic colour. It was present in the eighteen-sixties when he was writing his earliest poems; it came out conspicuously in *The Return of the Native*, gathered momentum in *The Mayor of Casterbridge* and *Tess of the D'Urbervilles*, appeared defiantly in *Jude*, and continued without abatement through his last volumes of verse. It is Hardy's view of the world, the irony in the constitution of things, the clash between human plans and that otherwise disposing order of the universe which, in its magnitude and sweep, extinguishes purpose with the same casualness that a forest fire would exhibit in burning up a colony of ants. Man *happens* to be in the path of the destroying force.

Thomas Hardy has sometimes been compared with Shakespeare in respect of the inexorable nature of his tragedies. As soon as the characters get caught in the tragic current, no power on earth can stop the inevitable catastrophe, no matter how strong may be our romantic eagerness to have the stream blocked or diverted. That is true in a sense, but Hardy's idea of Fate differs from that of Shakespeare in that there is so little consideration attached to the *will* in the fashioning of results. It is true that what we call *accident* does appear in Shakespeare, particularly in an early play like *Romeo and Juliet*, but in his great tragedies it assumes a relatively unimportant function, and a great deal (though not all) of responsibility is chalked up to the human account. The Hardian irony is not the *Macbeth* irony. It is not retribution. Hardy described Fate as 'crass casualty,' an impersonal purblind order which makes for calamity. It may be represented by Nature in the sense of the elements, or by social convention with its sanctions, penalties, and stigmas. Its chief ironic operation is through coincidence. One of Hardy's best-known poems is based upon this treatment of circumstance - 'The Convergence of the Twain (Lines upon the Loss of the "Titanic")' - where the iceberg and the ship happen to meet at one particular moment at one precise intersection of the parallels:

> Alien they seemed to be:
> No mortal eye could see
> The intimate welding of their later history ...
>
> Till the Spinner of the years,
> Said 'Now!' And each one hears,
> And consummation comes, and jars two hemispheres.

The logic of irony is so worked out by Hardy that it has left a general impression that he has strained the mechanism of his method. Whenever Fate seems by some freakish turn to run the danger of being spoiled of a victim, an accident is conscripted to depress the rising scale. The explanatory letter to Angel Clare which Tess slips under the door of his bedroom is not discovered till the day of the wedding, when it is too late. The same delay cancels whatever hope she entertained in the despatch of another letter to Brazil. It is delayed by storms. Clym's visit to his mother takes place on the same day as the mother's visit to the son, but their failure to meet in time is responsible for the blasting remorse which follows. And so on. This is the way the current of life is supposed to move. There may be quieter backwaters, but these are just eddies that try to twist themselves against the tide; finally, they are all pulled into the general gravitation. Happiness may come to life but it 'is only an occasional episode in the general drama of pain.'

This conception of life and fate is partly the result of the hold which physical science was exercising upon the mind of England in the mid-nineteenth century – the belief that human decisions and human actions are as much the effects of physical laws as the combination of gases. And, partly, it may be explained by Hardy's own temperament. He said that was the way he saw life. Romance might be left to other minds. He was a philosophical realist, 'vocal to tragedy.' George Eliot, his contemporary, was likewise under the spell of the scientific spirit, but she worked out a different aspect of law where the moral signals were flown: 'What we have been makes us what we are ... Our deeds our angels are for good and evil.' Not so with Hardy: his great epic-drama *The Dynasts* is the most complete expression in literature of the iron government of Fate where men, to use Napoleon's words, are as 'thistle-globes in Heaven's high gales.'

Complete pessimism, however, is not the final impression which is made on the reader. The dark tones are relieved by the personality of Hardy himself, by his immense sympathies and by his perception of the fine grain in the human material. To offset this idea of sheer waste, there are pictures of the holiest forms of renunciation, of devotion in the midst of suffering that rises into the sublime. Matching the stratagems of Wildeve for the possession of Eustacia, Diggory Venn, the reddleman, devotes himself by day-and-night vigil to restoring Wildeve to Thomasin Yeobright, when every self-regarding interest of his nature would tend to widen the cleft between them. Standing over against the sensuality of Troy, the dragoon, is the staunchness of Gabriel Oak, who might very well furnish the example in literature of whatever is sound in an English heart. That faithfulness of love which is unto death is enduringly shown in the character of Marty South, and is expressed in her lament at the grave of her lover, Giles Winterborne. The imaginative grandeur with which Hardy can invest a figure, alone and in darkness upon a heath, cannot surpass as an evidence of genius the lyrical intensity of that cry which ends the story of *The Woodlanders*.

## UNDER THE GREENWOOD TREE

*Under the Greenwood Tree* is the second published work of Hardy. It was written in the spirit of reaction from the melodramatic

*Desperate Remedies.* It contains no terrors, no blood-freezing incidents, no trace of the sombre philosophy. Hardy first entitled the story *The Mellstock Quire* – then changed it to *Under the Greenwood Tree, A Rural Painting of the Dutch School,* the very title anticipating the quietness of the pastoral setting and the uneventfulness of the plot. The novel received kindly treatment at the hands of reviewers, who described it as a 'simple sketch of a rural courtship,' and complimented the author on having written a story which might persuade people 'to give up valuable time to see a marriage accomplished in its pages.'

It has been called a love-idyll, which is a correct description if we have in mind only the main theme of the courtship of Dick Dewy and Fancy Day. There are no violent emotional disturbances of the kind that shook or wrecked the natures of Hardy's great characters – Tess, Eustacia, Clym, Henchard, Boldwood, and Jude – no clutch of circumstance. The only evidences of entanglement come from Shiner and Maybold, but here the deeps are not fiercely agitated, and in this respect the novel is the least characteristic of Hardy as we know him from the bulk of his production.

But it is in this story where Hardy taps a source of power which was never to fail him in his long career. His command of pictorial description, of atmospheric background, is unsurpassed in English literature and perhaps unequalled except by Scott and Conrad. It differs considerably from the use of Nature in most of the fiction of the late eighteenth and early nineteenth centuries, where background was created out of the void for the purpose of decoration, having no organic relation with story or characterization. Hardy is not only a great master of landscape, accurately portraying its light and shade, its wildness and serenity; he has the artist's feeling for harmony between the drama and the stage setting. Egdon Heath, in *The Return of the Native,* is the classical illustration of this dramatic fusion. The Wessex landscapes merge into the life horizons. Lascelles Abercrombie, writing of *Tess,* remarks:

It is with a more than logical propriety, that the scenery of Tess's life changes from the prodigal beauty of the Vales of Blackmoor and Froom, to the grim upland winter of Flintcomb Ash with its hard soil immensely exposed to scathing rain and windy snow; and that her occupation correspondingly changes from idyllic dairying under the humorous Crick, to aching toil among the swedes, at reed-drawing, and on the threshing-machine, under the eye of a vindictive curmudgeon ... The human narrative, the surrounding nature, the accompaniment of intellectual and emotional significance, all weave inextricably together.

*Under the Greenwood Tree* contains many nature descriptions as beautiful as they are true. The opening paragraph of the book, with the sob of the fir-trees, the whistle of the holly, the hiss of the ash, the rustle of the beech, is the overture to Hardy's symphonic interpretations. It is his almost invariable method to preface an incident by a pastoral note. When the incident becomes a crisis, our minds are prepared for it by an orchestral accompaniment. Though not so elaborate here as in some of the other stories, yet the technique may be seen in the 'Confession' of the Third Part, in Dick's journey to Yalbury Wood, in Fancy's visit to Elizabeth Endorfield, in Maybold's reflections at Grey's Bridge, and in the prelude to the wedding.

The novel also introduces another distinctive feature of Hardy's genius – his intimate characterization of rustic folk, his firsthand portrayal of their dialect, their rich loamy observations on their own customs and manners, and their quaint philosophy. It is in the treatment of such people that Hardy allows full rein to his humour, nearly always held in rigid check in his verse. Generally, he makes his main characters the protagonists in the struggle with Fate, but allows his subordinate figures to live and laugh and love, and to take the sun as well as the rain in the course of a life season. He resembles Shakespeare here in the handling of the sub-plots and the comic characters who glide along on easier currents. He is like Scott whose local types – Edie Ochiltree, Peter Peebles, Cuddie Headrigg, Old Mause, and many others – constitute a human interest often more abiding than the love-stories which make up the conventional properties of romance.

The portraits of Hardy's peasants are convincing. The Wessex clay is on their shoes. In this story their dances and carols and talk, their resistance to innovation focused in the battle between the 'strings' and the organ, their reminiscences of the good old days, furnish a social document of the period. That Hardy was drawing from real life is indicated by records in his own family. His grandfather had played the 'cello in Puddletown Church, and though the Dewys are not exactly a family portrait, yet it is impossible not to see many resemblances in the composite picture. Mrs Hardy (the second wife) makes this illuminating point of biography:

The actual name of the shoemaker 'Robert Penny' in the same story was Robert Reason. He, like the Tranter and the Tranter's wife, is buried in Stinsford Churchyard near the tombs of the Hardys, though his name is almost illegible. Hardy once said he would much have preferred to use the real name, as being better suited to the character, but thought at the time of writing that there were possible relatives who might be hurt by the use of it, though he afterwards found there were none. The only real name in the story is that of 'Voss', who brought the hot mead and viands to the choir on their rounds. It can still be read on a headstone, also quite near to where the Hardys lie. It will be remembered that these headstones are alluded to in the poem entitled 'The Dead Quire':

> There Dewy lay by the gaunt yew tree,
> There Reuben and Michael, a pace behind,
> And Bowman with his family
> By the wall that the ivies bind.

The reference to the change from Reason to Penny is significant, for Hardy has fashioned the very names to fit the rural comedy. No heavy clouds are going to burst upon characters with such names, any more than they would break upon Dogberry, Bottom, or Sir Toby. What bitter fate could visit Grandfather William, whose face was like 'the sunny side of a ripe ribstone pippin,' or strike down the tranter, who could come out of the wash-tub 'smelling like a summer fog?' And what novelist could provide such tragic atmosphere at the moment of introducing such a personnel as Farmer Shiner, Elias Spinks, Thomas Leaf, Michael Mail, Billy Chimlen, Dick Dewy, and Fancy Day?

# H / Pratt as Teacher: The Lectures and Addresses

**Huxley**

(Undergraduate lecture, Victoria College, 1932 or later)

Huxley was the greatest exponent and interpreter of science and the scientific spirit throughout the nineteenth century. He was the champion of free investigation of all matters that might be examined by the human reason. He was at the centre of a controversy which lasted for many years, particularly in the sixties, a controversy not only between the conservative and liberal forces within science itself but between science and orthodox theology. Huxley has become a text not merely on the scientific curriculum but on the English course in arts because he became a master of style. He was born in 1825 in the period of the great industrial expansion, of Reform Bills and Poor Laws, and in his early years he came under the influence of great writers and scientists like Carlyle; Charles Lyell, the geologist; and Charles Darwin. Lyell had brought out his work, *The Principles of Geology,* which put the age of the earth at several million years, and stirred up opposition from the orthodox theologians who based all their geology and anthropology upon the Bible. The sky, the sea, the land, the brute, and man were the creative miracles of Divine power. In 1831 Darwin sailed away on the *Beagle* on his famous voyage, and when he returned Huxley was eleven years old and undergoing a religious training which became more and more obnoxious to him. He was taught that the world was made in six natural days, that the deluge which occasioned the building of Noah's ark was universal, that the Garden of Eden was a literal garden, that Jonah lived for three days inside the whale, that the moon stood still while Joshua slew his enemies. What worried Huxley most was that those doctrines were imposed upon his mind for acceptance on pain of reprobation in this world and damnation in the next. Huxley did not abandon all religion but he abandoned orthodox theology, which meant the literal acceptance of the Bible. What saved him from complete atheism was Carlyle's *Sartor Resartus*. At thirty-five Huxley said, '*Sartor Resartus* led me to know that a deep sense of religion was compatible with the complete absence of theology.' Twenty years later, at the time of Carlyle's death in 1881, he wrote:

> Few men can have dissented more strongly from [Carlyle's] way of looking at things than I, but I should not yield to the most devoted of his followers in gratitude for the bracing influence of his writings, when, as a very young man, I was essaying without rudder or compass to strike out a course for myself ... There is nothing of permanent value except the sense of having worked according to one's capacity and light, to make things clear and get rid of cant and shams of all sorts.

Carlyle had also an influence on Huxley's style. At first glance, one might imagine the two styles absolutely opposite: Carlyle's mystical, visionary, allegorical; Huxley's plain, clear, rational, expository, but Huxley's prose is often very imaginative, full of striking and accurate metaphors and similes. Huxley had then in compensation for his religious or theological disillusionment a deep sense of duty, of honesty in the facing of facts and in the drawing of inferences. His first thorough training was in anatomy. In 1845 he won the gold medal in anatomy and physiology, and soon after was appointed as assistant surgeon on the *Rattlesnake*, which was to survey the waters of Northeast Australia, Torres Straits, and the Great Barrier Reef. That trip on the *Rattlesnake* was to be for Huxley and the world of science what the voyage on the *Beagle* was to be for Darwin. Huxley spent his time in dissecting and studying the structures of invertebrates. He was an expert draughtsman and he filled his notebooks with minute descriptions and drawings of organisms which had hitherto not received much attention. He also saw enough of the Australian aborigines to make it easier for him to understand the relation between primitive man and the anthropoids. Darwin had also written about the primitive types he had seen:

Perhaps nothing is more certain to create astonishment than the first sight in his native haunts of a barbarian – of a man in his lowest and most savage state. One's mind hurries back over past centuries and then asks, could our progenitors have been men like these men, whose signs and expressions are less intelligible to us than those of the domesticated animals. I do not believe it is possible to describe or paint the difference between savage and cultivated man.

So Huxley's voyage made him think of theology in terms of anthropology. When he returned to England Huxley was received as a scientist of considerable achievement and greater promise by the leading scientists of his day. He was made a Fellow of the Royal Society at twenty-six. In 1855 Huxley began his first lectures to working men at the lecture theatre in Jermyn Street. Those lectures to laymen became nationally popular. Huxley is an outstanding example of a master scientist who could make a technical subject as clear as day to an untechnical audience, hold their attention for hours with his gift for clarity and luminous illustration. He could address an expert gathering at the Royal Institution which included such famous authorities as the geologist Lyell, Michael Faraday, Alfred Wallace, the codiscoverer of evolution with Darwin himself. Wallace commented on Huxley's lecture before the Zoological Society in London – a lecture upon some parasites in the liver of a zebra which had died in the zoological gardens. He said:

He did not read the paper, but with the help of diagrams and sketches on the blackboard, showed us its main points of structure, its mode of development, and the strange transformations it underwent. I was particularly struck with the wonderful power of making a difficult and rather complex subject perfectly intelligible and especially interesting to persons who were absolutely ignorant of the subject. I was amazed too at his complete mastery of the topic, and his great amount of technical knowledge of the structure and development of the lower forms of animals.

Huxley believed in the education of people generally. 'I want,' he said, 'the working classes to understand that science and her ways are great facts for them – not because fellows in black with white ties tell them so but because there are plain and patent laws of nature which they must obey under penalties.' The labourers of London venerated him.

The most dramatic event in the life of Huxley of course was the publication in 1859 of Darwin's *Origin of Species*. It might be called the greatest scientific event of the nineteenth century, rivalling or even surpassing in its influence upon human thought the discoveries of Copernicus and Sir Isaac Newton. It nearly blew up England because it had tremendous applications to the teaching of history, philosophy, psychology, and particularly of religion. Darwin versus the Church, the Church versus Darwin. For some years before 1859 Darwin and Huxley had discussed the theories involved, and Huxley had admitted his general acceptance of the position, and now when the storm broke Huxley undertook the championship of Darwin through the media of the press, the scientific journals, and the public platforms. Darwin, who though a great writer was not a good speaker, refused to enter the lists, and Huxley said: 'Dear old Darwin either cannot or will not defend himself. Therefore I shall constitute myself Darwin's bulldog.' The most memorable clash came in June 1860 at the meeting of the British Association at Oxford, at which Bishop Wilberforce decided to kill Darwin and Huxley once and for all by an oration which lasted for one hour. Here is the account of that meeting:

Bishop Wilberforce was greeted with loud cheers and the waving handkerchiefs of the ladies. He was at the height of his great reputation, as a wit, a controversialist, and a pillar of the Church of England. It was true that he was known as Soapy Sam because of his verbal facility and smooth assurance with all manner of people, but his industry was unquestioned and he did more than anyone else to set a new standard for the clergy. In short, the forces of orthodoxy could not have selected a better man to cast public abuse and ridicule on the *Origin of Species*. He spoke for a full hour with loose scientific arguments, with bright bantering allusions and with outbursts of rounded eloquence, ending in a solemn protest against the outrageous and degrading doctrine, which conflicted with Holy Writ. His audience was carried away by storm. Even those who were most resentful of his unfairness conceded the brilliance of his effort. His success apparently could not have been more complete. But in the course of his brief and amateurish discussion of genealogies, he had turned smilingly to Huxley and said something to this effect: 'I should like to ask Professor Huxley, who is sitting by me and is about to tear me in pieces when I have sat down, as to his belief in being descended from an ape. Is it on his grandfather's or his grandmother's side that the ape ancestry comes in?' As the bishop continued his tirade, Huxley remarked in an undertone to Sir Benjamin Brodie: 'The Lord hath this day delivered him into my hands.' The audience of course called for Huxley but greeted him with hardly a cheer. A slight tall figure, stern and pale, very quiet and very grave, he went quickly about his task. He exposed the ignorance and the reasoning power of the bishop. He made a lucid statement of Darwin's main ideas. He took up the insolent question regarding his ancestry: 'I asserted – and I repeat – that a man has no reason to be ashamed of having an ape for his grandfather. If there were an ancestor whom I should feel shame in recalling, it would rather be a man – a man of restless and versatile intellect – who, not content with an equivocal success in his own sphere of activity, plunges into scientific questions with which he has no real acquaintance, only to obscure them by an aimless rhetoric, and distract the attention of his hearers from the real point at issue by eloquent digressions and skilled appeals to religious prejudice.'

The effect was tremendous. One lady fainted. Another jumped up on her chair. The applause which had increased during his speech ended in an ovation rivalling the bishop's.

In the many disputes that went on for years it was assumed that Huxley's proof of man's kinship with the apes and the lower animals, of the physical basis of life, of the great antiquity of man and of the still greater antiquity of the earth, to say nothing of the stellar universe, it was assumed that the whole position destroyed the notion of a non-physical human soul. Hence God was denied his job of creation and man his possession of immortality. To all this Huxley replied that he did not deny the existence of God or of immortality. He merely affirmed, 'I do not know,' calling himself an agnostic, the Latin term for I know not, which is distinct from atheist, meaning I deny God. To say I do not affirm is not the same thing as I deny. Huxley demanded evidence.

A very poignant letter was written by Huxley to Charles Kingsley, who had sent a letter of consolation to Huxley upon the death of his child. It is one of the great personal letters of the nineteenth century, and it shows Huxley's conflicting emotion upon his personal loss. Kingsley had held out to him the hope of immortality as a solace for his bereavement. I shall read parts of it because only in this way can one realize the contemporary scene of mid-nineteenth-century England, how intense the convictions were upon the religious issues. A great deal of the poetry of Tennyson, Browning, and Arnold is built upon that basis – the acceptance or rejection of a faith and all that it involved or what they thought it involved.

## D.H. Lawrence

(Undergraduate lecture, Victoria College, 1934 or later)

The most thoroughgoing representative of primitivism in poetry and also in fiction is Lawrence. He is as far removed as could be from the humanistic rationalist who thinks that the human brain is the last perfect word in the evolutionary scheme, that it is intellect which saves man from animal degradation. Lawrence deplored this ascendancy of reason and logic over instinct and intuition. Evolution has sharpened the brain but demoralized the soul and thwarted and starved man's fundamental impulses. It has debased and perverted sex. The admirers of Lawrence thought that it was his virtue to rehabilitate sex, put it in its natural place in life where shame would not enter nor mock modesty. In his *Fantasia of the Unconscious* he tried to point out that the great dynamic centres of our life are non-mental. It is not the brain but the solar plexus and the lumbar ganglia that are the centres of action. They control the subconscious life, which is infinitely more important and vital than the conscious processes. The prime evil of modern existence is the suppression of life in its complete physical sense. That is the burden of his poem 'Cypresses.'

We can see that when this point of view is put into literature it can become a wonderful source of power. It is close to the earth, and we have only to look into the stories of Hardy and the poems of Robinson Jeffers to see how these writers can harness the tides. Lawrence can burn up the turf. He can blind the reason with smoke and fire. He has a jungle imagination, rich and luxuriant – his word painting is unforgettable. John Macy in his preface to *Sons and Lovers* says, 'To find a similar blending of minute diurnal detail and wide imaginative vision we must go back to Hardy. [Lawrence possessed like Hardy] a sense of the earth, of nature, of the soil in which human nature is rooted.'

Lawrence was a source of perplexity to his friends, particularly to Middleton Murry. They were friends but artistically opposed. Lawrence thought Murry was devoid of a sensuous nature, and Murry regretted Lawrence's 'descent into mindlessness.' Murry referred to Lawrence's revindication of the way of the flesh, his attempt to make the world innocent, to base love once more on the real and not on the ideal. He would, if he could, have exterminated forever idealization in human love.

Lawrence's wife, Frieda, after her husband's death published a book upon him called *Not I but the Wind*. It is written sympathetically but frankly. Here are two astonishing passages which bear out the opinion of those who knew him intimately, that the brain processes of Lawrence himself could explain his own peculiar attitude towards that abode of the intellect. Lawrence wrote to his mother-in-law:

I am no Jesus that stays on his mother's lap. I go my way through the world, and if Frieda finds it such hard work to love me, then dear God, let her love rest, give it a holiday. O mother-in-law, you understand, as my mother finally understood that a man doesn't want, doesn't ask for love from his wife, but for strength, strength, strength. To fight, to fight, to fight, and to fight again. And one needs courage and strength and weapons. And the stupid woman keeps on saying love, love, love and writes of love. To the devil with love – Give me strength, battle strength, fighting strength O you women.

Then Frieda relates this incident:

My daughter Barbara, now grown up was coming to stay with me. She was coming for the first time. I was beside myself with joy to have her. But Lawrence did not share my joy. One day at our evening meal came this outburst. 'Don't you imagine your mother loves you,' he said to Barbara. 'She doesn't love anybody, look at her false face.' And he flung half a glass of red wine in my face.

That's the domestic picture. The inner check of the humanist with its appeal to law and restraint did not have much chance against those atavistic urges that according to Lawrence sprang from the solar plexus. His poem on the 'Baby Tortoise' is another fine subject for a primitivist, a picture of a low form of life. The tortoise is a pioneer of life, moving through the immemorial ages. The Lawrentian emphasis upon blood and the cellular processes, the reflexes.

His apologists who claimed that he was putting love in its proper place must have been studying the life of the glorified apes in true romantic fashion. Still literature could come out of it.

**[Robinson Jeffers]**
(Undergraduate lecture, Victoria College, 1945 or later)

There are certain ideas and attitudes that constantly recur in the writing of Jeffers. They are insisted on so often that many readers have complained that he sets out to bully them into acceptance: (1) his naturalistic view of humanity, that man is a biological phenomenon, (2) a deterministic concept of history, and (3) an extreme individualism or isolationism. He is a disciple of Nietzsche and Spengler and Darwin, Freud and Jung, but he has made an inverted conception of evolution in the sense that man represents a descent not an ascent. Man is an ignoble by-product of evolution. He is half-animal, and the other half is certainly not angel. Jeffers is caught by the movement of science, especially by astrophysics, the immensity of the time-space concept as illustrated by Sir James Jeans's *The Mysterious Universe*, and Bertrand Russell, and *The Modern Temper* by Joseph Krutch. The effect produced by advancing science was to show the sense of helplessness and terror, the feeling of homelessness in the midst of vast non-human forces indifferent to humanity. It develops a terrible opposition between the human consciousness and the unconscious power which is alien to life. In *The Women at Point Sur* Jeffers makes Barclay express it. Barclay sees infinite worlds: 'It seemed to Barclay the cloud broke and he saw the stars, / Those of this swarm were many, but beyond them universe past universe / Flared to infinity, no end conceivable. Alien, alien, alien universe.' Man is helpless and insignificant. He is the last least taint of a trace in the dregs of the solution. Jeffers says in *Roan Stallion*, 'Humanity is the mould to break away from, the crust to break through, the coal to split into fire, the atom to be split.' Man then is in an indifferent universe, he is caught in a net, his values have no justification in the cosmic setting. And this dwelling on such factors has caused Jeffers to emphasize the littleness of man and preoccupy himself with the ignoble and the horrible. Hence he sings the praises of death and extinction and of inorganic life where consciousness hasn't entered. Man's solution is extinction and he hopes that when the end of civilization comes it will be swift and dramatic not slow and unexciting. The characters, whenever they feel pleasant, rhapsodize over annihilation. Barclay cries out, 'Annihilation that beautiful / Word.'

It is interesting to notice how writers react differently to the same set of circumstances. Some of the nineteenth-century writers laid the idea of progress over the idea of evolution. Tennyson believed that 'men may rise on stepping stones / Of their dead selves to higher things.' Meredith, Huxley, and Matthew Arnold had their moorings in the sanctity of the moral law. To Jeffers it is a movement backwards, getting worse all the time. His characters are pathological in their impulses, they are introverted, and the idea of incest assumes a large and grotesque proportion in Jeffers's mind. And against the dynamic beliefs of men like Whitman, Sandburg, and Lindsay in the future and greatness of America, Jeffers writes about the Perishing Republic.

What are the things then that Jeffers admires? Two main classifications, inanimate inorganic things like rocks, the sea with its rocky floor and so forth, and organic life symbolizing power like hawks and eagles. In the hawk he says that he finds all the qualities which man in general lacks, and here is Jeffers's blind spot. The hawk has courage, energy, simple-minded devotion to the one aim of living by the hunt, and great capacity for suffering pain. The hawk is not troubled by a multiplicity of motives, no conscience prevents the flow of his energy in one direction. He has too a haughty defiance of death.

One might ask what would turn a writer into such a creed. A hard question to answer, as it is in the case of Hardy and Housman. Jeffers said that his life had been a very happy one and that he would gladly live several centuries, a curious contradiction with his poetry. His determinism has been related to his early upbringing, for his father was a Calvinist theologian, and the son may have been caught early in that predestination web. But his study of biology taught him one thing: that the greater, more developed the brain, the greater the agony, and the attainment of human consciousness has produced a more refined brute but left man a brute nevertheless.

This glorification of power, of things elemental, led him, according to a reviewer, to extol Hitler. Not that he accepted the Fascist programme but because Hitler was the instrument of that destruction of civilization, that obliteration of humankind, which Jeffers has long considered as necessary and good. As far as the politics of Fascism was concerned, Jeffers didn't take sides.

There are many similarities between Hardy's philosophy and that of Jeffers, but there is one tremendous difference. Jeffers glorifies power and has little place for pity. Hardy is infinitely sympathetic to the human lot and attacks Power as symbolized by Fate.

It is hard to see how mankind can live on the Jeffers programme. A writer discussing 'The Enigma of Robinson Jeffers' indicts Jeffers as follows:

> Stated in terms of ideas, Jeffers' response is an ideology. Stated in terms of the emotions, his response is hysterical. Human beings are often brutal, Nature is sometimes violent, and life is indeed a mystery, but to respond as Jeffers does by rejecting humanity and saluting the peace of death is to come to a conclusion which is not only barren, a result which pleases Jeffers, but false, and thus in the end without interest and without value.

The response spoken of is Jeffers's reaction to nineteenth-century science, the First World War, and the Carmel coast, the stage of much of his poetry and the source of his conception of Nature as violent, indifferent to man, or even hostile and evil. His work is emotional hysteria. Another writer said, 'Jeffers either knocks you out cold or makes you fling his books down in madness or disgust.'

## *King Lear*

(Public lecture, Old Victoria College Library, 15 February 1950)

All Shakespearean tragedies begin by shaping a dark cloud on the horizon which augurs inevitably a storm. The lines may be drawn very definitely in an expository prologue as in *Romeo and*

*Juliet,* followed by the clash of swords between the servants of the two houses upon whose feud both lovers are to be broken. In *Julius Caesar* there is the variability of the Roman commoners, who are soon to assemble and be swayed first by the more sedate and direct notes of Brutus and then by the subtly passionate oratory of Antony. In *Othello* the conversation between Iago and Roderigo indicates that things are not going to turn out too smoothly for the Moor. In *Macbeth,* the internal mutterings of the hero over the witch scenes - so foul and fair a day - point to a fall in the barometer. And many other examples.

This expository scheme is followed in *King Lear,* but nowhere are we hurled into the rising action more precipitately; nowhere are we more conscious of the early closing of doors. Lear enters the arena after less than a hundred lines has been spoken. The conflict starts with that incredulous 'Nothing' in repetition of Cordelia's 'Nothing, my lord' [I.i.87-8], and when Kent loyally intervenes after Lear's exile of Cordelia from his home and heart, we get the first stroke of the bell in the tragic struggle: 'Be Kent, unmannerly, / When Lear is mad' [I.i.145-6].

That the tragedy essentially resides in that fight within the mind of Lear is indicated by his continuous reference to it. It is not only Kent's fear but Lear's. It is true that Kent in his opening reference didn't carry the later significances. He might just there have meant no more by his statement than any honest and steadfast friend would mean by saying to another when the latter had made a decision which was both absurd and unjust, 'Have you lost your wits? Have you gone mad to do that?' Something like that indeed, but still it is like the opening gong in the ring. A word is used which is going to be repeated many times before the drama ends. The circumstance of physical death which normal tragedy demands is just a circumstance compared to that deterioration of mind which, with its own fluctuations, constitutes the dramatic progression. Such references show Shakespeare's preoccupation with mental turmoil and catastrophe in comparison with which the mere stopping of a pulse is just a matter for the stethoscope.

A rapid survey of the plot of *King Lear* would show the effect of the successive scenes upon a mind which had committed itself to the renunciation of Cordelia. It is true enough that in the first scene there is not much anticipated catharsis through the incapacity of the old king to penetrate the blandishments of the two elder sisters and the frankness of Cordelia. There is little sympathy awakened for him in those outbursts of rage which occasioned the redistribution of his territory. The test is called childish and freakish, but the implausibility of the first scene has never been much of a perplexity to criticism. It is usually passed by with the remark that opening scenes are often just postulates which the spectator is asked to grant, like the bond story in *The Merchant of Venice*. The tragic flaw, here call it rashness or emotional instability, has the effect of starting the action, but by no means determining it, as there are so many other factors more vital, as the play will show. Accept, then, the initial presupposition, and devote the critical interest to the rest of the play, for, after the first scene, the matter of childishness or presumed senility of judgment becomes lost in the sequel.

And likewise the motivation for the behaviour of the two elder daughters does not call for much emphasis. It has been pointed out that sometimes only a slight motivation is sufficient to get us into the sweep of the action. After his division of Cordelia's inheritance between Goneril and Regan, Lear announces his intention to stay in alternate months at their homes, reserving a hundred knights and retaining only the royal name and dignity. Goneril and Regan have watched his exhibition so far and noticed his intention, putting it down to the infirmity of age, and they realize what they may have to put up with when the king quarters himself and his hundred attendants on them. Then in the third scene, Goneril is incensed that Lear struck Oswald, her steward, for chiding the Fool. This came on the top of a series of annoyances and irritations. When he returned from hunting, he must have his whims satisfied immediately. He and his hungry knights must fling themselves around the table in a unanimous attack upon the venison. Goneril won't come down to see him and Lear begins to notice the neglect. When she does appear she complains about the Fool and the insolent retinue, and insists that he must curtail them. Lear prepares to leave after uttering one of the most violent curses upon a daughter to be found in drama. He saddles his horses and makes for Regan's castle, having despatched the disguised Kent to announce his coming. When he eventually faces Regan, she takes the same attitude as her sister, and Lear, Gloucester, Kent, and the Fool go out into the storm.

Before the storm scenes, Lear has given full rein to his explosive character and irritability, and had the drama been confined to the first two acts, if we could imagine such an abridgment and still call it *Lear,* we might say that the sisters had a case. Indeed one writer has claimed that our sympathies in those acts are somewhat with them, but such a claim ignores the fact that we know from the whole play that there was infinitely more behind the expulsion of Lear than a matter of household economics. If the play had just been an account of the sufferings of Lear for the embarrassments to which he subjected his daughters through rashness and riotousness on the part of himself and his knights, it would be more of the nature of a domestic squabble. If it were a matter of Goneril saying to Regan 'We simply cannot put up with the old gentleman. Did you hear what he said when the horns sounded after the hunt? "Let me not stay a jot for dinner. Go get it ready" [I.iv.8–9]. Did you hear that? We must limit his retinue and have some semblance of order in this house. We'll give him an attendant or two, make him keep regular hours and go to bed early,' then whatever inconveniences he would suffer would be in proportion to his conduct, that is, to the motivation. But the result that is soon to occur is so out of keeping with this initial cause that we feel we are not moving in a world of wrongdoing equated with desert, where poetic justice reigns, but in a world of high tragedy where there are no ready explanations that satisfy the moral sense.

Shakespeare began the play with an account of those irritations, but we know that such is in line with his method of introducing just a measure of causation. Iago had some reasons, just to create an air of plausibility, but the perpetration of his villainy was so thorough and fiendish that since Coleridge's time, such reasons have been conceived as a hunt for motives to cover an unexplained blackness of heart. It doesn't take long to see that this condition was present in the nature of the two sisters. Side by side with the apparent motivations little symptoms of the malignant growths are indicated. Even in the first scene there are traces of intrigue, jealousy, and ambitious design: the glibness of the declaration of affection taken at verbal value by the father, but surfeiting to Cordelia and Kent; the collusion between the two sisters against Cordelia and against the father, the whisperings, secret implications, suggestions that pass from flank movements into frontal attack upon the king. We are prepared for the dismissal of the retinue by the cold enunciation in which the successive limitations are suggested. And all the motives are driven underground with Regan's question – 'Why need one?' [II.iv.263]. The motive hunt is over, and the hounds are going round in circles having mistaken the scent of the fox.

That Shakespeare is presenting a condition of utter moral corruption, and painting it ruthlessly is shown in many scenes after the end of Act II. We are not surprised at his refusal to allow any trace of loyalty between the two sisters in their common crime. That Goneril should poison Regan towards the end might be taken for granted, and it is a matter of no moment which sister might get there first with the arsenic. That is relatively simple. But we are startled into recoil at other depths which are complete in the malignancy when the superficial motives are gone. There is not an area unvisited. We see it from the eyes of Lear, Kent, and the Fool, but that there should not be a square millimetre unexposed, Shakespeare adds the terrible scene of the blinding of Gloucester. I have seen the play acted about half-a-dozen times and there are two sentences which never cease to ring or clang long after in memory, and they come from Regan. She answers Lear's statement 'I gave you all' with 'And in good time you gave it' [II.iv.250], where the callous core within the flippant shell would be difficult to match, and yet it is matched and surpassed by her remark after the blinding of Gloucester – 'Let him smell / His way to Dover' [III.vii.93–4]. If there is a more brutal sentence in all literature than that, I haven't heard of it. Webster couldn't do better than that – or worse. For straight flint it hasn't an equal. Even Richard III could take lessons from her and he would be in the kindergarten class, and Iago himself, had he heard it, might be imagined as lifting his eyebrows and taking out his notebook to add a memorandum to his agenda: 'Effective, but scarcely subtle.' And that sentence of the daughter and that deed come after Lear's cry: 'Let them anatomize Regan and see what breeds about her heart' [III.vi.76]. Well, that's beyond the cardiograph to answer.

It is against such a background that the tragedy is developed. The theme is usually stated as the effect of ingratitude and cruelty upon the soul of Lear, but the special point of interest here is to trace the growth of that internal conflict to the accompaniment of a changing idiom. The struggle is to preserve his sanity. The fear of madness is expressed so often that it is equivalent to a refrain, and the adaptation of the speech to all the mental variations is one of the most remarkable triumphs of Shakespearean expression. Shakespeare has to take a king, an absolute monarch, proud, intolerant of opposition, accustomed to having his commands and his whims obeyed unquestioningly, and put him on his knees in rags to beg for charity, and later to acknowledge his faults and ask for forgiveness.

He is introduced in the first scene with all the ceremonial of royalty. He is attended by Cornwall, Albany, his three daughters, Kent, and Gloucester, who is sent out to call in the King of France and the Duke of Burgundy. His opening speech is an address from the throne. The royal 'we' is used throughout, 'Meantime we shall express our darker purpose' [I.i.36]. He calls for a map, and with a wave of his hand Britain is divided into three parts which are to be distributed to his daughters. The royal will is weighted with the terms of the syntax. The sentences move like mechanized columns under undivided authority. The answers of Goneril and Regan are also in perfect stride. Look at Regan's language:

> I profess
> Myself an enemy to all other joys;

Which the most precious square of sense possesses,
And find I am alone felicitate
In your dear highness' love. [I.i.72–6]

That last line, 'And find I am alone felicitate,' is well groomed to the demands of documentary grammar, and the king's complacency with the perfect mechanism is indicated in his reply:

To thee and thine hereditary ever
Remain this ample third of our fair kingdom
No less in space, validity, and pleasure
Than that conferred on Goneril. [I.i.79–82]

Then suddenly there is a jarring shift in the gears. Cordelia's 'Nothing, my lord' jolts him into a bewildering exclamation as if he hadn't heard aright. 'Nothing.' 'Nothing?' 'Nothing.' 'Nothing will come of nothing, speak again' [I.i.87–90]. Five times the word is repeated as this revolt from authority and routine takes time to sink in, and then the royal syntax breaks into a roar so violent that Kent has to intervene at the risk of his position and his life. But in the midst of the violence Lear has expressed himself in a statement which is of paramount importance to the tragedy – that of his special love for his youngest daughter: 'I loved her most, and thought to set my rest / On her kind nursery' [I.i.123–4]. Nevertheless his last words to Cordelia and the King of France are irrevocable: 'Therefore, be gone' [I.i.264].

And from this exit of France and Cordelia, the first obvious portent of trouble for Lear is in the conversation of Goneril and Regan climaxed in a phrase which has all the slangy flavour of underworld thugs: 'Let's hit together' [I.i.303–4].

The opportunity comes very soon. Goneril commands the steward to put on a weary negligence in the presence of the king and retinue, and she prepares a letter to her sister. Lear begins to notice the neglect, which comes to a head with Goneril's demand for a reduction of his knights, whom she describes as a rabble. As in the case of Cordelia, it takes some time for the situation to be comprehended fully by Lear. Goneril's reference to his dotage and the cold terms of her censure have a similar effect, but greatly magnified, as 'Nothing, my lord.' Again he wonders if he has heard correctly. Is it an illusion? 'Are you our daughter?' 'Does anybody here know me?' [I.iv.218, 226]. Cordelia keeps entering his mind, and the remorse for her banishment contributes as much to Lear's unsettlement as Goneril's ingratitude. 'O most small fault.' 'Beat at this gate' [I.iv.266, 271]. A few lines further on, Lear's abstraction in the midst of the Fool's conundrums indicates this one side of the double fixation. 'I did her wrong' [I.v.24] – a favourite device of Shakespeare, where an irrelevant remark in a stretch of dialogue shows what is really possessing the speaker's mind. And the first act ends on an invocation paraphrasing the earlier metaphor: 'Beat at this gate' by the terribly simple and direct 'O let me not be mad, not mad, sweet heavens. / Keep me in temper, I would not be mad' [I.v.46–7].

It is this conflict which runs through the play. Lear has to go through the same experience with Regan in the second act as he did with Goneril in the first. There is the same incredulity at Regan's 'Oh, Sir, you are old' [II.iv.147], the same bewilderment, the same effort to gain control of himself after each shock, the attempt to straighten himself up with the vestiges of kingship when approaching collapse, the appeal to the heavens to give him patience, the appeal to Goneril in the presence of Regan – 'I prithee daughter, do not make me mad' [II.iv.218], and then turning to Regan again, as if ashamed of any appearance of his weakness:

> You think I'll weep;
> No, I'll not weep.
> I have full cause of weeping; but this heart
> Shall break into a hundred thousand flaws,
> Or ere I'll weep. O fool, I shall go mad. [II.iv.282–6]

The third act is overwhelming in its terror. The demand for magnitude in high tragedy is met to the full in this act. It is devoted to the description of two storms – the physical one on the heath. There is no storm in Shakespeare which is so long, so destructive. It is ominous like a supernatural portent, for the gods are invoked throughout. It is pictured in direct description by Lear and his followers. It is given obliquely by their moods. The other storm is in the heart of Lear. That this one is greater – in fact the one to which the other is incidental – is indicated: 'Where the greater malady is fixed, / The lesser is scarcely felt' [III.iv.8–9]. The fear expressed so often is now realized because Lear enters a darkness blacker than the night itself. He is, for Gloucester, the 'ruined piece of Nature' [IV.vi.134]. There is no scene of mental abnormality comparable to it, for in *Hamlet* the nature of his mental condition can and does provoke an argument. The Ophelia scenes, the Lady Macbeth scene, as vividly drawn as they are, do not possess this to the same degree, this type of shattering power, this kind of anticipatory struggle before the precipice is reached. It is true that Lady Macbeth's words 'These deeds must not be thought / After these ways; so, it will make us mad' [II.ii.30–1] are an ironic foreshadowing, but there is no insistence on the fear. But in *King Lear* the ground is bitterly disputed and Shakespeare shows the variation of the struggle through the action and the idiom. Lear is undergoing a transformation from his royal apparel to rags, from that authoritative sweep of his hand over the map of Britain to his gesture to Kent and to the Fool to precede him into the shelter of the hovel. The manipulation of the idiom is an engrossing study in itself. In his speeches he frequently begins with the regal note and then suddenly lapses into a cry, or in the reverse order. As in the opening speech of the second scene of the third act, 'Blow winds and crack your cheeks' [III.ii.1], the words run along in the sublime manner, an indictment of high heaven full of prosecuting terms, then change and return. When John Gielgud was here three or four years ago, he commented in an address upon the way a Lear passage ended. Taking his cue, I imagine from Granville-Barker's comparison of the Promethean Lear with the human Lear, he read this speech as a contrast of mood and language:

You cataracts and hurricanoes, spout
Till you have drenched our steeples, drowned the cocks.
You sulphurous and thought-executing fires,

> Vaunt - couriers of oak-cleaving thunderbolts,
> Singe my white head. [III.ii.2–6]

And further on: 'I tax not you, you elements, with unkindness ... Here I stand your slave, / A poor, infirm, weak, and despised old man' [III.ii.16, 19–20]. From 'sulphurous and thought-executing fires' down to that. First, the language one might expect of the monarch resisting disobedience, then the cry, then a resurgence of the early Lear: 'But yet I call you servile ministers, / That have with two pernicious daughters joined / Your high-engendered battles' down again to ''gainst a head / So old and white as this' [III.ii.21–4]. This ascent and decline is portrayed continually in the third act with the decline progressing from scene to scene as madness takes hold:

> But I will punish home.
> No, I will weep no more. In such a night
> To shut me out ...
> O that way madness lies; let me shun that.
> No more of that. [III.iv.16–18, 21–2]

But there *is* more and it comes in a scene or series of scenes which must strike an audience tremendous blows. This, I should suppose, must be the supreme tax for actors on a stage. The mad scenes fittingly appear in the middle or climax of the play. The mental break-up has come before the physical. And in the portrayal Shakespeare uses, as it were, a curtain, swaying with the wind, now opening slightly, to give, very momentarily indeed, a glimpse of Lear uttering a few fragments from his past experience, then closing to bar us from every sight or sound of rationality.

That curtain movement has its undeniable meaning in the unfolding of the mental tragedy. The memory of his former authority and his sudden and fruitless reassertion of it and the patchwork of design and uncontrol show the stubbornness of his resistance to his supreme fear. To look back for a moment, there is a good example of this alternation between authority and entreaty when Lear finds Kent in the stocks. His first response is that of indignation and disbelief: 'They durst not do it. / They could not, would not do it' [II.iv.22–3]. When he learns the truth that it was done by Regan and Cornwall with the connivance of Goneril, he tries to stem his rage: 'O how this mother swells up towards my heart,' followed by a moan of capitulation, 'No Regan, thou shalt never have my curse,' and this followed by a demanding question, 'Who put my man in the stocks' repeated several times in a high key before the king's tremulous 'I gave you all' [II.iv.56, 170, 182, 250].

So in the third act with the storm on, the challenging words 'Close pent-up guilts, / Rive your concealing continents, and cry / These dreadful summoners grace' conclude on a broken utterance: 'I am a man / More sinned against than sinning.' A little later it is 'My wits begin to turn. / Come on my boy? art cold? / I am cold myself' [III.ii.57–9, 67–9]. As the act proceeds, the darkness increases, broken luridly by his references to his daughters, who have now become a symbol of all evil in the world. The fear with which Lear started has given way to the thing feared – a madness for the time so complete that the king has become oblivious to the reality. All the great actors have pronounced upon the difficulty of representing these scenes. The earlier formalities of utterance, even the explosions of rage, were easy in comparison. All the knowledge of the context must be in the mind of the audience to escape any absurdity of situation.

Lear's passion is projected in passages, some in brief fragments like twisted oddities that shake us as much by their dislocations as by their undercurrent of meaning, such as 'No, I will be a pattern of all patience, / I will say nothing' [III.ii.37–8] and his reflection on Tom o' Bedlam: 'What have his daughters brought him to this pass?' 'Off, off you lendings, come, unbutton here' [III.iv.63, 108–9]. 'They told me I was everything. 'Tis a lie, I am not ague-proof' [IV.vi.104–5]. These are put over against longer speeches where the shutters open to illuminate his mind for a moment or two upon the nature of the world in which he lives and suffers and is to die. And between the two extremes of expression we have the mixture, as in his dialogue with the blind

Gloucester: 'O, ho, are you there with me?' This is followed by an orderly judgment in blank verse, to be succeeded by the word 'kill' repeated six times in the same line [IV.vi.145, 187].

Dowden[?] and Bradley reflect upon the change in the character of Lear through his suffering. His arrogance, his selfishness and vanity have been consumed in the fires. He has been brought closer to humanity when he has been stripped of his officialdom. There in the hut he takes pity on the houseless wretches, and he comments upon the injustices of the world, the value of real human qualities as contrasted with the emptiness of mere rank and authority without moral sanctions, and being alone with Cordelia now is worth more than the whole world to him. What a poignantly dramatic exit for Lear. He dies under the illusion that Cordelia is alive and with him.

... Those last speech fragments of Lear have been described as the highest pinnacle ever reached in tragic drama. But before they are spoken, Shakespeare had continued the mental conflict which one might think had ended in complete blackness and disruption in the preceding scenes. It is, however, maintained, and this shunting of the mind through doors that open and shut is staggering in its realistic psychology. In the fourth act Shakespeare throws Lear into broken prose, as is his custom in portraying mental cleavage, and it draws the sympathy of Gloucester in 'O ruined piece of Nature ...' The prose continues as Lear adds: 'What, art mad? A man may see how this world goes with no eyes.' Then Lear's return to a shade of clarity is indicated by blank verse as he describes injustice, as he recognizes Gloucester, a change calling for Edgar's comment 'O matter and impertinency mixed. / Reason in madness' [IV.vi.134, 150–1, 174–5]. The door is ajar part of the time, but Shakespeare pushes it open with the restoration of Cordelia and the prospect of their union, even in prison, is in sight:

Come let's away to prison;
We two alone will sing like birds i' the cage.
When thou dost ask me blessing, I'll kneel down
And ask of thee forgiveness. So we'll live,

And pray, and sing, and tell old tales, and laugh
At gilded butterflies, and hear poor rogues
Talk of court news; and we'll talk with them too,
Who loses and who wins, who's in, who's out,
And take upon's the mystery of things,
As if we were God's spies. [V.iii.8–17]

The idiom within the blank verse mould itself is so different from that of the monarchical Lear, different in its conversational tenderness, in its devotional ecstasy, but still with a few lines added in the old ring of resolution: 'Have I caught thee? / He that parts us shall bring a brand from heaven, / And fire us hence like foxes' [V.iii.21–3].

... Behind everything is the unspeakable evil in the sisters, like the evil in Iago or in Iachimo, like the evil in the feud between the Montagues and Capulets. That kind of evil is not going to fritter away in a pointless lethargy. The physical storm is so great, so continuous, that we know it is not just meant for the refreshment of crocuses. The passion itself of Lear is a tide which cannot be dammed up or swept into another channel. The sub-plot with its own tragedy paralleling the main plot is meant for the reinforcement of the Lear catastrophe. The pathos of the Fool and his departure from the scene so comparatively early contributes to the same result, and that which has been the emphasis all through the play, the approach and onset of madness, the wearing down of the mind before the final stroke on the body, this has had so many ironic pressures that there could be no backing away from the last scenes. In fact Shakespeare, not satisfied with driving the nail home, clinches it in the last fifty lines, if we are right in assuming that, after an announcement of death in unequivocal terms, his following exclamation 'the feather stirs' [V.iii.266] shows Lear is under an illusion of life. Again he comes to it in his last utterance, which has placed under tribute the finest powers of interpretation in the record of Shakespearean criticism.

Still, whatever there may be of illusion, it does not take the form of the terrible mania of the third act. If we were reading *Lear* for the first time, as if it were a new discovery, but with a knowledge, however, of the other tragedies, and if we had just finished the *Lear* of the storm, we might anticipate with perplexity just what Shakespeare would do with him in the last quarter of the play. Is the picture going to be left there hung with crape? Even in the central acts, in the midst of the sombre, terrible magnificence, Shakespeare throws out a few flashes, conveyed by short sentences and phrases – hints of dramatic futurity. The clouds themselves are stabbed. The blind Gloucester makes his own penetration, for after his discovery of the treachery of Edmund and the loyalty of Edgar, he utters one sublime paradox which reversed the lower rationalistic values governing the conduct of Edmund: 'I stumbled when I saw' [IV.i.19], uncovering a truth which Lear was bitterly learning. And then the very fact of Lear's indictment is given validity by the rock-base on which he stands and which will reveal itself towards the end. So Shakespeare could not present a complete maniac to his audience. Though he has brought him close to the condition indeed, there is enough variation in the comments of Edgar, Gloucester, and Kent to show that the curtain quivered when it appeared closed. Dark as may be his spiritual night, it must not end in absolute and final blackness. Neither would Shakespeare's treatment be in keeping with his art if he brought the king back to full sunlight. The storm and the spiritual agony had produced a wreck, but they had pitched it on the shore, not sunk it. 'Matter and impertinency mixed' [IV.vi.174]. An illuminating phrase. The sudden bursts of energy, reassertions of kingship and authority, indicated the kind of insulation that was resisting the bolts. The chief interest, as in all the tragedies, is in a spiritual battle, which is here the story of the Shakespearean Lear, where the yards are gained and lost and recovered, again lost, and the strife ever renewed. That Lear is going to be enfeebled both in body and mind would be granted. Strong as he is physically at the beginning, he is still eighty years and upwards, and in the course of the time covered by the play, both his age and his terrible experience would stumble him towards his grave. But during this passage

Shakespeare brings him in out of the mental storm as he did out of the physical, and though there is enough reverberation from the thunder of the third act to make us cast an occasional glance at the horizon, yet Shakespeare restores him to an awareness of what is going on. There is the recognition of Cordelia just before the fifth act begins; there has been the partial restoration through sleep and the care of a physician, and from there on, the blank verse of Lear himself has its own technical justification. The joy of seeing Cordelia, though on her way to prison, is one of rapture controlled by meaning, and even the contrasted agony at her death closes with the reflection that if the feather stirs, 'It is a chance which does redeem all sorrows' [V.iii.267]. This scene reveals, too, a further transformation in his nature. The third act had shown him in those sparse clarified moments as discounting rank and privilege, so here at the conclusion there isn't a shred left of the royal, formal Lear. In these final scenes the catharsis of pity and fear is produced by the united power of incident and poetry. It is high tragedy with magnitude without question, with its characters of high estate brought low in the ceremonial sense, yes; in dramatic rather than narrative form, yes; in language with pleasurable accessories? Yes, but here enters the wedge of a problem. Does this catharsis imply any degree of reconciliation on the part of the audience to the combined deaths? To many it does not, and the mind may never come to rest, though the passion be spent. The feeling of waste of the good may lie too heavily upon us to afford any reconciliation or solution. There is something which baffles definition here. How is it possible to find pleasure in the representation of such suffering and death? Apart from any pathological reason like sadism, we wouldn't find such pleasure in actual life, but on the stage the situation must be different unless we deny high tragedy a place among the arts. The word 'pleasure' indeed is too inadequate, too misleading to describe the emotion of the audience. But the attraction *is* there: otherwise we would never go to see the play or read it. And the nature of that attraction has often been explored. There is the artistic satisfaction of watching a work of craftsmanship in the construction and coordination of scenes, in the development of the characters, in the subjection of a great theme to an equally great treatment, and, to use a quotation from C.E. Montague, 'in the gradual admission of the playgoer to an exceptional measure of intimacy with the deeply moved mind of the dramatist.' But underneath it all, or above it all, one can point to the poetry, which not only makes persuasive the inevitability of the tragedy but gives it a weird irresistible fascination. The emotion is brought to such a pitch of exaltation and refinement that it translates us, as it were, to another realm of existence, where in the midst of the fiery purgation, gold actually does come from the furnace. No matter how high tragedy may be defined, there will always be a remainder standing outside the plot – something that can only be half resolved – it may be by the sight of a face or by the emotional impact of a scene, or something sacramental in the poetry covering the action which effects the transfiguration. It is not Goneril, Regan, and Edmund who are with us at the end. Their intrigues accomplished, they are taken in hand and disposed of by Nemesis in the conventional manner. Their lifeless bodies are in the presence of Lear but unnoticed by him. No one now refers to them. Even before their deaths Lear cut short Cordelia's question 'Shall we not see these daughters and these sisters?' with 'No, no, no, no' [V.iii.7–8]. What we have with us is a picture, not of a king and a princess-queen, but that of a father and daughter, the father restored momentarily to sanity, asking forgiveness of the daughter, and the daughter saying 'There is nothing to forgive,' and then after the death of Cordelia, the exit of Lear, where the tragic poignancy of the scene is sublimated by a fire of poetic expression never excelled in Shakespeare. The language of these last two speeches could not afford any further reduction in simplicity. Were it attempted, the result would be an inarticulate cry, and the repetition of that one word 'never' [V.iii.309] five times in one line nearly reaches down to it. That line is the hardest thing imaginable to read, and I do not profess capacity to do it any measure of justice. There are very few words spoken by the characters after this passage – no surveys of the tragic situation, no formal encomiums, no tableau effects. Only the ink has to be dried on the final chapter, and it is fitting that Shakespeare should give that short task to Kent, for the chapter is his own as well as that of his master.

## *Paradise Lost* with Special Reference to the First Three Books
(Lecture to the Graduate English Club, University of Toronto, later 1940s)

*Paradise Lost* is not only the greatest epic in English poetry; it is one of the greatest in world literature. Very few critics have disputed this claim, but their objections have been based mainly on the ground of its theology and theory of the universe, not on the ground of its poetry. It has all the qualities of the epic in the accepted classical sense – greatness of theme, elevation of treatment, proportion and magnitude, the sustained effect of the heroic; in fact, everything that may be summed up in the word 'sublimity.'

This word is hard to define; its meaning must rather be felt in the impact which the poem possessing it makes upon our minds and emotions. Certain objects and forces and natural phenomena call for the term, such as a range of mountains; a flight of eagles; storms; cataracts; struggles on the immense scale, whether physical or moral, involving the fate of nations and people; and whenever the description, generally in verse, rises to the height of the occasion, 'sublimity' is ascribed.

Milton was native to his subject and medium. It has been said of him that 'no one ever soared so high and sustained his flight so long.' This statement may be applied to most of his major work, both prose and verse, but it is supremely true of the *Paradise Lost*. He was conscious of the tremendous scope of his task and superbly confident of his ability to achieve it. That self-confidence would sound like a boast, were it not true that his work thoroughly justifies his belief. The invocation of twenty-six lines at the beginning of Book I states his theme, *The Fall of Man*; his purpose, to assert Eternal Providence; and his high ambition, to accomplish something not yet attempted, and beyond the flight even of the ancient classics: [I, 1–26 quoted].

It took some time for Milton to decide on his subject. That it would be ambitious we can discover from hints in his early writings. Would it be something similar to the Arthurian legend? Would it be couched in dramatic form? In any case it would be a work which in his own words 'the world would not willingly let die.' Having made his choice eventually as to material and epic treatment, there was a long period before he got to work substantially upon his composition. The delay was caused by the Civil War between the Royalists and the Parliamentarians, which engaged Milton's arduous activities till well after his total blindness in 1652. This period was, apart from a few noble sonnets, devoted to controversial prose containing some of the richest passages in the language and anticipating an essential element in *Paradise Lost* – the hatred of oppression – and, coupled with it, the emphasis on individual freedom and responsibility.

Indeed, so eloquent does Milton become when the thought of tyrannical power takes hold of him that he ran the risk in the early part of the poem of giving the dramatic supremacy to Satan, of exalting his courage, endurance, and will power to such a degree as to make an undue demand upon our sympathies. Milton himself, being a rebel all his life, played up that spirit of defiance. The picture is so powerfully portrayed that famous Romantic writers like Blake, Shelley, and Byron considered the first two books of the *Paradise Lost* the best of the twelve, and Satan as the real epic hero.

Was Milton conscious that the grandeur of Satan's portrait might evoke such a response? In a sense, was he carried away by Satan through his own enthusiasm for qualities which Satan undeniably possessed?

These questions have been raised. Obviously, it was inevitable that Satan's stature had to be magnified because he was the chief adversary of God, and the word 'Satan' is used in the Old Testament sense as 'The Adversary.' Here in the *Paradise Lost* the action required that the opponent must be worthy of the steel. Hence we have those wonderful passages following the invocation: [I, 40–53 quoted]. Though fighting a forlorn cause Satan is not subdued in mind: [I, 105–9 quoted]. And still further in Book I the rebel hosts, despite their defeat and consignment to the lake of fire, possess something of their original greatness. Satan retains his leadership and the admiration of his followers: [I, 587–605 quoted before the following:]

> The fellows of his crime, the followers rather
> (Far other once beheld in bliss) condemned
> Forever now to have their lot in pain,
> Millions of spirits for his fault amerced
> Of heaven, and from eternal splendours flung
> For his revolt, yet faithful how they stood,
> Their glory withered. As when heaven's fire
> Hath scathed the forest oaks, or mountain pines,
> With singed top their stately growth though bare
> Stands on the blasted heath. [I, 606–15]

This figure of speech in the last sentence is Milton at his best for apt comparisons. The ruin itself is like that of an abandoned castle reminiscent of its former majesty.

Book II deals with the consultation of the fallen archangels as to what is to be done in the future. The principal rebels like Beelzebub, Belial, Mammon, and Moloch enter into debate, and their advice is consistent with their characters. For instance, Belial is thus described:

> On the other side uprose
> Belial, in act more graceful and humane;
> A fairer person lost not heaven; he seemed
> For dignity composed and high exploit:
> But all was false and hollow; though his tongue
> Dropped manna, and could make the worse appear
> The better reason, to perplex and dash
> Maturest counsels: for his thoughts were low;
> To vice industrious, but to nobler deeds
> Timorous and slothful. [II, 108–17]

Some advise a war of reprisal; others are against it, but the final decision is made that, as force of arms is impossible, an attempt be made to circumvent the Almighty by the invasion of Paradise and bring about the Fall of Adam and Eve. Who will undertake the immense and dangerous journey? Satan offers himself for the task of finding the new world, and is saluted by the cheers of millions of spirits.

From now on, the attention is concentrated less on the might and unsubmissive will of Satan than on his guile and deception. His stature is altered. To suit his purpose he takes on the shape of a meaner angel to get inside the gate of Paradise. He is described as the 'fraudulent impostor' who outwits Uriel, the Regent of the Sun, and contrives to enter the garden, where he sits as a cormorant on top of the Tree of Knowledge and later in the Temptation as a serpent; then, to climax the degradation of form, he returns to Pandemonium, where he meets with a universal hiss from the fallen beings, now likewise transformed into his shape.

Right through the whole poem Milton stresses the freedom of the will as against predestination, but it is a freedom which must always be under the rule of reason. It must serve goodness and right, that is, it has to be under divine guidance. Again and again, he reverts to this principle as if there were a danger of misinterpretation. Several characters are spokesmen for freedom. God speaks to His Son concerning Satan: [III, 98–117 quoted].

The same doctrine is preached to Adam and by Adam to Eve. Good and evil are in man's choice, the latter resulting when reason is obscured by passion. Adam says about man: [IX, 348–52 quoted].

Satan is motivated by envy, revenge, and immortal hate. He identifies himself with evil. Milton makes him say: 'But of this be sure / To do aught good never will be our task, / But ever to do ill our sole delight' [I, 158–60].

Springing out of this idea of choice is Milton's belief that not only good and evil but happiness and misery have their home in the mind of man. Some of his noblest lines are fashioned out of this moral stand towards life. Although he called his blindness 'a sorer affliction than old age,' yet his greatest poems issued from it. When at the age of forty-four he became blind, he began a series of poems with a sonnet upon the loss of his sight. This should be read with passages strongly autobiographical from the third book of the *Paradise Lost* and from *Samson Agonistes*, where the blind Samson towards the end of the poem mirrors Milton's own condition.

Here is the sonnet: [XIX, 'When I consider ...,' quoted in its entirety].

Book III of the *Paradise Lost* opens with a glorious hymn to light: [1–40 quoted]. And this is succeeded by a poignant description of the darkness which has fallen upon Milton: [III, 40–50 quoted]. Still the section ends on the heroic note: [III, 51–5 quoted].

Literally, hundreds of references to the opposition of light and darkness; to suffering and endurance; to the spiritual necessity of retiring into one's inner life as a bulwark against despair are strewn through the last poems. In the *Paradise Regained* he shows how superior is that inner rule to the reign of the earthly monarch: 'Yet he who reigns within himself, and rules / Passions, desires and fears, is more a king' [II, 466–7].

When some friend offered to Milton his sympathy upon the calamity which had overtaken him, Milton's reply was: 'It is not blindness that is intolerable! What would be intolerable would be to lack the capacity to endure it.' That relation between his life, his duty, and his genius is evidenced on practically every page of his major prose and verse.

## THE MEDIUM

The choice of blank verse as the medium for the epic was as natural to Milton as the selection of the subject. It is not enough simply to define the form as unrhymed iambic pentameter. That is the *norm*, of course, but to write a poem of approximately ten thousand lines, every one consisting of ten syllables and five stresses, and each stress an iambic where the accent falls on the second syllable – to do that would be to achieve a homicidal monotony. Milton avoids this by an almost miraculous use of variations from the norm. This basic line may recur only once in a half-dozen or more lines, but its recurrence is welcomed as it helps to establish the type of verse.

A few lines here would indicate the norm and its variations.

Sometimes it isn't easy to detect the norm as the stress could vary slightly with the vocal reading, but the iambics are fairly evident in 'In adamantine chains and penal fire,' 'That witnessed huge affliction and dismay,' 'And justify the ways of God to men.'

The most noticeable change in accent is the substitution of a trochee for the iambic at the beginning of a line: '*Fast* by the oracle of God.' '*Regions* of sorrow, doleful shades.' '*Better* to reign in hell.' This replacement may be found, but less frequently, at other positions in the lines.

Accompanying this change is the *number* of accents in the line; occasionally only *three*, one for each word, as 'Immutable, immortal, infinite' – ten syllables, but three stresses as denoted by speech. And a line containing seven accents may be found, as 'Rocks, caves, lakes, fens, bogs, dens, and shades of death' – a much-quoted line in the midst of a long passage of harsh consonants and grim images where Milton is depicting a universe of death.

And just as the accentuation varies, so does the breaking pause or caesura. No one before him except Marlowe and Shakespeare achieved anything approaching this technical mastery of harmonics. To get its full effect Milton used the verse paragraph as the unit of thought and imagery far beyond the capacity of the couplet or stanza.

Passages could be found almost at random to illustrate these qualities and justify the praise accorded to Milton by Tennyson in the lines: 'O mighty-mouthed inventor of harmonies, / O skilled to sing of Time and Eternity, / God-gifted organ-voice of England.'

Two might be chosen from Book I which exhibit them all – the magnificence of the imagery, the variety of cadence, the use of the open vowels, the musical roll of personal and geographical names, that resounding parade of the syllables – now fast, now slow, and according to the required tempo, all organized to produce the grandest oratory in verse ever fallen on human ears. The first is a description of Mulciber:

> Men called him Mulciber; and how he fell
> From heaven, they fabled, thrown by angry Jove
> Sheer o'er the crystal battlements; from morn

To noon he fell, from noon to dewy eve,
A summer's day; and with the setting sun
Dropped from the Zenith like a falling star,
On Lemnos the Aegean isle. ... [I, 740–6].

The second is the more elaborate picture of Satan arousing his legions after their defeat: [I, 283–307 quoted].

## Address on Wordsworth at Cornell

(Lecture, Cornell University, c. 1946)

This is not in any sense an ambitious lecture. I have no new light to throw upon the text of Wordsworth, nothing to add to the historical and biographical research. Indeed so much has been done in recent years upon the poetry, tracts, and letters by such authorities as Legouis, Garrod, de Selincourt, Dicey, and your own Professor Broughton, and others, that the margin left for another investigator must be exceedingly slim. I do not call myself a Wordsworthian specialist in any technical sense, but only a teacher who for twenty years has enjoyed his best poetry and has tried to present it in the classroom. I have had a hobby of watching the responses of students year by year to the presentation of Wordsworth, and I have been struck with the variability of interest, ranging from irritation and boredom to delight and admiration. I should say there is no other poet of the Romantic period who makes such a deep division among his readers, and elicits such positive reaction for and against. Coleridge does not divide us in like manner, partly I presume because the *Biographia Literaria* secures our critical allegiance more than the 'Preface to the *Lyrical Ballads*' and partly because we do not dissect or read that large mass of inferior verse which Coleridge wrote as we do that of Wordsworth. Shelley and Keats on the formal or aesthetic side rarely come in for critical attack, and Byron, though obviously open to assault in this respect, yet keeps an amazing popularity. It is this strange curve with its high peaks and deep troughs that I should like to present. I have in mind mainly my own personal observation of students in the University of Toronto for twenty years.

When I came up to the University of Toronto, very raw from the high school of Newfoundland, I went in to my first lecture in English literature delivered by a man who was later to become my great friend and esteemed colleague, Professor Pelham Edgar. He began his lecture with a terrific generalization: 'The world today,' he said, 'is divided into three great classes - Wordsworthians, anti-Wordsworthians, and those who have never heard of him. We shall ignore the third division,' which by the way constituted eighty per cent of his class, 'and consider the first two types.' I remarked to myself, 'I belong to the second class - the antis,' for my high school knowledge had given me a nodding acquaintance with Lucy Gray, Susan Gale, Betty Foy, and Simon Lee, Goody Blake and Harry Gill. The prescriptions were restricted to poems like 'We are Seven' (which was held up to us as a masterpiece of pathos like the death of Little Nell), 'She was a Phantom of Delight,' 'The Reverie of Poor Susan,' and several of the shorter pieces, which we found afterwards were included because their brevity appealed to the Minister of Education, who, with a very limited budget, had been informed by the Minister of Finance that he had to economize on the size of the textbooks. With that initial attitude I faced my professor, who fortunately was able to subdue the antagonisms of his class though it took him twenty lectures to do so.

I found indeed that Wordsworth was unpopular in survey courses where just a few lectures were delivered upon him, whereas in honours classes or in graduate studies, interest became intensified. He could never be conquered by occasional sniping from flank and rear either by professor or student. He had to be taken by frontal assault with all the energy necessary to come to grips with his life, philosophy, and poetry. And it was a mistake to introduce him by way of the *Lyrical Ballads*, despite the chronological reason and the importance of the 'Preface.' We could easily appreciate the soundness of the critical reviews which greeted their publication, for we realized that with all the target practice of Wordsworth and Coleridge up to 1798, only twice did the flag go up for a bullseye[?] in 'Tintern Abbey' and 'The Ancient Mariner.' It required such poems to overcome the feeling of profound bathos derived from the cumulative mawkishness of most of the other poems of the volume.

That Wordsworth shares in common with Donne, Blake, and Keats the power to pull us back to him after intervals of separation is seen in the revivals of interest in his life and work. And the strongest pull, strange to say, does not come from what is usually regarded as his main characteristic, his nature poetry. That suffers from the many vicissitudes through which our theories pass when we try to place man in his evolutionary setting. The hold which Thomas Hardy exercised over the thought of the last generation, perpetuating as it did the scientific interest of the mid-nineteenth century, has loosened the sway of the Romanticists. We lost the habit of interrogating nature as a kind mother whose task it was to lead us from joy to joy, who never did betray the heart that loved her. We look upon life with the eyes of Thomas Huxley, who saw the ethical and the cosmic in perpetual struggle, and England became not only a land noted for its Cumberland dales but for its Wessex heaths and Suffolk coasts. We do not have to go far through any anthology of contemporary poetry before we realize what a grasp realism has upon the mind and imagination of writers today.

Supporting this realistic attack on nature poetry was the criticism of the new humanism, and Wordsworth, who had been let out for an airing during the years of the First Great War, slid again into the shadows during the twenties and suffered almost total eclipse in the early thirties. And the anti-Wordsworthians had their day of triumph when the late Irving Babbitt, surveying the battlefield with his centrality of vision, brought up his armoured divisions of inner checks and norms of rational behaviour. It was an interesting spectacle when Mr Babbitt, having completed his series of lectures at the University of Toronto, faced the staff in English for discussion and controversy. He had a large following among the students, but drew little support from the English professoriate, who had spent twenty per cent of their working hours attempting to show how Wordsworth was the third-greatest English poet. The discussion, as I remember it, became quite personal, as if an old friend and master who was responsible for a good slice of the livelihood of his disciples had been libelled and slandered. Mr Babbitt stuck to his guns and emptied his batteries on Rousseau, Romance, and Wordsworth as the arch-villain of the piece, whose ideal of life was to merge himself in the landscape, to develop vertigo as he tried to locate the voice of the cuckoo, and to drown himself in a swamp of recollected emotion. The arts would never recover respect until we had relegated to a subordinate position the Romantic welter of feeling which drowned reason – the one function of man which elevated him from the brutes. I can remember the contempt in his voice as he read what was to him the absurd 'Tables Turned': 'One impulse from a vernal wood / May teach you more of man / Of moral evil and of good, / Than all the sages can,' and I must say it did not seem difficult for students to follow his points ...

This particular humanistic emphasis struck hard at Wordsworth, and it could not be easily countered by trying to separate the poetry as such from the natural philosophy which it enshrined. The question continued to be raised as to the validity of the intellectual substance on which the musical score was built. And the objection was not lessened much by pointing out, in comparison with Milton, that the *Paradise Lost* was built on a scrapped cosmogony. The Miltonic harmonies and images were so incredibly sustained that the imagination of the readers capitulated to the trans-stellar march of the expeditionary forces which Milton sent into conflict.

Wordsworth's style suffers from a manner which became a mannerism – the use of parenthesis and appositional phrases which have an aggravating way of dragging a reader down from high ground. We are of course familiar with this method of writing in much of contemporary verse, but the fault here, if it is a fault, does not seem to be serious when the whole texture of the composition is homely and conversational. The threads do not appear to be so ragged when the coat is used cleaning out the parish pump, but they become a scandal in a sanctuary. It is Wordsworth's frequent indifference to harmony of tone, or possibly his justification of flats, which is responsible for so many of his explanatory passages which really belong to footnotes. Look at the great passage on the Simplon Pass:

The brook and road
Were fellow travellers in this gloomy Pass,
And with them did we journey several hours
At a slow step. The immeasurable height
Of woods decaying, never to be decayed,
The stationary blasts of water-falls,
And everywhere along the hollow rent
Winds thwarting winds, bewildered and forlorn,
The torrents shooting from the clear blue sky,
The rocks that muttered close upon our ears,
Black drizzling crags that spake by the wayside
As if a voice were in them, the sick sight
And giddy prospect of the raving stream,
The unfettered clouds, and region of the Heavens,
Tumult and peace, the darkness and the light
Were all like workings of one mind, the features
Of the same face, blossoms upon one tree,
Characters of the great apocalypse,
The types and symbols of Eternity,
Of first and last, and midst, and without end.

This grand paragraph of verse is succeeded by the following lines:

That night our lodging was an Alpine House,
An Inn, or Hospital, as they are named,
Standing in that same valley by itself,
And close upon the confluence of two streams.

So in the sequel to his description of France:

But Nature then was sovereign in my heart,
And mighty forms seizing a youthful Fancy
Had given a charter to irregular hopes.

In any age, without an impulse sent
From work of nations, and their goings-on,
I should have been possessed by like desire ...
France standing on the top of golden hours,
And human nature seeming born again.

Then this:

Bound, as I said, to the Alps, it was our lot
To land at Calais on the very eve
Of that great federal day.

It is the sort of thing we get in 'The Thorn,' where the footnote or addendum is given as explanation: the familiar – 'I've measured it from side to side: / 'Tis three feet long, and two feet wide.' It is as if Milton, having written:

All night the dreadless angel unpursued
Through heaven's wide champaign held his way, till morn,
Waked by the circling hours, with rosy hand
Unbarred the gates of light,

should have added as integral to the lines: 'By the dreadless angel I mean of course, Abdiel.' Anticlimaxes are very disturbing when they are embodied in high speech. This interruption of the oratory in Wordsworth is conditioned to some extent by the nature of autobiographical verse which reveals not only the formation of Wordsworth's intellectual and moral beliefs but the geography of his travels. It is conditioned by his lack of humour, by his evangelical seriousness, which would argue that since the spirit of the Universe breathed on all forms of life, then all such manifestations are equally sacred and entitled to the full share of the divine afflatus in their interpretation. Or possibly it was conditioned by his short-windedness. Wordsworth was fine with the hundred-yard dash. It is a fine sight to see him come up to the tape in highest fettle. But his arterial system, though capable of extraordinary bursts, was very susceptible to coronary threats. Certainly the aesthetic let-down is not compensated for by a doctrine of pantheism or mystical union with nature, and even the sublime 'Ode to Immortality' is not helped by any variation on the cult of the noble savage or the noble child, where the huge epithets in the verse lie upon the youngster, 'heavy as frost, and deep almost as life.' The seriousness of the philosophy, the obviousness of the didactic intention have little value without the cooperation of the readers to accept the terms. And the terms generally are not accepted. And whenever, in the hundreds of passages, the ethical purpose is stripped of all its poetic garments, the result is a bare abstraction. Hence the symphonic appeal which applies to Milton in his long poems does not apply to Wordsworth, for the great passages in *The Prelude* and *The Excursion* are sporadic and produce the impression that whenever he got comfortably seated at the keyboard his hand fumbled at the diapason, and what began as a march ended in a rout.

The revival of interest in Wordsworth today may be traced mainly to the world crisis. We have found in his work a repository of illustrations and quotations which have lifted our hearts out of the abyss. To the purist or dilettante in search of essences or quintessences, who wants the gravy without the beef, this defence of Wordsworth may have no appeal. But to those who think that literature should lay hold on mind and heart and should trouble the pools of human healing, there is a profound justification in reading what was written in the period between 1798 and 1815. Of course we have to decide upon whether a subject is worth expression. We may join the chorus of critics who complain that Wordsworth pushed his theory of subject matter and diction to absurd lengths. We may explain his lapses to a lack of humour, a defect which he shared with Milton and his archangels, but having made our complaints we confess to astonishment at the manner in which a great theme summoned the trumpet to his lips. We may smile forbearingly at his ecstasy over wild pinks, celandines, and pet lambs. We may regard as bathos his poem on the redbreast and the butterfly, and ask him what should be the biological diet of a robin if not worms and bugs and butterflies. We may throw overboard the whole nature fallacy, but the themes of human freedom and justice, of resistance to oppression, the right to breathe, are as old as the race. These are the permanent qualities of the spirit of man which are brought into relief and rated at their proper value when threatened with extinction. It is then that the poet, in common with the statesman, has the opportunity to underwrite the deed with the word and to blow the spirit of flame through the dying coals.

Both the poetry and prose of Wordsworth during that decade bear testimony to a man who was looking at a subject steadily and as a whole, carrying over into a life and death struggle the same intense democratic enthusiasm that marked his revolutionary days. The proud rebellion of his spirit, which made him reproach his own country sometimes for her lethargy and sometimes for her active collaboration with a tyrannical regime in France, which made him risk his life in Paris, made him later fling himself into the struggle against France when Napoleon invaded Switzerland and even before, when the young rising general was shaping up into the stature of an aggressor and dictator.

The parallels between his age and our own are many and striking. Indeed, with a change here and there in a date or a name, the letters and tracts and poems could pass for documents contemporary with 1914–1918 and 1938–1945. With such minor changes one could see him at Westminster flaying the appeasers of 1938 and 9. Look at the analogy between the Convention of Cintra and the Munich negotiations, with the record of treaty signatures and broken pledges. That tract of Wordsworth has been too much neglected in the classroom, at least by us. It should be taken as a companion piece to his sonnets and to his autobiographical verse. Professor Dicey in his *The Statesmanship of Wordsworth* made the claim (and I quote) that 'at the very crisis of the great war between England and Napoleon ... Wordsworth tendered to English politicians and to the people of England the wisest counsel expressed in the noblest language.' He exonerates him of any inconsistency in his apparent change of front from 1792 to 1802:

The strongest among Wordsworth's convictions were that France had a right to choose for herself her own form of government and that England had in 1793 no right to invade France and force upon her a government which she detested. To both of these convictions Wordsworth clung through life. In 1802 Wordsworth, then a man of 31, and at the very height of his power as a poet and a thinker, began pressing upon England the necessity and the duty of waging a remorseless war against France for the overthrow of that Napoleonic despotism which threatened destruction to the freedom of England and of every other European country which still possessed or claimed national independence ... My object is to consider the development rather than the variation of Wordsworth's political creed during the years from 1793 to 1802, which rendered it not only natural but almost inevitable that the man who loathed the war between England and France in 1793 ... should from 1802 ... onwards press upon England with heart and soul the necessity, or rather the duty, of war against Napoleon ...

I do not profess to be anything of an historian, hence I quote when judgments are given on the political issues of the period, but I wish to point out that those political sonnets belong to great literature in the way they lay hold upon our convictions. They have the quality of siren alerts warning of danger and summoning men to the fire brigades and to the clearing away of physical and moral debris, or, to change the figure, they were in 1802 and [180]3 what the beacon fires were on the Dover headlands in 1588 or what the national appeals were in our[?] own[?] time[?]:

*To the Men of Kent, October, 1803*

Vanguard of liberty, ye men of Kent,
Ye children of a soil that doth advance
Her haughty brow against the coast of France,
Now is the time to prove your hardiment!
To France be words of invitation sent.
They from their fields can see the countenance
Of your fierce war, may ken the glittering lance,
And hear you shouting forth your brave intent.
Left single, in bold parley, ye of yore,
Did from the Norman win a gallant wreath;
Confirmed the charters that were yours before; –

No parleying now. In Britain is one breath;
We are all with you now from shore to shore:
Ye men of Kent, 'tis victory or death!

It is not easy to visualize these two partners of the *Lyrical Ballads*, Coleridge and Wordsworth, with sabres or bayonets in their hands, Coleridge on a charger in a cavalry brigade, or Wordsworth answering to the rapped command of the drill sergeant and going at the double to the barricades. Both of them for a time had the ambition, and though we can easily imagine Coleridge holding a death grip onto the reins to preserve his narcotic balance, we can more readily understand that fixity of purpose and courage which, carrying Wordsworth through the French Revolution, would not have failed him before Napoleon's grenadiers:

Wisdom and spirit of the universe.
Thou Soul, that art the eternity of thought.
And givest to forms and images a breath
And everlasting motion! not in vain,
By day or starlight, thus from my first dawn
Of childhood didst thou intertwine for me
The passions that build up our human soul;
Not with the mean and vulgar works of Man;
But with high objects, with enduring things,
With life and nature; purifying thus
The elements of feeling and of thought,
And sanctifying by such discipline
Both pain and fear – until we recognize
A grandeur in the beatings of the heart.

Could not the following paragraph taken from the Tract be dated 1940?

It is a frightful spectacle – to see the prime of a vast nation propelled out of their territory with the rapid sweep of a horde of Tartars; moving from the impulse of like savage instincts; and furnished, at the same time, with those implements of physical destruction which have been produced by science and civilization. Such are the notions of the French armies; unchecked by any thought which philosophy and the spirit of society, progressively humanizing, have called forth – to determine or regulate the application of the murderous and desolating apparatus with which by philosophy and science they have been provided. With a like perversion of things, and the same mischievous reconcilement of forces in their nature adverse, these appetites of barbarous men are embodied in a new frame of polity; ... And at the head of all, is the mind of one man who acts avowedly upon the principle that every thing, which can be done safely by the supreme power of a state, may be done.

## [Principles of Poetic Art]

(Place and date of delivery unknown)

The general topic assigned to the speakers tonight presents an initial difficulty, that of cross-division, of treating a common subject without trespassing upon another person's property. The job, I should imagine, imposes the lightest burden upon the first speaker in the series, the heaviest on the last, merely the result of order.

I should like, however, to state what I consider to be a few principles which underlie the poetic art, and merely in passing to refer their application to the kindred arts.

The natural method of showing the relationship is an historical one – out of the question here simply because of time. It may only be stated without argument that the beginnings of art in the broad sense reveal the close contacts between many of its forms, contacts which lose some of the more obvious relationships later on. We may regard poetry as having its origins, if one may speak of origins at all, in that most primitive channel for the display of emotion, the ballad dance where verse and singing and dancing were merged in one expression. Today they not only constitute three art-types, but each type in itself has differentiated into numerous forms, the inevitable result of a process which has invaded science, industry, education, in fact, all life, that of specialization. Out of the ballad then have emerged and crystallized the poetic forms known as the song, the lyric, the epic, the ode, the elegy, and the rest, and the growth has been subject to the same laws which govern the historical movements of music, painting, sculpture, and architecture. The terms 'romantic,' 'classical,' 'realistic,' 'futuristic' are applied in much the same sense to all the variations of art. All art then may be considered as an attempt to represent, interpret, modify reality, to create illusion, and to make it pass as authentic currency; and to accomplish this end each art has chosen its own medium, which is its normal basis of differentiation.

In the first place the psychological distinction between the arts or art groups has been made familiar to us by the great work of Lessing, for the argument of the *Laocoön* is that the difference between poetry and painting and sculpture is that in poetry the effect is produced by progression, by a time-sequence. We have to wait until the end before we get a complete artistic fusion of the elements, whereas in painting or sculpture we get it by juxtaposition, all the elements being apparent at once to the mind.

But the primary aesthetic principle which unquestionably underlies all forms of art, the principle which is the ground of their relationship is obviously that of rhythm. We may claim that the end of art is to achieve an aesthetic effect; to realize the conception of beauty. That may be so, but it is possible to stage a debate upon this claim until the word aesthetic or beautiful has been stretched until it becomes nebulous. We still adhere, however, to the very idea of rhythm, and talk about it as if we were on mutual ground, as if we felt and knew that here was something which was in the very constitution of our life, in the ordering of our universe, present in a field of wheat as in the movement of a planet. It is a term which is essential in the technical vocabulary of any art. In poetry this rhythm is described as periodicity, the definite recurrence of time-periods containing syllables of speech, their position determined by stress or accentuation. Rhythm of course is to be found in poetic prose, but here it is less marked, because more irregular. In verse it is this very fact of greater regularity, covering at the same time variation, which constitutes its rhythm. It might be possible to work out a scale showing the degree in which rhythm is present, from the most precise ordering of the periods to the last pitch of irregularity beyond which the ear fails to detect any governing movement, as in flat prose. We are all familiar with certain experiments in literature where writers in reaction against licence and extravagance endeavoured to fit poetic speech within exact moulds, experiments in precision, clarity – in adherence to a formula. The most logical of such experiments in English literature is in Pope, in his *Essay on Criticism,* where nearly every couplet and sometimes the line itself is complete in its meaning, where the accent falls uniformly on the second syllable of the foot, where Pegasus takes on the carriage and rate of a motor truck: 'Tis more to guide than spur the Muse's steed, / Restrain his fury than provoke his speed.' Over against this is the demand for freedom, for fuller rhythms, for overflow, characteristic of the great Romanticists like Coleridge, Shelley, Keats, the 'Ode to the West Wind' being an outstanding illustration. Outside of these rhythms may range the movements of free verse or poetic prose, the most notable being those of the Authorized Version of the Bible: 'The Lord is my shepherd, I shall not want' or 'Consider the lilies of the field, / How they grow. They toil not, neither do they spin, / And yet I say that Solomon in all his glory was not arrayed like one of these.'

I might take two striking examples from the greatest master of musical prose in contemporary drama, John Synge, one a comic passage from *The Tinker's Wedding*, the other a tragic passage from the *Riders to the Sea*. You remember where Michael Byrne and Sarah Casey have put the priest in the sack after his refusal to marry them, and Mary Byrne, the old mother, is trying to soothe him.

The other is Maurya's lament over the body of Bartley, who has been drowned. She has now lost all her sons in the same way.

The appeal of these rhythms is to be found in the purest human speech at its highest emotional levels.

Leaving aside, however, the intricate question of prose measurements, and keeping within the field of metrical poetry, what a stretch of horizon between such a type of rhythm as 'Sing a song of sixpence, a pocket full of rye' to 'Darkened so, yet shone above them all the Archangel,' in the *Paradise Lost*. Those who understand music and its notation can find the analogies here far better than I am capable of doing.

The relation between poetry and painting is that, allowing the differences of medium, both artists may describe their effects in terms of tone colour and all the nuances of light and shade, the painter making the visual appeal direct, the poet vicariously by means of language, word-painting. This naturally opens up a territory impossible to explore at this moment, the power which the inevitable word has to evoke imagery and thought. The marvel of Shakespeare's diction, it is said, is its immense suggestiveness, the power of radiating through single expressions a life and meaning which they do not retain in their removal to a dictionary. When we describe Keats as, next to Shakespeare, the greatest English colourist, we mean he can so tap the resources of language to make an actual assault upon the eye, and not only that, but to make you taste, hear, smell, and touch that which exists primarily only in figure. Look at the stanza describing Porphyro's preparation of the feast for Madeline:

And still she slept an azure-lidded sleep,
In blanched linen, smooth and lavendered,
While he from forth the closet brought a heap,
Of candied apple, quince and plum and gourd;
With jellies smoother than the creamy curd,
And lucent syrops, tinct with cinnamon;
Manna and dates, in argosy transferred
From Fez; and spiced dainties, every one,
From silken Samarcand to cedared Lebanon.

What then would be the relation of poetry in the orthodox sense to architecture and sculpture? Apart from the medium again, apart from the three-dimensional plane in which these artists work, poetic architecture is clearly the question of design and construction, seen in its most elaborate form in dramatic and epic achievement. It is rather the intellectual than the emotional side of the process, though the two phases must never be sharply separated. It is the poet's ability to shape his material, to adjust word to word, line to line, canto to canto, scene to scene, act to act, that makes him an architect. It is Matthew Arnold's criticism of the Romantic movement on its extreme side that too much attention was given to the beauty of individual phrases and images, subordinating simplicity of outline and proportion to loose ornamentation. How does the work look at a distance? In perspective 'How has the day gone?' is better known to the general staff than to the soldier in the smoke. The supreme example of architecture in English verse is the *Paradise Lost,* where many years of labour in designing the ground-plan and in rearing the superstructure meant the severest intellectual toil. Hence the word serves the phrase, the phrase the line, the line the verse paragraph, the paragraph the section, the section the larger division, the division the epic. It is just this question of craftsmanship, of studied proportion, of integrity of construction which makes the *Hyperion* of Keats so much finer architecturally than the *Endymion,* which places *Othello* in the big four of Shakespeare, and which makes the *Antony and Cleopatra,* as glorious as it is in its passages, just fall short of the ultimate classification.

## The Outlook for Poetry

(various locations, 1936)

I have been asked to read a short paper upon the outlook of contemporary poetry and to offer some reflections upon the Canadian scene. The question is sometimes raised as to what direction the Canadian literary movement should take. Should writers be advised with regard to the selection and treatment of subjects? Is it possible to create a distinctively Canadian poetic literature, a literature differentiated from all others in the sense, for example, that the Anglo-Irish production is in a class by itself?

It is not easy to answer these questions because of the danger of putting limitations upon the creative spirit. Considerations of space and time, local manners, national idiosyncrasy may be and have been taken as the basis of sterling literature, but they are only important factors amongst other factors equally important.

Literature in its most vital sense may be regarded as a relation between life and language, and the authority of language whether in speech or print is rooted in the personality of the one who uses it. There is an eastern proverb which stresses the responsibility of speech, the irrevocable nature of it. A word is a soul, and the one who speaks it has pledged his character to it. It is claimed that this emphasis is pre-eminently an Oriental quality, and the more simple the life the more true it is - the gentleman's agreement, which regards the signed contract as only an artificial bolstering of the faith. When the word goes out it cannot be recalled. The Hebrew literature reflects this truth in so many forms. Words possess hidden potencies: they cast spells either of favour or malediction. When Isaac gave his blessing to Jacob, mistaking him for Esau, it was final, the later knowledge of the deceit having no power to revoke the gift. It is this contact between life and letters of which I want first to speak.

The survival condition of a literature, as of a species, lies in its power of adjustment; its capacity to represent adequately an experience. Out of a thousand statements one survives because of some dramatic fitness between a crisis and its utterance, between a view of life and its articulation. When the language begins with the intensity of a passion we get the element of literature.

If we take the peaks of literary expression in the last one hundred years, we find that they emerged out of the emotional and intellectual strife between religious faith and science. We are familiar with the upheavals of the mid-nineteenth century when Huxley's assaults on dogmatic theology produced all kinds of responses. Some men fell back into a general state of atheism and created literature out of it. Some accepted the old dualism that what might be true in science might be false for religion and the converse, and many a mystical utterance of the highest exaltation came out of that paradox. Some hurried for refuge into the Roman Communion and composed immortal lyrics and hymns out of that. Others welcomed the freest intellectual inquiry on the assumption that no theory of light could prevent a man from seeing and no theory of heat could keep one from warming his hands at a fire. Each type of mind put up its own defence, and where the convictions were profound high reaches of literary expression were attained.

Then how is that lesson of a century ago being learned today, and how is it being inscribed in the literary documents? We are witnessing much the same ebb and flow of the struggle though the armies on both sides are more numerous than ever. The growing immensity of the universe has created the most diverse impressions. To some minds it has emphasized the insignificance of man making his short and crippled biological step, only to cease like any other animal organism of past ages, and yet see what Hardy and Housman made out of that belief, or the way Bertrand Russell could build up his paragraphs to give them the drum-like accompaniment of a Dead March.

But others have noticed a significant trend of scientific literature in the growing idealism of the contemporary scientists where there is a junction effected between science and romance in the larger sense of the term, and when you have such a union, the cause of literature is immensely served. When investigation has not stifled the spirit of wonder and awe, when problems receive solutions that are found not to solve, when outposts are abandoned and direction signs reversed, there is left enough mystery to shake complacency and to nourish faith. The very complexity of life, as well as the staggering figures of stellar computation, rather than belittling the human species, has increased the importance of those who formulate the laws and make the calculations. I think we are on the verge of a fresh release of poetic energy from mystical sources as soon as the intellectual arrogance of the specialist disappears. The very concentration on a focus blinds the eye to everything but the illuminated point, and we forget how tremendously vital to literature is the vast penumbra outside, the half-tones, the guesses, the shadows, the gropings in a world but dimly realized. A fair proportion of the poetic literature today is indirectly a plea for suspended judgment, where the writers, conscious of the cleavage between science and faith, yet convinced of ultimate reconciliation, side-step the abstract logic and call upon the imagination to furnish similes which act as a marvellous buttress to faith. One of the most perfect sonnets ever written expresses this point of view, that of Blanco White, where the intimation of immortality is supplied by the very nature of darkness – that when the noonday sun reveals the insect on the leaf, it blinds the eye to the multitude of stars that need night for their discovery: 'If light can thus deceive, wherefore not life?'

It was to offset a narrow scientific naturalism that the Irish literary movement started, following the rise of French symbolism. Anatole [France?] expresses the new direction when he states: 'An argument pursued on a complex subject will never prove anything but the ability of the mind which conducts it ... [T]he things which touch us most nearly, which seem to us loveliest and most desirable are precisely those which will always remain vague to us and in part mysterious.' And so Yeats:

> The scientific movement is ebbing a little everywhere, and I am certain that everywhere literature will return once more to its own extravagant fantastical expression, for in literature, unlike science, there are no discoveries, and it is always the old that returns. Let us go forth, the tellers of tales, and seize whatever prey the heart longs for, and have no fear. The earth is only a little dust under our feet, the ultimate reality is a dream reality, an imaginative existence, the world of the arts which God gave to man before he gave them wheat.

The interaction between science and the humanities has been profound, and the literature known as humanism has been moulded either in sympathy with or in antagonism to scientific results. With some of the writers the conception of God is thrown into the discard, or where the concession is granted, it is regarded as a nursling idea, a sign of man's immaturity which will ultimately disappear as human needs grow less with the advancement of physical well-being through the agency of science. This is an old idea to receive perpetual discouragement when the machine turns on the mechanic or when the latest announcement in chemistry is that of a gas of more than diabolical virtues. Still, even here the best pages of the humanistic account are those expressing undercurrents of feeling which are wistful, where the heart tries to repudiate the logic of the head, passages full of the low chords of lamentation over a glory that is gone. But the more hopeful side of humanism as expressed in the work of its more distinguished exponents is the emphasis given to the idea of worth, the ultimate value that is ascribed to the human soul, and that idea is pressed home upon us whenever we come in contact with great personal sacrificial decisions.

This has always been the greatest material for poetry and it is along this road that poetry is to have its greatest triumphs. Whenever tragic literature, in staging the conflicts between man and nature or fate, brings out the refinement upon his face, the exaltation through suffering, it forces us to give our interpretation of life deeper implications, to make the pattern a nobler and more comprehensive one. This constitutes the main problem for idealistic literature, to get the anomalies explained, to find a place for man in a setting that makes sense to our baffled understanding, and the more we find ourselves in the presence of sacrificial deeds, the closer we get to the heart of life and the heart of the universe.

If we were asked to name two antithetic programmes of conduct, one doing justice to man's noblest aspirations, and the other catering to his egotism, what should we name? For the first we should agree on the Sermon on the Mount; for the other, I should refer to a speech which Shakespeare puts in the mouth of Falstaff, where the opportunist outlook on life, the materialistic ethic, is expressed with such economy and such finality. This has been described as the greatest negation of the moral ideal in literature, where we have expressed within half a page a standpoint which a less inspired writer might take half a play to unfold. Though we may be disarmed by its frankness and by its partial justification through its reference to war, yet when it is taken as a general philosophy of conduct, it is to be interpreted as the extreme statement of ignoble common sense. Falstaff is debating the value of a thing called honour, which is to his mind to be weighed like a commodity:

PRINCE HAL
... Why thou owest God a death.
FALSTAFF
Tis not due yet: I would be loath to pay him before his day. What need I to be so forward with him that calls not on me? Well, tis no matter; honour pricks me on. Yea, but how if honour prick me off when I come on? how then? Can honour set to a leg? No. Or an arm? No. Or take away the grief of a wound? No. Honour hath no skill in surgery then? No. What is honour? A word. What is that word honour? Air. A trim reckoning. Who hath it? He that died o' Wednesday. Doth he feel it? No. Doth he hear it? No. It is insensible then? Yea to the dead. But will it not live with the living? No. Why? Detraction will not suffer it. Therefore I'll none of it. Honour is a mere scutcheon; and so ends my catechism.

Swinging to the other side of the pendulum and ever keeping in mind the ultimate values of action, we have the statement 'He that loses his life for my sake shall find it' as the sternest and most challenging idealism in literature.

The note of authority in the literature of today, both in its permanent and fugitive forms, comes from the sincerity of the challenge, where the writer in prophetic tones and with the prophet's awareness of actuality not only points to the catastrophe ahead, but indicates the heroic measures to avoid it. The true prophet refuses to scrap the last shred of hope for the world, for he believes there is sufficient good in human nature both in heart and intelligence to respond to enlightened direction. For him the world isn't just chaos even if, as someone remarked, 'it is a spiritual kindergarten where millions of bewildered infants are trying to spell God with the wrong blocks.'

It is an amazing but to some extent an assuring fact that the most stirring revivals of literature have come out of periods of the deepest confusion, that when the anarchic elements were appearing to take control by their sheer mass, there is a return to sanity and light under inspired leadership. That sacrificial offerings are found on the altars on such dawns, supplying as they do the test to the reality of the change, is the supreme tragic fact of our race, but the fact must be confronted like the presence of some disease deep in the vitals. The new way of life for us and for literature lies in the deed or in a belief stated in terms of the pulse behind human sympathy and justice. It is the deed following the motive which supplies the dynamic, whether it springs out of the unforced goodness of the heart, an instinctive thing native to the blood, as we say, or out of the pull of forces where the right finally gains the ascendancy ... No one will deny the charm of metaphysical verse. It will always delight us by its sweet wit, its fantastic phrasing, its clever turns, its exquisite shading, but the poetry which may spring out of a great deed has more than the fragrance of roses, more than the music of nightingales.

The subjects for Canadian poetry, that is, poetry written by Canadians, are knocking perpetually at our front doors, and it is interesting to watch the response of the younger Canadian writers. What is their outlook? What is their pulse beat? What are their dominating passions? Are they segregating into groups? How much of experiment and originality is there in the production? The *Canadian Poetry Magazine*, which we are trying to produce and maintain, represents within its very restricted spatial limits a good cross-section of the poetic interest, and I think it does reflect the complexity of the modern literary scene. We have tradition with its sanctities of form and content, its love of myth and romance, and the simplicities of heart and utterance, and we need it, will always need it. We have the modern spirit, definitely anti-romantic, crashing into creeds and ideals, relentlessly exposing existing structures and lighting up the precipices which many people believe to be ahead of the world. And we need that too. That is the reason why a favourite mode of contemporary writing is satire, obvious or concealed. The old pastoral sympathies and conventions are not much in evidence, and in their place are devastating attacks on industrialism and war and social hypocrisy. The main movements reflect the dominant temper of a generation which is facing the future with more alarm than hope, in the presence of the blind alleys of our economic life. There is no doubt that the general result is in the direction of a reinvigorated language, and away from the precious and the merely decorative. The old shyness about the use of scientific or mechanical terms in poetry is gone, for whether a poem is written in defence of the machine or, as it generally is, as an indictment of it, one thing is certain: that motors and cranks and pistons and cylinders are fitting into the measures of the verse today as smoothly as the time-honoured reaping hook and the plough. The material of poetry is at the blast furnace as it is at the hearth. Romance or idealism in poetry does not mean withdrawal from the grit and grind of life and the fashioning of 'Kubla Khans,' as beautiful as the process may be. It consists rather in the discovery and reassertion of values for the human family, aesthetic or social or religious, or all three combined. And there are many paths leading to this discovery. I think that the wise attitude to take to any new movement is one of catholicity, a liberalism, such as science might adopt towards a new physical hypothesis, a willingness to examine the merits of a position. A sheer conservatism never makes any progress when it becomes blind to its own origins, when it fails to recognize that what is now a settled respectable routine was once a cause fought on the barricades by ragged battalions. This is the lesson of toleration for the new. Give any cause its right of expression, its demand for a hearing, but after that, what? Examination and criticism, by all means. It is a mistake to claim that the heaviest fires today proceed from the conservative batteries. That attack is mild compared with the heat and scorn poured upon the older orders by the new schools. And it is an easy but fallacious reasoning to claim that the more violent and extreme forms of the present will be accepted and orthodox modes of the future. What is more likely to happen, if one might make an inference from the analogy of literary history, is that the very violent forms will subside and disappear like the effervescence on a tankard of Stein.

A renaissance of Canadian poetry can only be effected by a conjunction of public interest, the operation of critical taste, and of poetic productivity. The last certainly is active enough if one may judge by the inundation of the editorial office by manuscripts which have swept in like a Johnstown flood. The second factor is tremendously essential, for we do not half appreciate what we owe to reviewers, columnists, and literary critics. That conjunction of forces is having a most pronounced effect today in raising the level of Canadian creative effort. The great purpose is to get interest aroused, cultivated intelligent interest. Let us get people talking about poetry, about our Canadian future, get them criticizing it, appreciating it. Our worst foe is complacency. If the critical batteries open fire, at least they will have the effect of getting the attention of the public directed upon the whereabouts of the targets.

## [**The Golden Mean in Poetry**]

(Place of delivery unknown, c. 1938 or later)

I believe in the Golden Mean in poetry as I do in life. I know there is a good deal of controversy today over the significance or relevance of meaning in poetry. There are some who relegate meaning to prose and seek to divest poetry of ideas and intelligible meaning. They claim that it is the tune, the verbal melody that counts, that it makes little or no difference if the words or the lines or the stanza or the whole poem conveyed meaning. I think there is some defence of that position if meaning is identified with propaganda on a low level. I am reminded of a verse which was published during the First World War when there was a spate of invective on both sides. A writer bored with the verse propaganda wrote this:

God heard the embattled nations loudly shout –
'God strafe England and God save the king,
God this, God that, and God the other thing,'
Good God, said God, I got my work cut out.

But I can understand how propaganda can be construed on such a high level that the message may accomplish its purpose without the reader being aware of it, as for instance in the parables of Jesus, which are moral messages as well as poetry of the highest kind. It depends on the nature of the message. On the one hand you may have that, but at the other extreme you may have verse which yields up no ideas, no sense, no significance whatsoever. Such writers depend merely upon the syllabic, a kind of mouth music which, important as one element, yet taken by itself reduces poetry to the level of the kindergarten or even lower. I think that all the major poetry of the world which belongs to the great tradition is complex, containing a number of elements in varying proportions: tune, ideas, and images and emotional suggestion. That to me is the Golden Mean.

## [The Music of Language]

(Place unknown, 1939 or later)

I am going to commence this brief paper by quoting an excellent passage from the *Music of Language* by Mr Campbell-McInnes. It is on page fifty-two under the caption of 'The Power of Words':

> By this magical art, the great literary writers are able to convey to the imaginative reader of literature, characters of their own creation, whom he has never seen, yet so vital in verbal description, that their very names arouse mental images of their persons as 'true' realities. Hamlet, Macbeth, Shylock, Othello, Romeo, Juliet, Falstaff, Brutus, Julius Caesar – symphonic characters conceived in the mould of the music of language.

The expression which caught my attention and admiration, particularly, was the last. And I am going to take a few passages from the play *Othello*, the most perfect, though not necessarily the greatest, of the Shakespearean dramas. Shakespeare is devoting his imagination mainly to the portrayal of two characters, and I think it is the finest study in contrast in the whole gallery of his portraits. The art of individualization in drama is to build up a system of character points through action and speech. Action of course is the easier medium because the plot itself is the least Shakespearean part of a Shakespeare play: it is generally borrowed in the main outlines, and a murder or an intrigue is a very obvious way to characterize a murderer or a villain. But when the man is made to speak, not simply to act, it is then that the hand of the master is disclosed. Iago is the ultimate villain of Shakespeare. He is diabolically shrewd, calculating, deliberate, cold-blooded, the realist in the most sinister sense of that term. Othello is romantic, imaginative, tempestuous, passionate, the idealist in the most visionary sense of *that* term. To exhibit that contrast Shakespeare gives each a philosophy, a temperament, and what concerns us most here, an idiom. Even if we didn't have their names attached to their speeches, we should know who was speaking. Iago talks in a matter-of-fact, prosaic, cryptic, staccato, cynical manner. Any observations he makes on goodness and love and ethics are ironic and are delivered with a shrug of the shoulders and a Mephistophelean chuckle. Othello speaks in the grand manner, approaching at times the sublime. A passage from *Othello* looks like a passage from the *Paradise Lost* in the elevation of the sentiment, though he adds what generally Milton lacks – the stormy note of passion.

Here is a bit of Iago's conversation with Roderigo:

Love! It is mere lust of the blood and a permission of the will. Come, be a man. Drown thyself! drown cats and blind puppies. I have professed me thy friend and I confess me knit to thy deserving with cables of perdurable toughness; I could never better stead thee than now. Put money in thy purse; follow thou the wars; defeat thy favour with a usurped beard; I say, put money in thy purse. It cannot be that Desdemona should long continue her love to the Moor, – put money in thy purse.

There is his speech on good reputation (III.iii.155–61).

Compare this with Othello's blank verse:

O, now for ever
Farewell the tranquil mind! 'farewell content.'

Farewell the plumed troop, and the big wars,
That makes ambition virtue. O, farewell.
Farewell the neighing steed, and the shrill trump,
The spirit-stirring drum, the ear-piercing fife,
The royal banner, and all quality,
Pride, pomp, and circumstance of glorious war.
And, O you mortal engines, whose rude throats
The immortal Jove's dread clamours counterfeit,
Farewell, Othello's occupation's gone. [III.iii.347–57]

Now the amazing thing in this play, which is a source of difficult exegesis for some interpreters, is that Iago, on two occasions, speaks with another accent and another rhythm than his own. In such a statement as 'Put money in thy purse' or 'Love is just a lust of the blood,' no one can mistake the Iago touch or tone. In thought and expression he is there to the manner born. And in that cold logic with which he presents to Othello the quarrel between Cassio and Montano, a logic which convinces the whole three of them that he is telling the truth, in a masterpiece of ironic understatement that is fundamentally false – in that logic he is the supreme villain. But when he sees Othello coming down the stairs and knows that the poison has done its work, he says this:

Look, where he comes. Not poppy, nor mandragora,
Nor all the drowsy syrups of the world,
Shall ever medicine thee to that sweet sleep
Which thou owedst yesterday. [III.iii.330–3]

We say, 'Why that's a new accent.' That type of speech is like Othello's, but that is just Shakespeare's little trick of making the villain assume the tones of his victim in the moment of capture. It is intentional. He is playing on an organ for a moment of triumph, just for a moment, as Othello plays on it all the time. Iago is mocking Othello.

That great mandragora passage is a wonderful illustration of the music of language. There is little that is original or striking in the thought as such. In bold, bald terms of prose all that Iago says is: 'O, you are not going to sleep so well after this.' That's all. That's the prose of it, but 'Not poppy, nor mandragora' is the poetry of it, and it is accomplished by the music of language.

There is one other illustration. In that same scene, the great Instigation scene, the two utterances are again merged into the one idiom:

IAGO
Patience, I say; your mind perhaps may change.
OTHELLO
Never, Iago. Like to the Pontic sea,
Whose icy current and compulsive course
Ne'er feels retiring ebb, but keeps due on
To the Propontic and the Hellespont,
Even so my bloody thoughts, with violent pace,
Shall ne'er look back, ne'er ebb to humble love,
Till that a capable and wide revenge
Swallow them up. Now, by yond marble heaven,
[*Kneels*] In the due reverence of a sacred vow
I here engage my words.
IAGO
Do not rise yet.
[*Kneels*] Witness, you ever-burning lights above,
You elements that clip us round about,
Witness that here Iago doth give up
The execution of his wit, hands, heart,
To wrong'd Othello's service. Let him command
And to obey shall be in me remorse,
What bloody business ever. [III.iii.452–69]

Iago is saying this in mocking paraphrase, the simulation of Othello's speech and gesture. But apart from these instances, Iago is epigrammatic, rational, gnomic. It is just this restraint, this controlled speech of Iago which never overflows the intellectual limits, it is this which prevents Iago from stepping into the sublimely tragic class of heroes.

To go from Shakespeare to Milton, we pass from a dramatic to an epic genius where the emphasis is more upon periodic movement, upon resonance, upon taxing the resources of language to yield up harmonic combinations; Milton could not make a character talk like Falstaff or like Iago. He wasn't concerned much with the inner exploration of character, with the revelation of subtle and complex moods. His characters talk much alike in style, however different they may be in ideas. Belial, Moloch, and Satan are conceived in the vocal style of Michael, Abdiel, and Raphael, that is, they are blowing trumpets continually, though they summon their hosts to different banners. Milton rarely leaves the rare altitudes of the sublime, and he has given us the most imperial oratory which has ever fallen on human ears. No one knew better how to perpetuate and amplify the blank verse tradition of Marlowe, how to get not merely the sound but the actual taste of words, how to vary stress to avoid monotony, where to place the breathing pause, how to pull out the diapason, how to retard and accelerate the tempo. His freedom in the handling of blank verse is amazing. Though the normal line of blank verse consists of five unrhymed iambics, that is, five stresses in ten syllables, the only element that is constant in his epics is the ten syllables, from which he never departs except by elision. All the other elements are varied. Sometimes there are four stresses, sometimes three, and the perfectly normal line may be found only once out of five or eight or even ten lines in the verse paragraph. An instance of Marlowe's freedom is seen in this line of ten syllables, which has only three rhetorical stresses though the normal mechanics would consist of five: 'And ride in triumph through Persepolis.' An instance of Milton's freedom: 'Eyeless in Gaza, at the mill, with slaves.' There are a few examples where Milton wants to show the effects of disobedience not so much in ideas as in sounds, where nearly every word in the line is stressed, where both accent and quantity are made to crack like the strokes of a whip: 'Rocks, caves, lakes, fens, bogs, dens and shades of death.' The Miltonic tradition is perpetuated by Shelley, Keats, and Tennyson. Tennyson in his *Death of Arthur* was trying to get the full consonantal and vowel resonance of his master: 'So all day long the noise of battle rolled / Among the mountains by the winter sea.' This is a classic example of the imitation of the Miltonic use of the open vowels.

The reason why I like the 'Cargoes' of Masefield is because it is a bit of conscious artistry elaborated and successfully achieved. Everyone knows how certain consonants are elementally associated with certain moods. I have no doubt that a biological theory can be made to fit this natural conjunction of sound and sense. The gutturals abound in the growls, the sibilants and mutes in the oaths, though the s may equally apply to the curse and the caress, the open vowels in epic declamation, the liquids in serenades and lullabies. Take an illustration first from Shakespeare, from Henry IV's soliloquy on sleep. Look at the l's and the s's:

And lulled with sounds of sweetest melody?
O thou dull god why liest thou with the vile
In loathsome beds, and leav'st the kingly couch
A watch case or a common 'larum bell?

Now turn to the most magical of Masefield's short pieces. Notice the breadth of it in spite of its brevity. The first two stanzas are romantic, the third is realistic; the three are in full accord with theme and imagery. He gives us a dip into the past centuries and then we are flung right into the dusty smoky present on board of a dirty British coaster:

Quinquireme of Nineveh from distant Ophir
Rowing home to haven in sunny Palestine,
With a cargo of ivory,
And apes and peacocks,
Sandalwood, cedarwood, and sweet white wine.

Stately Spanish galleon coming from the Isthmus,
Dipping through the Tropics by the palm-green shores,
With a cargo of diamonds,

Emeralds, amethysts,
Topazes, and cinnamon, and gold moidores.

Dirty British coaster with a salt-caked smoke stack,
Butting through the Channel in the mad March days,
With a cargo of Tyne coal,
Road-rails, pig-lead,
Firewood, iron-ware, and cheap tin trays.

It is an excellent example of the sound echoing the sense. After the deluge of liquids and labials in the first two stanzas, we are almost knocked down by the mutes and the gutturals blended with the sibilants in the conclusion.

A good deal of attention today is given to a newly discovered poet, Gerard Manley Hopkins. Hopkins carried on extensive correspondence with Sir Robert Bridges, himself an expert on prosody, and the claim that Hopkins made was that the mechanics of metre must always be subordinated to the sensitiveness of the ear – not a new claim indeed but rather a fresh insistence. Read what you have to say, see where the emphasis naturally falls, and mould the lines accordingly. In such experimentation, the unstressed syllables may be left out and the vacancy filled up by lingering over the stress or by the rhetorical pause. As I indicated, this is not new but a re-emphasis of the value of substitution, which the eighteenth century had forgotten. Tennyson, who was a superb experimenter, gives us a beautiful example of substitution where one word has the time value of two words or three:

Break, break, break,
On thy cold grey stones, O Sea.
And I would that my tongue could utter
The thoughts that arise in me.

There are just three words in the first line but as they stand as independent units of stress, they take as much time in delivery as the seven words of the second line:

Break, break, break,
At the foot of thy crags, O Sea.
But the tender grace of a day that is dead
Will never come back to me.

I might turn now to the Irish dramatist, Synge, for examples of a type of speech which belongs to that borderland between unmeasured prose and metric poetry, where the loveliest rhythms not based on accent come out of selected human speech.

In the first illustration the words actually laugh; in the second, they shed tears.

## [**Meaning and Modernity**]

(Place unknown, 1944 or later)

To try to untangle the many threads in the poetic complexity today might bring back to mind Synge's reference to the string in the *Riders to the Sea*. The string's perished with the salt water and there's a knot in it you wouldn't loosen in a week. Though that time indicated is much too short. And the most pernicious tangle relates to the matter of meaning in poetry. It has had a long history.

The Metaphysicals and the French Symbolists of the late nineteenth century have had an enormous influence upon writers today. The two schools are closely related. The Metaphysicals, Donne, Vaughan, Herbert, Crashaw, made a lot of use of verbal paradox or wit, by taking ideas which were on the surface unrelated, and juxtaposing them, with the result that the reader received a shock as if he were intellectually protesting against irrelevant or contradictory ideas within the same context. Sometimes the figures of speech were not so much paradoxical as bizarre or far-fetched; hence the phrase 'metaphysical conceits,' criticized by Dr Johnson, though Johnson, with his characteristic flashes of illumination, had to concede that occasionally the conceits, though far-fetched, were, in his own words, often worth the carriage, especially when driven by the masters of that mode.

But generally they produced irritation as being unnatural and illogical. The metaphors were mixed, often deliberately, the passion and the mood of sincerity alternated with cynicism and wit and surface brilliance, and the straining for clever and smart effects. They mixed up the styles, the grand manner and the colloquial, even doggerel.

The Symbolists revived a form of this but went a step further, and their followers went not just a step but a mile farther. They took over the paradoxes, the mixtures of styles, but they tended to leave the images unrelated, without any intellectual thread to bind them together. Generally the Metaphysicals could be counted on to supply a general idea, as with Donne, who could run it through his poems. The Symbolists were often satisfied to leave the images unassimilated. And certainly the later disciples of the Symbolists made the medley their most important characteristic, and left their readers at loose ends, often infuriated at their inability to extract any sense or meaning, a vexation which was increased by the demands which the writers made on their readers, first, that meaning was altogether irrelevant, or second, that the reader did not have the requisite intellectual or aesthetic capacity to get to the kernel of the poem, which claim was intellectual arrogance at its most nauseating.

The Freudian psychology, its psychoanalysis, travelled far beyond its field of psychology and psychiatry in its use of method. It gave a powerful stimulus to the commonest method of writing both in fiction and poetry of the last generation, the mode of free association or emotional sequence. Poems became strings of non-governed ideas, that is to say, not governed by any kind of rational design. It issued in a phase of automatic writing; practically anything might emerge from that dark depth called the subconscious. It is said that the films sometimes used that method in shooting a number of dramatic scenes which didn't seem to have much relation to one another, but they were meant to get the audience in an emotional condition for a later more evolved and coordinated act. That free association method in writing has given rise to more irritation and boredom on the part of readers than any technique ever instituted, and more untalented people have surreptitiously got into the hall of creative art by that kind of spurious pass than are countable.

The age has been very strident in its distrust of the rational processes. Occasionally a genius arose who made his life philosophy the deïfication of this subconscious self and the damnation of reason, like D.H. Lawrence, but Lawrence's powerful fiction and his burning poetry could be followed through in their plots and characterizations and verse sequences by the understanding as well as by the feelings. Still as he was the great primitivist of the last generation he lent his support to those who wanted reason to abnegate her position.

On the periphery of those movements were schools like Dadaism and Surrealism where meaning was pitched into the abyss. That mania called Dadaism had its home in Zurich during the First World War, but they were fired out of the place by the shocked inhabitants, so they went to Paris where the colony gave them a home. They issued a manifesto starting with the proclamation 'Dada has no meaning.' 'Art is a private matter ... Any work of art that can be understood is the product of a journalist.' The cult was founded by Tristan Tzara to proclaim utter contempt for the public, and it was launched with a series of practical jokes which outraged people. To show their abhorrence of convention they announced they would hold their first meeting on Easter Friday hoping for a rainy Friday, which it was, and the first speech was made in a graveyard and at night in pouring rain. Finding Zurich too hot or too wet for them they went to Paris, where they engaged a hall and invited the public. Tzara began proceedings by reading a newspaper article aloud while an accomplice kept ringing an electric bell so that no one could hear a word of what he said.

Dada was against all tradition in the arts. A novel was written about contemporary Paris, and to show his contempt of such an established element as local colour, the novelist put into the novel Redskin Indians, mermaids, and unicorns. It was contempt for all popular judgments they were showing, in fact contempt for all judgments except that of the artist himself. It was irresponsibility at its worst. It relieved art, and poetry in particular, of all social value and social function. Behind it all it was contended by the advocates that poetry should be pure poetry, pure and undefiled, the poetry of escapism due to disillusionment, and preoccupation with form to the exclusion of matter.

This repudiation of logic and the normal relationships between ideas, this renunciation of the rational mind, was stimulated by the Freudian craze, to break down the barriers between the conscious and the subconscious life in order to release the subconscious elements for literature and art. The type state was of course the dream, with its unexpected, irrational, and fantastic arrangements. Hence in the waking state automatic writing became a very common exercise. Get away from the personal and conscious volitions. So, the surrealists in art gave examples in Paris by taking cuttings from illustrated papers and pasting them together fortuitously (Max Ernst) or by taking the grained surface of wood or stone to make charcoal rubbings. Later the leader was André Breton, who set up his manifesto in 1924. He called it psychic automatism, a procedure to register dream states, or thought's dictation in the absence of all control exercised by the reason, and outside all aesthetic or moral considerations: 'Empty the mind completely of all familiar associations and get at reality. Get at the dream state with all of its illogicalities.' It is true that Yeats said something like that, but not even Yeats could get away from the feeling of bewilderment when he saw the literary crimes which were committed under the name of that ism and its kindred phobias. The *Poetry* magazine of Chicago had such a phase in the early thirties ...

We certainly have supped full of fads in recent years. Schools have been born, have grown up, and died, some in a decade, some in a year, some in a month. Some day there may be a solid, perhaps, definitive work of literary criticism entitled fads, coteries, cracks, and clacks of the earlier twentieth century. Some of them have been highly controversial, highly entertaining, like stunts in jugglery and acrobatics and a good deal of clowning. Advertising has been used on a tremendous scale to get across the best seller. Dadaism was news for popular consumption though the exponents expressed their scorn for the public.

And was there ever a writer more publicized than Gertrude Stein or any writer more keen to catch the public eye than that renowned lady? Her trip or tour through the United States a few years ago was like a triumphal march, something like Shaw's, who himself is the cleverest salesman of his wares of all the literary artists. The parties given to Gertrude Stein in New York were described in Madrid and Paris and Vienna. She was so conscious of her own public importance that she made a bet with Madeline Carroll that more people would turn to look at her as they walked down Broadway than at Madeline. A third person agreed to accompany them to record the looks and remarks that might be overheard. It is said that Madeline didn't have a chance. She was snowed under. For every one who said 'There's Madeline,' there were ten who said 'Look there's Gert.'

People are still trying to explain the Stein legend. They hesitate to ascribe a piece of sheer and colossal nonsense to a person who had a very clever mind and who in normal moments could write fine and intelligible prose. But thousands of people could write fine and intelligible prose, while very few people were ingenious enough to write meaningless prose and have it accepted as the hidden operations of genius. Besides readers could point to her early work and say: 'There is nothing wrong with that kind of writing.' And admirers like Sherwood Anderson and Hemingway, who were personal friends, claimed that she had influenced their style. When such writers were asked how, they answered that she had taught them the value of repetition, of the short sentence, and a few other things.

When *Portraits and Prayers* came out I made a survey of the reviews of the book in the American and English periodicals, anxious to get to the bottom of the phenomenon to see whether it was a problem for literature or for abnormal psychology. The book was designed to give portraits of Cézanne and Matisse, Eliot, Edith Sitwell, Hemingway, and others. Here is her portrait of Cézanne: 'The Irish lady can say that today is every day. Caesar can say that every day is today, and they say that every day is as they say. In this way we have a place to stay, and he was not met because he was settled to stay. When I said settled to stay

I meant settled to stay. When I said settled to stay I meant settled to stay Saturday.' You may observe there is a little progression there. The day is Saturday, which wasn't mentioned before. 'In this way a month is a month. In this way if in as a month if in as a month where, if in as a month where and there. Believe they have water too.' That remark really does come out of the blue and can't be put down to repetition.

The critics laughed or wept or swore over this book as of later books. One remarked:

> She has not invigorated but debilitated the language by getting rid of connotation. Her only rhetorical device is repetition. She says a thing not twice but twenty times. She would have been more successful if she had stuck to nonsense, deliberate nonsense, child's nonsense. Anyone with a good ear can make pleasant sounds and succession of sounds if he does not bother with sense. The difficult thing is to make equally persuasive sounds that do make sense, which is precisely what all the great stylists have accomplished.

About this time when she was travelling, the members of the Paris colony turned against her. Stein had made some remarks about Dadaism with which she first was in cooperation and sympathy. In a pamphlet called 'Testimony against Gertrude Stein,' they charged her with both not understanding and misrepresenting the artistic life of Dadaism, in her *Autobiography of Alice B. Toklas*. 'Hollow tinsel Bohemianism and egocentric deformation,' said Tristan Tzara of the lady. 'Underneath the baby style it is easy to discern a really coarse spirit, straight clinical megalomania,' wrote Tzara, which remark was wirelessed to New York and came out in the New York papers when Gertrude was attending the afternoon parties in her honour. She replied to the reporters: 'Tzara regards as nonsense anything which does not come within the enclosure of his comprehension.' This gives one some idea of the feuds which go on within the sacred folds. Most of the critic-disciples of Stein took this lame attitude – there must be something behind it all or she wouldn't have such a reputation and be such a brilliant conversationalist. She is very clever in herself, but they showed a lamentable lack of exposition when they tried to explain the alleged hidden profundities.

Louis Bromfield was here last week, and I asked him at a little party what he thought of the literary scene today. The talk came round to Gertrude, whom he knew very well indeed. She was a phenomenon, the most brilliant talker he ever knew. When she came into a room full of guests she was like a high-voltage electric current. Her talk had originality but it was the originality and unexpectedness of a child. It has been called baby talk with infinite repetition. No one in adult life had talked just this way before outside of an asylum. But she never got inside the words; her craziness didn't take the anti-social form. She was a real entertainer, a performer of a spectacular literary stunt.

How much of it is buffoonery and self-promotion? The stories that have been built up around her are very entertaining. Bennet Cerf, who was her publisher, sent her a cheque when she was in France just after the War. He was in a playful mood and wrote out the cheque 'Pay pay pay to Miss Gertrude G.G. Stein Stein S. One thousand dollars dollars dollars. Signed Random House B.C.' The banker in the town wouldn't cash the cheque and Gertrude sent back the cheque to Cerf. 'Dear dear dear Bennett Bennett stop your nonsense and send a sensible cheque.' The style wasn't suited to banking. Stories like that sent Gertrude's sales soaring. It is very difficult to find the dividing line between the genuine and the spurious, between the whole wool and the shoddy. The public liked to be fooled, it is said, but how long can they stand the same joke being perpetrated on them?

She is reported to have given this as a partial explanation of her work. At the end of her American trip her manager, who had been besieged by people to explain Stein's[?] art[?], asked her to give him some kind of a plausible, rational account which he could transmit to the hungry American reading populace. 'Give us a break Gert or they are going to do me in.' She replied, 'If I wrote in normal English prose, however good it was, would I get anywhere? Now thousands are asking: what does Gertrude mean? Why, students and professors are talking about me at the common tables and in the faculty dining rooms,' which of course they were doing. 'Is there anything wrong in publicity? Besides,' she added, 'this is the first time in a century that people have found out that a rose is red.' It certainly made people buy her books and gape at her photograph.

I suppose if one were asked to name two extremes in types of expression among outstanding names today one might instance Gertrude Stein on one side and Hopkins on the other, that is in work which could be taken as characteristic. And the difference may lie in two functions of language. There is the function of denotation, where words are used in their plain scientific or dictionary sense, their primary significance, where the word 'house' means a building with a foundation and rooms and stories of rooms, fireplaces, and baths if any, a place for people to live in. That is, say, the primary meaning. On the other hand you may say, 'O I don't mean that at all. I mean a mansion in the skies, or I mean a love nest, or the human heart, which can enclose a number of individuals in its folds.' Here you have moved away from the primary meaning, that of denotation, and you have imposed upon it a secondary meaning, an associational meaning, a suggestive meaning we call connotation.

Now supposing we get irritated over those secondary images and say, 'O for goodness sake talk sense - a house means a building of wood or brick and not an illuminated manuscript,' you are arguing for plain primary significations. Then to emphasize your protest against suggestive association or too much of it, you say, 'A house is a house, a house is a house, let me tell you that a rose is a rose is a rose is a rose,' and then you present your readers with a volume of three hundred pages which carries out those repetitions not three times but three hundred times. That is the only wisp of intelligence that I can get out of the Stein method, but why a whole book to declare that simple fact? That repetition has become today the last word in banality. It has gone infinitely beyond the artistic needs and justifications. That is what is meant when she has been criticized for debilitating the English language and foisting a piece of folderol on the public.

Certainly the trick got people talking, discussing the art. It is the extreme side of a mode or a technique which is pushed to its most extreme and grotesque forms.

On the other hand there is the danger in the extreme employment of the opposite form, the extravagant use of connotation wherein poetic values largely reside, the suggestive power of words. The Metaphysical poets and the Symbolistic poets stress this secondary value with the adoption of themes that are vague and shadowy yet full of mystical appeal. Of course our language is full of connotation. Take a word like 'rose.' How much more is it than a botanical specimen, how it has entered into the great allegories of our literature. Take a word like 'death.' How much more is it than the departure of breath and pulse from the body. Naturally this goes without debate. There is often a good deal of difficulty of interpretation. One person may get this meaning out of a line, another a different one, but the great mystical and metaphysical poems of literature have a large common zone of interpretation. Realizing this, then, an experimenter might say: 'I am going to take the idea of connotation as a nucleus. I am going to develop it to its limit,' and along come other artists and say, 'We'll go you one better,' until finally the technical apparatus blows into a thousand pieces, and the ideas and emotions intended to be conveyed from the crucible go up in the same blast. A technique of difficulty which within its limits is legitimate enough becomes a technique of confusion, which renders up no significance, no analysis or interpretation of life whatsoever.

We can see the pendulum swinging between what is called pure art and outright propaganda. Again we are dealing with the perils of extremes. Writers have lost the sense of the golden mean. I have heard writers claim that the only subject nowadays worthwhile is the class struggle, having in the background of their minds a totalitarian ideology that has become the most vicious enemy to art and literature ever devised, that there are penalties prescribed if you don't swing into line. That is putting fetters on the human spirit, when some external authority demands and decrees that you must write in a certain way. You may have propaganda and didacticism fraying the sleeves of the texture so that the art is lost, or you may have them on such an elevated and passionate level that the moral and social work may be done without the reader being conscious of it. A writer dealing with a spate of invective that rushed out from certain quarters in the First World War composed these four lines:

God heard the embattled nations sing and shout;
Gott strafe England and God save the king,
God this, God that, and God the other thing,
Good God, said God, I've got my work cut out.

You may have that kind of propaganda or I may assert Eternal Providence 'and justify the ways of God to men,' or the prophecies of Isaiah or the parables of Jesus.

At the other end is the attempt to relieve poetry not only of propaganda but also of ideas. And the most irritating of all the mannerisms was the exploitation of private imagery. It might have been a personal joke known perhaps only to one other person or to a very few. Edith Sitwell tried out a few of her tricks, like her use of the phrase 'Emily-coloured hands.' 'Why Emily?' someone asked. 'O Emily, that's the name of my maid.' Then again 'Martha-coloured scabious.' 'Martha?' 'O that's the name of an old nurse named Martha who wore a scabious coloured dress.' Such tricks became the rage till not only the critics, reviewers, but the book-buying public got fed up with the silly obscurities, which had too much of the colour of patent medicine advertisements. The writer's sense of humour must have been pretty diluted to have resort to such fakirism. Critics asked the writers, 'What are you constructing? We appreciate the occasional exquisiteness and delicacy of the parts on display, but what are you trying to assemble, a clock or a sewing machine?' There was no answer except that communication was irrelevant. The common people were ignored by a type of artistic snobbery and pretension which was infuriating to say the least.

One of the most extreme exponents of this arrogance was Pound, who worked out a private symbolism of his own, drawn from the minor classics and from medieval writers. He used names without representing the faiths possessed by the men named. He answered his critics and his humble readers alike by saying that he gloried in his splendid isolation: 'I mate with my free kind upon the crags.' He delved into the remote works of the Middle Ages so profusely that even Eliot of all men had to take a crack at him with this statement: 'Pound is attracted to the Middle Ages apparently by everything except that which gives them their significance.' No one was surprised later when Pound, to show his aristocratic aloofness from the society of ordinary people, joined Mussolini and his fascist crew, and later was saved from the extreme sentence of the Allied Courts on the ground that he had gone crazy.

Pound's statement was: 'I beg you, my friendly critics / Do not set about to procure me an audience, / I mate with my free kind upon the crags.' That is to say that the doctrine is that a poet should talk only to himself, that he has nothing to say or offer to the community in which he lives.

The disciples of Eliot, Pound, Hopkins, outdid their masters at first. Auden, Spender, Day Lewis were obsessed with the fad, deliberately constructing barriers between their own thought and the interpretation of their readers. They used Hopkins's ellipses, and Eliot's dislocations and remote allusiveness, to render their meanings opaque. Auden would have a private joke with his friend Spender and would put it in his poems, and naturally only Spender had the key. Sometimes he would write a longish poem without any light breaking through for the reader until he came to the last line: 'Of course, you know the farm was in Devonshire,' when hitherto there wasn't even the suggestion of a barn or a pump, a cow or a hen. It is true that the lines themselves often were euphonic, and the apologists for this genre would claim that the rhythms themselves were the justification, but that is reducing the art of poetry to the level of the nursery. The fad contained in itself the seed of its own dissolution. That kind of verse is easy to write because no one can question the path that freedom of association may take. An editor who adheres to it may be the most gullible person in the world.

A short time ago (*Time*, July 17, 1944) editor Max Harris of a little magazine of Adelaide called the *Angry Penguins* introduced the work of a new poet named Ern Malley with a thirty-page rhapsody explaining with deadly and Dadaistic earnestness why Malley was 'one of the two giants of contemporary poetry.' Then an Australian airman, Lieutenant Jas MacAuley (who fought in New Guinea), and Corporal Harold Stewart revealed that they were Ern Malley. Forced to kill an afternoon's leave, they created poet Malley by leafing through the *Oxford Dictionary of Quotations* and other inspirational works and lifting whatever hit their fancy. Here are some samples of Malley's masterpieces:

> There have been interpolations, false syndromes
> Like a rivet through the hand
> Such deliberate suppressions of crisis as
> 'Footscray' [A Melbourne suburb whose malodorous tanneries
> are the subjects of malodorous jokes.]
> I have split the infinitive
> Beyond is anything.

Hoaxers MacAuley and Stewart confessed that they culled the first three lines of 'Culture as Exhibit' from the U.S. report on mosquito breeding grounds. Here are the lines: 'Swamps, marshes, barrowpits, and other / Areas of stagnant water serve / As breeding grounds.' But MacAuley and Stewart were out to kill more than an afternoon. As Ern Malley they wrote: 'For some years we have observed with distaste the gradual decay of meaning and craftsmanship in poetry. Harris and other *Angry Penguins* writers represent the Australian outcrop of a literary fashion prominent in England and America, a distinctive feature of which seemed to us to render its devotees insensible of its absurdity.'

The editor had to reply as the hoax was being printed all over America. It got into *Time*. And the Surrealist Harris made the lamest explanation, which put him further to confusion. He wrote: 'If 50,000,000 monkeys with 50,000,000 typewriters tapped 50,000,000 years, one of them would produce a Shakespeare sonnet. I hope MacAuley and Stewart have not produced such a phenomenon. It is not their claim of exposure but time that tells the story. Time will explain that a myth is sometimes greater than its creators.' He must have been hard put to it to find such an explanation. It would have been much more to his credit had he admitted the hoax and joined in the laugh at himself.

But the form of complete freedom of association will always remain open to such wide attack. It is not really a form, an art form, but a mannerism which has assumed a worldwide notoriety. That claim to complete freedom is on a par with the complaint of the inexperienced tennis player that the net interfered with his game.

It is interesting to watch some of the more able writers renounce their fads. Some of them do, some of them don't. The outstanding English poets of the new generation a few years ago were social reformers. They had a message for their times which they were conveying in their prose but failed to deliver in their verse. And the social propaganda, the thing nearest to their hearts, won out. And their later work showed a return to sense and meaning. What made those two Australian soldiers mad was to see a group of men in control of a magazine spending their time in the midst of a terrible war printing absolute gibberish and trying to pass it off as significant literature.

It is very hard to see the value of any artistic medium which is utterly contemptuous of communication. It is illogical because the very process of publication, on which all are agreed, argues the desirability of an audience, however restricted. And it is essentially inartistic because expression as such is a challenge to someone or other to offer criticism or appreciation. To repeat, this does not imply that a meaning may not be difficult. A certain measure of difficulty is often an aid to emotional suggestion, but the difficulty implies the existence of a problem, which implies the possibility of a solution.

There has been a decided swing away from Eliot by writers who had become weary of his early nihilism, just as the later Eliot swung away from his earlier self to some extent, his continual mood of apathy and negation, his poetry of dry bones and churchyards and hollow skulls, that circling procession of images of decay and dust and death, even if the writer is doing it in protest against the living death condition of the world. An indication of this revolt is seen in Day Lewis's volume in which he criticizes himself as well as his fellow craftsmen for neglecting the people, the readers:

*Overture to Death*

I fear this careful art
Would never storm the sense ...

When madmen play the piper
And knaves call the tune.
Honesty's the right passion,
She must call to her own.
Let yours be the start and stir
Of a flooding indignation
That channels the dry heart deeper
And sings through the dry bone.

And the meaning is very pointed in lines written in fear of death by an air raid:

We cannot meet
Our children's mirth at night
Who dream their blood upon a darkening street.

Stay away Spring,
Since death is on the wing
To blast our seed and poison everything.

If you go through an account of the great poetry of the world you will find material, content, ideas in abundance. The poets expressed moral judgments too in a great deal of their poetry. You cannot get pure poetry in the absolute sense as you may get pure music, because words unlike notes are not abstractions. They possess meanings in their own right and in their context. And to limit the function of words to their sounds alone reduces poetry to mouth music which might belong to the speech of an Ojibway completely lacking in meaning to the hearer. Poetry is not just a volatile essence abstracted from substance. It is a very complex process, which instead of excluding, abstracting this, that, and the other alleged non-poetic elements assimilates them.

About the most sensible account of this controversial subject that I have come across recently is given by Day Lewis in his *A Hope for Poetry*:

> To the idea of poetry as exclusive, esoteric, a-moral, the private affair of the poet, moving in a different world from prose, creative of its own reality, I should oppose the idea of poetry as catholic, diverse in function, moral, everyone's business (potentially at any rate), assimilating, not rejecting prose meaning, a way of synthesizing and communicating reality ... [I]t is better to err on the side of catholicity than of exclusiveness: that poetry's language is, as Hopkins said, a heightening of the idiom of the common speech of its age. We refuse no contact with life. We enter it. It should be rooted in common and garden life.

I might mention another quality in contemporary poetry, the mixture of vocabularies, the grave rhetoric mixed with the colloquial and slangy. The French writer Laforgue specialized in this mode. Pound used it a lot. Browning had this conversational style before them all, and of course Donne had it long before. Eliot acknowledged his debt here to Laforgue. With this goes the manner of teaming up great or at least remote names of the past with those of the present. Pound laid this erudition on with a steam shovel till people got weary of his pedantry. Eliot had the gift of assimilation which Pound didn't possess.

## 'The Immortal Memory'

(*Daily News*, [St. John's, Newfoundland] 26 January 1949: 3)

I cannot begin to express adequately my appreciation of the honour of being invited to come down to Newfoundland to propose this toast. When I received the official invitation from the

President of the St Andrew's Society, my first thought was the responsibility attached to the undertaking. I couldn't see how any speech of a half-an-hour, more or less, could justify a total flight of 3000 miles, and my next thought was that this was an expression of downright Newfoundland hospitality, an invitation to a homeboy to come back and be with his ain folk for a few days. That is the main thrill for me tonight. This is my fourth visit to Newfoundland since I left in 1907, and had the gods, who control the economic as well as the moral laws, been a little less stringent in their economy, the visits would have been more frequent and more prolonged. I cannot get over the feeling that I am a citizen of two worlds. I revere my adopted country, which like a foster mother (or shall I say an aunt) has given me a home, security, a modest stipend, though not so modest an income tax. On the other hand, there is the natural mother by ties of birth and sentiment. The point is often put to me in the form of a question: 'Are you a Canadian who has come from Newfoundland, or a Newfoundlander who has come to Canada?' I don't acknowledge the distinction implied except to answer that I can toast the health of Canada and Newfoundland, just as a Newfoundland Scotchman can give the double toasts to this country and to Scotland as either the land of his birth or that of his ancestors. In a sense, we are living in two separate suites in the same apartment block, and both the aunt and the mother can be saluted on both cheeks.

Another inducement to make this visit was that the subject tonight has always been close to my academic interest and to my heart. I know that it would be next to impossible to give an address on Burns which would convey new material or throw fresh light on his character or his poetry. For a century and a half now Burns Clubs and Societies have been holding the anniversaries of the Bard, reciting his poems, singing his songs, sounding his praises, and addresses have been delivered until now there is not much to be added except by way of a footnote. But that is no reason why we should not go on reciting his poems, singing his songs, any more than we should stop singing the songs of Schubert, for Burns is to poetry what Schubert is to music, Burns dividing the lyric crown only with Shelley in British poetry and, in respect of lyrics challenging musical composition for their setting, having no one to share his throne in the literary realm of the world.

That may look like an extravagant assertion springing out of the proceedings of an anniversary, a kind of a family or clan prejudice, but that is the considered judgment of most of the literary historians. An Oxford professor of poetry claimed recently in an address in Toronto that he couldn't summon up enough heart or energy to dispute any Scotchman who said that Burns was the greatest poet that ever lived.

There are qualifications here of course, but as this is Burns Nicht they should be passed over lightly. It would be irrelevant to place him on a parity with Shakespeare for the simple reason that Shakespeare was first and foremost a dramatist, and Burns wrote no drama in the technical sense, and it would be equally irrelevant to place him with Milton for Burns wrote no epics in the technical sense. One must get common ground and the same measuring units to do the gauging, but there is a ground of tremendous area where Burns is supreme in English poetry, and though it is in lyrical acres, so to speak, where he reaps the richest harvest, yet it is amazing how fruitful was his cultivation of other fields.

We know that his literary gods were the outstanding satirists of the eighteenth century, that he worshipped at the shrines of Dryden and Pope just as Byron did, but he could equal both those masters in the one field in which they were pre-eminent, that of scorching satire. He knew that they got their effects by the unsurpassed use of the heroic couplet, by the use of the last phrase or even the last word of the second line. But he didn't make himself a slave of their special metre. He took another form, and while it was not original with him any more than the heroic couplet was original with Dryden and Pope, he appropriated it to himself by the masterly use of the scorpion sting in the final lines of the stanzas by which he consigned the censorious hypocrites, not to oblivion (his victims might have wished he had), but rather to a purgatorial immortality. Pope never did anything better in stinging a victim than Burns did in his extempore epigram on the Lord Advocate in the Court of Session:

He clenched his pamphlets in his fist,
He quoted and he hinted,
Till, in a declamation mist,
His argument he tint it.
He gaped for't; he graped for't,
He fand it was awa' man;
But when his common sense came short,
He eked out wi' law, man.

A phrase like 'declamation mist,' tinting the argument, and the comparison between common sense and the law of the day would have won the plaudits of Dryden and Pope.

There was only one writer in the next generation who could match his art in this respect, and that was Byron. If William Fisher, Black Russell, Moodie, and the others had only known how their names would come down the generations in the way they have, they might have abated their zeal in getting Robin so often on the cutty stool, however much from orthodox standards he may have deserved that place of confession and hypothetical repentance.

And of equal merit with the satires are his dramatic narratives. He could pack his homespun philosophy, his wit, his probing analysis of motives, his tenderness and humanity into his lines, by a mode of expression which even the great Romantics hadn't learned. Burns's poetry was the first rich outcropping of real humour since the Elizabethans. Wordsworth and Shelley, great as they were in their crusading approaches to poetry, had no humour, Wordsworth especially being as devoid of it as one of Milton's archangels. Indeed, it might be said, as it is actually, that no sustained and genuine humour had entered English verse for 150 years before Burns, and then it came in a flood. Wit, yes, in abundance, but before his time practically no humour.

Burns introduced this quality in a novel and difficult way. He did not satisfy himself with just the easy conventional manner of taking types comic in themselves and hence giving him an initial advantage, but he took traditional themes generally considered as serious and to be treated in a sublime manner. The Miltonic approach dominated English literature down to the time of Tennyson and even after. Burns didn't wait for the twentieth century to invert the treatment of old themes. Burns handled the conceptions of the Auld Licht with uproarious levity or biting scorn. Theological ideas which dwelt at length upon the sovereignty of God but ignored his Fatherhood might be rebutted in lengthy treatises which might never be read except by the Divines of the day and not by many of those. Burns turned them inside out, made targets out of them, ran high explosives through them, and the world has been listening to the echoes of the detonations ever since. He brought the Devil up from Pandemonium, examined him with a superb piece of descriptive and humorous analysis, and put the old fellow under a microscope as if he were a human bacillus. The last time that Satan was seen in the form of a star or a planet was when Meredith trained a telescope upon him on a starry night in the celebrated poem 'Lucifer in Starlight.' Since then Satan has forfeited not only those qualities of ambition and design which made him such a picturesque study in moral dynamics, but also his mass. He has become the classical example of degradation of energy. And also the etiquette of admission into Heaven and Hell has changed. Both realms have taken on the character of big public museums with the doors thrown wide open but extending a special invitation to the antiquarian. Burns anticipated many aspects of this modern view. 'The Address to the Devil' is sheer Burns. It is so original in treatment that it is difficult to trace its genealogy.

His excursions into narrative verse were most fruitful. In fact, of all his long poems it would be hard to place any one ahead of 'Tam O'Shanter.' I have been greatly interested in the recent assessments of Burns's genius by the scholars, and I find that 'Tam' is regarded generally as the greatest of his works, even greater than 'The Cotter's Saturday Night,' as fine as that is, but other poets of the late eighteenth century in England might have written it or at least have approximated it, with slight changes in locale – Goldsmith for instance – but none could have written 'Tam.' It is as much Burns as his dark eyes and black hair. There was nothing like it anywhere in the previous history of narrative verse for gusto, mirth, high spirits, devil-may-care abandon, and for the speed of those four beats to the line which travels like a jet. And yet though we could select a single poem and give it pre-eminence, Burns's most important gift to the world was his contribution to song. We know him best through his lyrics in Johnson's *Musical Museum* and Thompson's *Selected Songs*. Johnson and Thompson came to him with Scotch airs, some of them without words and some with inadequate words, and Burns undertook to revise and limber up the language or create new lyrics. We have more than three hundred of them, the finest aggregation of lyrics to be read or sung in the world's treasury – love songs, drinking songs, ballads, elegies, patriotic songs – the classification is almost inexhaustible. The undercurrent was his love of freedom, of honest labour, of personal independence, and of the simplicities and essentials of humanity.

I should like to mention here the remarkable and peculiar appeal which the vernacular has over the merely literary, or shall I say the scholastic expression. The Scotch claim that there are no authentic English synonyms for many of their terms. Gloaming is not twilight though the physical or optical effect may be the same. He met her in the twilight, 'Well, what about it?' the Scot might reply. He met her in the gloamin', 'Well, that's another matter.' A 'chiel' or a 'bairn' carries a connotation a wee bit different from that of a 'child.' 'Are the children all in?' the mother says to the father at the fall of night, and the father, sinking deeper into his chair and gazing more abstractedly at the smoke rings from his pipe, says – 'Oh, there's no hurry, they'll be back in a little while.' But 'Are the bairns all in?' and daddy immediately puts on his cap and goes after them. This happens especially when the question is made all the more musical by the pulling out of the tremolo stops. It is this familiar use of the vernacular, richly endowed with associations rooted in the soil, that Burns took as his poetic capital. He used words like musical notes, and he built up on them both libretto and score. I was talking some time ago to a professor of poetry in the University of Aberdeen, and he was putting up a claim that 'Auld Lang Syne' was the most nostalgic song ever written. Of course he was Scotch, and one of my English friends said, 'What about "Home Sweet Home?"' 'Oh,' he said, '"Auld Lang Syne" is poetry and "Home Sweet Home" is not,' and he went into a long analysis of the two songs, claiming that in 'Auld Lang Syne' we had verse equal to the music, and in 'Home Sweet Home' the words were too sentimental and undistinguished, and did not reach the musical setting. Well, I am not an authority by any means on music, but I do know this – that over the range of thousands of songs which have come down to us, the vast proportion of the songs as words do not measure up to the songs as music in the sense of combination of notes. To take an air which has survived centuries and write a lyric equal to it is a most difficult accomplishment and is very rare. The words which are set to the great classical productions, as you know, are often thin and lacking in evocative quality, but they gain a kind of vicarious value from the music. The reason, I suppose, is that the musician if he composed the words may not have been a poet, or the person other than the musician who set the words didn't have the lyrical fire. The music has a way of tyrannizing over the words. I am of course referring to genuine songs and not to the monstrosities wheezing out of the jukeboxes, where both music and words have found today a new low or new high in the record of mass laryngitis.

But in Burns we have the complete marriage of the two parties. What he did to the national folklore is immeasurable in its value. Airs which might have dispersed and died were kept alive by his vitality. He did the same work for song that Shakespeare did for the poetic drama. There were two forms, straight drama as represented by Ben Jonson and represented today by Shaw and Somerset Maugham, straight drama in that it intentionally excluded romantic elements of the harmonies of language, and there was straight or pure poetry, which steered clear of the realistic area. Shakespeare took the two and made each revitalize and enhance the other. So the national bard of Scotland did just that. He took two forms more separated possibly from each other than poetry and drama – two arts, music and the verbal lyric – and he combined them with such power and beauty that even the historians of other lands confess they haven't an equal to him in their literature.

It has often been pointed out that Burns's mode of composition differed from that of the Romantic poets of England, in fact from that of verse writers generally. He would listen to someone humming an air and, fascinated by it, he would learn it and sing it to himself over and over. He took some time to do it, and I understand that, while he had a fair bass voice, it wasn't anything extraordinary. Then he would write the poem, or if the air had words he would revise them, but it was the tune which came first. With a writer like Wordsworth or Shelley, the emotion was followed by the poem without going through the mediating process. This is a very interesting point because some of the greatest lyricists of the world had very little ear for music in the normal orthodox sense of music. Milton and Browning had that ear, it is true, but many who were known principally for lyrics had little or none, like Shelley and Tennyson. Neither had Swinburne. Of all the English poets whose verse depended largely upon sound, Swinburne would rank very high indeed, but he could hardly tell one note from another. And even William Butler Yeats, the greatest poet of this century writing in English, confessed in a lecture some years ago in Toronto, that he knew nothing of music, and look what lyrics the man wrote! And the Canadian Bliss Carman, perhaps the most rhythmic of all the poets of his generation, said that he could only identify the song 'God Save the King' because people stood up when they sang it and they didn't have to stand with other songs. Of course, one could match every writer here mentioned with another who had musical appreciation, but the result remains that the two arts in some respects are distinct, one dealing with the music of words and the other with the music of notes.

With Burns, however, we have a man most susceptible to tunes, to simple folk airs. Indeed he was haunted by them, but this susceptibility to a folk song is one thing and the susceptibility to a complex, intricate symphony is another. It is that first susceptibility that Burns possessed and really all that he needed for his great work.

I should like to give just two instances which are typical. The last great lyric he composed was the result of a tune. Just before his death he asked his friend Jessie Lewars, who had come to nurse him in his fatal illness, to play him her favourite tune. She did so with a gay lilting melody – 'The robin cam to the wren's nest, and keekit in, and keekit in.' Burns hummed it, altered the tempo and almost at once produced – 'O wert thou in the cauld blast, / On yonder lea, on yonder lea!' He was always experimenting with tempo, discovering how a gay tune could be made into a serious and pathetic one by slowing down the movement.

Another instance is this. Burns stated that he had ever been fascinated by an old tune called 'Hay Tuttie Taitie.' He said in a letter to George Thompson, 'I am delighted with many little melodies which the learned musicians despise as silly. But "Hey Tuttie Taitie" accompanied by Fraser's hautboy fills my eyes with tears.' 'There is a tradition,' he goes on to say, 'that the song was Bruce's March at the Battle of Bannockburn.' That tradition, we know, is without foundation, but we do know that 'Tuttie Taitie' was the spirited air of a Jacobite song which may have been composed about the year 1718. It runs:

Fill, fill your bumpers high,
Drain, drain your glasses dry,
Out upon him, fye, oh fye,
That winna do't again.
When you hear the trumpet sound,
Tuttie Taitie to the drum,
Up your swords and down your guns
And to the rogues again.

Burns got his start from this air, but certainly his idea from the Bannockburn field. Burns's friend, John Syme, gives an account of the poet's 'Ode to Bannockburn': 'In 1793,' he writes, 'we set out on horseback. It took him by the moor-road, where savage and desolate regions extended wide around. The sky was sympathetic with the wretchedness of the soil. It became lowering and dark. The winds sighed: the lightnings gleamed: the thunder rolled. Burns enjoyed the awful scene. He spoke not a word, but seemed wrapt in meditation. What do you think he was about? He was charging the English army along with Bruce. Next day he produced me the famous address of Bruce at Bannockburn.'

I never think of 'Scots wha hae' without thinking of the Englishman who went with his golfing outfit to the golf course which is on the field of Bannockburn. He observed that the players, all but himself, were Scotchmen, and he remarked to his caddie, 'How is it, caddie, that they are so few Englishmen on this course? All I see are Scotchmen,' to which the caddie, noticing that the Englishman was a bit of a dub at golf, replied, 'Ah weel, sir, if you keep on diggin' into the turf with your mashie the way you're doin', I hae nae doots you'll soon uncover a braw puckle of 'em.' That story illustrates another point which characterizes Burns, the peculiar appeal which the vernacular has over the merely literary, or shall I say, the scholastic expression. Translate that phrase into 'a vast number' or 'a goodly host' and all the juice is extracted from the mutton.

It is claimed that the nature of the Lowland Scot has been so explored by Burns that there isn't a facet of his personality left out of the picture. Burns's poems mirror the social, economic, political, and religious life of his day. I put this question to my same friend, the Aberdonian professor: 'Why is it that most of the stories about Scotchmen concern their alleged, I say their alleged, parsimoniousness?' *Punch*, for instance, as you know, always ran a column with its famous illustrations on British characteristics. *Punch* was subject to epidemics, the rash following a definite graph. One year it was the Yorkshireman who came in for it, then it was the Welshman, then the Irishman, then the Cockney, but the Scotchman came in for the heaviest pasting. I referred to a story now quite old and repeated with many variants. *Punch* had the English people laughing over the Aberdonian who came to London, saw a penny on the road, dived for it, was run over by the tram and killed, and the coroner's jury brought in a verdict of death through natural causes. The Aberdonian professor countered: 'That describes a trait grossly exaggerated. It isn't parsimoniousness. It is just thrift, economy, putting away the pennies for a rainy day,' and so on, and he added, 'If you claim that Burns is the representative poet of Scotland why should parsimoniousness be lacking in his pen portraits of Scotchmen as such. It was just thrift.' The two best-known poets of Scotland, Sir Walter Scott and Burns, were as generous as Santa Claus in instinct, but as for Burns, what could anyone do if he had to earn a living out of the farming conditions under which he worked? Any generalization has a weak link in the chain. We forget that the word 'general' does not mean absolute, and we are always on dangerous ground when we talk about national characteristics such as economy when it really springs out of an oatmeal necessity. I was reminded of a story related to me by my wife concerning a grocer who lived in a town in Ontario where she was brought up. She said that on going into the grocery store one day to make a purchase she noticed a large placard just inside the door carrying this notice: 'Credit, yes, we give credit but only to people seventy years and over and accompanied by their parents.' I thought this story too good to be true, so I took a trip to the town, went into the store, saw the same proprietor and the same sign. I asked him his name. He said, 'My name's Murphy.' Well, that showed me how a generalization may be open to exceptions. The name might just as easily have been Jones or Smith as Murphy or Rob Roy MacIntosh. So, gentlemen of the St Andrew's Society, let that slanderous formula against the Scotch character be dismissed with the contempt it deserves, and let me conclude with a remark or two about Burns's work.

Apart from the legitimate drama and the traditional epic, Burns's range was exceedingly wide. And that is all the more remarkable when we know that most of his poems were woven out of his personal experiences. Everything was grist for his mill. He resembles Thomas Hardy in this respect, that a raw particular observation or a feeling became transmuted into precious metal. He ran to rhyme and rhythm because he couldn't help it. On one day he could puncture a theological dogma, a sermon in which the preacher treated his congregation to a description of the tortures of the damned. On another day he could take you inside of a cottage and show you the simple fare of an honest tenant farmer. On another he could pronounce a grace over haggis, though let me observe just here that I have attended some Burns's dinner celebrations where by a glance at the plates I could see that the homage paid to the national dish was largely theoretic. But let that observation pass if you will. On another day he could inscribe a few lines of gratitude which would make the Earl of Glencairn known to the future as one who had befriended the poet. On another he could turn his sympathies towards a field mouse or a daisy, and on another he would give the brush-off to a parasite, whether human or insect, and on another he would turn his metrical attention to Jean or Mary or Bess, and make those local characters the perpetual heroines of song.

## [**The Function of a University**]

(Address at the Installation of the Chancellor and of the President, Memorial University of Newfoundland, St John's, 18 October 1952)

I wish first to express a deep sense of honour at being invited down to my native heath to deliver an address on this most historic occasion. It is historic in that it is the founding of a University in the complete sense which, if I can assess the calibre of Newfoundlanders, will develop into a great institution of learning. The occasion is also unique in that it has a double function – the installation in the same ceremony of two men of such distinction, who have been associated so long with the interests of Newfoundland, Chancellor Lord Rothermere and President Raymond Gushue. That is a happy combination.

I am also bringing a message both personal and official, from President Sidney Smith of the University of Toronto. As a former teacher of President Gushue, he wishes to convey to him his warm pedagogical greetings; as a President representing his institution, he transmits to your Chancellor and President and to your University his administrative best wishes for your future.

For myself, let me repeat, it is a joy to be on Newfoundland soil again, after an interval of three years, and to see the faces of so many friends in this audience, and to breathe the atmosphere which is as native to me as it was more than thirty years ago when I left the shores to go to the University of Toronto. It is like coming home or (shall I say?) going from one room to another in the same house.

I must confess that I found some difficulty in selecting a title for this address, for I realized that anything I might say about the function of a University has been said before. But restatements are always necessary since we are apt to get into the habit of forgetting or glossing over the embodied truths.

We are all making a common journey, an uncertain and dangerous one. We are reading every day about humanity at the crossroads. Every scientist is talking about the gulf ahead of us which must be bridged. It is at once a physical and a spiritual gulf, and all kinds of workers are needed in that supreme engineering.

If we were living in a Utopia, we would be building ivory towers along our coasts instead of lighthouses. The lighthouse is necessary because the sea is rough, and the harbour is not only a destination for trade but a haven for security. Life is ever a sequence of calls and answers, and I am sure that no breed of people understands that more vitally than the Newfoundland race, familiar with the full significance of an SOS in a storm. Nothing can stir the blood more than that little trinity of letters. The call and the answer! Men have been hailing objects – reefs, promontories, icebergs, submerged steel. They have been hailing one another, friends and strangers, across centuries and continents. The dead have chimed in with the living and the living with the dead. The scientists have been tapping to one another through laboratory walls, and how the history of medicine has illustrated that process. Everyone is asking – 'what have you found?' But the highest question of all is – 'what are you going to do with what you have found?' And here philosophy, the social sciences, and literature in general must earmark for special attention the humane character of the discovery, whether it is shown by direct impression or oblique implication. A scientific result always stands in need of a physician to supervise a moral operation.

The University, I believe, speaks for this full expression of the human spirit, where the intellectual and moral issues in their highest sense are in alliance. This point must always be presented because in the last forty years we have gone through a destructive period where the very essence of the University idea has been challenged and spurned. A totalitarian gospel has been preached to the world with such unambiguous frankness that it literally and metaphorically disarmed the democratic audiences. The principle that truth should be pursued for its own sake was put on the level of a medieval superstition, a kind of Christian senility. It is very significant that such a gospel began with the burning of books, the imprisonment, torture, exile, and death of the leading scientists and writers. The first blows fell on the teachers and preachers.

It is against such a monstrous assertion that a free institution like a University sets its face. To repeat the theme, it presents a gentleman's agreement between science and the humane studies. Without narrowing the definition of the latter, it does emphasize through the teaching of literature that the greatest stories of our race revolving around the most revered and loved names in the history of life have been concerned with elemental justice and freedom and truth.

Therefore, at the beginning of every University term, the teachers have no other recourse than to offer without apology the same principles of academic faith – the free prosecution of ideas, the right to form an independent judgment in conformity with evidence. One would think that this battle had been fought and won centuries ago, that the issue might have been closed once and for all, except as a matter of doctrinaire discussion. But the issue *does* remain open, for we have witnessed in this generation a huge step back into the dark ages – many an instance when a scientist could not dare to record a reaction in a test-tube until first he could prove to the authorities that the result did not conflict with a twisted ideology.

The least that a university requires of its students is their honest industry and the exercise of unfettered intelligence upon their tasks, and a becoming modesty attending the spirit of inquiry. That spirit tries to travel a golden mean between stagnation and a brash, uncritical acceptance of novelty for its own sake. Above all, the governing attitude is that of a reasonable toleration. A stand-pat position makes no progress because it becomes blind to its own origins - because it fails to recognize that what is now a settled and respectable routine was once a cause fought on the barricades by ragged battalions. That is the lesson of toleration for the new. Give a belief its right of expression, its demand for a hearing, but after that, examination and criticism by all means. On the other hand, there is the capricious attitude which is contemptuous of tradition, not realizing the multitude of speculations which have gone the way of bubbles and fads.

All of us have blind spots which we sometimes ignore. The very concentration on a focus blinds the eye to everything but the illuminated point, and we forget how tremendously vital to science and literature is the vast penumbra, the half-tones, the guesses, the shadows, the gropings in a world but dimly realized. How often do we exclaim - why, the incredible thing has happened! Those figures in the shadows have walked out into the light. The mark of the educated man is not in his boast that he has built his mountain of facts and stood on the top of it, but in his admission that there may be other peaks in the same range with men on the top of them, and that, though their views of the landscape may be different from his, they are nonetheless legitimate. Without the adventurer there would be no exploration, but whenever the fog comes in, the wise navigator slows down and doubles his watch. A withheld judgment is not a case of suspended animation.

May I now add a few specific applications.

The University keeps a watchful eye on a number of student types: one who says, 'I know nothing about the subject but it is my profound opinion'; another who every night goes to sleep with one set of convictions and wakes up with another; and a third, quite rare, who with a terrific thirst for knowledge of all sorts asks for more subjects than are on the curriculum, and develops a blurred and watery vision which sees men as trees walking; and a fourth who, limiting his vision to a microbe or – let us say – to etymology as if it were the whole of literature, forgets that there are other teachers and investigators in adjoining rooms and clinics. The intensity of that insight is of great importance, naturally: the danger lies in the unconsidered isolation.

Specialists are like parents – their subjects are their children, to whom they give their jealous protection and encouragement, and the students who study such subjects, quite affectionately think that the parents are better than those who are fathering other broods, and when those rivalries become acute, the University has to exercise its role of a United Nations Organization in miniature to achieve peaceful and successful cooperation. It must continue to play that role – a great agency to place the humanities and sciences in good stride along the same or parallel highways.

This is, however, only one side of an introduction to a University. The students come to make it their home for a period ranging from one year to four or more, depending upon post-graduate aspirations or upon conditions other than these. The University undertakes to offer intellectual nourishment. Some of the food may be hard to chew and digest, but the difficulty is scaled according to principles long known to experts in dentition and digestive physiology. Part of the food may be bitter but, we hope, not sour. There are no ration cards to distribute. The supply is limited only by their capacity to assimilate it. There is an abundance of products, some natural, some synthetic. The University now becomes their host, and the meals are varied, so much so indeed that there may be a bewildering hesitation over the courses and the individual plates. The host is quite indulgent in this respect. The students are encouraged to lift the covers off the dishes and inspect the contents. More than that, there are preliminary courses prepared which they can taste and, if the taste pleases them, the course may be made a steady diet. If it does not, they can tell the host, who will inform the cook of their idiosyncrasy.

I have often wondered at the parallel between the physical and mental capacities. In fact, either side of our natures may be illustrated by similes drawn from the other. I have found that students in the University of Toronto, for instance, have certain allergies and immunities. Some claim that their reasoning powers are good but their memories are poor, and vice versa. I remembered a claim made by a professor in mathematics that he could tell by the look of a student whether he would succeed or fail in mathematics. He said the face never was mistaken. He pointed out to me a man who was ploughed twice in geometry. 'Why,' I said, 'that person led his class in theology.' 'Quite true,' he replied, 'I advised him, when he came in to see me, to go into theology. I could tell by the glare in his eyes.' I use this illustration just to show that, though there may have been a blind spot in the eyes of that theologian for geometry, there might likewise be a blind spot in the eyes of the geometrician for theology. There are philosophers who are allergic to languages, and scientists who can get little out of pure letters. And there are artists and writers who are content to dwell in their ivory towers and look at their own shadows on the walls. These limitations may be inevitable, like the physical blind spots, but what should be and could be avoided are the spots of prejudice and intolerance. Behind all those specializations and varieties of points of view there should always be conceded the significance of a cultural and civilizing process designed to promote the interest of truth.

We know that any given fact is not a static object found to be self-contained at the moment of its discovery. It is alive and vocal, calling out for its immediate family, its blood relations. All its cousins, near and far removed, come in to take a look at its face, its complexion, its pulse, to find out what position it should occupy in the family circle. It enters a world of functions and values. Starting as it may, in a realm of abstract thought, it is soon led under the compulsion of a governing theory into the field of human deeds. And that field requires its own exploration and assessment. The philosopher, the scientist, the statesman, the student of literature, cannot ignore that fact in the ultimate sense. All their utterances, decisions, and conclusions in the past have become the elements of our human drama. As in the past, so in the present. That we are all of the one family, being members of one another, whether we like it or not, is shown by that inexorable continuity of thought in the history of mankind. To catch that rhythm of life, to hear calls and answer them with the highest moral courage and intelligence is the greatest function of a university. And may God speed you.

## In Quest of the Humanities

(Address to the Humanities Association of Canada, Learned Societies Conference, University of Western Ontario, 29 May 1953)

When Professor Tracy asked me to give an address on some phase of the humanities, I wondered if there was anything fresh that might be offered on the subject. The place of the humanities in our modern life has been stated so often from so many points of view that I feel a touch of presumption in making this appearance. But I accepted the invitation and I had to select a title. After many rejections because of difficulties of definition I finally chose 'In Quest of the Humanities,' though a waggish friend of mine asked me if I should not spell 'In Quest' as one word, with more than a hint that the subject had been stretched out cold on a mortuary slab, awaiting dissection. However, it *is* two words and the search implies a profound belief in the existence, vitality, and ultimate significance of the object pursued.

To allow pessimism and despair to inundate the mind would further the very conditions we are trying to avoid. That this danger is real may be seen in the fact that a large group of outstanding commentators and analysts have surrendered themselves to the counsel of despair. They have read the evidence in the story of the last forty years and in the signs on the horizon today. That is the reason why rereadings are necessary, and messages of hope and faith need to be run through the bulletins of realism. There is a mental therapy in hope, in the expression of a positive faith that a tunnel, however dark the passageway, has an exit into some measure of sunlight. To believe otherwise means inertia, frustration, and continuous darkness.

Many of us in this room remember how, thirty-five years ago, after the tumult of the War, we listened to addresses from university platforms, pulpits, and public halls, bolstering the heart with words of encouragement, while hammers, shovels, and derricks were engaged in clearing away debris and building new structures. It required a good deal of courage to proclaim a dawn after the storm, and less than ten years ago, following a chaos even greater than the first, it required still more courage. But the message today must be the same, and must be driven home with unfaltering application because never in history have the ideals of life been so challenged and spurned. Before the Second World War began, the totalitarian gospel had been preached to the world with such unambiguous frankness that it literally and metaphorically disarmed the democratic audiences. It could not be believed by many who thought it was diplomatic bluff. The principle that truth should be pursued for the sake of truth was put on the level of a medieval superstition - a kind of Christian senility to be displaced by the doctrine of blood, race, and soil. The democracies woke up later to find that the new Gospel was put to a bitter and cruel realization.

Nevertheless, the humanities have no other recourse than to present without apology the same principles - the free prosecution of ideas, the right to form an independent judgment in conformity with evidence. One would think that this kind of battle had been fought and won centuries ago, that the issue might have been closed once and for all, except as a matter of doctrinaire discussion. The fact that one can enlist on behalf of freedom, justice, and truth the most honoured and loved names in the history of life would make us recoil from the New Order which was presented to the world. It is very significant that it began with the burning of books, the imprisonment, torture, exile, and death of the leading scientists and writers. The first blows had fallen on them as teachers and preachers. Education became indoctrination. And what a step back into the Dark Ages it was when a scientist could not dare to record a reaction in a test-tube until he could prove to the authorities that the result did not conflict with a twisted political ideology.

To repeat, it required courage and an incredible buoyancy of heart to make those utterances. Some thinkers found it impossible to float with such a cork, Shaw, for instance, going down for the third time with the cry that human efforts were useless, as men would continue to fight so long as they had fists. Others were caught by the snarl in the constitution of life; that any scientific discovery or invention was seized upon immediately as a means of destruction though it could just as easily be used to promote the welfare and perpetuation of life, and probably was so intended.

An uncannily ironic feature of the last great struggle was that tons of plasma should have been delivered from Canadian and American ports and sunk in mid-Atlantic before it could replenish the veins on European battlefields. That it should be so shed and not given a chance to flow along life-giving channels is the most ghastly waste of function that the mind can conceive. If the offering of a life could be attended by the saving of another, the sacrifice could find its place in the Christian faith, but otherwise the process could stand for a symbol of the ironic in its ultimate rigour. Ever since his life began, man has been calling for blood in all that polarity of mood from vengeance to redemption, from the curse to the prayer. The range of his need has ever outpaced the spread of his knowledge.

But there are several points of view from which the landscape may be surveyed, according to the adjustment of the telescope. It is not just a matter of complete pessimism nor of unqualified optimism. Both are lines of least resistance. The problem is an honest facing of two realities, two groups of challenging facts. We deplore the debris in the wake of a storm, a flood, a fire, but men *do* get to work to clear up rubble, to rebuild demolished homes, to assuage stricken souls. The picture is never complete without regarding the rehabilitating process of love as well as the destroying power of hate. Both may coexist in a single soul as we know too well, and it is one of the tasks of education and, in the wide sense, of the humanities to develop the former and to arrest and diminish the latter either directly or obliquely.

A life without a faith, without a tolerant kindliness, without a love for one's fellow beings, without a will to improve their lot is about the most dismal condition into which human nature can slump. Neither is it enough to reduce the values of life to the will to endure, though that reduction may have an element of sublimity evoking our admiration, for the stoic reserve does throw a man back upon his own resources, which postulates a spiritual basis, a sense of inward dignity. Nevertheless, very few members of the human family possess enough stamina to keep their chins up in the fog of 'Dover Beach,' however admirable that poem from the standpoint of expression. A melancholy roar, sustained indefinitely, can drown volition and initiative, and one turns readily for compensation to the affirmations of Arnold where culture and conduct are united. To know the best in the history of literature and life and to make that best prevail may be regarded as a classical rendering of the Christian faith. All the elements which give meaning to life are implicit in that faith. The realist, the stoic, the prophet might at the end of their climb find common ground. The desperate cruelty of existence may be seen in the lament over Jerusalem and that cry of abandonment on the cross, but with that was his belief in love human and divine stubbornly held, sublimely contrasted with the ignorance of his enemies. It is a hard faith as everyone knows who has tried to maintain it when failure, suffering, and death crawl like shadows over the hopes.

It is meeting with resistance today as much as ever. The word 'Utopia' like the word 'optimism' may cause men to shrug their shoulders, but after the shrug, a story may be flashed through the skies of some sacrificial deed which makes us ashamed of our meannesses and pettinesses, and the pulse begins to beat at a faster rate, and we are made aware of what the world might become if great moral forces were harnessed to the general will.

There is a danger, I think, in making too rigid a distinction between the humanities and the sciences, or between the theoretical and the practical interests. It is the actual deed which gives concrete value to the theory. The distinction is one of emphasis, not one of absolute opposition. We know that any given fact is not a static object found to be self-contained at the moment of its discovery. It is alive and vocal, calling out for its immediate family, its blood relations. All its cousins near and far removed come in to take a look at its face to find out what position it should occupy in the family circle. It enters a world of functions and values. Starting, as it may, in a realm of abstract thought, it is soon led under the compulsion of its governing theory into the field of human deeds. And that field itself needs its own exploration and assessment. After the scientist in theory and the technician in practice have launched their results, we ask what is their relation to human life. There should here be no apology for the use of the abused word 'utilitarian' when it is given the high connotation of the abatement of human misery and the advancement of human welfare. It is difficult to find any great quest of life, such as justice and freedom, which is devoid of some shade at least of utility, though the adjective has degenerated.

## Introduction to Roy Campbell
(Toronto, November 1953)

My first introduction to the work of Roy Campbell was when I visited London in the early twenties. I had the good fortune to meet John Squire, editor of the *London Mercury*, which had a long review of Campbell's *Flaming Terrapin*. Squire said he had never seen anything like this in print before, and certainly he had never seen such a human phenomenon in the flesh before. I immediately bought *The Flaming Terrapin*, and was held in the grip of it from beginning to end. I had never read anything like it, and I went to a gallery to see a portrait of its author by Augustus John, which pictured him as a very thin man, a wraith, enveloped in flames. (He lost the wraith, but retained the flames.) I thought, what is going to be the future of this writer who at a little over twenty years of age could so blaze himself on the literary horizon? Would he be a meteor or an enduring star?

When I got back to Canada, I was on the lookout for his later publications, and everything I read of his was like a new revelation. The work which struck me most was his *Flowering Rifle*, which I read at a single sitting in the library of Queen's University, where I was lecturing at the Summer School. It was a huge poem of something like 6000 lines in the heroic couplet which made me so oblivious to my environment that I forgot to give my afternoon lecture. The students speculated on my absence – was I caught in a motor accident, or was it a normal lapse of memory? As a matter of fact, I spent the afternoon on the golf course as a corrective, but that was no use as the putts would not go down, so concentrated was my attention on *Flowering Rifle*. So over-stimulated I remained, that finally I had to go to William Butler Yeats for a sedative, and 'The Lake Isle of Innisfree' lowered my temperature.

I was so anxious to find out about the actual life of Campbell that I got hold of his autobiography, which made any book on adventure and romance read like a seed catalogue to a person who didn't want to do any gardening or farming. (I was interested in the first paragraph of a review which an English critic wrote on Roy Campbell's autobiography. It runs this way: 'A reviewer who is honest enough to confess that he has never in his life strangled a whale with his bare hands, or speared a man-eating shark from horseback, or bitten an octopus to death under water, or caught an enormous black mamba with ground bait and six trout hooks, now takes up his footling pen with an air of apology.') I am going through it again to find out if there is anything in the realm of the genus homo which he has not done. He spent holidays in Rhodesia hunting leopards, baboons, lions, buffaloes, and giraffes. He did deep-sea diving after octopuses, roped steers, roped wild horses for a living, became a champion of water-jousting and an outstanding bullfighter in Toledo, bet on the Dempsey-Carpentier fight when all of his French friends were hostile to his bet. He dug himself out of bankruptcy by the bet.

When I read all this, I wondered how I could introduce him without clutching at my solar plexus. I am still a wee bit nervous, though I have read enough of his kindness and chivalry to set me at my ease.

But all these things are merely incidental to his career. He wrote up his life in prose and verse. He could do the short satiric epigrammatic poem of four lines. When I was in Halifax in the late twenties, I was walking along Barrington Avenue with Fred Clarke, who had been Professor of Education first in a South African university, then at McGill, and later at the University of London, England. Clarke had the Campbell verses off by heart. He recited the quatrain of 'Some South African Novelists,' which has been so much anthologized:

You praise the firm restraint with which they write,
I'm with you there, of course,
They use the snaffle and the curb all right,
But where's the bloody horse.

Well, here's the ruddy horse himself. Will Mr Roy Campbell step into the arena?

# Notes

The first date and place of publication or delivery (where known) of each item in this volume have been given under the item's title in the body of the work, so the notes offer source information only about previously unpublished typescripts and those quotations whose sources Pratt noted or I have subsequently identified. Items listed as coming from the E.J. Pratt Collection refer to the collection in the library of Victoria University in the University of Toronto. The numbers cited in this context (e.g., 9.70.2.1–3) refer to the box (9), file (70.2), and page numbers (1–3). The text of Pratt's own footnotes are followed by '[EJP],' but because they are often sketchy and in unconventional form, I have expanded the information (unless this has been given in a previous note, in which case I have condensed Pratt's note) and regularized the format.

Textual notes and explanatory notes are grouped together under each item, with the textual notes preceding the explanatory notes.

The following abbreviations are used in the notes:

Special Collections

PCVU Pratt Collection, Victoria University in the University of Toronto

Books

CPMP John Milton. *Complete Poems and Major Prose*. Ed. Merritt Y. Hughes. New York: Odyssey Press, 1957

CPWTH Thomas Hardy. *The Complete Poetical Works of Thomas Hardy.* Ed Samuel Hynes. Oxford: Clarendon Press, 1982–5

CWRB *The Complete Works of Robert Burns.* Ed. and intro. J.A. Mackay. 2nd ed. Ayrshire: Alloway Publishing Ltd, 1990

OHLP E.J. Pratt. *On His Life and Poetry.* Ed. Susan Gingell. Toronto: U of Toronto P, 1983

POT *The Poems of Tennyson.* Ed. Christopher Ricks. London: Longmans, 1969

MY David G. Pitt. *E.J. Pratt: The Master Years, 1927–1964.* Toronto: U of Toronto P, 1987

RS William Shakespeare. *The Riverside Shakespeare.* Ed. G. Blakemore Evans. Boston: Houghton Mifflin Co., 1974

TY David G. Pitt, *E.J. Pratt: The Truant Years, 1882–1927.* Toronto: U of Toronto P, 1984

Other

ms manuscript

ts(s) typescript(s)

## A. Pratt as Story-Teller

'A Northern Holiday'

Appearing under the byline 'The Rev. E.J. Pratt,' this article is Pratt's earliest known publication. The trip described in this light journalistic work was part of a tour Pratt took in the Notre Dame Bay area with his friend W.H. (Billy) Pike to sell the dubious concoction they called Universal Lung Healer to help finance their university education. For a fuller account of this journey and an assessment of Pratt's first publication, see TY 79–80.

Explanatory Note

5 'Koch.' Robert Koch (1843–1910) was a German bacteriologist and Nobel laureate in medicine, who established the bacteriological cause of many infectious diseases and studied many maladies, including malaria and sleeping sickness.

'A Western Experience'

For a more detailed account of Pratt's western experience, see 'Westward Ho,' *TY* 104–12.

Explanatory Notes

6 'student ... services.' Pratt is referring to the way in which the Methodist Church staffed its prairie mission fields with young student ministers from the East.

9 'Mr. M–.' William ('Billy') Magoon, with whose family Pratt boarded during his 'Western Experience,' *TY* 107

'"Hooked": A Rocky Mountain Experience'

Explanatory Note

11 'Lake O'Hara.' This lake, like all the other geographical features named in this narrative (except Edmonton, Alberta), is in the province of British Columbia.

## B. Pratt as Theologian: Thesis Extracts

'The Demonology of the New Testament in Its Relation to Earlier Developments, and to the Mind of Christ'

The first extract comes from about the mid-point of the thesis, following a historical and cross-cultural account of demonology and some preliminary remarks on the similarities and differences between historical demonological phenomena and those described in the Synoptics. The second extract follows Pratt's detailing of the disparities between the Gospel reports of four demoniacal cases apart from the Gadarene incident discussed in extract one. After claiming 'there is nothing to warrant the general distrust of the main historical points' (8.61.18), Pratt goes on to examine the nature and actuality of the cures Christ is reported to have effected and to point out that a convalescent period was sometimes indicated.

The title at the head of p. 1 differs slightly from that on the title page, the former reading 'The Demonology of the Synoptics in Its Relation to Earlier Developments, and to the Mind of Christ.'

I have parenthetically inserted into the body of the text the biblical references Pratt relegated to footnotes.

I have capitalized words naming sacred things or manifestations of the divine in accordance with Pratt's usual, though not consistent, practice.

Textual Notes

18 'It could ... feeding.' This sentence is at least awkward if not garbled. The word 'It' appears first to refer back to the term 'the narrative' in the previous sentence, but the present sentence only makes sense if the 'It' is understood to refer forward to the phrase 'the simple statement of Matthew.'

19 'Evangelists.' Evangelist

21–2 'In his ... effectively.' This sentence seems garbled.

25 'so that the Satanic.' so that Satanic

28 'parents'.' parent's

Explanatory Notes

17 'Strauss.' David Friedrich Strauss (1808–74), a Christologist whose *A New Life of Jesus*, 2 vols (London: Williams and Norgate, 1865) enormously influenced Pratt's own view of Christ as a historical person and moral exemplar

18 'Gadarene incident ... "showpiece".' Strauss, vol. 2, 183 [EJP]

18 'Baur ... Volkmar.' Baur is almost certainly Ferdinand Christian Baur (1792–1860), professor of Evangelical Theological in the University of Tübingen and D.F. Strauss's teacher. Volkmar is probably Gustav Volkmar (1809–93), known for his commentaries on Old Testament Apocrypha.

*Studies in Pauline Eschatology and Its Background*

The first extract is the concluding part of the chapter headed 'Significance of Concepts'; the second ends the final chapter, 'Conclusions.'

Textual Note

29 'effluence.' affluence. This reading follows the Revised Version of *The Wisdom of Solomon*, intro. and notes by Rev. J.A.F. Gregg (Cambridge: Cambridge UP, 1909).

Explanatory Notes

28 'stars or heavenly bodies.' See Gilbert Murray, 'Hellenistic Philosophy,' *Hibbert Journal* 9 (1910): 20, for discussion of the deification of the sun, moon, and stars in Plato, Aristotle, and the Stoics [EJP].

28 'likeness of Christ.' Henry Beach Carre, 'The Ethical Significance of Paul's Doctrine of the Spirit,' *Biblical World* 48 (1916): 204 [EJP]

29 'Philo's adjectives.' Philo Judaeus, 'On the Giants,' *The Works of Philo Judaeus*, vol. 1, trans. C.D. Yonge (London: George Bell and Sons, 1890) 334 [EJP]. Philo Judaeus (Philo of Alexandria) (*c.* 20 B.C.–A.D. 50 was a Jewish philosopher and biblical commentator who sought a synthesis between Jewish and Greek (especially Platonic) thought.

29 'An eternal ... radiance.' Philo, 'On Joseph,' *Works* vol. 2 (1894) 483. The 1894 translation reads 'everlasting day, free from all participation in night or in any kind of shade, inasmuch as it is surrounded uninterruptedly by a brilliant display of inextinguishable and unadulterated light.'

29 'the Omnipotent ... light.' Pratt does not indicate his elisions after 'Omnipotent' and 'light.'

29 'Wisdom ... power.' James Drummond, *Philo Judaeus; or the Jewish-Alexandrian Philosophy in Its Development and Completion* (London: Williams and Norgate, 1888) 217 [EJP]

29 'of the stars.' In Philo as quoted in Drummond: of stars

30 'The monarchical ... throne.' 'Have courage, Enoch, do not fear, and [they] showed me the Lord from afar, sitting on His very high Throne,' 2 Enoch 20:3 [EJP].

30 'happens.' In Philo: occurs

30 'incorporeal ... body.' Philo, 'Questions and Solutions,' *Works* vol. 4 (London: H.G. Bohn, 1855) 334 [EJP]

30 'living.' In Philo: being

30 'The souls ... spheres.' Edwyn Bevan, *Stoics and Sceptics* (Oxford: Clarendon Press, 1913) 111n, trans. from the Latin [EJP]

30 'My divine ... empty name.' Quoted by Frantz Cumont, *Astrology and Religion among the Greeks and Romans* (New York: G.P. Putnam's Sons, 1912) 179 [EJP]

31–2 'One might ... speech.' Adolf Deissmann, *Bible Studies; Contributions Chiefly from Papyri and Inscriptions, to the History of the Language, the Literature, and the Religion of Hellenistic Judaism and Primitive Christianity*, trans. Alexander Grieve (Edinburgh: T. and T. Clark, 1901) 79 [EJP]

32 'Body ... dimensions.' R.D. Hicks, *Stoic and Epicurean*, Epochs of Philosophy (London: Longmans Green and Co., 1910) 23 [EJP]

34 'A clearly schematized ... prophets.' W.M. Ramsay, 'The Teaching of Paul in Terms of the Present Day,' *Expositor*, 8th ser., 4 (July 1912): 91 [EJP]

36 'Hebrew terms ... Greek expressions.' Earlier in his concluding chapter, Pratt summarizes how Paul used the Greek term *'pneuma'* (cf Hebrew *'ruach'*). *Pneuma* denotes 'the intellectual, volitional and emotional processes ... Its prevalent usage, however, is to indicate the conformity of human life on the earth with the life of Jesus ... On its distinctively post-earthly or eschatological side it characterizes the new organism given by God to the Christian – a heavenly and incorruptible organism which replaces the earthly and perishable one of flesh and blood' (194–5). Similarly, Pratt notes that Paul used *'psyche'* (cf *'nephesh'*) to designate 'the life of the individual in its personal and social relations, and specifically the emotions such as distress and pain, tenderness and solicitude, and even volitional processes ... But the term ... has little, if any, explicit reference to the life after death, and in this lies its main difference from preceding apocalyptic thought which used *psyche* and *pneuma* interchangeably in this relationship' (193). The Parousia or Day of the Lord (cf the Day of Yahweh) is throughout Paul's letters 'the appearance of Jesus Christ, who from the time of his ascension existed in the heavens, and whose reappearance was to be the signal for the passing away of the present aeon and the inauguration of the consummated kingdom' (195).

## C. Pratt as Essayist

'Thomas Hardy'

Textual Note

46 'tread.' In Hardy: head

Explanatory Notes

43 'recent anthology.' *An Anthology of Modern Verse*, chosen by A. Methuen (London: Methuen, 1921), is dedicated 'To Thomas Hardy O.M. Greatest of the Moderns.'

44 'another volume four years later.' *Poems of the Past and Present* was actually published in 1901, although the volume was dated 1902.

44 *'Tristram and Isolde.'* The work is in fact entitled *The Famous Tragedy of the Queen of Cornwall at Tintagel in Lyonesse* (1923). The reference to 'others' that follows is misleading because Hardy's *Collected Poems* (1925), *Far Phantasies, Songs, and Trifles* (1925), and *Winter Words in Various Moods and Metres* (1928) were all published after Pratt's essay had appeared.

44 'eighty-two.' At the time of publication of this essay, Hardy was, in fact, just about eighty-four (b. 2 June 1840).

44 'Abbotsford ... Row.' Abbotsford on the Tweed was the estate of Sir Walter and Lady Margaret Scott; Dove Cottage, Grasmere, was home to William and Dorothy Wordsworth; and Cheyne Row, Chelsea, was the address of Thomas and Jane Carlyle.

46 'Not a plough ... Gunpowder Plot.' *The Return of the Native* (London: Macmillan, 1920) 17

47 'Only ... pass.' Pratt quotes the first two of the three stanzas of 'In Time of "The Breaking of Nations,"' CPWTH 511.

47 'the viewless ... wheel.' Forescene, Part First, *The Dynasts, Parts First and Second* (London: Macmillan, 1913) 8

47 'as a violent ... locality.' *Jude the Obscure*, vol. 1 (New York: Harper and Bros, 1905) 45

48 'Breathe ... rare.' Pratt quotes stanzas one and five of the six-stanza 'To An Unborn Pauper Child,' CPWTH 116–17.

48 'Clym ... Eustacia.' Characters in *The Return of the Native*

48 'Fanny ... Troy.' Characters in *Far from the Madding Crowd*

49 'Will of Schopenhauer ... Unconscious Principle of Von Hartmann.' Arthur Schopenhauer (1788–1860), author of *The World as Will and Representation* (1818), argued that human existence is driven by a blind Will to survive. Eduard von Hartmann (1842–1906), author of *Philosophy of the Unconscious* (1869), argued that the world process is activated by inexplicable forces of nature, which he termed the Unconscious.

49 'happiness ... pain.' Pratt is recalling the final words of *The Life and Death of the Mayor of Casterbridge*.

49 'the intolerable ... feel.' *The Dynasts*, Part First, IV.v., 100

49–50 'If but ... pain.' 'Hap,' CPWTH 7

50 'Nature ... joy.' William Wordsworth, 'Lines Composed a Few Miles

Above Tintern Abbey …,' *The Poetical Works of William Wordsworth*, vol. 2, ed. Ernest de Selincourt (Oxford: Clarendon Press, 1944) 262, lines 122–5

50 'songs of a factory girl … Asolo's happiest four.' A reference to Robert Browning's *Pippa Passes* (1841), a dramatic poem in which the title character, a young silk-mill worker, compares her own life with those of the four apparently happiest people in her town, Asolo

50 'He hath … paths.' Job 19:8

51 'Cytherea Graye … Sue Bridehead.' Pratt here refers to scenes in *Desperate Remedies* and *Jude the Obscure*, respectively. I have not been able to locate the source of the words Pratt quotes, but he is likely recalling a critic's description of the effect of the scene in *Jude*.

51 'At once … unaware.' 'The Darkling Thrush,' *CPWTH* 137

51 'passage to *The Dynasts*.' The choice of the preposition 'to' here, which seems unidiomatic, may be governed by Pratt's thinking of the lines he quotes as the closing passage to *The Dynasts*.

52 'But … fair.' *The Dynasts*, Part Third, After Scene, 256

52 'fills.' In CPWTH: thrills

52 'sound.' In CPWTH: sounds

52 'It may … spring.' 'Apology,' *CPWTH* 531–2

52 'may be.' In *CPWTH*: may indeed be

52–3 'We may reject … body blow.' Hardy articulates his idea of impersonal Casualty in the poem 'Hap,' *CPWTH* 7, and uses the Aeschylean concept of the President of the Immortals in the final paragraph of *Tess of the D'Urbervilles*.

53 'infatuation or mania of Boldwood.' In *Far from the Madding Crowd*

53–4 '"Now, my own, … good things.' *The Woodlanders* (New York: Harper and Bros, 1905) 364

54 'I stand … This bird.' 'The Blinded Bird,' *CPWTH* 446

'Golfomania'

For another account of Pratt's 'Golfomania' see *TY* 207–9 and 274.

Explanatory Notes

55 'this college.' Victoria College is the Arts and Science college of Victoria University in the University of Toronto.

56 'Professor Thomson.' There were two professors named Thomson at the University of Toronto at the time Pratt wrote this essay, both

of whom taught at University College and both of whom he would likely have known. Robert Boyd Thomson was an associate professor of phanerogamic botany, and Joseph Ellis Thomson was an assistant professor of mineralogy.

56 'new treatise.' Cyril Tolley, *The Modern Golfer* (New York: A.A. Knopf, 1924) 31–2, 35

56 'which is standing on edge.' In Tolley: when it is standing on an edge

56 'tend.' In Tolley: help you

57 'Hagen ... Duncan.' Walter Hagen (1892–1969) is described by the *Encyclopedia of Golf*, Webster Evans, comp. (New York: St Martin's Press, 1971) as 'The greatest figure in American and international golf immediately before the First World War and through the 1920s' (100); Gene Sarazen (b. 1902) was one of a very few players to have won both American and British Open championships in the same year; Macdonald Smith (1890–1949), popularly known as Macsmith, narrowly missed winning the U.S. and British Opens several times, but was Canadian Open champion in 1926; John Taylor (1871–1963) was one of the so-called Triumvirate of Vardon, Taylor, and Braid, who won sixteen British Open championships among them; Henry Vardon (1870–1937) won his place in the Triumvirate by taking the British Open a record six times; Arthur Havers (b. 1898) was British Open champion in 1923, the year before Pratt's essay was published; George Duncan (1883–1964) won the British Open in 1920, and was renowned for the speed with which he played his shots.

59 'Theobald.' Lewis Theobald (1688–1744), the main satiric target of Alexander Pope's *Dunciad*, published in 1734 an edition of Shakespeare noted for its many valuable restorations and conjectural emendations, including the one Pratt cites in his essay describing the death of Falstaff from *Henry V*, II.iii.

59 'any pen.' In Shakespeare: a pen

59 'very unhappy.' In Shakespeare: most unhappy

59 'these fatal holes.' In Shakespeare: these holes

'The Fly-Wheel Lost'

Explanatory Notes

62 '"Work in Progress".' 'A Work of Progress.' The provisional title

was suggested by Ford Madox Ford, the editor of the *Transatlantic Review*, which, in 1 (April 1924), published the first fragment of the work that was to become *Finnegans Wake*.

63 '"Afterwards".' Whether Pratt was speaking of an unpublished or a published poem is impossible to tell from the context, but 'Afterwards' was not among the poems published in the offending number (37) of *Poetry* (Chicago) in February 1931 of which Pratt writes later in the article (see next note but one below).

63 'Sterne ... Wadman.' Pratt refers here to Laurence Sterne's *Tristram Shandy*.

64 'objectivists.' It was in fact Louis Zukofsky, the guest editor of *Poetry* (Chicago) 37 (February 1931), who in a comment entitled 'Program: "Objectivists" 1931' gave this group its name; but he was under presure from Harriet Monroe to identify the poets published in this number as part of a movement.

64 'Sandburg ... Lowell.' American modernist poets: Carl Sandburg (1878–1967), Edgar Lee Masters (1868–1950), (Nicholas) Vachel Lindsay (1879–1931), Edwin Arlington Robinson (1869–1935), Amy Lowell (1874–1925)

64–5 'Am on ... birds.' Louis Zukofsky, '"A" – Seventh Movement,' *Poetry* (Chicago) 37 (February 1931): 242–6

65 'Laundry-To-let.' In Zukofsky: LAUNDRY-TO-LET

65 'bro' [no period].' In Zukofsky: bro'. [period]

65 'through.' In Zukofsky: thru

'Canadian Writers of the Past: Pickthall'

Pratt's essay is Part VI of the *Forum* series evaluating major figures in Canada's literary history.

Textual Note

68 'might as well have been.' might have been

Explanatory Notes

66 '*The Countess Cathleen* ... "The Hound of Heaven".' Both W.B. Yeats's play *The Countess Cathleen* (1892) and John Millington Synge's unfinished verse drama *Deirdre of the Sorrows* (1910) treat of figures in Irish mythology; Dante Gabriel Rossetti's poem 'The Blessed Damozel' (1850) concerns the yearning of a damsel in heaven for a lover on

earth. I have been unable to discover a work entitled 'The Shepherdess of Sleep,' but Pratt may have had in mind a poem by Alice Meynell (1847–1922), 'The Shepherdess,' which refers repeatedly and redundantly to a 'shepherdess of sheep.' This poem was part of Meynell's *Later Poems* (1901), and she and her husband befriended Francis Thompson, whose devotional poem 'The Hound of Heaven' (1893) is the monologue of someone in flight from, but pursued and overtaken by, God's love.

66 'industrial blasts from Chicago.' A reference to the realist verse of Carl Sandburg

66 '"In No Strange Land".' Francis Thompson's poem 'In No Strange Land' (later entitled 'The Kingdom of God') first appeared in *Athenaeum*, 8 August 1908. John Lane, who published Pickthall's *The Drift of Pinions* in both New York and London (in Canada, Montreal's *University Magazine* was the publisher), also published two of Thompson's early volumes.

66 'hounds ... rain.' Pratt quotes lines 65 and 68 from Algernon Charles Swinburne's dramatic poem *Atalanta in Calydon* (1865), rpt in a facsimile of the first edition with a preface by Dr Georges Lafourcade (London: Oxford UP, 1930) 3

66 'the lisp.' In Swinburne: With lisp

67 'horns of elfland.' Tennyson, The Splendour Falls,' in *The Princess* (see POT, vol. 2, 231, line 10)

67 'Moira O'Neill ... Charlotte Mew.' Moira O'Neill (*c.* 1870–?) was the pseudonym for the Irish writer Mrs Agnes Higginson Skrine. Her *Songs of the Glens of Antrim* (1900) is described by Stephen Gwynn in *Irish Literature and Drama in the English Language: A Short History* (1936) 139, as 'one of the very few books which, if all copies were destroyed, could probably be reproduced from oral tradition.' Katherine Tynan (Hinkson; 1861–1931), another Irish poet, came to the attention of W.B. Yeats, who published a selection entitled *Twenty-One Poems by Katherine Tynan* (1907). Charlotte Mew (1869–1928) was a protégée of Thomas Hardy. Her book *The Farmer's Bride* (London: The Poetry Bookshop, 1916) was published in North America as *Saturday Market* (New York: Macmillan, 1921).

67 'Hart House Theatre.' Hart House Theatre at the University of Toronto was instrumental in getting significant numbers of Canadian

plays on the boards at a time when interest in a national drama was only beginning to make itself felt.

68 'Andrea del Sarto.' Robert Browning's dramatic monologue 'Andrea del Sarto' (1855) reveals to the reader a spiritless artist who uses his faithless wife as a model for his painting of the Virgin, having allowed his passion for her to become a substitute for artistic passion.

68 'Your face ... Dorette!' *The Wood Carver's Wife and Later Poems* (Toronto: McClelland and Stewart, 1922) 84, 86–7. Pickthall's text has stanza breaks between the last three lines Pratt quotes here.

68 'a number of her letters.' No such letters are among those few preserved in the Pickthall Collection at Victoria University, and I have not been able to locate them elsewhere.

69 'Hudson.' William Henry Hudson (1841–1922), a naturalized British subject, is remembered for his account of his early life in Argentina, *Far Away and Long Ago: A History of My Life* (1918), and his picture of folk life on the Wiltshire downs, *A Shepherd's Life: Impressions of the South Wiltshire Downs* (1910).

'Canadian Poetry – Past and Present'

Explanatory Notes

70 'Mattagami ... little Bateese.' The name 'Mattagami' is associated with Duncan Campbell Scott (see 'Spring on Mattagami') that of 'Tantramar' with Sir Charles G.D. Roberts (see 'The Tantramar Revisited'), and that of the 'Basin of Minas' with both Bliss Carman (see 'Arnold, Master of the Scud') and Roberts (see his short story collection *By the Marshes of Minas* [1900]). *Tecumseh* (1886) is a verse drama by Charles Mair, and Little, or more correctly Leetle, Bateese is the title character of W.H. Drummond's poem 'Little Bateese' (1901).

71 '*Oxford Book of Modern Verse*.' Yeats's anthology first appeared in 1936.

71 'with one exception.' Probably Merrill Denison, who by the 1930s was living in New York, his work in Canadian radio and print having earned him an American reputation. He became, as Arthur Phelps lamented, 'one more emigration statistic' in the American brain drain. (See Dick MacDonald, *Mugwump Canadian: The Merrill Denison Story* [Montreal: Content Publishing Ltd, 1973] 103.) The Canadian novelist to whom Pratt subsequently refers as the only one 'to possess a big international reputation' at this time is probably Mazo de la

Roche, who by the time Pratt's essay appeared had published six of her Jalna novels, one of which Pratt had reviewed in 1929 (see section F, pages 137–8), though Morley Callaghan, who had published six novels and two short-story collections, is also a possibility.

72 'Trossachs.' A glen in southwest Perthshire, Scotland, made famous by Sir Walter Scott's descriptions of its beauty in *The Lady of the Lake* and *Rob Roy*

73 'Here the spirit ... evermore.' Charles Sangster's 'Lyric to the Isles' is part of 'The St. Lawrence and the Saguenay,' *The St. Lawrence and the Saguenay, and Other Poems* (New York: Miller, Orton, and Mulligan, 1856) 12–13.

73 'breath.' In Sangster: breaths

73 'Where is ... light.' Charles Mair, 'The Fire-Flies,' *Dreamland and Other Poems* (Montreal: Dawson Brothers, 1868), rpt in *Dreamland and Other Poems; Tecumseh: A Drama*, intro. Norman Shrive (Toronto: U of Toronto P, 1974) 115

73–4 'Broad shadows ... villages.' Archibald Lampman, 'A Sunset at Les Éboulements,' *The Poems of Archibald Lampman*, ed. D.C. Scott (Toronto: George N. Morang, 1900) 273–4

74 'A vireo ... bassoons.' D.C. Scott, 'An Impromptu,' *The Poems of Duncan Campbell Scott* (Toronto: McClelland and Stewart, 1926) 135

74 'his fellows.' In Scott: its fellows

74 'The scarlet ... hills.' Bliss Carman, 'A Vagabond Song,' in Bliss Carman and Richard Hovey, *More Songs from Vagabondia* (Boston: Copeland and Day, 1896), rpt in *The Poems of Bliss Carman*, ed. with intro. John Robert Sorfleet (Toronto: McClelland and Stewart, 1976) 68

74 'asters on.' In Carman: asters like a smoke upon

75 'editorial office.' Pratt was editor of the *Canadian Poetry Magazine* from August 1935 to September 1943. See section E of this book for selected editorial comments.

75 'Quiller-Couch.' Sir Arthur Quiller-Couch (1863–1944) prolific author of fiction, poetry, and literary journalism, as well as a leading anthologist of his time

75 '"To Spring".' Gray's ode is entitled 'On the Spring.'

76 'literary hara-kiri.' What Pratt means here by 'literary hara-kiri' is better explained in the second paragraph of 'English Meat *and* Irish Gravy,' 90–1 in this volume.

76 '"Works in Progress".' Pratt's distaste for James Joyce's 'Work in Progress' and for the work of his followers is discussed at greater length in 'The Fly-Wheel Lost' 59–65 in this volume.

77 'fine frenzy ... lunacy.' 'The lunatic ... / The poet's eye in a fine frenzy rolling,' *A Midsummer Night's Dream*, RS V.1.7–11.

78 'Oxford satirists.' Pratt discusses these Oxford satirists and their critical reception at greater length in '[Meaning and Modernity]' 250–64 in this volume.

79 'three university quarterlies.' The three Canadian university quarterlies publishing at the time Pratt's essay appeared were the *University of Toronto Quarterly* (first pub. October 1931), *Queen's Quarterly* (first pub. July 1893), and the *Dalhousie Review* (first pub. April 1921).

79 '*Globe and Mail* ... editor.' Pratt's relationship with the *Globe and Mail*'s literary editor, William Arthur Deacon, can be partially explored in his correspondence with Deacon, which is preserved among the letters in the W.A. Deacon Collection, Thomas Fisher Rare Book Library, University of Toronto. See also Clara Thomas and John Lennox, *William Arthur Deacon: A Canadian Literary Life* (Toronto: U of Toronto P, 1982) and TY and MY.

'Dorothy Livesay'

Explanatory Notes

81 '*Green Pitcher*.' *Green Pitcher* (Toronto: Macmillan, 1928)

81 'The thought ... before.' Dorothy Livesay, 'Time,' *Signpost* (Toronto: Macmillan, 1932) 22

81 'We ... wore.' Emily Dickinson, Poem 887, *The Complete Poems of Emily Dickinson*, ed. Thomas H. Johnson (London: Faber and Faber, 1970) 420–1

81 'Amy Lowell's manifesto.' Amy Lowell's 'manifesto' appeared in *Some Imagist Poets* (Boston: Houghton Mifflin, 1915).

82 '*Day and Night*.' *Day and Night* (Toronto: Ryerson Press, 1944)

82 'Lorca.' Federico García Lorca (1898–1936), Spanish poet and dramatist, murdered by the followers of Francisco Franco, the Spanish fascist leader, at the outbreak of the Spanish Civil War

83 'You dance ... token.' 'Lorca' 24

83 '"Serenade for Spring".' In Livesay: 'Serenade for Strings'

83 'O God ... a man.' 'Serenade for Strings' 30, 32

84 'One step ... shout.' 'Day and Night' 16

## D. Pratt as Commentator

'The Decay of Romance'

This was the first of twenty-one articles in Pratt's series of 'Literature' columns for this relatively short-lived general-interest magazine, published from 1933 to 1936. Pratt recast this essay as a lecture which he delivered to the Association of Canadian Bookmen in March 1936, and excerpts were published as 'Some Tendencies in Modern Poetry,' *Literary Bulletin* (The Association of Canadian Bookmen) 1.1 (1936): 8–9. The only significant addition to the text reproduced here is the last paragraph excerpted in the *Literary Bulletin;* it reads:

It would be a rash prophet who would attempt to forecast with any degree of confidence the goal to which all these strivings lead. Are they just eddies in a current, or do they constitute the main stream? There can be little question that they may reflect the dominant temper of a generation which is facing the future with more alarm than hope, with a mind compact of bewilderment before the blind alleys of our economic life. We have seen on all sides the fierce indictment in poetry as in drama and fiction, of the industrial system of the machine age with its terrible efficiency and its vast roll of the unemployed. But how the tune would change if in the next ten or fifteen years there was a change in the heart of the world and all machinery was placed under tribute to human happiness. Then motors and cranks and pistons and cylinders would fit into the measures of the verse with the rich association of the reaping hook and the plough. Fire can warm, dissolve, and purify, produce gold as well as ash, even though the Promethean penalty has to be paid in every age for the lesson of the control. The material of poetry is at every blast furnace as it is at every hearth, and if the world is going to move through the redemptive processes of human effort, out of its present confusion into sanity and light, its literature will emerge from frustration into a sense of growth and accomplishment. It may never return to the catchwords and mottoes of fifty years ago, for the lines of Browning 'I stoop, I pick a posy, I look up all's blue' fall like pseudo-cultural strain upon our hearing today. Still tremendous gain will be made if poetry can gather from the new horizon enough colour to keep on asserting the values that belong to the heart.

Explanatory Notes

85 'Russell.' George William Russell, pseud. AE (1867–1935), Irish author, one of the major figures of the Irish Literary Renaissance

86 'Strachey ... Hackett.' Lytton Strachey (1880–1932) was the most important of the English Victorian-era biographers. His *Eminent Victorians* (1918) was prefaced by a statement of his methods, which were to avoid 'scrupulous narration' and to 'attack his subject in unexpected places,' shooting 'a sudden revealing searchlight into obscure recesses, hitherto undivined.' Emil Ludwig (1881–1948) was a predominantly political biographer, but he also published *Genius and Character* (1927), a general study of the biographical art. André Maurois (1885–1967) was a prolific biographer of literary figures, who also published *Aspects de la biographie* (1928). Francis Hackett (1883–1962) published a number of biographies of European monarchs.

86 'The Guard ... dismayed.' Pratt quotes first a phrase attributed to General Pierre Jacques Étienne de Combronne, commander of a division of the French Old Guard at Waterloo. Though cited by the French journalist Nicolas Balisson de Rougemont as de Combronne's retort to a demand for surrender, this rejoinder was likely de Rougemont's invention, for de Combronne himself denied having used the phrase. Pratt then cites line 10 from Alfred, Lord Tennyson's 'The Charge of the Light Brigade' (1854).

86 *'Fiery Particles ... White Chateau.'* See C.E. Montague, *Fiery Particles* (1923) and *Rough Justice* (1926); Erich Maria Remarque, *All Quiet on the Western Front*, trans. A.W. Wheen (1929); Robert Sherriff, *Journey's End* (1929); Sean O'Casey, *The Silver Tassie* (1928); and R.C. Berkeley, *White Chateau* (1925).

87 'starry night.' A reference to George Meredith's 'Lucifer in Starlight' (1883), which pictures a restless Prince Lucifer flying over the world, but upon looking up at the stars, confronting in the skies 'the army of unalterable law' (line 14), *The Poems of George Meredith*, vol. 1. ed. Phyllis B. Barlett (New Haven and New York: Yale UP, 1978) 285.

87 'All night ... light.' John Milton, *Paradise Lost* VI, lines 1–4

87 'In the false ... way.' Carl Sandburg, 'Blue Island Intersection,' *Complete Poems* (New York: Harcourt, Brace and Co., 1950) 166

'Changing Standpoints'

Explanatory Notes

88 'Isle of Wight.' Tennyson lived on the Isle of Wight while writing *Idylls of the King*.

88 'Francis Thompson.' A late nineteenth-century poet best known for 'The Hound of Heaven' (see note to page 66 in this volume in notes on 'Canadian Writers of the Past: Pickthall'). Pratt subsequently paraphrases the opening two lines from Thompson's 'To the Dead Cardinal of Westminster.'

89 'I'm sick ... steam.' Rudyard Kipling, 'M' Andrew's Hymn, '*Verses, 1889–1896*. The Writings in Prose and Verse of Rudyard Kipling, vol. 11 (New York: Charles Scribner's Sons, 1899) 214

89 'white sheets into red ... subdued to the machine it works upon.' A reference to Shakespeare's sonnet 111: 'And almost hence my nature is subdued / To what it works in, like the dyer's hand' (lines 6–7), RS 1769

89 'Giovannitti.' Arturo Giovannitti (1884–1959), the editor of the Italian Socialist Federation organ *Il Proletario*, became active in the 1912 Lawrence, Mass., textile-mill strike as an orator and relief worker. Along with his friend and fellow union organizer Joseph Ettor, Giovannitti was arrested and charged with being an accessory before the fact in the fatal shooting of 29 January 1912 of striker Annie LoPizzo, because the men were held to have incited and procured the commission of the crime by advocating the strike. After eight months in prison, the men were brought to trial along with striker Joseph Caruso, who was charged with the actual shooting. All three were acquitted after a three-day trial, a victory that was fought for and celebrated by the labour movement around the world.

89 'blows ... law.' Pratt's first quotation from Giovannitti, *Arrows in the Gale* (Riverside, Conn.: Hillacre Bookhouse, 1914) 18, is a paraphrase of lines 7–8 of the 'Proem'; he then quotes lines 21–4 of the same poem. 'The Walker' can be found on pp 21–7.

90 '*Justice*.' John Galsworthy's play *Justice* (1910) criticizes the legal process, prison administration, and society, all of which are responsible for the victimizing of a lawyer's clerk sentenced for forging a cheque to help a woman in trouble.

## 'English Meat *and* Irish Gravy'

Textual Notes

91 'reflexives.' reflections

Explanatory Notes

92 'Irish bull.' As Pratt suggests, a bull is a self-contradictory proposition, and the qualifier 'Irish' frequently prefixes the term. Pratt may well have known Maria Edgeworth's substantial 'Essay on Irish Bulls,' which was republished in 1832 along with *Castle Rackrent* in the Baldwin and Craddock Edgeworth series. The essay ironically critiques the ascription of bulls and blunders to the Irish, and lauds their ingenious, inventive use of English.

92 *'Twenty Years A-Growing.'* Maurice O'Sullivan, *Twenty Years A'Growing*, rendered from the original Irish by Moya Llewelyn Davies and George Thomson, with an introductory note by E.M. Forster (London: Chatto and Windus, 1933)

## 'New Notes in Canadian Poetry'

This essay was reprinted in Peter Stevens, *The McGill Movement* (Toronto: Ryerson Press, 1969) 32–5.

Explanatory Note

93 *'The Shrouding.' The Shrouding* (1933)

## 'With Hook and Worm'

Explanatory Notes

95 *'The Compleat Angler.'* Izaak Walton's *The Compleat Angler* (1653). The page numbers listed below are drawn from John Buxton, ed., *The Compleat Angler* (Oxford: Oxford UP, 1982). I have not recorded the variant spellings or the deletion of the italicizing of, or parentheses around, some words and phrases in the modernized English of the text Pratt cites.

95–6 'As for ... sauce.' Walton 366, 262, 238

95 'As for money, neglect.' As for money (which may be said to be the third blessing) neglect

96 'letter to Coleridge.' The letter, dated 28 October 1796, can be

found in its entirety in *The Works of Charles Lamb*, ed. Sir Thomas Noon Talfourd (London: Bell and Daldy, 1867) 13–14.

96 'Wordsworth ... sonnets.' See William Wordsworth, 'Written Upon a Blank Leaf in "The Complete Angler"' (1819) and 'Walton's Book of Lives,' Ecclesiastical Sonnets Part III, Sonnet V (1822) in *William Wordsworth: The Poems*, vol. 2, ed. John O. Hayden (New Haven and London: Yale UP, 1977) 398, 485.

96 'Hallam.' Arthur Henry Hallam (1811–33), whose early death became the subject of Tennyson's poem *In Memoriam*

96 '*Lives*.' Izaak Walton, *The Lives of Dr. John Donne, Sir Henry Wotton, Mr. Richard Hooker, Mr. George Herbert* (1670)

96 'sick ... aims.' A reference to line 204 of Matthew Arnold's 'The Scholar Gypsy,' *Poetical Works*, ed. C.B. Tinker and H.F. Lowry (London: Oxford UP, 1950) 261

96 'I knew ... soul.' *The Compleat Angler* 364

'Simplicity in Poetry'

Explanatory Notes

97 'Harold Hobson.' I have not been able to locate the Hobson article, and Pratt's text does not set off the quotation in such a way as to make clear where Hobson's words end. Pratt's biographer, David G. Pitt, writes to me in a letter of 25 August 1987 that he suspects Pratt quotes him at greater length than the one paragraph I have ascribed to him here.

98 'I'd rather ... horn.' William Wordsworth, 'The World Is Too Much With Us,' *The Poems*, vol. 1, 568

98 'Breathes ... strand.' Sir Walter Scott, 'The Lay of the Last Minstrel,' *The Poetical Works of Sir Walter Scott* (New York: Thomas Crowell and Co., 1894), Canto Sixth, 40, lines 1–6

98 'Is there ... that.' Robert Burns, 'Song – For A' That and A' That,' rpt as 'Is There for Honest Poverty,' in CWRB 535–6

99 'his Fool's passing.' The words which Pratt quotes are spoken by Lear over the body of Cordelia, but they are often interpreted as referring to Lear's Fool as well.

99 'We twa ... syne.' Robert Burns, 'Auld Lang Syne,' CWRB 251–2

## 'A Study in Poetic Development'

### Textual Notes

101 'lyricist.' lyrist

101 'Bells," and "The.' Bells,' 'The

### Explanatory Notes

101 'Had I ... dreams.' 'He Wishes for the Cloths of Heaven,' *The Variorum Edition of the Poems of W.B. Yeats,* ed. Peter Allt and Russel K. Alspach (1957; rpt New York: Macmillan, 1965) 176

102 'I will ... core.' 'The Lake Isle of Innisfree,' ibid. 117

103 'I am content ... blest.' 'A Dialogue of Self and Soul,' ibid. 479

103 'Covered ... mythologies.' 'A Coat,' ibid. 320

## 'The Comic Spirit'

### Explanatory Notes

104 'Any ... fellow-beings.' Henri Bergson, *Laughter: An Essay on the Meaning of the Comic,* trans. Cloudsley Brereton and Fred Rothwell (London: Macmillan, 1911) 134

104 'The passion ... formerly.' Thomas Hobbes, 'Human Nature,' *The English Works of Thomas Hobbes of Malmesbury,* ed. Sir William Molesworth, vol. 4 (London: John Bohn, 1840) 46

104 'a sudden conception of eminency.' In Hobbes: sudden conception of some eminency

104 'inferiority.' In Hobbes: infirmity

104 'Spencer.' Herbert Spencer (1820–1903), founder of evolutionary philosophy and author of numerous works, including *First Principles* (1862), *Principles of Biology* (1864–7), *Principles of Sociology* (1876–96), and *Principles of Ethics* (1879–93)

105 'Sir Oswald Mosley.' Sir Oswald Mosley (1896–1980), the leader of the British Union of Fascists from 1932 to 1940, was noted for his powerful oratorical skills.

## 'Slang – Why and Why Not'

### Textual Notes

106 'world," "You.' world, you

110 'were heightened.' was heightened

Explanatory Notes

106 'parent society.' The Society for Pure English was founded in 1913 by a committee consisting of Henry Bradley, Robert Bridges, Sir Walter Raleigh (see note immediately below) and Logan Pearsall Smith.

106 'Robert Bridges ... Henry Bradley ... Sir Walter Raleigh.' Robert Bridges (1844–1930) was made poet laureate of Britain in 1913 following the Oxford University Press publication of his *Poetical Works* (1912). In his long association with the press, he is credited with having done a great deal to enhance accuracy and taste in printing. He helped found the Society for Pure English and edited its tracts, which addressed such matters as grammar, pronunciation, etymology, and handwriting. Henry Bradley (1845–1923), a philologist, is chiefly remembered for his work on the *Oxford English Dictionary*, of which he eventually became chief editor. Sir Walter Raleigh (1861–1922), a popular teacher and critic, was the first holder of the chair of English literature at Oxford.

107 'an American philologist.' I have been unable to identify the philologist in question.

107 'Ring Lardner.' Ring Lardner (1855–1933) first came to public attention as a sports writer and columnist in Chicago and New York, but his talent for reproducing the vernacular, particularly sports vernacular, later made him a success as a short-story writer. *The Love Nest and Other Stories* (1926) is a typical and well-known collection.

108 'the Gardens.' Toronto's Maple Leaf Gardens, besides being the home arena of the Toronto Maple Leafs Hockey Club, is also the locale of many other sporting and entertainment events.

109 'English as she is spoke.' An allusion to the misbegotten work of Jose de Fonseca and Pedro Carolino, *English as She Is Spoke: The New Guide of the Conversation in Portuguese and English* (1855), whose hilarious blunders sufficiently amused Mark Twain that he wrote an introduction to a 1923 reissue of the book.

## E. Pratt as Editor: The *Canadian Poetry Magazine* Editorials

'Foreword' to vol. 1, no. 1

The 'Foreword' was signed 'The Editors.'

'Entering the Second Year'

Explanatory Notes

116 'Governor-General.' Lord Tweedsmuir addressed the audience assembled in Convocation Hall, University of Toronto, for the first Canadian Poetry Night, 24 November 1937, and presented the 1936 Governor General's Awards for Literature at that time. His address, 'Return to Masterpieces,' and a complete description of the program were printed in 2 (December 1937): 5–23. The first Tweedsmuir medal, awarded in 1937 for the best poem appearing in that year in the *Canadian Poetry Magazine,* was awarded posthumously to Annie Charlotte Dalton for 'Wheat and Barley.' The first Governor General's Award for Poetry went to Pratt himself for the 1937 publication of *The Fable of the Goats and Other Poems.*

117 'article ... Pierce.' Pierce's essay, 'The Interpreter's House,' an intelligent survey of the history of Canadian poetry in English and its supportive organs, argues that 'Canada was not discovered until our poets found it, nor was this land explored until our poets made it known'; *Canadian Poetry Magazine* 2 (June 1937): 5.

## F. Pratt as Reviewer

A.D. Watson's *Robert Norwood*. Toronto: Ryerson Press, 1923

Explanatory Notes

118 'projected series.' Watson's book on Norwood was the first in the Makers of Canadian Literature Series. It was Lorne Pierce, instigator of the series, who asked Pratt to write the review (TY 260).

119 'Great art ... beautiful.' Watson 117

Flos Jewell Williams's *New Furrows*. Ottawa: Graphic Press, 1926

James O'Donnell Bennett's *Much Loved Books: Best Sellers of the Ages*. Toronto: Boni and Liveright McLean and Smithers, 1927

The nature of Bennett's enterprise in his weekly columns and the collection of them may well have provided a model for Pratt's own columns in *Canadian Comment*. Both writers offer commentary on Lord Macaulay, Sir Francis Bacon, Samuel Pepys, Izaak Walton, Charles Lamb, and Charles Dickens.

Explanatory Notes

121 'Polonius-Montaigne.' This description of Pepys is ascribed in Bennett (281) to James Russell Lowell.

121 'verra pious.' Quoted in Bennett 157

121 'The minute ... circumstances.' Quoted in Bennett 198

121–2 'What did ... ill.' Pratt substantially and interestingly alters Boswell's text as quoted by Bennett, 119:

> He sometimes could not bear to be teased with questions. I was once present when a gentleman asked so many as, 'What did you do, Sir?' 'What did you say, Sir?' that he at last grew enraged, and said 'I will not be put to the *question*. Don't you consider, Sir, that these are not the manners of a gentleman. I will not be baited with *what* and *why*; what is this? what is that? why is the cow's tail long? why is a fox's tail bushy?' The gentleman who was a good deal out of countenance, said, 'Why, Sir, you are so good, that I venture to trouble you.' JOHNSON. 'Sir, my being so *good* is no reason why you should be so *ill*.'

Laura Riding's *Contemporaries and Snobs*. Toronto: Cape Nelson, 1928

Explanatory Notes

122 'the will ... independence.' Riding 10

122 'whatever.' In Riding: any

123 'creative self-consciousness ... terms.' Riding 129

123 'professional conscience.' Riding 128

123 'their poetry ... written.' Riding 30

123 'written.' In Riding: being written

123 'little hill of nonsense.' Riding 52

123 'writing ... society.' Riding 98
123 'There is ... poetry.' Riding 9

Robert M. Gay's *Ralph Waldo Emerson*. Toronto: Doubleday, Doran and Gundy, 1928

Textual Note
124 'transcendentalism.' transcendalism

Explanatory Notes
124 'externalities ... efficiency.' Gay 1
124 'The compensation ... helpful life.' Gay 176
125 'one ... knew.' Gay 100
125 'Tennyson ... violets.' The descriptions of Tennyson, Macaulay, and Landor are all from Gay 202.

Emil Ludwig's *Goethe*. Toronto: Ryerson Press, 1928

Textual Notes
127 'and proposed.' proposed
127 'paint.' plant
128 'pace.' In Ludwig and in Pratt: place

Explanatory Notes
125 'This ... traits.' Ludwig vi
125 'Thus he will.' In Ludwig: He will thus
125 'humanly comprehensible.' In Ludwig: comprehensible
125 'not otherwise seen.' In Ludwig: seen in this way
125 'in their obscuring of.' In Ludwig: in obscuring
125 'the unification of.' In Ludwig: uniting
125 'traits.' In Ludwig: traits of character
126 'art of dress.' Ludwig 6
126 'quaint little beggars.' Ludwig 5
126 'If blustering ... mice.' Ludwig 75–6
126 'an imaginative career.' Ludwig speaks of Goethe's father as clearing the way for his son's 'imaginative life' (76).
127 'seemed ... eye-sockets.' I have not been able to find such a passage in the biography, though Ludwig quotes Johann Gottfried

Herder as saying to Goethe, 'You're all for the eye!' (107), and later, in explaining how as an amateur anatomist Goethe had discovered the human intermaxillary bone, Ludwig writes, 'his eye was unprejudiced ... That eye was thinking while it gazed' (205).

127 'devastated ... keys.' Ludwig 154

127 'deaf, running his fingers.' In Ludwig: very hard of hearing; whose fingers are rushing headlong

127 'mutually ... countenance.' Ludwig 175

127 'gaze.' In Ludwig: to gaze

127–8 'When ... mastery.' Quoted on 31 as epigraph to ch. 2 of vol. 1, with an elision of the phrases between 'energies' and 'till'

J. Middleton Murry, ed., *The Letters of Katherine Mansfield*. 2 vols. Toronto: Macmillan, 1928

Textual Note

128 'Introductory Note.' Introductory

Explanatory Notes

128 'In arranging ... life.' Murry, vol. 1, vii

129 'God forbid ... *writing*.' Murry, vol. 2, 2

129 'marvellous.' In Murry: gorgeous marvellous

129 'You know ... not.' Murry, vol. 1, 307

129 'time I.' In Murry: time when I

129–30 'The nights ... there?' Murry, vol. 1, 13

129 'nights here.' In Murry: nights

130 'As soon ... quarter to 2!' Murry, vol. 1, 103

130 'sit in.' In Murry: sit up in

130 'For some ... fever.' Murry, vol. 1, 40–1

130 'Keats ... live.' Pratt is not really quoting here. Mansfield does, however, write of Wordsworth and Coleridge, as well as of the writers Pratt mentions, 'those are the people with whom I want to live' (vol. 1, 143).

130 'Nowadays ... Ball.' Murry, vol. 1, 234

130 'the movement ... experiment.' Murry, vol. 2, 62. Pratt interpolates the word 'is' and adds 'just an experiment,' though Mansfield uses the word 'experiment' only later in her letter when she explains

to Walpole her choice of the word 'task' in her review; she had tried to describe what he seemed to want to do: 'perhaps "experiment" was nearer my meaning' (63).

130 'one of those ... future.' Murry, vol. 2, 66

Edwin Arlington Robinson's *Sonnet*. Toronto: Macmillan, 1929; Elinor Wylie's *Angels and Earthly Creatures*. Toronto: Longmans, Green and Co., 1929; and Bliss Carman's *Wild Garden*. Toronto: McClelland and Stewart, 1929

The review included brief comments on Kathleen Millay's *The Hermit Thrush* and Alice Mary Kimball's *The Devil Is a Woman* not reproduced here. In the copy text, asterisks separate the parts of the review, each part being headed by bibliographic information.

Explanatory Notes

131 *'The Children of the Night.' The Children of the Night* (1897) is a revised and expanded reissue of Robinson's first book, *The Torrent and the Night Before* (1896).

131 *'The Man ... Twice.'* The volumes appeared in 1916, 1923, and 1924, respectively.

131 '"Job the Dejected".' In Robinson: 'Job the Rejected'

131 'crowns ... won.' This phrase does not appear either in *Sonnets* or in the earlier *The Children of the Night*.

132 'The Sheaves.' *Sonnets* 72

133 'hands ... chilled ... fires.' An allusion to 'Dying Speech of an Old Philosopher,' by Walter Savage Landor, which ends 'I warmed my hands before the fire of Life; / It sinks, and I am ready to depart.' *Poems*, ed. Stephen Wheeler, *Complete Works*, 15 (London: Chapman and Hall, 1935) 226. Landor prided himself on the classical elegance and perfection of his art; hence the parallel with Wylie's 'technical excellence,' 'chiselled' lines, etc.

133 'The laureate.' Bliss Carman was crowned with a laurel wreath and named 'unofficial laureate' in 1921 at a Canadian Authors' Association dinner in Montreal.

134 *'Book of Lyrics ... Sea Children.' Low Tide on Grand Pré: A Book of Lyrics*

(1893), *Songs from Vagabondia* (1895), *More Songs from Vagabondia* (1896), *Last Songs from Vagabondia* (1901), and *Echoes from Vagabondia* (1912); *Songs of the Sea Children* (1904)

134 'old sorceries.' 'Moment Musicale,' *Wild Garden* 11

134 'morning ... oracles.' See 'Nature Lore,' which in speaking of Nature refers to 'Her morning revelations / Her twilight oracles,' *Wild Garden* 4.

134 'Far fleeing ... fame.' 'A Dream Garden,' *Wild Garden* 27

134–5 'Because ... deserving.' *Wild Garden* 47–8

K.A.R. Sugden's *A Short History of the Brontës*. Toronto: Oxford UP, 1929

Explanatory Notes

135 'It seemed ... proportion.' Sugden v

135 'seemed.' In Sugden: seemed then

135–6 'multitude ... west.' Sugden 5–6

136 'and bilberry.' In Sugden: or of bilberry

136 'hard labour ... between.' Sugden 21

136 'riotous ... cubs.' Sugden 22

136 'Little ... gentleman-like.' Sugden 28–9

136 'I have ... soul.' Sugden 34

136 '*Jane Eyre, Shirley,* and *Villette*.' All novels by Charlotte, published in 1847, 1849, and 1853, respectively

136–7 'We have ... work.' Elizabeth Rigby reviewed *Jane Eyre* in *The Quarterly Review* (December 1848): 162–76. The excerpt appears in Sugden 49.

136 'Jane Eyre.' In Sugden: her; In Pratt: *Jane Eyre*

137 'make Jane Eyre.' In Pratt: make *Jane Eyre*

Mazo de la Roche's *Whiteoaks of Jalna*. Toronto: Macmillan, 1929

Under the heading 'Whiteoaks of Jalna – A Review,' the review began '*Whiteoaks of Jalna*, Mazo De la Roche.'

Explanatory Notes

137 '*Jalna*.' *Jalna* (Boston: Little Brown, 1927)

138 '*The White Monkey*.' John Galsworthy, *The White Monkey* (1924)

138 'character of Wakefield ... development.' De la Roche did in fact develop this character in later books, most notably *Wakefield's Course* (Boston: Little Brown, 1941).

André Maurois's *Byron*. Toronto: Ryerson Press, 1930

Explanatory Notes

138 '*Ariel* and *Disraeli*.' *Ariel*, the life of Percy Bysshe Shelley, and *Disraeli* appeared in 1923 and 1927, respectively.

138 'Jukes ... Kallikaks.' The fictitious names of a New York and New Jersey family, respectively, whose case histories over several generations compiled by nineteenth-century sociologists showed an abnormally high incidence of poverty, disease, criminality, mental retardation, etc. These case histories were used to justify eugenic policies in the United States.

139 'Fairweather.' Most sources, including Maurois (10), cite Foulweather Jack as the nickname of Byron's ancestor.

139 'It seemed ... tree.' Maurois 13

139–40 'All Scotland ... him.' Maurois 24–5

140 'The subject ... other.' Maurois 176

141–2 'My days ... thy rest.' On This Day I Complete My Thirty-Sixth Year,' *Poetical Works of Lord Byron*, Poetry vol. 7, 2d ed., ed. Ernest Hartley Coleridge (London: John Murray, 1905) 86–8

142 'now in ... afraid.' Maurois 535

142 'A few moments ... dead.' Maurois 537

Frank H. Shaw's *Famous Shipwrecks*. London: Elkin Matthews and Marrott, 1930

Textual Note

143 'not even need.' In Shaw; In Pratt: not need

Explanatory Notes

142 'Q-boat.' Also called hush-hush or mystery ships, these First World War British destroyers disguised as trading vessels were used to decoy German U-boats. Their name is an abbreviation of the Latin *quaere* (to seek, look for, inquire).

143 'size ... security.' Shaw 81

143 'maritime.' In Shaw: perfect maritime

143–4 'Here ... decks.' Shaw 83
144 'the two ... courage.' Shaw 123 refers to 'that two-o'clock-in-the-morning brand' of courage.
144 'some form ... gale.' Shaw 319

Wilson Follett, ed., *The Collected Poems of Stephen Crane*. Toronto: Longmans, Green, 1930

Explanatory Notes
145 'two books.' *The Collected Poems* not only reprints earlier work, but adds previously uncollected poems. Its three sections are 'The Black Riders and Other Lines,' 'War Is Kind and Other Lines,' and 'Three Poems.'
145 'Once ... simplicity.' Follett, ed. 7
146 'I saw ... ran on.' Follett, ed. 26
146–7 'Do not ... kind.' Follett, ed. 77–8. Pratt quotes stanzas 1, 3, and 5.

Dormer Creston's *Andromeda in Wimpole Street*. Toronto: E.P. Dutton, 1930; and Émilie and Georges Romieu's *Three Virgins of Haworth*. Toronto: E.P. Dutton, 1930

The Romieu book, subtitled 'Being an Account of the Brontë Sisters,' was translated from the French by Roberts Tapley [Robert Stapley?].

Explanatory Notes
147 Last year ... printed.' Pratt had reviewed Leonard Huxley's *Elizabeth Barrett Browning* (Toronto: Macmillan, 1929) for *Saturday Night*, 4 January 1930: 8, under the title 'The Brownings Again.'
147 'If a prince ... not do.' Creston 45
148 'a friend ... floor.' Creston 45
148 'Perseus.' The description of Robert Browning as 'Perseus, the Deliverer' is Creston's: 57.
148 'a swift-walking ... hair.' Creston 57
148 'with a pale.' In Creston: his pale
148–9 'and as ... world.' Creston 241, 250
149 'odd ... children.' Romieu viii
149 'Creakle ... Squeers.' Creakle is the headmaster of Salem House in *David Copperfield* and Wackford Squeers the headmaster of Dothe-

boys Hall in *Nicholas Nickleby.*

149 'Cowan's ... Wilson ... black marble.' The Rev. William Carus Wilson, trustee of Cowan's Bridge School, is the prototype for Brocklehurst in *Jane Eyre*. Pratt is probably remembering Brontë's reference to Brocklehurst as 'a black pillar' rather than quoting accurately from the novel.

150 'Héger.' See 136 in this volume.

150 'islanded by the dead.' Romieu 134

150 'Swinburne ... Maeterlinck.' In fact, Maeterlinck was not born until seven years after Charlotte Brontë's death, and Swinburne was only in his teens at the time.

John Masefield's *The Wanderer of Liverpool*. Toronto: Macmillan, 1930

Explanatory Notes

150 'Poet Laureate.' The title was bestowed in 1930.

150 '*Dauber ... The Everlasting Mercy ... Reynard The Fox*.' published in 1913, 1911, and 1919, respectively

151 '*Salt Water Ballads ... Gallipoli ...* "Consecration".' *Salt Water Ballads* was published in 1902 and *Gallipoli* in 1916. 'A Consecration' prefaced *Salt Water Ballads*, promising that the commoner and the oppressed would be the subject-matter of the songs and tales.

151 'The sight ... done.' Masefield 12–13

152 'When ... San Francisco.' Masefield 31

152 'The Bosun ... here.' Masefield, *Dauber* 14

153 'Of course ... neglected.' The unsigned review appeared in *The New Statesman*, 15 November 1930: 180, under the title 'She Walked the Water.'

153–4 'In the morning ... below.' Masefield 26

153 'the anchorage.' In Masefield: her anchorage

154 '*Watchers*.' In Masefield: watchers

154 'And another voice ... spray.' Masefield 81–2

Joseph Auslander, trans., *The Sonnets of Petrarch*. Toronto: Longmans, Green, 1931

Explanatory Notes

155 'Lesbia ... Julia.' Lesbia is associated with Catullus; Corinna and

Julia with Robert Herrick; Cynara with Horace (and later with Ernest Dowson), Beatrice with Dante.

156 'Never ... rivalries.' CXII, Auslander, trans., 112

156 'the theatre ... sorrow.' Auslander translates CXXIII as 'Wherein all Nature in the Theatre to her Sorrow' 123.

157 'Felicitous ... hook.' CLXXVII, Auslander, trans., 177

157 'some soft.' In Auslander: one soft

Kenneth Leslie's *By Stubborn Stars and Other Poems*. Toronto: Ryerson Press, 1938

The review was accompanied by the following congratulatory stop-press announcement: '*By Stubborn Stars* has just received the Governor-General's Award for the outstanding book of poetry in Canada for 1938. Congratulations to Kenneth Leslie!'

Explanatory Notes

157 '*Windward Rock*.' *Windward Rock* (New York: Macmillan Co., 1934)

158 'The day ... distils.' 'By Stubborn Stars,' *By Stubborn Stars* 6, 12

158 'There is ... we know.' 'The Misty Mother' appeared in the *Canadian Poetry Magazine* (January 1936): 33. The poem was revised to become an untitled part of the sonnet sequence 'By Stubborn Stars' for its book-form publication.

Verna Loveday Harden's *Postlude to an Era*. Toronto: The Crucible Press, 1940

Explanatory Notes

158 'Verna Loveday Harden.' Verna Loveday Harden also published two Ryerson Press chapbooks, no. 118, *When This Tide Ebbs* (1946), and no. 183, *In Her Mind Carrying* (1959). The former includes on the front-cover verso a bio-bibliographical note on this little-known poet:

> Verna Loveday Harden is a native of Toronto and her verse began to appear in the newspapers of that city when she was twelve years old. She has contributed verse, short articles and poetry reviews to Canadian and American publications. Only one other collection of her verse has been made, *Postlude to an Era*, a Carillon Chap-Book in 1940. She is former Secretary of [the]

Canadian Authors' Association, Toronto Branch, and the Canadian Literature Club of Toronto.

The poems in the present collection have appeared in *Canadian Poetry Magazine, Saturday Night, Christian Science Monitor, Toronto Daily Star, Chatelaine, Alberta Poetry Yearbook,* and *Trinity University Review.* The title poem won the Macnab Historical Association's Poetry Award for 1945.

159 'To One in Bedlam.' See his *Verses* (1896).

159 'Happy fool ... O happy fool.' Harden, 'To an Idiot, September, 1938,' *Postlude* 12

159 'You have.' In Harden: You will have

Watson Kirkconnell's *The Flying Bull and Other Tales*. Toronto: Oxford UP, 1940

Explanatory Notes

160 'linguist ... scholar ... artist.' Despite Pratt's subsequent claim for parity of achievement, Kirkconnell is probably better remembered for his translations and anthologies of world literature and Canadian poetry written originally in languages other than English than for his own creative writing. See for example his *Canadian Overtones: An Anthology of Canadian Poetry Written Originally in Icelandic, Swedish, Hungarian, Italian, Greek, and Ukrainian* (Winnipeg: Columbia Press, 1935). His annual reviews (1938–65) of Canadian literature written in languages other than English for the 'Letters in Canada' survey of the *University of Toronto Quarterly* are further testament to his passionate scholarly dedication to the promotion of literatures in the non-official languages in Canada.

161 'In time ... peaks.' 'The Bus Driver's Tale of the Magyar Violinist,' *The Flying Bull* 134

Alan Crawley, ed., *Contemporary Verse: A Canadian Quarterly*

Explanatory Notes

161 'a national organization.' the Canadian Authors' Association

161 '"Three poems".' 'Surrealism in the Service of Christ,' 'The Mermaid,' and 'The Cry,' *Poetry* (Chicago) 58.1 (April 1941): 9–11

Earle Birney's *David and Other Poems*. Toronto: Ryerson Press, 1942

Explanatory Note

163 'Professor Sedgewick's phrase.' Garnet Sedgewick was head of the Department of English at the University of British Columbia, where Birney was first a student and then a friend and colleague of Sedgewick's. The phrase comes from Sedgewick's endorsement of the book, which appeared, along with those of L.A. MacKay (Classics, UBC) and Pratt, on the back of the dust-jacket of the first edition. Pratt's endorsement reads:

> Earle Birney's poems are original in their daring use of phrase and imagery. He has the gift of vitalizing language by infusing fresh meanings into words while preserving their basic connotation. Ideas are packed into his lines. What he says is worth saying and it is said well. 'David' is a superb story, dynamic in its feeling, musical in its elaborated metrics – an intense human drama placed against a brilliantly executed backdrop of the mountains.

Mona Gould's *Tasting the Earth*. Toronto: Macmillan, 1943

Mona Helen Gould (b. Prince Albert, Saskatchewan, 25 January 1908) had a career as a newspaper writer, women's-page editor, advertising copy-writer, and publicity writer for such organizations as the Red Cross, Sick Children's Hospital (Toronto), National Clothing Drive, and the Salvation Army, in addition to her film-script writing for Associated Screen News and her poetry writing. She also published *I Run with the Fox* (Toronto: Macmillan, 1946).

Textual Note

163 'NostAlgia.' In Gould: NostAglia

Explanatory Notes

163 'B.K. Sandwell.' As editor of *Saturday Night*, B.K. Sandwell published a number of the poems in the volume Pratt reviewed. In his 'Foreword' Sandwell deems Gould to be 'exceptionally successful' in revealing the 'ordinary man and woman in the moments when they are not ordinary, without any ... sense of intrusion.'

163 'And even ... eagerness.' 'This Was My Brother,' *Tasting the Earth*

4. This poem was used by General Motors for their Victory Loan campaign and quoted by the *Globe and Mail* as 'the finest war poem of the 2nd Great War,' according to *Canadian Who's Who* for 1949–51. That publication also reported that the poem was to be reproduced in bronze in both English and French and erected at Dieppe.

A.M. Klein's *The Hitleriad*. New York: New Directions, 1944

Explanatory Notes

164 '*New Provinces* ... *Hath Not a Jew*.' Published in 1936 and 1940, respectively

164 'Ludwig Lewisohn.' Ludwig Lewisohn wrote a foreword for the 1940 publication of *Hath Not A Jew* ... which Miriam Waddington reprints in her *Collected Poems of A.M. Klein* (Toronto: McGraw-Hill Ryerson Press, 1974).

164 '"Soirée of Velvel Kleinburger".' This poem first appeared in the *Canadian Forum* (August 1932): 424–5.

165 '*The Hitleriad*.' 'The Hitleriad,' *First Statement* 2.1 (August 1943): ii–3 [lines 1–109] and 2.3 (October 1943): 4–7 [lines 303–451]

165 'I am weak ... bird.' 'Out of the Pulver and the Polished Lens' 80–4, in *A.M. Klein: Complete Poems*, ed. Zailig Pollock (Toronto: U of Toronto P, 1990) line 211. The copy text does not preserve Klein's stanza break before the last line quoted here.

165 'at length [no period].' In the versions of 'Out of the Pulver and the Polished Lens' published in *Hath Not a Jew* ... and the *Complete Poems* there is no punctuation after 'at length'; in the versions published in the *Canadian Forum* and *New Provinces* there is a period. Pratt's text has no period.

165 'Dryden ... Achitophel.' See John Dryden, 'Absalom and Achitophel' (1681); Zimri is Dryden's name in the poem for George Villiers, 2nd Duke of Buckingham, and Achitophel that for the 1st Earl of Shaftesbury, the leader of Whig party opposition to the succession of the Catholic James II to the throne of England.

165–6 'He drew ... iscariots.' *The Hitleriad* 114–25, in *Complete Poems*, 2.585

166 'Goering ... Ley.' Hermann Goering (1893–1946) founded and

headed the Gestapo. Joseph Goebbels (1897–1945) was Hitler's propaganda minister, propagating anti-Jewish sentiment through his control of German radio, press, cinema, and theatre. Alfred Rosenberg (1893–1946) was the author of *The Myth of the Twentieth Century* (1930), a book which provided Hitler with spurious philosophical and scientific authority for his racist theories. After 1941, Rosenberg was minister to the East European countries and therefore responsible for Nazi atrocities there. Joachim von Ribbentrop (1893–1946) was Hitler's foreign minister. Robert Ley (1890–1945) served as head of the German Workers' front after the suppression in May 1933 of independent trade unions.

166 'Heil ... Berlin.' *The Hitleriad* 1–7, in *Complete Poems* 2.581

## G. Pratt as Prefacer: Forewords and Introductions

'Foreword' to Jack McLaren's *Our Great Ones: Twelve Caricatures Cut in Linoleum.*

Explanatory Notes

168 'Jack McLaren.' J.W. McLaren (1896–1954) was an illustrator and cartoonist who in 1922 became a member of the Toronto Arts and Letters Club, to which Pratt belonged.

168 'Merrill Denison.' Merrill Denison (1893–1975) is best remembered as a playwright who was at the forefront of the Little Theatre Movement in Canada in the 1920s, but he also left his mark as a journalist, broadcaster, historian, raconteur, and conservationist.

'Foreword' to Samuel Morgan-Powell's *Down the Years*

Explanatory Notes

169 'vindicated by his signature.' Morgan-Powell reviewed Pratt's own first book, *Newfoundland Verse*, in the *Montreal Star*, 5 May 1923: 15, calling Pratt a 'Poet of Inspirational Power.' Thereafter Morgan-Powell regularly gave favourable reviews to Pratt's books. Summaries of these reviews can be found in Lila and Raymond Laakso with Moira Allen and Marjorie Linden, 'E.J. Pratt: An Annotated Bibli-

ography,' in Robert Lecker and Jack David, eds, *The Annotated Bibliography of Canada's Major Authors*, vol. 2 (Downsview: ECW Press, 1980) 205, 209, 212, 215, 215–16.

170 *'Memories That Live.'* Morgan-Powell, *Memories That Live* (Toronto: Macmillan, 1929)

'Canadian Poets in the USA – A.J.M. Smith'

The other poets introduced and sampled in the way Smith was were Ralph Gustafson, Kenneth Leslie, and Leo Kennedy.

Explanatory Note

170 *'News of the Phoenix.'* In 1943 the book was published by both Coward-McCann in New York and Ryerson Press in Toronto.

'Introduction to the Life and Work of Melville'

Explanatory Notes

171 'Doughty.' Charles Montagu Doughty (1843–1926), author of *Travels in Arabia Deserta*

172 *'Typee ... Omoo.'* Though Pratt discusses *Typee: A Peep at Polynesian Life* second, in was in fact Melville's first novel, published in 1846. *Redburn: His First Voyage* appeared in 1849, after *Omoo: A Narrative of Adventure in the South Seas* (1847), making the latter Melville's second work, not his third, as Pratt indicates.

172 *'Evangeline* and *Hiawatha.' Evangeline, A Tale of Acadie* (1847) and *The Song of Hiawatha* (1855) are narrative poems by Melville's contemporary Henry Wadsworth Longfellow. The former represents the lives of Acadian lovers separated by the French and so-called Indian wars; the latter recounts the life and death of the titular Native hero, who, before he dies, predicts the White man's advent, and advises his people to accept the newcomers.

173 'Harper fire of 1853.' In the fire that destroyed the offices of Melville's publisher, Harper and Brothers, the plates of all his novels and most of the copies of his seven published books in stock were lost.

173 *'Cyclopedia of American Biographies.'* Likely *Appleton's Cyclopedia of American Biography*, ed. James Grant Wilson and John Fiske (New York:

Appleton, 1888), in which Melville was accorded little more than half a page, while the entry on Henry Wadsworth Longfellow ran to five and a half pages.

173 *'British Survey of American Letters.'* I have been unable to locate either a periodical or a book with this title or a close variant of it.

173 'Stevenson, Stoddard, O'Brien, and Jack London.' Pratt is following Raymond Weaver, *Herman Melville: Mariner and Mystic* (New York: George H. Doran, 1921), who lists Robert Louis Stevenson, Charles Warren Stoddard, Jack London, and Frederick O'Brien among the eight named as Melville's 'ample and rapidly multiplying progeny' (24).

174 'Marryat, Cooper, and Dana.' Captain Frederick Marryat (1792–1848), James Fenimore Cooper (1789–1851), and Richard Henry Dana (1815–82)

174 'the first ... forecastle.' Weaver 24

174 'hatch ... forecastle.' In Weaver: and show the world what passes in a ship's forecastle

175 'Not long ... experience.' Preface, *Mardi and the Voyage Thither,* Works of Herman Melville, vol. 3, ed. Harrison Hayford, Hershel Parker, and G. Thomas Tanselle (Evanston and Chicago: Northwestern UP and the Newberry Library, 1970) vii

175 'Stevenson.' Robert Louis Stevenson (1850–94), Scottish-born novelist, short-story writer, and essayist. He identified Melville as 'a howling cheese' in a letter from the Pacific of 6 September 1888 to Charles Baxter, cited in Jay Leyda *The Melville Log: A Documentary Life of Herman Melville, 1819–1891,* 2 (New York: Harcourt, Brace and Co., 1951) 809.

175 'a man who had once lived among cannibals.' In Weaver 21: a man who lived among the cannibals! (letter from Melville to Nathaniel Hawthorne 1? June 1851)

176 'Jonathan Edwards.' (1703–58) American Puritan theologian and preacher

176 'Toby ... Ghost.' Toby, a fellow crewman of Melville's when he served on the *Acushnet,* is Richard Tobias Greene. Melville wrote about him in *Typee* and its sequel, 'The Story of Toby.' Dr Long Ghost,

whom Melville writes about in *Omoo*, was the medical officer aboard the *Julia* when Melville signed on, and their friendship grew closer when they were put ashore on Tahiti for their ineffectual resistance to a mutiny.

176 'a parcel ... captain.' This description of the *Acushnet* crew appears in *Typee* and is quoted in Weaver 162.

177 'order ... descent.' Weaver 25

177 'broiled in Hell Fire.' In a letter to Nathaniel Hawthorne, 29 June 1851, Melville writes, 'Shall I send you a fin of the *Whale* by way of a specimen mouthful? The tail is not yet cooked, though the hell-fire in which the book is broiled might not unreasonably have cooked it ere this' (quoted in Weaver 319–20).

177–8 'though ... fright.' Pratt here quotes the last sentence of the third-last paragraph of ch. 42 of *Moby Dick*, 'The Whiteness of the Whale.'

179 'Burton.' Robert Burton (1577–1640), author of *The Anatomy of Melancholy* (1621), a miscellany of theological, classical, and Elizabethan learning

179 'Paley.' William Paley (1743–1805) was the author of *Evidences of Christianity* (1794) and *Natural Theology* (1802). He found proof for the existence of God in the design apparent in natural phenomena and the mechanisms of the human body.

From 'Introduction' to Thomas Hardy's *Under the Greenwood Tree or the Mellstock Quire*

I have not reproduced the first section of the Introduction, 'Life of Thomas Hardy,' because it is an unremarkable and sketchy bio-bibliographical account.

Explanatory Notes

181 'Festival ... Plot.' The passage comes from ch. 3 of Book First, 'The Custom of the Country,' in *The Return of the Native* (London: Macmillan, 1920) 17

181 'He had ... days.' The passage comes from ch. 8 of *The Woodlanders* (London: Macmillan, 1920) 72.

181–2 'Only ... die.' The poem comes from *Moments of Vision and Miscellaneous Verses* (1917), rpt in CPWTH 511.

183 'crass casualty.' The final lines of 'Hap' read: 'Crass Casualty obstructs the sun and rain, / And dicing Time for gladness casts a moan ... / These purblind Doomsters had as easily strown / Blisses about my pilgrimage as pain,' CPWTH 7.

183 'Alien ... hemispheres.' The poem comes from *Satires of Circumstance* (1914), rpt in CPWTH 289.

183 'Angel Clare ... Clym's visit.' Angel Clare and Tess are characters in *Tess of the D'Urbervilles*, and Clym Yeobright is a character in *The Return of the Native*.

183 'is only ... pain.' Pratt is recalling the final words of *The Life and Death of the Mayor of Casterbridge*.

184 'What we have ... evil.' George Eliot uses as a heading for ch. 70 of *Middlemarch* the lines 'Our deeds still travel with us from afar / And what we have been makes us what we are.'

184 'thistle-globes ... gales.' *The Dynasts*, in *The Poetical Works of Thomas Hardy*, vol. 2 (London: Macmillan, 1924), 204, Part Second, II, vii

184 'in Heaven's.' In Hardy: on Heaven's

184 'Matching ... between them.' Pratt refers here to *The Return of the Native*.

184 'Standing over ... English heart.' Sergeant Troy and Gabriel Oak are characters in *Far from the Madding Crowd*.

185 'Henchard, Boldwood.' Michael Henchard is the central character of *The Mayor of Casterbridge* and Farmer Boldwood appears in *Far from the Madding Crowd*.

185–6 'It is ... together.' Lascelles Abercrombie, *Thomas Hardy: A Critical Study* (London: Martin Secker, 1924), 110–11

186 'Edie Ochiltree ... Old Mause.' Edie Ochiltree is a character in Scott's *The Antiquary*; Peter Peebles appears in *Redgauntlet*; and Cuddie and Old Mause Headrigg, in *Old Mortality*.

187 'The actual ... bind.' Florence Emily Hardy, *The Early Life of Thomas Hardy, 1840–1891* (London: Macmillan, 1928) 122

187 'the sunny ... fog.' *Under the Greenwood Tree* (New York: Harper and Brothers, 1905) 18, 47

## H. Pratt as Teacher: The Lectures and Addresses

### Huxley

The text is taken from a three-page ts (10.72.62–4). The phraseology, quotations, and ordering of material in this lecture all point to Pratt's heavy reliance on Houston Peterson's *Huxley: Prophet of Science* (London: Longman's Green and Co., 1932), and the dating of the lecture is based on the publication of this book.

Explanatory Notes

188 *'The Principles of Geology.'* Charles Lyell's *The Principles of Geology,* 3 vols (1830–3)

189 *'Sartor Resartus.'* The chapters of *Sartor Resartus* entitled 'The Everlasting No,' 'Centre of Indifference,' and 'The Everlasting Yea' map a spiritual crisis like the one Carlyle experienced in his early days at the University of Edinburgh, where he was studying for the ministry.

189 *'Sartor Resartus* ... Theology.' Quoted in Peterson 8

189 'Few ... sorts.' The comment was made in a letter to Lord Stanley of Alderley, 9 March 1881. Quoted in Peterson 8–9

189 'bracing.' In Peterson: bracing wholesome

189 'sorts.' In Peterson: sort

190 'Perhaps ... man.' Charles Darwin, *Journal of Researches,* quoted in Peterson 43

190 'haunts.' In Peterson: haunt

190 'these men, whose signs.' In Peterson: these? – men whose very signs

190 'cultivated.' In Peterson: civilized

190 'Faraday ... Wallace.' Michael Faraday (1791–1867) laid the foundations of classical field theory in physics, developed the first dynamo, and discovered both electromagnetic induction and the compound benzene. Alfred Russell Wallace (1823–1913) was a naturalist whose special contribution to the evidence for evolution was in biogeography, a science he systematized. He wrote the two-volume *The Geographical Distribution of Animals* (1876), and later published a supplement, *Island Life* (1881).

190–1 'He ... animals.' Peterson 68

190 'us its.' In Peterson: us clearly its
191 'the wonderful.' In Peterson: his wonderful
191 'especially.' In Peterson: extremely
191 'of the subject.' In Peterson: whole group. (Wallace was referring to Huxley's discussion of parasites.)
191 'topic.' In Peterson: subject
191 'the working ... penalties.' Quoted in Peterson 81
191 'there.' In Peterson: these
191–2 'Bishop ... bishop's.' Peterson 120–2. In Peterson, the third sentence quoted begins a new paragraph.
193 'letter.' The letter, dated 23 September 1860, is quoted in Peterson 125–33. It makes clear Huxley's deeply considered agnosticism and simultaneous sense of sacred responsibility to tell the truth as he knows it. His point, as a man of science, is that he lacks evidence to decide the issue of human immortality either way. He affirms that science has taught him to be careful not to adopt a view because it accords with his preoccupations; rather in such circumstances, one should require more complete and persuasive evidence than in a situation where one is predisposed to be hostile to the idea. Thus, on the matter of immortality, since it would be comforting to him to believe that his son as a distinct personality lives on, Huxley would require the most rigorous proof to believe it.

## D.H. Lawrence

The text is taken from an untitled ts (10.35.7–8), the first page of which has centred at the top a holograph addition that is either the number 20 or 2a. The holograph notes at the end of the ts indicate that the comments on Lawrence were part of a series of lectures on poetry since the turn of the century. The dating of this lecture is based on the reference to Frieda Lawrence's book (see first note to p 195 in this volume).

### Explanatory Notes

193 'that it is intellect.' that is intellect
194 '*Fantasia of the Unconscious*.' *Fantasia of the Unconscious* (1922) is a non-fictional work.
194 'Cypresses.' 'Cypresses' is from the 'Trees' section of *Birds, Beasts and Flowers* (1923).

194 'To find ... rooted.' John Macy, 'Introduction' to *Sons and Lovers*, Modern Library edition (New York: Random House, 1922) vi–vii

194 'to Hardy.' In Macy: to two older novelists, Hardy and Meredith

194 'descent into mindlessness.' I have not been able to find this exact phrase in Murry's writings about Lawrence, but his reviews of *The Lost Girl* in *Athenaeum* and of *Women in Love* in *Nation and Athenaeum*, as well as the book-length work *Son of Woman* (London: Jonathan Cape, 1931), repeatedly make this point in other words.

195 'I am ... women.' The letter, dated 10 November 1923, is quoted in Frieda Lawrence, *Not I but the Wind* (New York: Viking Press, 1934) 143.

195 'stays.' In Lawrence: lies

195 'holiday.' In Lawrence: holidays

195 'keeps on saying.' In Lawrence: keeps saying

195 'battle strength, fighting strength.' In Lawrence: battle-strength, weapon-strength, fighting-strength

195 'O you women.[period]' In Lawrence: give me this you woman!

195 'My daughter ... face.' Frieda Lawrence 179

195 'this outburst.' In Lawrence: the outburst

195 'to Barbara ... "She.' In Lawrence: to Barby; 'she

195 '"Baby Tortoise".' 'Baby Tortoise' is from the 'Reptiles' section of *Birds, Beasts and Flowers* (1923).

[Robinson Jeffers]

The text is taken from an untitled ts (10.38.5 and 7), the second of two on Robinson Jeffers in the PCVU. Ts1 (10.38.1 and 3) has two pages, and begins with a biographical note that helps to explain Pratt's interest in Jeffers: 'Jeffers was educated in the classics, in medicine and forestry. There are so many pictures drawn from biology and chemistry. A description of an injured brain after a fractured skull, of broken bone ends grinding together as the injured man drags himself along the beach. His scientific education gives him a feeling for the immensities of space.' The dating of this lecture is based on the references to Hitler and Fascism in the lecture.

Explanatory Notes

196 *'The Mysterious Universe.'* Sir James Jeans's *The Mysterious Universe* (Cambridge: Cambridge UP, 1930) begins by pointing out that hundreds of thousands of earths would fit into most stars with room to spare, and that the total number of stars is comparable to the number of grains of sand on all the beaches of the world. Ts1 refers to Russell's *Power: A New Social Analysis* (London: George Allen and Unwin Ltd, 1938), citing a passage that links insanity, power, and science (34). It is, however, likely that Pratt had in mind such passages as the one describing the modern universe in *The Impact of Science on Society* 16–17 and the lectures that were published as chs 3–5 of Part Three of *On the Philosophy of Science*, ed. Charles A. Fritz, Jr (Indianapolis: Bobbs-Merrill, 1965) 104–36. Delmore Schwartz (see first note to page 198 in this volume) mentions the early philosophical writings of Russell in addition to citing Joseph Wood Krutch's *The Modern Temper* (New York: Harcourt, Brace, and Co., 1929) (see especially p 8) as containing analogues to Jeffers's view of the universe.

196 'It seemed ... universe.' *The Women at Point Sur* (New York: Boni and Liveright, 1927) 103

196 'this.' In Jeffers: his

196 'alien universe.' In Jeffers: alien universes

196 'Humanity ... split.' *Roan Stallion, Tamar, and Other Poems* (New York: Modern Library, 1935) 13

196 'to split into.' In Jeffers: to break into

197 'annihilation ... Word.' *The Women at Point Sur* 30

197 'men ... things.' 'In Memoriam,' Canto I, lines 3–4, POT 318

197 'Perishing Republic.' The holograph addition 'Read' that follows here indicates that at this point Pratt read Jeffers's 'Shine, Perishing Republic' to his students.

197 'Two main ... blind spot.' See Frajam Taylor's 'The Hawk and the Stone,' part II, of the two-part article 'The Enigma of Robinson Jeffers,' part II of which appeared in *Poetry* (Chicago) 55.1 (October 1939): 39–46. We know that Pratt was aware of this article because he quotes from part I of the essay by Delmore Schwartz (see first note to page 198 in this volume). Schwartz discusses the narrative poem *Give Your Heart to the Hawks* at length, as well as other occurrences of the hawk in Jeffers's poetry.

197 'predestination web.' Cf Pratt's own background as he describes it to Ronald Hambleton in 'An Experience of Life,' OHLP 42.

198 'Stated ... value.' Delmore Schwartz, 'Sources of Violence,' part I of 'The Enigma of Robinson Jeffers' 33; in a parenthetical note Pratt identifies Schwartz and the month and year of the *Poetry* number in which the article appeared.

198 'are often.' In Schwartz: are quite often

198 'false.' In Schwartz: also false

198 'Jeffers ... disgust.' In all probability Pratt is referring to Rolphe Humphries, who in 'Two Books by Jeffers,' *Poetry* (Chicago) 40.3 (June 1932) writes, 'He either knocks you, or leaves you cold' (154).

*King Lear*

The text is a composite of two items in the PCVU: a tape, which I have transcribed, and a ts (10.73.161–74). The tape records an address Pratt made in the Old Victoria College Library on 15 February 1950, according to David G. Pitt in an enclosure with a letter to me dated 25 August 1987. Pitt explains that the tape, which bears the date 15 December 1960, was probably cut from another on that date. He adds, 'The *Lear* lecture was given with minor modifications on at least two subsequent occasions in the early 1950s.'

The twelve-page ts (there is no ts page 162) is used to supplement and conclude the transcribed text, which was chosen as the central copy text because of its greater conciseness and more concentrated focus on *King Lear*. However, where the ts text makes a particular point clearer, it has been preferred. Pratt's quotations from the play seem most often to be from memory, rather than made in a scholarly way, but in the body of the text, I have provided parenthetical act, scene, and line references, and marked line endings. I have not recorded Pratt's expansions of Shakespeare's contractions (e.g., 'do it' for 'do't') or variant spellings or word division in the notes.

Textual Notes

201 'equated with desert.' equated by desert

207 'uncontrol.' On tape: control

209 'Dowden.' This name, indistinctly pronounced, occurs only on the tape.

209 'with him.' The taped address ends here, the balance of the text being excerpted from the ts, 10.73.169–70a, 170b, 173, 174. The ts picks up at this point with a discussion of how the action of the early scenes of Act III are in complete conformity with the speech of the characters, and how the scenes if taken out of context might appear comic. Pratt notes that in his experience, however, audiences do not find comic relief in the scenes. Even the Fool is seen as a medium for commenting on the action, a fact which makes him unique in Shakespeare. A plot summary of occurrences up to Lear's last words follows.

210 'like foxes.' The ts goes on to discuss several directors' and critics' views of the inevitability of *Lear*'s conclusion before taking up the matter of what Pratt calls 'tragic inevitability.'

Explanatory Notes

202 'Why need.' In Shakespeare: What need

203 'Regan and see.' In Shakespeare: Regan; see

205 'anybody.' In Shakespeare: any

205 'heavens.' In Shakespeare: heaven

206 'scarcely.' In Shakespeare: scarce

206 'John Gielgud.' Sir John Gielgud (b. 1904), actor, particularly renowned for his performances in Shakespearean plays, most notably *Hamlet*

206 'Granville-Barker.' Harley Granville-Barker (1877–1946), English dramatist, actor, producer, and critic, author of *Prefaces to Shakespeare*

207 'have ... joined.' In Shakespeare: will ... join

208 'towards.' In Shakespeare: toward

208 'boy? art.' In Shakespeare: boy. How dost, my boy? Art

208 'What have.' In Shakespeare: Has

209 'Dowden ... Bradley.' Ernest Dowden, the author of *Shakespeare: A Study of His Mind and Art* (1875) and *Shakespeare Primer* (1877), would almost certainly have been known to Pratt. A.C. Bradley's classic *Shakespearean Tragedy* (1904) focuses on the psychological analysis of character.

209 'Those last speech fragments.' Pratt is referring to Lear's words as he enters 'with Cordelia dead in his arms' (10.73.169).

210 'the feather.' In Shakespeare: This feather

213 'in the gradual ... dramatist.' C.E. Montague, 'Delights of Tragedy' in *A Writer's Notes on His Trade* (London: Chatto and Windus, 1946) 227. Pratt paraphrases rather than quotes Montague.

*Paradise Lost* with Special Reference to the First Three Books

The text is taken from a ts (10.75.1.17–33). This ts is, however, incomplete, and is therefore supplemented with reference to a holograph draft of the lecture (10.75.1.1–15). There are also two incomplete carbons in the PCVU: the black is of 1–3, 5, and 6, the blue of 7–10 of the ts. David G. Pitt informed me in a letter of 25 August 1987 that this talk, 'or one version of it,' was one of several Pratt gave in the later 1940s to the Graduate English Club at the University of Toronto.

In this lecture, Pratt quotes long passages from Milton, but I have reproduced the quotations only if Pratt does substantial analysis of the lines or if the text would make little sense without them. Otherwise I have merely indicated in square brackets which lines he quoted.

Textual Note
218 'of the darkness.' of darkness

Explanatory Notes
215 'the world ... die.' In the preface to Book II of *The Reason of Church Government Urged against Prelaty* (1642) Milton sets out the principles that will guide him as a poet. Among them is the statement that 'by labour and intent study (which I take to be my portion in this life) joined with the strong propensity of nature, I might perhaps leave something so written to aftertimes, as they should not willingly let it die' (CP&MP 668).

217 'a sorer ... age.' The phrase comes from the Familiar Letter 14, to Henry Oldenburg, Agent for Bremen, 1654 (trans. from the Latin). See John S. Diekhoff, *Milton on Himself* (New York: Humanities Press, 1965) 35–6.

218 'It is ... endure it.' See *The Second Defense* (1954): 'To be blind is not miserable; not to able to bear blindness, that is miserable.' *Milton on Himself* 97

219 'O mighty ... England.' See 'Experiments. Milton: Alcaics,' POT 652

Address on Wordsworth at Cornell

The text is taken from a ts (10.75.3.1–5); in the PCVU ts the page numbered 10.75.3.2 is clearly out of order, its text following logically from that on 10.75.3.5. The provisional dating of the lecture is based on Pratt's friend E.K. Brown's having chaired the Cornell English Department between 1941 and 1944, and this dating accords with Pratt's reference to having taught at the University of Toronto for twenty years.

Textual Notes

222 'bullseye.' Only the letters 'bu' are legible, the rest of the word being obscured by a reinforcing ring. I am indebted to Professor Robert Gibbs for this conjectural reading.

226 'compensated for.' compensated

Explanatory Notes

220 'Legouis ... Broughton.' Emile Legouis (1861–1937), Wordsworth biographer; Heathcote Garrod (1878–1960), Wordsworth critic; Ernest de Selincourt (1870–1943), Wordsworth editor and critic; Alfred Venn Dicey (1835–1922), legal scholar, who also published a book on the statesmanship of Wordsworth; Leslie Broughton (1877–1952), Romantics scholar

221 'Pelham Edgar.' For an account of Pratt's relationship with Pelham Edgar, see *TY* and *MY* passim. An unpublished account appears in a ts entitled 'Highlights and Lowlights: Reminiscences of University [1953]' (9.69.1.5, 7, 9).

224 'The brook ... streams.' *The Prelude* (1805 ed.), VI, lines 553–76

224–5 'But nature ... day.' *The Prelude*, VI, lines 346–51, 353–4, and 355–7

225 'All night ... light.' The lines open Book VI of *Paradise Lost*.

226 'heavy ... life.' Pratt here quotes the last line of section 8 of the 'Ode: Intimations of Immortality From Recollections of Early Childhood.'

226 'poem ... butterfly.' Pratt is referring to 'The Redbreast Chasing the Butterfly.'

227 'that decade.' Wordsworth's 'great decade' is usually reckoned to have ended with the publication of *Poems in Two Volumes* in 1807.

227 'looking ... whole.' Pratt is here recalling Matthew Arnold's

'Sonnet to a Friend,' which lauds Sophocles as one 'who saw life steadily, and saw it whole' *Poetical Works*, ed. C.B. Tinker and H.F. Lowry (London: Oxford UP, 1966) 2.

227–8 'at the ... against Napoleon.' A.V. Dicey, *The Statesmanship of Wordsworth* (Oxford: Clarendon Press, 1917) 5 and 54

228 'of 31.' In Dicey: of over thirty-one

228 'consider.' In Dicey: consider and explain

228–9 'Vanguard ... death.' 'To the Men of Kent' was published in *Poems in Two Volumes* (1807) and rpt in Ernest de Selincourt, ed. *The Poetical Works of William Wordsworth*, vol. 3 (Oxford: Clarendon Press, 1946) 120

229 'we can ... grenadiers.' Pratt's references to the difficulty of envisaging Coleridge and Wordsworth as soldiers arise at least in part from Wordsworth's having enlisted after Napoleon violated the Treaty of Amiens (1802) and war between England and France was renewed in May 1803. Coleridge had fled an unhappy college experience in 1792 by enlisting in the Dragoons, but his tenure as a soldier was brief and never repeated.

229 'Wisdom ... heart.' *The Prelude* (I.401–14, 1850 ed.)

229–30 'It is ... done.' *Concerning the Relations of Great Britain, Spain and Portugal, to each other, and to the common enemy at this crisis; and specifically as affected by the Convention of Cintra*, rpt in *The Prose Works of William Wordsworth*, ed. Rev. Alexander B. Grosart, vol. 1 (London: Edward Moxon, Son, and Co., 1976) 162–3

229 'It is a frightful.' In Wordsworth: It is, I allow, a frightful

230 'notions.' In Wordsworth: motions

230 'these appetites.' In Wordsworth: these revolutionary impulses and these appetites

230 'barbarous men.' In Wordsworth: barbarous (nay, what is far worse, of barbarized) men

230 'polity; And.' In Wordsworth: polity; which possesses the consistency of an ancient Government, without its embarrassments and weaknesses. And

[Principles of Poetic Art]

The text is taken from an untitled ts (9.70.5.1, 3, 5, 7)

Textual Notes
234 'designing the ground-plan.' designing ground-plan
234 'and which makes the.' and the

Explanatory Notes
230 'speakers.' I have not been able to discover the occasion or the names of the other speakers referred to here.
231 'Laocoön.' Gotthold Ephraim Lessing's *Laokoön* (1766) has become a classic of modern aesthetics.
232 ''Tis ... speed.' 'An Essay on Criticism,' *The Poems of Alexander Pope*, ed. John Butt (New Haven: Yale UP, 1963) 146, lines 84–5
232 'The Lord ... these.' Pratt cites the opening of Psalm 21 and Matthew 6:28.
232 'comic passage.' The speech comes late in Act Two. See J.M. Synge, *Plays*, ed. Anne Saddlemeyer (London: Oxford UP, 1969) 55.
232 'tragic passage.' The speech comes near the end of the play. See J.M. Synge, *Plays* 12–13.
233 'And still ... Lebanon.' John Keats, 'The Eve of St. Agnes,' *The Poems of John Keats*, ed. Jack Stillinger (Cambridge, Mass.: Belknap Press, 1978) 236.

The Outlook for Poetry

The text is taken from a ts (9.70.12–16). In a letter to me of 25 August 1987, David G. Pitt wrote: '"The Outlook for Poetry" (or major portions of it) was delivered under a different title before the English and History section of the Ontario Education Association on 14 April 1936. Parts of the same had already been aired in March 1936 before a session of the Association of Canadian Bookmen ... Much of the same under the title "Tendencies in Modern Poetry" was delivered at the C.A.A. [Canadian Authors' Association] convention in Vancouver on 14 July 1936.'

Textual Notes
234 'Canadian literary.' Can. lit.

237 'states.' stated

238 'half a play.' half a page. (The reading in the copy-text does not make sense. In all probability 'page' was accidentally copied from the preceding line.)

240 'ascendancy ....' Pratt goes on to tell his oft-repeated story of a man's failed and fatal attempt to rescue a woman stranded on an ice-floe on the Niagara River below the Falls. See OHLP 128–9.

241 'withdrawal ... physical ... A sheer.' withdraw[ ] ... phys[ ] ... sheer. (Several letters are missing because of damage to the edge of the page.)

241 'literary history.' lit, history

Explanatory Notes

237 'One of the most perfect sonnets.' Pratt is here echoing Coleridge's judgment that 'Night and Death' was one of the finest and most grandly conceived sonnets in English.

237 'If light ... life.' Pratt's University College colleague W.J. Alexander may well have introduced Pratt to the sonnet by including it in his school anthology *Shorter Poems* (Toronto: Eaton, 1924) 32.

237 'Anatole [France].' I have not been able to identify the source, but the substance of the passage resembles a number of comments made by Anatole France (1844–1924), Nobel Prize-winning novelist and man of letters.

237 'The scientific ... wheat.' I have not been able to identify the source of this quotation.

239 'Why thou owest ... catechism.' *1 Henry IV*, RS, V.i.126–40

239 'He that ... find it.' Christ's statement appears in both Mark 8:35 and Luke 9:24.

240 '*Canadian Poetry Magazine*.' See 'Section E: Pratt as Editor' 111–17 in this volume.

241 'Stein.' Pratt is likely punning here, referring both to an earthenware mug for beer and to the sudden widespread fame of Gertrude Stein. See '[Meaning and Modernity]' 254–7 in this volume.

242 'Johnstown flood.' Johnstown, Pennsylvania, was the site of a flood on 31 May 1889 that resulted in the loss of about 2,200 lives.

[The Golden Mean in Poetry]

The text is taken from a half-page untitled ts (9.70.4.1). The intermittently legible holograph at the bottom of the page begins with the phrase 'Circumscribing the field,' and asserts that 'poetry may deal with any facet of experience ... provided it is artistically done,' before stating that 'Poetry in its highest flight has spread its wings for long spiritual voyages.' Shakespeare's *Tempest,* the poetry of Milton, Francis Thompson's 'The Hound of Heaven,' and the Archbishop's reply to the temptation in T.S. Eliot's *Murder in the Cathedral* are cited as examples of poetry in high flight. Pratt then comments on the Utopian and pessimistic strains in poetry, before the text becomes almost totally illegible. The provisional dating of this ts is based on its reference to *Murder in the Cathedral* (1935).

Explanatory Note

242 'God ... out.' Pratt never identifies the author or source of these lines, though he repeatedly quotes variants of them. See, for example, '[Meaning and Modernity]' 259 in this volume.

[The Music of Language]

The text is taken from an untitled ts (10.41.9.1–4). The dating of the paper is based on the reference to Campbell-McInnes's book (see first note to page 243 in this volume).

Textual Note

246 'it is accomplished.' it accomplished

Explanatory Notes

243 'By this ... language.' J. Campbell-McInnes, *The Music of Language* (London: Frederick Harris, 1939) 52

243 'Caesar –.' In Campbell-McInnes: Caesar, Cassius, Iago, Ophelia –

244 'Love ... purse.' *Othello,* RS, I.iii.337–9. The word 'Love' Pratt takes from Iago's previous speech.

247–8 'And ride ... winter sea.' The lines quoted in this paragraph are from Christopher Marlowe's *Tamburlaine the Great: Part I,* II.v.49 (see Irving Ribner, ed., *The Complete Plays of Christopher Marlowe* [New

York: Odyssey Press, 1963] 72); John Milton's *Samson Agonistes,* line 40 and *Paradise Lost,* II, line 621 (see CPMP); and Tennyson's *The Passing of Arthur,* lines 170–1 (see Christopher Ricks, ed., *The Poems of Tennyson* [London: Longman's, 1969] 1747).

248 'And lulled ... bell.' *II Henry IV, RS,* III.i.14–17

248–9 'Quinquereme ... trays.' 'Cargoes' was one of the John Masefield poems selected by Pratt's colleague, University College Professor of English W.J. Alexander for his high school anthology *Shorter Poems* (Toronto: Eaton, 1924), (see 340), which also reprinted Pratt's 'The Ice-Floes.'

249–50 'Break ... to me.' See Ricks, ed., 602.

[Meaning and Modernity]

The text is taken from a ts 10.72.90, 92, 94–5, 98–101. The dating of this lecture is based on references to Day Lewis (see first explanatory note to page 250 in this volume) and the 'Angry Penguins' article (see note to page 261 in this volume).

Textual Notes

250 'of the late.' of late

253 'early thirties.' The ts continues with an account of the infamous number (37) of *Poetry* (Chicago) that the objectivists of 1931 took over. Because Pratt provides the background information and his reaction to this number in 'The Fly-Wheel Lost' (64–5 in this volume), I have not reproduced it here.

257 'foisting.' hoisting

258 'How much more ... literature.' The awkwardness of phrasing here makes it unclear whether Pratt intended the clauses to be read as questions or exclamations. I decided to reproduce the copy text exactly as it stands, despite the awkwardness, because of this lack of clarity.

258 'texture so that.' texture that

Explanatory Notes

250 'Synge's.' John Millington Synge (1871–1909), Irish playwright.

250 'the phrase "metaphysical conceits".' Dr Johnson, in the famous passage from 'The Life of Cowley,' of course criticized not the term

but the practice of the metaphysical poets. In his discussion of the metaphysical influence on modern poetry, as in much of this lecture, Pratt is leaning heavily on Cecil Day Lewis's *A Hope for Poetry* (Reprint with a Postscript) (Oxford: Basil Blackwell, 1944). See ch. 9 for the discussion of metaphysical poetry.

252 'Dada has no meaning.' Tristan Tzara's 'Dada Manifesto' (1918) contains, though does not begin with, the statements 'Dada Ne Signifie Rien' and 'L'art est une chose privée, l'artiste le fait pour lui; une oeuvre comprehensible est produit de journaliste'; rpt in Jean-Jacques Pauvert, ed., *Sept manifestes Dada* (Holland: Libertés Nouvelles, 1963) 15.

252 'A novel ... unicorns.' Pratt is here modifying Day Lewis's statement that following Dada theory 'you could write a novel about contemporary Paris and introduce into it Redskins, mermaids and unicorns' (86–7), which statement in turn is a modification of Malcolm Cowley's projections about the Dada writer: 'if he was writing a novel about modern Paris, he need not hesitate to introduce a tribe of Redskins, an octopus, a unicorn, Napoleon or the Virgin Mary.' *Exile's Return: A Narrative of Ideas* (London: Jonathan Cape, 1935) 161.

253 'Max Ernst.' The German visual artist Max Ernst (1891–1976) was one of the founders of Surrealism.

253 'André Breton.' The French writer André Breton (1886–1966) wrote three manifestos (1924, 1930, 1934) for the Surrealist movement and opened a studio for Surrealist research. The instructions about how to achieve a Surrealist state that Pratt gives here seem to be a paraphrase of the 1924 manifesto, 'Secrets of the Magical Surrealist Art.' See André Breton, *Manifestos of Surrealism*, trans. Richard Seaver and Helen Lane (Ann Arbor: U of Michigan P, 1969) 29–30.

254 'Madeline Carroll.' Madeline Carroll (1909–87) was a British-born stage and screen actress best known for her roles in such films as *The Thirty-Nine Steps, The Prisoner of Zenda,* and *North West Mounted Police.* Stein's visit to America between 24 October 1934 and 4 May 1935 came at a time when Carroll was at the height of her popularity as an actress. Though I have been able to find no record of the Stein-Carroll contest, Elizabeth Sprigge in *Gertrude Stein: Her Life and Work* (New York: Harper and Bros, 1957) 185, recounts an incident in which a young black woman recognized Stein on the street.

254–5 'The Irish ... water too.' Gertrude Stein, *Portraits and Prayers* (New York: Random House, 1934) 11

254 'settled to stay.' In Stein: settled

255 'month ... month ... month ... month ... month.' In Stein: mouth ... mouth ... mouth ... mouth ... mouth

255 'She ... accomplished.' I have been unable to identify the source of this quotation.

255 'Testimony ... Stein.' 'Testimony against Gertrude Stein' appeared as a supplement to *Transition* (February 1935).

256 'Louis Bromfield.' Louis Bromfield (1896–1956) was an American-born journalist and novelist whose work includes the Pulitzer Prize-winning novel *Early Autumn* (1926). He was among the American expatriates who, for an extended period, made their home in France. He became a good friend of Stein's after 1929, initially because they shared an interest in gardens, then because they had in common the status of expatriate Americans, and finally because they came to admire each other's writing.

256–7 'She is reported ... red.' Elizabeth Sprigge reports Stein as saying to her publisher, Alfred Harcourt, 'Remember this extraordinary welcome that I am having does not come from the books of mine that they do understand like the Autobiography but the books of mine that they did not understand' (185).

259 'God ... cut out.' Though Pratt repeatedly quotes these lines in similar contexts, he never identifies their author or source.

260 'I mate ... crags.' 'Tenzone,' *Personae: The Collected Poems of Ezra Pound* (New York: Horace Liveright, 1926) 81. When Pratt quotes the line in fuller context in the next paragraph, he quotes the last two lines from the previous stanza, though his text gives no indication of the stanza break.

260 'Pound ... significance.' I have been unable to identify the source of this comment.

261 'introduced ... its absurdity.' Pratt's text in these two paragraphs quotes freely rather than with scrupulous accuracy from the article 'Angry Penguins,' *Time*, 17 July 1944: 99, but the pseudo-poem he quotes is reproduced accurately.

263 'I fear ... bone.' 'Self Criticism and Answer,' in *Overtures to Death*

(1938), rpt in *Collected Poems* (London: Jonathan Cape with the Hogarth Press, 1954) 207–8

263 'We cannot ... everything.' 'February 1936,' rpt in CP 170

264 'To the idea ... life.' Cecil Day Lewis, *A Hope for Poetry* 97–9

264 'We refuse ... garden life.' In Day Lewis: It asserts finally that poetry always has been and always should be rooted in common and garden life.

'The Immortal Memory'

The article was subtitled 'Toast Given by Prof. E.J. Pratt at Burns Night Dinner, Tuesday, Jan. 25.'

Textual Notes

265 'worlds.' words

265 'shall I say.' shall say

271 'lyricists.' lyrists

272 'keekit in, and.' keekit it in, and

Explanatory Notes

265 'since I left.' Pratt left Newfoundland to pursue a BA at the University of Toronto.

267 'He clenched ... man.' 'Extempore in the Court of Session,' CWRB 273

267 'William Fisher ... Moodie.' William Fisher was the model for the hypocritical Kirk Elder in 'Holy Willie's Prayer,' and Revs John Russell of Kilmarnock and Alexander Moodie of Riccarton had their quarrel over parish boundaries memorialized in 'The Twa Herds: Or, The Holy Tulyie.'

267 'cutty stool.' A low stool in church on which sinners, especially those guilty of unchastity, were required to sit as a public sign of repentance

268 'The Address to the Devil.' CWRB gives the title as 'Address to the Deil' 161.

269 'Johnson's ... *Songs*.' Burns became literary editor of James Johnson's *The Scots Musical Museum* in all but title, according to Hugh Douglas, *Robert Burns: A Life* (London: Robert Hale, 1976) 131, whereas

George Thompson often failed to respect Burns's wishes about those of his songs included in *A Select Collection of Original Scottish Airs*.

272 'The robin ... keekit in.' 'The Wren's Nest,' CWRB 571

272 'O Wert ... lea.' James Mackay in a headnote to 'O, Wert Thou in the Cauld Blast' records the tune as 'Lenox Love to Blantyre' (567), but W.E. Henley and T.F. Henderson in the *Complete Poetical Works of Robert Burns* (Boston: Houghton Mifflin and Co., 1896–7) identify the song as 'The Wren' in their introductory note to the poem (315).

272 'an old tune.' The title of the old tune is variously recorded, but Mackay's edition has 'Hey, Tuti Tattey' (314). Pratt runs together loosely quoted fragments from Burns's letter of 'about 30 August 1793' in J. de Lancey Ferguson, ed., *The Letters of Robert Burns*, vol. 2, 1790–6 (Oxford: Clarendon Press, 1931) 194–5.

272 'In 1793 ... Bannockburn.' The poem Pratt calls 'Ode to Bannockburn' is 'Scots, Wha Hae.' See Smye's letter to Dr Currie in Rev. J.C. Higgins, 'The Life of the Poet,' in *The Book of Robert Burns*, vol. 3 (Edinburgh: Scott and Ferguson and Burness and Co., 1891) 252–5. Pratt runs together loosely quoted fragments from the letter.

[The Function of a University]

Taken from *The Proceedings on the Occasion of the Installation of the Right Honourable Viscount Rothmere of Hemsted as First Chancellor and Raymond Gushue as Second President October Eighth and Ninth Nineteen Hundred and Fifty-two* (St John's: Memorial U of Newfoundland 1952) 19–22, the article was entitled simply 'Dr. E.J. Pratt's Address.' See MY 444–6 for an account of the occasion, a picture of Pratt giving the address, and identification of the persons he mentions.

Explanatory Notes

276 'after ... three years.' Pratt's trip to Newfoundland in 1949, besides providing an opportunity to visit family and friends, was the occasion of his Burns Night address, 'The Immortal Memory'; see 264–75 in this volume.

276 'more than thirty years ago.' It had in fact been forty-five years since Pratt left Newfoundland.

279 'watery ... walking.' A blind man whose sight Christ restores responds to his healer's question, 'Do you see anything?' with 'I see men, but they look like trees, walking' (Mark 8: 24).

In Quest of the Humanities

The text is taken from a ts (9.70.2.1–3). The information about audience, location, and date of delivery of this address was provided by David G. Pitt in a letter of 25 August 1987 to me.

Explanatory Note

281 'Professor Tracy.' The words 'Professor Tracy' are cancelled in the ts, suggesting that Pratt may have used the text of the address on more than one occasion. The original reference to Professor Tracy was no doubt to Clarence Tracy, who was at the time a professor of English at the University of Saskatchewan and secretary-treasurer of the Humanities Association. However, as Pitt writes in his letter of 25 August 1987, 'it was the President, Roy Wiles, who had sent Pratt the invitation to speak, and to whom he replied, agreeing to do so.'

Introduction to Roy Campbell

The text is taken from a ts (9.71.9), which, in a letter to me dated 25 August 1987, David G. Pitt asserts is the text of the introduction Pratt used in Toronto. There are two other tss of introductions to Roy Campbell in the PCVU. Ts1 (9.71.5) is a single-page fragment which refers to Campbell's upcoming visit to Assumption College, Windsor. Ts2 (9.71.7) is a single-page text of an introduction which Pratt may have used when, as Pitt records, Pratt 'had the pleasure of introducing [Campbell] to a Canadian audience' in Montreal in early November 1953 (TY 280) and 'a few days later' in Toronto (*MY* 458–9). For more details on Campbell's visit, see Bruce Whiteman, *The Letters of John Sutherland, 1942–1956* (Toronto: ECW Press, 1992).

Explanatory Notes

285 'John Squire.' The meeting with Squire took place 2 August 1924 (TY 279). *The Flaming Terrapin* (1924) is a lively allegorical narrative of the Flood, which Pitt claims was an important influence on both *The Great Feud* and *The Cachalot* (TY 280).

285 '*Flowering Rifle.*' Pratt's account of his reaction to *Flowering Rifle* (1939) is, David G. Pitt argues convincingly in his letter to me dated 25 August 1987, 'typical Prattian hyperbole, aimed here at ingratiating himself with Campbell – in which he succeeded.'

286 'autobiography.' *Broken Record* (1934) was the first of two autobiographies; the second, *Light on a Dark Horse,* appeared in 1951.
286 'A reviewer ... apology.' I have been unable to identify the source of this quotation.
287 'You praise ... horse.' 'Some South African Novelists' appears in Roy Campbell's *Adamastor* (London: Faber and Faber 1930) 104.

# Index

www.ingramcontent.com/pod-product-compliance
Lightning Source LLC
Chambersburg PA
CBHW051512100726
47898CB00005B/1419

* 9 7 8 1 4 8 7 5 8 1 1 4 5 *